TROLLOPE

MICHAEL SADLEIR

———

TROLLOPE

A
COMMENTARY

LONDON
OXFORD UNIVERSITY PRESS

Oxford University Press, Amen House, London E.C.4

GLASGOW NEW YORK TORONTO MELBOURNE WELLINGTON
BOMBAY CALCUTTA MADRAS KARACHI KUALA LUMPUR
CAPE TOWN IBADAN NAIROBI ACCRA

First published by Constable and Company Ltd., 1927
Second Edition 1928, Third Edition 1945
First issued in OXFORD PAPERBACKS *1961*

Printed in Great Britain

CONTENTS

7

ANTHONY (*continued*)

Damaging Effect of the Autobiography—The Revival—
Acceptance and Understanding—Refusal to Pass Judgment
—Worldly Proficiency and Good Manners—The Evolution

THE BOOKS (*continued*)

of his Talent—*The Three Clerks*—A Relapse—*Doctor Thorne* —Trollope's Heroines—*The Bertrams*—*Castle Richmond*— *Orley Farm*—*The Claverings* and *The Belton Estate*—He Knew He Was Right—*Dr. Wortle's School*—First-Rate Second-Rate —And *The Way We Live Now*—Second only to *Doctor Thorne*.

APPENDICES:

A*

ILLUSTRATIONS

FOREWORD

THIS NEW EDITION contains very little fresh material, but the text has been greatly simplified and condensed, and in places virtually rewritten. The book in its present form seems to me better suited to its subject than when it carried its original load of ornament.

I would ask permission to call readers' attention to a volume of essays, *Things Past*, which was published while this new edition was printing. In that volume are included three Introductions concerned with Anthony Trollope, written subsequently to this biography and originally prefixed to separate issues or re-issues of his work. These Introductions were purposely designed to supplement the "Commentary," and contain facts or thoughts about Trollope not recorded in the pages which follow.

M. S.

Summer 1944

WHEN ANTHONY TROLLOPE DIED, there passed not only the mid-Victorian novel but a social epoch also. This dual significance of Trollope—at once literary and social—sets him apart from the other novelists of his time and makes him one of the small group of English authors who, at any time, have expressed alike a period and an individual psychology.

To us in retrospect the mid-Victorian age resembles an interlude of tranquil contentment between the discontent and prodigality of the indignant 'forties, and the 'eighties with their æsthetic languors and their flushed imperialism. Not very long ago the England of the 'fifties to the 'seventies was the favourite butt of mocking innovators. To the critical eye of Edwardian and Georgian enlightenment the mid-Victorians appeared smug and hypocritical and selfish; their tastes seemed vulgar and their idealism smothered in the interests of material comfort.

This estimate, with all the faults inherent in a wide generalisation, had enough of truth to justify its prevalence and, among the recurrent young, its long acceptance. To youth the recent past is always a thing to be disparaged; and when to legendary dowdiness was added a certainty that in Victorian days daughters were stay-at-home and sons respectful to their parents, that age became more than usually abominable to a rising generation in revolt. The prejudice of persons more mature is less excusable, but as easily explained. The superficial observer, when contrasting any past epoch with his own, inevitably if unconsciously compares the worst survivals of the former with the best achievements of the latter. Thus he reflects on the social injustices of the eighteen-sixties; he notes contemptuously the exaggerated respect paid to rank, the outward rigidity of morals, the stilted conversations, the clothes and furnishings and fashionable amusements, which from their very unsuitability to the life he knows are judged absurd. He tells himself that nowadays there is at least more candour and courage; that freedom for young people and for women has supplanted an artificial discipline; that, while at any time a cat has claimed the privilege to outstare a king, the two may now converse and freely, seeing that both are living things and members of a commonwealth.

But all such reasoning, however naturally it may arise, is none the less a distortion of the truth. It gives a character to the mid-Victorian age which is mainly negative, mainly a falling short of the ideals of later epochs. Yet actually the age had many positive and admirable qualities and, if it is to be compared with modern days at all, the comparison should at least be fairly drawn and the two periods given as much credit for their good qualities as discredit for their bad.

Despite the fact that much of the criticism passed on the mid-Victorian period is superficial, tendentious and out of proportion, it has for long remained unchallenged. That this should be so offers disquieting proof of the power of one epoch over the reputation of its predecessor. If still too many persons misjudge the mid-Victorians and for tradition's sake speak slanderously of them, the fault is with the yellow eighteen-nineties, whose frail acidity curdled a generous cream. Time alone can set matters aright—has, indeed, begun to do so. Forces are already at work refuting and discrediting the long-accepted legend; and among them not the least is Trollope, who—re-discovered, re-appraised and re-appreciated—speaks from beyond the grave in sturdy vindication of his age.

For indeed, and to a peculiar degree, this mid-Victorian period is Trollope's period. He is the articulate perfection of its normal quality, and in his books lives the spirit of its dominant class—a spirit kindly but ardent; a spirit at once gay and thoughtful; a spirit as sympathetic to individual distress as it was indifferent to class-suffering; a spirit that combined a species of national self-satisfaction with eager personal striving, a ready personal generosity with the vaguest of general charity, a contented personal simplicity with a con-

ventional spaciousness of life; a spirit, in short, serious in its
aim to better self and thus to better others, but distrustful of
theories and aloof from large idealisms.

Specific reference to history, to politics and to contemporary
achievement in thought and deed is not found in Trollope.
He himself took little account of them. To him, as to the
majority of his less articulate fellows, the interpretation in
terms of his own life of such fundamental human impulses as
love, enmity, ambition, charity, honour and courage, was the
cardinal duty of man. Ideals, philosophies, laws and conquests
were indeed implicit in a right performance of that duty; but
they were subordinate to it, as the theory of friendship is
subordinate to its practice.

Let it be clear from the outset that Trollope's expression of
the mid-Victorian spirit has always the limitation of class and
background congenial to his taste. He is the chronicler, the
observer and the interpreter of the well-to-do, comfortable
England of London and the English shires. The industrial
north, whence came the wealth that gave the period prosperity,
is beyond his range of vision, and deliberately so. Newman,
Darwin, Arnold and Ruskin—with all that these names imply
of spiritual struggle, of scientific discovery, of the philosophies
of education, of beauty, and of economic ideals—might never
have lived in the world he made so peculiarly his own. Consequently any estimate of Trollope's mid-Victorianism must
accept the limits he set upon himself; any tribute to his unrivalled skill as social interpreter assumes that it is skill within
those limits.

To become the mouthpiece of any epoch would have seemed
to Trollope a pretentious and meaningless ambition. His
primary aim was to create character. That done, he was
concerned, consciously and literally, to portray an actuality
he knew, which actuality consisted mainly of the facts and
incidents of comfortable middle-class existence and of scenes
of country-house life, sporting and social.

In his book of reminiscences *The Passing Years* [1] the late

[1] London, 1924.

Lord Willoughby de Broke composed from traditional and remembered happening precisely such a picture of the English countryside during the 'fifties, 'sixties and early 'seventies as Trollope painted in a dozen novels. This volume of memories is a vivid record of the smiling England of the squirearchy. It is wise, because its author had great opportunity for wisdom; it is sympathetic, because he contrived in his own person to prolong into a different and more harassed age those simultaneous qualities of friendliness to all and dignified obedience to a great tradition, which were at once the strength and simplicity of the best type of mid-Victorian gentleman. Lord Willoughby defines what in his father's time was meant by "The County." The list includes all those people invited by Mr. Thorne to Ullathorne Sports in *Barchester Towers*. Anyone who reads *The Passing Years* and the same author's introduction to his anthology of hunting prose [1] will realise the rise, supremacy and decline of a benevolent squirearchy, and appreciate how faultlessly and how faithfully Trollopian fiction mirrors social fact.

It has been charged against Trollope that he lacks that inner flame of adventurous imagination which distinguishes genius from craftsmanship; that, in consequence, for all his truthfulness and sympathy he cannot rank among the supreme masters of English fiction. This judgment—even if it were unchallengeable—is out of proportion to its theme. It ignores a great part of the problem that Trollope presents. For, as has been said, his achievement can now be recognised as having a significance beyond the purely literary. His voice is the authentic voice of a well-marked and individual period of history, and in his work three decades of an essential England are embalmed.

2

Trollope's mid-Victorians inherited one period and left as legacy to their successors a wholly different one. Of what

[1] *The Sport of Our Ancestors.* Edited by Lord Willoughby de Broke. London, 1921.

kind their birthright and their bequest? Whence did they come? Whither did they tend? In what manner, during the time of its continuance, was their epoch distinguished from those that preceded and followed it?

At the very outset we are faced with a problem of terminology. The word "Victorian" has become so loosely comprehensive as to be almost meaningless. Much modern criticism of "Victorianism" seems to assume that English society and social philosophy were unchanging things from 1837 to the eighteen-eighties.[1] But in truth the Victorian period is three periods, and not one. Victorianism in a literal sense runs all the way from 1837 to 1902. But early Victorianism, from 1837 to 1850, is one social epoch; and late Victorianism, from about 1880 to the opening of the new century, is another. A third is mid-Victorianism, which joins the two and presents—from 1851 to 1879—an era more lauded by itself, more traduced by its successors, and therefore more difficult of impartial definition, than any other era of the last two centuries of English history.

3

But although the Victorian age is thus tripartite, its sections are closely interdependent. The qualities of each one arise, whether by evolution or by reaction, from the qualities of a preceding epoch. An essential preliminary, therefore, to any definition of the mid-Victorian spirit is an appreciation of its origins, a realisation of the events and social tendencies that led up to the 'fifties and 'sixties and influenced them.

During the eighteen-twenties Georgian society enjoyed its last unchallenged riot of fashionable dissipation. It seemed wholly unconscious that year by year the economic aftermath of a long war, the social dissatisfactions of the advancing century, and the strict personal morality of a growing evangelicalism were undermining its foundations. The buck of the

---

[1] A good example of the unhappy influence on logical argument of a failure to distinguish between the various "Victorianisms" is provided by Bonamy Dobree's essay on Addison in *Essays in Biography* (Oxford, 1925).

Regency, successfully and heedless of warning, prolonged through the distressful 'twenties his life of rowdy elegance. Government was still with the great families, who, by their wealth and thanks to nomination boroughs, kept their predominance intact. But the Reform Bill of 1832, by knocking from beneath the landlord class their chiefest prop, began in fact (though as yet imperceptibly) another epoch.

The years immediately subsequent to 1832 were years of apparent normality, of actual transformation. Though the structure of England had changed, the old order still persisted. Everywhere was expectation of displacement, nowhere was visible sign of it. But the enthronement of the middle class —as much for want of active opposition as from a national conviction of their efficiency in kingship—had been achieved and became permanent. The 'thirties ended with England a country under bourgeois rule.

If by 1840 the aristocratic families had lost their complete control of government, during the next ten years they were threatened with the further loss of their possessions. The middle 'forties were nervous times for English property. Even in 'forty-eight, when in reality the crisis was two years overpast, there were many who feared disaster and disruption. Abroad was open revolution; at home the more timid lived in terror of an outbreak, reading unhappily the final Chartist message as it was scrawled with menace across the walls of privilege. But rumour and newspaper report were more garish than fact. Even before the turn of the half-century the scene had once again changed utterly, and within three years of the turmoil of 'forty-eight a new era of serenity had flowered sumptuously beneath the glass arcading of the great exhibition in Hyde Park.

The strange evolution of mid-Victorian calm from the lurid unrealities of the 'forties began with the repeal of the Corn Laws in 1846. The morass of poverty and discontent, from which in 1841 Peel undertook to guide the suffering country, had lain directly in the path of the new bourgeois governing class. The obstacle had seemed impassable; indeed only by a trick of fortune was it surmounted. The period during which the Anti-Corn-Law League grew to full power was the period of Peel's personal conversion to Free Trade, and by a queer hazard he (and through him the starving masses) owed his victory as much to the mutual jealousies of the landed and the industrial employers as to the virtue of his cause. Simultaneously were generating the Factory Act of 1847 and the abolition of the Corn Laws of June 1846. The English country gentlemen supported the former for the same reason that the mill-owners and manufacturers clamoured for the latter—namely that the new legislation hampered their rivals but did not touch themselves. The manufacturing magnates were jealous of the County; the landed gentry saw themselves still as dispossessed rulers and not at all as co-members with the merchant-princes of an employing class. Thus it was that pride on one side and jealousy on the other blinded both landlord and industrial to a common interest. The reforms were carried through, and in the bitter recrimination which followed their triumph, Conservatism broke and scattered.

But if Peel split his party, he won the day for the people and, in effect, removed his country wholly from the fever zone of revolutionary uprising. When two years later Europe broke into revolt against the obstinate incompetence of military despotisms, England, now fairly launched on a period of commercial and agricultural prosperity, could play the interested but superior spectator. With the detachment of a nation which had managed its own revolution without a tithe of the shouting and disturbance necessary to Frenchmen and to Germans, Englishmen could afford to pity the oppressed, while thanking the special Providence of Britain for the wise ordering of their affairs. It is essential to remember the national self-satisfaction provoked alike in landed, professional, commercial and working-class England by the contrast in 1848 between affairs at home and those abroad. If even so relentless a critic as Macaulay could in an historical essay draw a proud comparison between the glorious English revolution of 1688 and the squalid European imbroglio of 1848, it is not surprising that the minds of persons less "difficult" and less articulate should yield to a consciousness of national well-being which bordered on the sanctimonious.

When in Prince Albert's famous Exhibition the trade supremacy of Britain won to its crowning glory, the pious complacency of press and public erupted like a volcano of beneficence on the benighted heads of races less gifted and less fortunate. England was indeed the Promised Land and all her sons and daughters chosen by Divine favour for happiness and plenty.[1]

It is thus that the approaches to mid-Victorianism appear from the vantage ground of our own time. They looked differently to eyes more nearly contemporary, and yet beneath the difference was a similarity. Consider mid-Victorian England as it appeared to Henry Adams—to the brilliant American who left behind him a detached and sensitive description of precisely that aspect of English society with which the student of Trollope is concerned—a description doubly valuable in that it is exterior to its theme.

Young Henry Adams crossed from Washington to London in 1861 as private secretary to his father, Charles Francis Adams, who had been appointed by President Lincoln Minister to the Court of St. James's at the most critical moment of American nineteenth-century history. He remained in England till 1868, with all his wits preternaturally sharpened by the delicacy of his situation. He was an understrapper to the Minister for the North in a society whose most fashionable

---

[1] An extract from Lady Eastlake's notorious review of *Jane Eyre* (*Quarterly Review*, December 1848) will show the sanctimony of which, even prior to 1851, the national character was capable :—

> Altogether the autobiography of *Jane Eyre* is pre-eminently an anti-Christian composition. There is throughout it a murmuring against the comforts of the rich and against the privations of the poor, which, as far as each individual is concerned, is a murmuring against God's appointment ; there is that pervading tone of ungodly discontent which is at once the most prominent and the most subtle evil which the law and the pulpit, which all civilised society, in fact, has at the present day to contend with. We do not hesitate to say that the tone of mind and thought which has overthrown authority abroad and fostered Chartism and rebellion at home, is the same which has also written *Jane Eyre*.

This spirit, which in 1848 was rather exceptional than pervading, came in the early 'fifties to supremacy.

members were for the South. He had long periods of apparent
leisure during which he was really doing the hardest work of all
—the work of preserving equilibrium, discretion and a calm bearing in the midst of a society whose very courtesy was hostile. He
had unrivalled opportunities of seeing the English on official
show, in unofficial undress; in town, in the country; personally friendly or from policy aloof. When in later years he
wrote the story of his life,[1] he recorded his impressions of
England in the 'fifties and 'sixties; and because he had to
perfection the genius and opportunity for onlooking, because
he could profit as little from applause of England as he could
suffer from her dispraise, his words are precious, giving as
they do precisely the guidance necessary to an understanding
of the prosperous but uncomfortable, arrogant but kindly
years, which lie at the very heart of mid-Victorianism.

Although Adams' personal intimacy with England did not
begin till after 1860, he gives in the early part of his autobiography occasional and, as it were, involuntary glimpses of
the social landscape of the 'forties.

> Mr. Adams (the writer's father) was one of the exceed-
> ingly small number of Americans to whom an English duke
> or duchess seemed to be indifferent, and royalty itself
> nothing more than a slightly inconvenient presence. This
> was rather the tone of English society in his time, but
> Americans were largely responsible for changing it.

Again:—

> The Paris of Louis Philippe, Guizot and de Tocqueville,
> as well as the London of Robert Peel, Macaulay and John
> Stuart Mill were but varieties of the same upper-class
> bourgeoisie that felt instinctive cousinship with the Boston
> of Ticknor, Prescott and Motley. England's middle-class
> government was the ideal of human progress.

Finally:—

> Every one now smiles at the bad taste of Queen Victoria

---

[1] *The Education of Henry Adams* was first *published* in 1918. It had been
written many, and privately printed several, years before.

and Louis Philippe—the society of the 'forties. But the taste was only the reflection of the social slackwater between a tide passed and a tide to come.

The implications of these sentences bear directly on our ultimate definition of mid-Victorianism. They show that the 'forties were noticeably non-snobbish; that toward rank and even toward royalty they were rather indifferent than servile. They show, also, that the 'forties were England's first period of bourgeois governance; that—as has already been remarked—the middle class were actually in command when the bad times came, and were not (as is often implied) substituted for a corrupt and selfish oligarchy by the forces of discontent. They show, finally, that the 'forties were a "between time" —a slack period of mid-century exhaustion, following on the death of one epoch and preceding the birth of another.

To an understanding of England in the 'fifties Adams makes two important contributions. The chances of his life had not yet brought him to settle in her midst, wherefore these observations are the one indirect, the other fleeting. But neither is the worse for its impermanence.

The first has reference to the English intelligentsia of 1858. Adams is at Harvard, whither James Russell Lowell returns after a spell of Germany:—

Lowell, on succeeding Longfellow as Professor of Belles Lettres, had duly gone to Germany, and had brought back whatever he found to bring. The literary world then agreed that truth survived in Germany alone, and Carlyle, Matthew Arnold, Renan, Emerson, with scores of popular followers, taught the German faith. The literary world had revolted against the yoke of coming capitalism—its money-lenders, its bank directors, its railway magnates. Thackeray and Dickens followed Balzac in scratching and biting the unfortunate middle class with savage ill-temper. . . . The middle class had the power, and held its coal and iron well in hand; but the satirists and idealists seized the press, and turned to Germany because at that moment Germany was neither economical nor military and a hundred years behind western Europe in the simplicity of its standard.

The cynical will note that in the matter of a querulous intelligentsia the 'fifties stood in the direct line of descent from Godwin to the present day. Then, as always, the "satirists and idealists" were in revolt against the monetary prosperity to which (though unadmittedly) they owed their personal survival; then, as always, they were in frenzied suicidal chase of new simplicities. But more essential to an understanding of mid-Victorianism is Adams' prophecy, within ten years of the period's beginning, of a coming reaction against material prosperity; for this reaction was to grow in strength and to claim a large share in the epoch's ultimate collapse.

In November 1858 Adams passed through England on his way to Germany (he was performing the pilgrimage proper to a Lowell pupil). From the window of a cab he looked on London and, in the few sentences that record this glimpse, he photographs the town:—

> Had he (Adams himself—the book is written throughout in the third person) known enough to know where to begin, he would have seen something to study more vital than Civil Law in the long, muddy, dirty, gaslit, dreariness of Oxford Street as his dingy fourwheeler dragged its way to Charing Cross.
>
> London was still London. A certain style dignified its grime; heavy, clumsy, arrogant, purse-proud but not cheap; insular but large; barely tolerant of an outside world and absolutely self-confident. The boys in the streets made such free comments on the American clothes and figures, that the travellers hurried to put on tall hats and long overcoats to escape criticism. No stranger had rights even in the Strand. The eighteenth century held its own. History muttered down Fleet Street, like Dr. Johnson, in Adams' ear. Vanity Fair was alive in Piccadilly in yellow chariots with coachmen in wigs; half the great houses, black with London smoke, bore large funereal hatchments;

every one seemed insolent, and the most insolent structures in the world were the Royal Exchange and the Bank of England.

Not only, therefore, for their intellectuals' sake can the late 'fifties claim a place in the stubborn continuity of English life. The merchant princes had already caught the grand manner of a vanished feudalism. Though the eighteenth century had passed and the despotism of the first estate was over, commerce could play the insolent as well as any nobleman; and if the foreigner expected that a bourgeois London would notice him any the more for being socially an equal, that foreigner would soon discover his mistake.

By 1861 Adams is settled in London. The American Civil War drags on. The immense majority of English opinion is for the South; Thackeray raves against Lincoln's brutality; the young secretary lives in uneasy loneliness. But as opinion veers round, as the war ends and the innate good sense of England triumphs over her too-ready sentiment, Minister Adams and his entourage became as intimate with their hosts as outsiders ever can.

Now, and for the first time, Adams detects patches of weakness in the solid wall of England's prosperous self-sufficiency.

For several years, under the keenest incitement to watchfulness, he observed the English mind in contact with itself and other minds. Especially with the American the contact was interesting. . . . The American mind was not a thought at all; it was a convention, a mere cutting instrument, practical, economical, sharp and direct.

The English themselves hardly conceived that their mind was economical, sharp or direct; but the defect that most struck an American was its enormous waste in eccentricity. Americans needed and used their whole energy and applied it with close economy; but English society was eccentric by law and for the sake of the eccentricity itself.

After enumerating various signs of English eccentricity, Adams proceeds:—

In 1863 the class of Englishmen who set out to be the intellectual opposites of Bright seemed to an American bystander the weakest and most eccentric of all. These were the trimmers, the political economists, the anti-slavery and doctrinaire class, the followers of de Tocqueville and John Stuart Mill. Numbers of these men haunted London society, all tending to free thinking, but never venturing much freedom of thought. Like the anti-slavery doctrinaires of the 'forties and 'fifties, they became mute and useless when slavery struck them in the face. . . .

These experiences of 1863 left the conviction that eccentricity was weakness. The years of Palmerston's last Cabinet —from 1859 to 1865—were avowedly years of truce—of arrested development. The British system was in its last stage of decomposition. Never had the British mind shown itself so *décousu*, so unravelled, at sea, floundering in every sort of historical shipwreck. Eccentricities had a free field. Contradictions swarmed in Church and State. A young American might dream, but he could not foretell the suddenness with which the old Europe, with England in its wake, was to vanish in 1870.

Here, then, is a new aspect of a period usually regarded as impenetrable alike in its prosperity and complacency. As early as 1863 the self-contained, unostentatious structure of Victorian England showed signs of scaling. It was to stand another fifteen, nearly another twenty, years; it might have stood much longer. But the 'sixties failed to reckon with the inevitable evolution of their own prosperity. The wealth of England was already seeking outlets in distant corners of the globe. Sooner or later, from the natural development of capitalist experiment abroad would be born the idea of empire; sooner or later that idea would turn to sentiment, and what had begun as economic commonsense would end in the hysteria of a slogan. And the main reason why (apart from ordinary lack of prescience) the 'sixties did not foresee the coming implication of their England with the outer world, was that they did not give to manufacture and to finance their due share of credit for the national wealth. Agriculture, for twenty-five years after the Abolition of the Corn Laws, enjoyed unreal prosperity. This Indian summer of the squirearchy lulled those concerned into a false expectation of perpetual sunshine, and taught them to think themselves the pivot of the national well-being. When in the 'seventies disaster came upon them, they were taken unawares; aghast at the realisation of their own financial insecurity and shocked to find that the industrials rather than themselves had been the country's real bread-winners, they lost their poise and with it their supremacy.

One final extract from Henry Adams, and his contribution has been made. Writing of the social scene in 1864—during the "truce time" earlier mentioned—he says:—

The Prince Consort was dead; the Queen had retired; the Prince of Wales was still a boy. In its best days Victorian society had never been " smart." During the 'forties, under the influence of Louis Philippe, courts affected to be simple, serious and middle-class—and they succeeded. Style lingered in the background with the powdered footman behind the yellow chariot, but speaking socially the Queen had no style save what she inherited. Balmoral was a startling revelation of royal taste. Nothing could be worse than the toilettes at Court unless it were the way they were worn. If any lady appeared well dressed, she was either a foreigner or " fast." Fashion was not fashionable in London until the Americans and the Jews were let loose. The style of London toilette universal in 1864 was grotesque—like Monckton Milnes on horseback in Rotten Row.

This survey comprises all that has gone before and even plots the way to what must follow. It is only necessary to set the implications of Adams' narrative upon a framework of chronology, to amplify a little the intriguing theme of the

woman-made revolution in the manners of polite society, and
our appreciation of the social tendency of mid-Victorianism
will be passably complete.

4

During the 'forties royalty was rather a reputation than an
influence. The Queen, keeping of her own discretion in the
background until with her husband's help she felt ready for
self-emphasis, was unrecognised by the people as a power and
unwilling at present to emerge as leader of the aristocracy.
The middle class, newly promoted to generalship, hovered
bewildered at the head of an unruly starving mob. But good
fortune and Peel's good sense transformed the scene and forestalled revolution. Prosperity, like a cup of wine, began to
pass from mouth to mouth; the disorderly rabble became a
band of eager and thriving workers. Only a gesture was
wanting, to swing the country alike to wealth and to comfort
both spiritual and material.

By the end of the decade royalty was prepared to make precisely this gesture. Prince Albert, invested with the romantic
prestige of a queen hitherto a little disregarded but now and
at long last self-assertive, stepped to the front and called the
world to wonder at the new and varied energies of England.

There was more to the royal gesture than practical leader-
ship. The crown's achievement was not only an achievement
in co-ordination and in guidance. Albert and Victoria reversed
the trend of manners by setting before the people the example
of their own domesticity. The end of the 'forties marked the
beginning of the Queen's emergence as the first and most
wifely lady of the land; it also—and in consequence—marked
the opening of the short sharp campaign which gave to the
feminine code of morals its final victory over that of men.

In few things did mid-Victorian society differ more completely from that which preceded it than in its moral tone. The
Georgian era and its aftermath had been a masculine era.
From the court downwards male ideals of conduct and enjoyment had been supreme. The easy acceptance of human

frailty that had characterised the eighteenth century contrived to persist—at least in London—until the 'forties were half run. But, outside London, the impulse to puritanism and to a graver view of life's responsibilities had rapidly gained ground. It had captured not only working folk, small shopkeepers and middle-class households, but the more thoughtful of the landed gentry also.

The origins of this spiritual transformation must—like those of the prodigality it challenged—be sought in the eighteenth century. During the last twenty years of that century there had crept into English minds, not only the ideas of liberty and humanity so forcibly proclaimed in France, but also the peculiar religious aspirations of the evangelicals. Throughout the 'teens, 'twenties and 'thirties of the new century these three impulses to self-assertiveness in politics, to mutual kindliness in social encounters, and to a sober delicacy in personal deportment had gradually but ever more strongly moved the nation, and in every rank of society. Sir Walter Scott, in one of his letters, tells of a great-aunt who, having enjoyed during the seventeen-sixties the novels of Mrs. Aphra Behn, insisted on re-reading them in the early eighteen-twenties. He sent her the books; but very quickly she returned them, saying:—

> Take back your bonny Mrs. Behn and, if you will take my advice, put her in the fire. Is it not a very odd thing that I, an old woman of eighty, sitting alone, feel myself ashamed to read a book which sixty years ago I had heard read aloud for the amusement of large circles, consisting of the first and the most creditable society of London? [1]

It is certain that the unconscious change of taste undergone by this old lady was but one of ten thousand similar experiences.

The evangelical seed, sown in the late eighteenth century, germinated slowly; but by 1845 it was itself in fruit and ready to seed again. One conspicuous sign of its maturity was the change that came over the conception of the ministry as a walk in life. Not only had the Anglican clergy become a different race of beings from their highly secular predecessors, but the

[1] *Lockhart's Life of Scott*, Vol. III. p. 513.

Church as a serious profession for serious youth was attracting thousands of candidates. Gladstone, in his *Essay on the Church*, remarks that during the 'forties quite half of the undergraduates at Oxford and Cambridge were reading for holy orders.

And this tendency toward a life in the service of religion was only one reflection of the changing face of England. To a growing majority of people the ways of fashionable life had become intolerable. Not unnaturally, seeing that they were the chief sufferers, women took the lead in the growing rebellion against a code of manners which, owing to the transformation of society, had lost touch with reality. With the aggressive virtue of a woman sovereign as weapon in their hands, the women of England rose and overthrew the despotism of masculine licence. A storm of disapproval broke over the night life of London; houses of entertainment and ill-fame were closed; a clamour—half political, half moral—was raised against the gambling, wenching rowdiness of the "men upon town."

When, therefore, in the bland sunshine of 1850 Victoria sat in prominence upon her throne, she surveyed a nation inspired with new and virtuous ambition. And not a nation only. The court—which would have been ready to flaunt an eighteenth-century tradition, to play the chief part in a revival of the regency—followed the sovereign's lead. Finding that the grand style, if it were to survive at all, must be surfaced over with the dowdiness of a Queen who had begun by looking dowdy on purpose and ended by becoming so; finding a frumpish rectitude *de rigueur* and elegance half-way to outlawry, the leaders of society took the hint and slid easily into the new deportment. Henceforward of all dull integrities that of the greatest ladies became the dullest and the most correct.

Astonishing, even to its promoters, must have been the thoroughness of the moral revolution of 1850. Everywhere resistance faded into acquiescence. Whatever chance of survival the fast set (and the complex interests which depended on them) might have had was swept away by the emergence of the royal household as the type *par excellence* of British domesticity. Morality curled up like a great wave and broke from above on the heads of the still unregenerate "bloods." Under this royal douche of rectitude, and already partially choked by the accumulating ash of bourgeois prudery, the fire of tolerated licence sputtered and died. Of course irregularities persisted, but they were driven underground; their existence was ignored, if not denied.

It is instructive to study the raffish literature of the 'thirties and early 'forties (the periodicals and books that catered for the various dissipations of London-after-dark) and to compare it with that of the middle 'fifties. Not only has the stream of it dwindled from a broad river to a tiny trickle, but, whereas the former shows a London in the essentials of licence and of crime the London of the Regency, the latter might concern a different city. To a greater or less degree the same transformation took place throughout polite society.

In many quarters, of course, the change was too sudden to be altogether real. But modishness has often grown to second nature, and the new decency was with time to prove itself largely genuine. Victoria and Albert made morality a *chic*; and what began as fashion, lingered, became a habit, and remained.

It is possible to welcome the new morality (some "tightening up" of decency was sorely needed) and at the same time to regret the inevitable pietism which evolved from it. The simultaneous discovery of commercial prosperity and of the loveliness of virtue convinced the English people of their mission to mankind. Where profit and propriety went hand in hand, there also went Divine approval. So it was that the 'fifties, potentially a decade of debauch, "went virtuous" and in sobriety lived out their time.

But with the 'sixties came change of another kind. Prince Albert is now dead. The Queen has gone into retirement. From dowdy society is withdrawn the very reason for its dowdiness. Across the slow ceremony of the London seasons cuts the fierce partisanship of the American war. The upper class, who had withstood unflinchingly the murderous incompetence of the Crimea and the bereavements of the Mutiny, wandered without a guide among the gilded mantraps of the parvenus. Jews, manufacturers and financiers grew rapidly more wealthy; edged their way further and further into the fastness of society.

There is room for them now; the garrison is thinning out. Many of the "families" have withdrawn from London or hidden themselves behind the solemn porticoes of Belgravia. A hush is on the town, and the faint whine of agitation sounds once more. Utopia-seekers find an audience again. A vague uneasiness begins to spread, and where before was happy boredom, now is less of boredom than of emptiness and— gradually—an inclination to fill the void with something, be it only discontent.[1]

The 'seventies bring royalty to the scene again. The Prince of Wales steps to the centre of the stage. Fashion of a new and cosmopolitan kind comes violently to life, and with it licence. The Prince seeks money and pleasure where they may be found. The Queen remains obstinately invisible. There is an uprush of republican propaganda which finds expression in scurrilous attacks on the Royal Family.[2] Bitter criticism of the immorality of privilege, blended with a resentment at the new intimacy between blue blood and dago money-bags, unites the sticklers for Englishry, the reformers, the bourgeois and the intelligent working-men. And in the background larger issues are developing. The agricultural prosperity comes abruptly to an end; the oversea extensions of industrial capital have spread so far and so successfully that the very contemplation of them provokes the vision of a Greater Britain. As the class who for a quarter of a century have ruled the land draw into retirement or, in self-preservation, invest their wealth in trade, the now triumphant money-power

[1] A vivid presentation of the *désœuvré*, restless London of the middle and late 'sixties—when Society, wayward and ill-at-ease, fluttered from crank to parvenu and thence to crank again—is given by Laurence Oliphant in his satirical novel *Piccadilly* (published in 1870).

[2] Once again contemporary evidence may be adduced. The series of satires on the Queen, the Prince of Wales and their entourage, which began with *The Coming K——* (Beeton's Christmas Annual for 1872) demonstrate the popular reaction to the new mode in royalty.

launches the country on the vivid adventure of Imperialism. The self-sufficiency of England is over; mid-Victorianism— as Trollope knew and loved it—is at an end.

5

So much for the social aspects of mid-Victorianism. But there were spiritual elements in the "make up" of the period, which no contemporary could detect. These elements have provoked fierce ridicule from hostile critics of later periods; but they have an intrinsic importance, because they reflect to a curious degree the material conditions of the period, having been created by them and being destined to a share in their destruction.

Modern hostility accuses the mid-Victorians of a prudery at once rigid and hypocritical, of intolerance and of a complacent pomposity. Are such strictures all or at all deserved?

In Austin Harrison's memoir of his father Frederic Harrison [1] may be found related in detail a conversation between the father and the son on the subject of personal continence. The father, asked point blank whether a man should ever take a mistress, appeals hotly to the teaching of religion and to the proscription of morality. "A man who cannot learn self-control is a cad." "There is only love in marriage." "A loose man is anti-social." In conclusion, "It is not a subject that decent men discuss."

This conversation—which must have taken place almost word for word as Austin Harrison records it—is highly illuminating. It goes a long way toward explaining the denigration of mid-Victorian morality, and the charges of hypocrisy and priggishness which were the small-talk of the eighteen-eighties and have been repeated ever since. And yet Frederic Harrison, when he spoke as he did, was neither hypocrite nor prig. He was not even consciously preaching a way of life. His words were a sincere expression of a genuine inability to imagine any son of his—indeed any member of his own class—so far defy-

[1] *Frederic Harrison : Thoughts and Memories.* By Austin Harrison. London 1926. Frederic Harrison lived from 1831 to 1923.

ing the teachings of Christianity, so far ignoring the claims of
the community on the individual, as even to consider an
irregular sexual union.

And this inability of Frederic Harrison lies at the very core
of his period's psychology. Two of the essential elements in
mid-Victorianism were moral thoughtfulness and a high sense
of duty toward community discipline. Men thought in terms
of morals as to-day they think in terms of science. The
individualism of the time was a sort of compliment paid to
man's integrity. It was as though society said to the individual:
"We leave you free to help the community or to hinder it.
Because you are an Englishman and a servant of the Queen
and a member of the Established Church—you will help and
not hinder; and you will help by denying to yourself the
indulgences that no one withholds from you. Because such
denial will be made of your own volition, you will yourself
become the more free and as a servant of the community the
more profitable."

This emphasis on personal rectitude for the sake of the community had two obvious results—the first a tendency to over-
gravity in judging the trivial and purely private actions of
oneself and other people; the second, a mobilisation of public
opinion against offenders. Both these results hastened the end
of the epoch and the revulsion against it. On the one hand,
mid-Victorianism stuck in the mud of its own seriousness; on
the other, renegades from its high standard of probity soon
found it easy, while paying lip service to the current dogmas of
morality, to go their own selfish ways under the cloak of their
conformity and to join in the hue and cry against those less
skilful than themselves, whose frailties were found out. So it
came to pass that a generation in revolt from mid-Victorianism
could with apparent cause mock at its pomposity and lash with
scorn the gap between its professions and its practice. But
they would more justly have blamed human nature for a failure
to maintain the most exacting (but at the same time the most
flattering and, in its way, the most pathetically honourable)
code of personal behaviour which a huge nation ever sought
to impose upon itself. Certainly the attempt at imposition

B

failed; certainly the burden laid on the ordinary mid-Victorian by the eminent and learned folk who governed him and by the high-principled women who ruled his private life was a burden too heavy to be borne. But there was a nobility in the very unreason of their idealism; and only an epoch unusually ambitious of perfectibility would ever have thought to aim so high.

The apparent intolerance and pomposity of the mid-Victorians demand a different explanation which, incidentally, will serve to gather up the social and spiritual threads which together form the texture of the period.

Without doubt the age was one of didacticism. Rules of conduct were laid down and rigidly imposed. But this readiness to codify virtue did not arise from any feeling of infallibility; rather it was evidence of a profound uncertainty—an uncertainty alike as to an ideal of conduct and to the fitness for rule-making of the very men who took it upon themselves to make the rules. Thus we arrive at a conclusion which can, alas, best be expressed in the jargon of the psycho-analysts—that mid-Victorian punditry suffered in many cases from an extreme form of the inferiority complex. That it should have done so appears natural and inevitable, once we refer back to the simple facts of social evolution.

The law-givers—social, political and ethical—of the 'fifties and 'sixties were for the most part children of poor and serious-minded men who, just because they were poor and serious-minded, had lived uneasy lives in the arrogant, still feudal world of the late eighteenth and early nineteenth centuries. The children of these men had been taught by cruel experience that the intelligence and virtue of their sort of person counted for nothing beside the dissolute selfishness of hereditary superiors. From the world of letters and of art typical cases may be cited. Thackeray, Charles Kingsley, Gilbert Scott, like many others who became in one way or another leading figures in mid-Victorian England, had spent unhappy childhoods among companions whose only superiority was one of birth or worldly circumstance. Naturally, when hazard of social change set them (and such as they) in seats of power, they inclined, one to bitter satire of his former enemies, another to didacticism, a third to self-assertion, and the rest to whatsoever expression of the inferiority complex was best suited to their various temperaments.

If among persons of intellect a smothered sense of insecurity produced a spirit of law-giving rather than one of sympathetic candour, among the less-gifted but often wealthier members of the middle class it created an exaggerated respect for social eminence and social decorum. Snobbery and respectability were born of unavowed but torturing doubts as to the validity and sanction of an enthroned bourgeoisie.

As between dog and underdog social climbing does not exist, only indifferent pride and sullen apathy. But with the coming of middle dog there creeps into social atmosphere the subtle taint of snobbery. Snobbery is the desire of middle dog to retain the power of patronising underdog, but yet to be on terms of affable equality with dog. Hence mid-Victorian emphasis on precedence; hence mid-Victorian love of "honourables"; hence mid-Victorian dread of too-emphatic searching into the unhappy squalor of the poor.

Respectability was similar in origin. The bourgeoisie had ridden to power on the wave of social reformation. A tide of royal principle and popular disgust, by engulfing the *ancien régime*, had transformed the middle classes from unimportant sandhills into the bulwark between land and sea. They took their new respectability with outward seriousness, with inward timidity. They realised their status, but were uncertain of it. Hence, forced to maintain the social rectitude which was, as it were, their charter, but at the same time willing to emulate the legendary dissipation of their predecessors, they evolved *la pudibonderie anglaise*—that curious blend of public virtue and of private licence, which was to become the affliction of their grandchildren and the mockery of foreign nations.

It has been the great misfortune of the mid-Victorians that, amid the jeers provoked by their few insincerities, their manifold virtues of energy, generosity and self-sacrifice have been forgotten. The snobs and the hypocrites were not more numerous among them than in any other generation; but during the mid-Victorian age this small minority, by hazard of historical evolution, were people of power and influence, and from mere opportunism contrived to create a moral code by talking about morality at the tops of their voices. The pity is that the noisy humbug of the few should have obscured the quiet merits of the many. Of the thousands of English families who lived their lives in contented and industrious well-doing, who from principle alone and by self-denial strove to fulfil their own high standard of personal integrity, no tradition has been formed. Yet these were the typical mid-Victorians, for they had ardour, courage and, in their self-subjection, a determined if a somewhat cumbrous idealism. Whatever their faults, their heavinesses and their self-delusions, these excellent folk were neither slothful nor blasé. To them life brought daily opportunity of adjusting self-indulgence to self-discipline. They held bravely to the pursuit of an ideal, and were warm in their genuine faith, if not in the well-doing of human nature, at least in its capacity for well-doing.

Of this acquiescent but scrupulous section of his countrymen Anthony Trollope is at once the mouthpiece and the unconscious advocate. In the face of his simplicity, his courage and his humour it is impossible to deny to mid-Victorian England qualities none the less admirable for being unspectacular. Trollope's England is neither portentous nor rococo; Trollope himself was neither prig nor moraliser. Who shall persist, against the evidence of his work and of his personality, in regarding as hypocritical, purse-proud and vulgar the epoch of which his fiction was so conspicuously a product, of which his *Autobiography* is so unmistakably a voice?

ANTHONY'S MOTHER

I

WHEN HENRY MILTON won a clerkship in the War Office and went from his father's Hampshire Vicarage to live in London, there went with him, to keep his house and help with his entertaining, his two sisters Mary and Frances.

This was in the year 1800 or thereabouts, and Frances Milton, once settled at No. 27 Keppel Street, Bloomsbury, found ample scope for her merry spirit and quick efficient hands in the building of her brother's home. She had already, as a girl of twenty, the genius for everyday enjoyment, the devouring interest in ordinary thrusting life, which never left her through the long, arduous years. A cheerful society of young men and women came to centre on Keppel Street, and there were card parties and tea drinkings and modest junketings of the kind which in those days were gaiety enough for children of the professional and learned classes.

One night a grave young lawyer, with a good presence and a reputation alike for scholarship and industry, came to Henry Milton's house. Thomas Anthony Trollope was a typical intellectual of the time. A Wykehamist, a Fellow of New College and an ambitious barrister, he had the reflective tradition and taste for gravity which carry persons of his kind portentously along their normal ways. Distrustful of any jokes but those with classical authority, solemnly ready for debate on abstract themes, in manner disapproving and in the small contacts of life the pedagogue, he was yet a being scrupulously honourable, and his heart, beneath the layers of shy dignity and sober clothing, was a true and tender one.

One can imagine him at Keppel Street. The first encounter

with his host's younger sister leaves him uneasy, almost resentful and, though he would not have owned to it, a little dazed.
She is so quick and mischievous and, by his standards, so
irreverent in the face of life's solemnity. But in the solitude
of his rooms he recalls her laughter and her malicious sparkling
eyes, and feels a stirring, a small excitement thrilling his
duty-ridden soul, which pleases while it shocks. Against his
better judgment (and, one may be sure, armed with some
serious excuse to salve his own conscience against frivolity)
he sees her again. They fall to talk of literature and, as he
praises the traditional virtues of English poetry and speaks
with grave disapprobation of the excesses of the school of
Wordsworth and of Coleridge, she sits and listens, silently
admiring—her pretty feminine submissiveness spread out
before his learning, her mouth demure, her quick eyes veiled.
Attraction grows, and Thomas Trollope decides that the visits
permitted by convention are too few. He has recourse to the
most time-honoured of all love's opening gambits; he sends
his lady a book, finding it necessary to write a long letter and
to enclose with the parcel two Latin odes and a translation
by himself.

Fanny Milton doubtless returned the book and discussed
the odes when next Thomas Trollope came to Keppel Street.
One may be sure that the subject thus happily begun was not
allowed to die. At each fresh meeting they would talk of
books more eagerly than ever, for there is no more profitable
pathway in the maze of love's first fumblings than that of
literature. The couple wandered to some purpose through
their preliminary uncertainties. When Thomas Trollope next
writes, it is with a ponderous playfulness which only a ripening
intimacy could provoke:—

Lincoln's Inn.
23rd Sept. 1808.

MY DEAR MADAM,

As your brother will probably have left Keppel Street
before my servant is able to get there with the umbrella he
was so good as to lend me last night, I take the liberty of
addressing this note to you expressing my best thanks for

the loan of it. At the same time I really hope you will indulge me in the request that it may henceforth be safely deposited in your house, since experience has shown that they are very apt to ramble from mine. Altho' the stern unrelenting heart of your brother may be inexorable, permit me, on the behalf of my trembling client now at your doors, to indulge better hopes from the clemency of the female disposition. In full expectation of this my humble request being complied with I shall consider myself as ever bound to pray etc. etc.

I am, my dear Madam,
with my best respects to your sister
whom I hope to enlist as an advocate
in my cause
your most true and very
humble servant
THOS. ANTH: TROLLOPE.

Fanny Milton's answer, undated and unsigned, is written on the blank sheet of her correspondent's own letter:—

MY DEAR SIR,

I am afraid you have applied to a very bad place, for *all my eloquence* has proved vain. Henry still feels it *impossible* to accept your umbrella, and therefore like an honest council I really advise you to give up the cause. To you I will confess that I think he sees this problem in a right point of view. Whenever the said umbrella met his sight I think it would give him a disagreeable sort of sensation. But as I was engaged on the other side, you may be sure I did not hint this to *him*. He desires me to say that he wishes you would prove you forgive his so pertinaciously insisting on having his own way, by giving him the pleasure of your company to dinner on Friday.

Thomas Trollope accepted the invitation. After dinner the young lady ventured to speak of a book she had read and enjoyed. He begged the loan of it, sat up half the night to finish it and, the next morning, wrote as follows:—

Lincoln's Inn
[*about October* 2 1808]

DEAR MADAM,

I have been much pleased with the perusal of the very sensible little book you did me the honour of lending me last night, and I have to return you my best thanks as well for the loan as for the recommendation of it.

When I had got home I could not persuade myself to throw it aside, intended as it was as a companion at my breakfast table this morning, without *just peeping* at a page or two; in consequence of this impatience I was led from chapter to chapter, tho' sitting without a fire after a walk home thro' the snow, till I had finished it. Whether this perseverance arose from the entertainment the elegant pages of Miss Edgeworth afforded me, or from some secret apprehension of not being able to find another leisure half-hour that might be dedicated to their perusal and the time should arrive prior to which I had received your strict injunctions to read them, I must leave to your imagination and conjecture.

> I am, dear Madam,
> with the highest respect and esteem,
> yours most devotedly,
> T. A. TROLLOPE.

The book in question (to judge from further comment made upon it in a letter not transcribed) was *The Modern Griselda*,[1] in which Maria Edgeworth points the moral of *Paradise Lost* and warns too-indulgent husbands that their wives, when petted into selfish unrestraint, will, in catastrophe, turn on and blame the very man that spoiled them. It is ironical that this tale should have been one of the earliest links between Fanny Milton and the man she was to marry. Little enough of spoiling lay in store for her, but rather gathering clouds of misfortune which turned her husband's grave affection—not to cruelty, but to the querulous exigence of a disappointed man.

[1] London, 1805.

About a month later Thomas Anthony Trollope took the
plunge. His letter of proposal is a long one—too long to
quote in full; but extracts from it, together with the young
lady's reply and his rapturous acknowledgment of her acceptance, will show how typical, at once of its maker and its period,
was the marriage-offer:—

Nov. 1 1808.

MY DEAR MADAM,

In the course of the last Spring I was no little delighted
with the subject a certain debating society had chosen for
their weekly discussion, which to the best of [my] recollection was in the words, or to the effect following: "Is it
most expedient for a man to make an avowal of his attach-
ment to a lady viva voce (*anglice* in a tête à tête), or by
epistolary correspondence?"

I well remember, and probably, my dear Madam, you
may also, that there was one, altho' not of this honourable
society, who expressed a most decided opinion upon the
subject; and to that opinion I now think myself bound to
submit.

This preface explains the motive of my now addressing
you. It will save me the necessity of a more explicit avowal,
and sufficiently declare to you that my future happiness on
earth is at your disposal.

If indeed, as I trust is the case, you are not entirely unaware that my chief delight has long since had its source
in your society and conversation; and if, permit my vanity
to indulge the hope, there has been the slightest degree of
mutuality in this delight, then perhaps—— I confess I
scarcely know what I was going to say, but perhaps you
would not require *three weeks* for passing a sentence on which
I must so anxiously depend.

There is no one perhaps that has a greater contempt for
those who are induced to contract alliances upon motives of
a pecuniary nature than I have; but at the same time I have
had experience enough to teach me that happiness is not
to be expected where the parties are no longer capable of
enjoying those necessaries and comforts of life to which they

B*

have been accustomed, and which are commonly incident to the rank and situation they hold in society.

With these sentiments, and believing them to be your own, as indeed they must be those of every sensible and considerate person of either sex, I deem it an indispensable duty, in addressing myself to you on this subject in which all my dearest interests are involved, to make an open declaration of what grounds I have to hope for the enjoyment of those comforts above alluded to.

My present income, tho' somewhat uncertain since part of it arises from my profession, is about £900 per annum; but as near £200 of this proceeds from my fellowship etc. at Oxford, this last emolument would drop, should I no longer be deemed a fit member of that society. I should also add that this income, trifling as it is, is subject to certain incumbrances, but as it is much beyond my present expenditure as a single man, they are gradually wearing away.

I must now draw this long letter to a conclusion; a letter perhaps chiefly to be remarked by its singularity, and particularly in its manner and style being so little adapted to its subject. If I have erred in this I must admit that it has been in a great measure with design, as my sole object has been to make a declaration which I could no longer conceal, and at the same time to state those circumstances, a knowledge of which, in case you should think the subject of my writing worthy your consideration, would be necessary for that purpose. In doing this in the most simple manner, and in rejecting the flippant nonsense which I believe to be commonly used on occasions of this nature, I doubt not I have acted as well in conformity of your sentiments as of those of, my dear Madam,

your sincere admirer and most devoted servant

THOS. ANTH: TROLLOPE.

[*No date—received 2nd Nov.* 1808]

It does not require three weeks consideration, Mr. Trollope, to enable me to tell you that the letter you left with me last night was most flattering and gratifying to me.

I value your good opinion too highly not to feel that the generous proof you have given me of it, must for ever and in any event, be remembered by me with pride and gratitude. But I fear you are not sufficiently aware that your choice, so flattering to me, is for yourself a very imprudent one. You have every right in an alliance of this kind to expect a fortune greatly superior to any I shall ever possess, and I agree too perfectly with you in your ideas on this point, not to think that you ought to be informed of the truth in this particular, *before* you decide on so important a subject. All I have independent of my father is £1300, and we each receive from him at present an annual allowance of £50. What he would give either of us, were we to marry, I really do not know.

In an affair of this kind, I do not think it any disadvantage to either party that some time should elapse between the first contemplation and final decision of it; it gives each an opportunity of becoming acquainted with the other's opinion on many important points which could not be canvassed before it was thought of, and which it would be useless to discuss after it was settled. I have to thank you for choosing that manner of addressing me, which I once so vaguely said I thought the best, but I have more than once since I began writing this, wished I had not said so. I have not, nor can I, express myself quite as I wish. There is something of cold formality in what I have written, which is very foreign to what I feel,—but I know not how to mend it.

FANNY MILTON.

Lincoln's Inn.
2nd November 1808.

MY DEAREST MADAM,

I am made most happy by the answer you have done me the honour of giving to my letter of last night, and my best thanks are due to you for the ready and very handsome manner in which it has been conveyed. I will not trouble you with another long letter, but will only say how anxious I am to *hear* confirmed by your lips what has been so gratifying to me *to read* under your hand. May I request you to

permit me to have the pleasure of calling upon you at half-
past three o'clock? or should you be engaged to-day would
you be kind enough to name any hour to-morrow morning?
One word by the bearer will be sufficient.

Yours most truly and devotedly,

THOS. ANTH: TROLLOPE.

The several love-letters which passed between the two
during their engagement are mainly of interest as revealing the
contrasted natures of the man and woman. Fanny Milton,
once free of the gravity of the proposal, becomes again the
chattering malicious little creature which she had been when
first her lover made her acquaintance; Thomas Trollope
appears in the ludicrous but rather lovable light of a very
serious slow-minded man, toiling valiantly in the wake of an
intelligence untrained but twice as rapid as his own, and, for
love of the music-maker, capering clumsily to her playful piping.

At the beginning of December she is at home at Heckfield
Vicarage. Her lover seems to have made discreet inquiries about
her dowry, to which she replies with charming frankness:—

Heckfield,
Hartford Bridge.
Dec. 2 1808.

Spite of being *quized* I should have written, as you desired,
yesterday, had it been possible to do so, but we did not
reach Reading till after four, and the postman had left the
Vicarage an hour before I arrived at it. My father did not
meet me, as he was obliged to dine out, but his servant did,
and I had a fine clear cold moonlight evening for my eight
miles jumble in his *patent cart.*[1]

---

[1] The mechanical preoccupations of the Reverend William Milton were at
once a serious drain on his resources and a favourite joke among his children.
He was for ever inventing types of vehicle and evolved in particular a non-
reversible coach, which was slung very low on enormous wheels. In explanation of this coach, he published a pamphlet with diagrams. T. Adolphus
Trollope (the old clergyman's eldest grandson) speaks in his reminiscences of
the coach-house at Heckfield with its crowd of strange and ineffectual model
coaches, and of an experimental contraption called "rotis volventibus" (*sic*)
which stood on the lawn and was a favourite, if dangerous, toy to visiting boyhood. (Cf. *What I Remember,* by T. Adolphus Trollope, Vol. 1. 19-20.)

Mrs. Milton, who I told you settled all these things, has been telling me what it is their intention to give me and this I am sorry to say is less at present than I hoped and expected. She says my father cannot now give me more than £1200 *stock* and another £100 for cloaths—that at his death I am to have the third of the little estate I mentioned to you, and at hers the third of £2000. I am afraid, nay I know, this is less than you must have expected—and this vexes me much.

                    Yours very truly,

                                        FRANCES MILTON.

As the correspondence proceeds Mr. Trollope becomes playful. He underlines words in imitation of his Fanny ("I have scored my 'howevers' to save you trouble"); scolds her for spoiling her eyes over fine needlework; expresses his extreme and proper anxiety to see her "on the Monday"; and concludes with this prudent reference to her money expectations:—

                                        [8 *December* 1808]

Very little has passed between your father and myself respecting what he should give you on our marriage. The first day I saw him he mentioned the sum of £1200 stock as expressed in your first letter, and I trust you will not think I went too far in replying that I had hoped he would not reduce the allowance he had formerly given to his daughter in the event of her marrying, provided it was with a person of whom he approved. Your father answered that he would take it into consideration. And in calling upon me yesterday told me that the £50 per annum would not be diminished. I find from him also that you are entitled to a property which you have hitherto omitted to mention to me. Indeed I apprehend that you meant to reserve it snugly for a little secret pin-money. I mean ⅛th of the patent coach, which Mr. Milton tells me he has made over to you! Pray are you to bear the same proportion of the expenses of it?

The letters follow one another at regular intervals. Literary discussion and allusion are frequent. Fanny Milton had developed a genuine, if a "young ladylike" interest in literature during her life in London, and Trollope's learning seemed to blend happily with her untrained enthusiasms.

The pair discuss Burns' poetry; she sends him an Italian sonnet written by herself; they appraise in detail the latest reviews; and there is much ado over the authenticity of the Rowley Poems.

But the intermixture of love-making with family gossip and literary opinion is sadly tenuous. The young woman tries now and again, with a timidity not without pathos, to tempt her punctilious lover into emotional asides. She has little success. He takes her playfulness literally or, lest he be thought behindhand in correct affection, reproves her for thinking that she only suffers from their separation. "I shall hope very soon for a letter," she writes, "and hope delayed, you know, maketh the heart sick. Now I am perfectly well at present and have no inclination to be sick myself, or what is much worse, that my heart should be so—so please write quickly!" The sad little jest—there is a quaver in the first sentence, for all the gaiety of the second—provokes a very cumbrous retort, meant perhaps humorously but in effect not very comforting:—

[28 *February* 1809]

"*Hope delayed maketh the heart sick.*"

What a singular quotation, my dear Fanny, is this that you have chosen for the conclusion of your last letter! And do you really think that there is any truth in this adage? or at the most can you entertain an idea that any heart can sicken with delay except that which beats within your own breast? But why need I put these questions to you? Your long silence since the receipt of my last letter has already given me a most decided answer in the negative; for charity alone must force me to put this interpretation on your not having written to me for nearly this fortnight past. No, my dear Fanny, if you really thought that such would have been the effect of your delaying *my* hopes of hearing *from you*, I cannot believe that you would have permitted such hopes to have been so long frustrated. But surely I have mistaken you; this passage must have been meant by you in pure irony and intended to convey an apology for having driven me from your thoughts so long; so I am content to accept it in the sense in which it was written, but trust you will not have the same necessity to have recourse to any apology of this nature in future.

Driven to explain what hardly in writing is explicable, the poor girl gives up her experiment in allusive badinage and puts the matter (emotionally speaking) in words of one syllable:—

Heckfield, March 1 1809.

How badly have you explained causes and their effects, and, if you have written what you think, how far are you from understanding the reason why my last letter did not tread closer on the heels of my former one! Must I tell you why it was? The wise ones would call me a "silly silly fool" for doing so, but I will not be accused of irony without trying to make you confess the accusation was unjust. First then I must confess that *I should have liked* to write to you before, but as you had never told me how often you wished me to write, I was afraid—not that you should deem my letters troublesome, I will not say I feared that—but that you might think I wrote *oftener than you* expected. Perhaps you will not understand this—it is I believe a little *female feeling*, and therefore it is hardly fair to expect you should. One other little private reason I had, which was that I calculated upon receiving an answer *immediately* if I let a tolerable length of time elapse—and I have already told you my heart does not like waiting when I expect a letter from you. Here, my dear father confessor, is my confession at full length. Will you give me absolution, or must I perform some penance first? and what must it be? not to wait ten days before I receive my sentence I hope.

Here a more sensitive man would have recognised his own lack of understanding and made silent resolutions for the future. But Thomas Trollope, in letter-writing as in the adventures of life, never knew when a subject or an occupation, having served its purpose, should be left alone. He continues tactlessly to labour this theme of letters exchanged. He harps to the extreme of prosiness on the respective anxiety of his mistress and himself for news of their beloved, until his persistence recalls (however unsuitably) the husband of Barry Pain's Eliza launched on the subject of his affection for his wife and hers for him. After five hundred words of tortuous elaboration of her phrase "dear father confessor," he makes this intolerable remark—intolerable for its stupidity, and for its wilful obscuring of the genuine affection that he had for her: ". . . I confess that it had never occurred to me to tell you that the oftener I heard from you the more I should be pleased, and that if you should write more frequently than I had expected your letter would only be the more grateful to me." Was ever clever man a clumsier lover?

But at last comes the climax of Fanny Milton's attempts to draw from him some unguarded expression of the love she did not doubt but longed to hear outspoken. The wedding day is fixed. In sudden panic need of reassurance she writes:—

Heckfield, May 2nd 1809.

I am rather in doubt, my dear friend, whether I *ought* to begin gossiping to you already. . . . It is a solemn business, my dear friend. Does not the near approach of it almost frighten you? I tremble lest you should love me less a twelvemonth hence than you do now. I sometimes fear you may be disappointed in me, that you will find me less informed, less capable of being a companion to you, than you expect, and then—but I am growing very dismal—this will never do. I must go and sun myself a little upon the heath.

This time the man is really touched. His letter must have been as difficult in the writing to one of his haughty shyness, as it is moving to the reader of this lop-sided, throttled love-story:—

4 *May* 1809.

Many thanks to you, my dear Fanny, for your letter of the 2nd, which I received late last night.

Though it pleases me to see your doubts removed, I scarcely know how to pardon their birth and existence. But perhaps they have arisen from the cold and flegmatic manner of telling you how anxious I always am of knowing you are well and particularly of receiving that intelligence from yourself. But, my dearest love, are you still to learn my character and sentiments? Still to be made acquainted with my lifeless manners, my stone-like disposition? Are you yet to be informed in what detestation I hold all ardent professions and in what admiration actions that want not the aid of declamation but boldly speak for themselves?

When I see a man vehement in his expressions without any apparent or sufficient cause, I am always inclined to suspect him. If he states to me a plain fact and takes unnecessary pains to inforce the truth of it, I immediately conclude it to be false. From these ideas, which perhaps you will say are not very liberal ones, tho' I think they are founded upon reason and confirmed by observation, it may not be improbable that I often seem to be too cautious of making use of what might be considered a natural and becoming warmth in my declarations; but I confess, whether it is from entertaining such sentiments as these myself or from any other cause, I always feel afraid of raising doubts to the prejudice of my own sincerity by professing too much or declaring myself in too vehement a manner.

Fanny's reply shows how happy his few sentences of candour have made her. She has been at long last given one chance of comforting and encouraging her dignified and self-sufficient lover. Instantly, womanlike, she concedes his every point. He has virtually entreated her forgiveness for his inarticulacy. There is nothing to forgive; he is right, as always, and it is she—poor weakling—who can only strive anew to be more worthy of his strength.

The remainder of the correspondence exchanged before the now imminent wedding is wholly trivial. Thomas Trollope has had his moment of unreserve; Fanny has won her little battle for a love-speech. Wherefore the two, each for a different reason, are content to write out the remaining days of their single life in purest commonplace.

On May 23 1809, Fanny Milton became Fanny Trollope, and began the married life which was to bring her face to face with poverty and sorrow, and to put such strain upon her courage, her endurance and her faith that only a great woman could support it. That she won her long struggle with fate, and came in the end to happy prosperous old age and to the love of famous sons, was the reward of her own indomitable spirit and has become her title to immortality.

II

THOMAS AND FRANCES TROLLOPE set up house in the same Keppel Street where first they met. For a while at least Henry Milton and his remaining sister Mary lived on at Number 47, within easy reach of the new household at Number 6, so that the circle of friends and the social background of Fanny's early married years were much the same as had been those of her girlhood.

She had, however, as foreground of her life the new engrossing occupations of her modest household and, more important still, of motherhood. The first child—Thomas Adolphus—was born in the year following the wedding. He was not for long the only one. The second son, Henry, was born in 1811; a third, Arthur William, in 1812; in 1813 came a daughter, who appeared and disappeared within twenty-four tragic hours; and on April 24 1815 the indefatigable woman gave to her husband his fourth son and to her country a great novelist.

Anthony was the last of the Trollope children born in Keppel Street. Between ambition and disappointment the father was growing dissatisfied alike with his home and his profession. When early in 1816 he decided to leave London, he first gave rein to the mania for rash experiment which was finally to ruin him.

At the time of his marriage, and although not himself a wealthy man, Thomas Trollope had considerable "expectations." His father, the Rev. Anthony Trollope, Rector of Cottered in Hertfordshire and sixth son of Sir Thomas Trollope, baronet, of Casewick, Lincolnshire, had married the daughter of Adolphus Meetkerke, a rich gentleman of Dutch descent who had an estate near Royston called Julians. When old Adolphus Meetkerke died, his property passed to his only

son, the brother-in-law of the Rector of Cottered, and as this
new owner of Julians remained unmarried, it was generally
accepted that his house and land and much of his money would
go to his sister's eldest son. Thomas Trollope, therefore, who
even before his father's death in 1806 had been a regular visitor
to Julians, was on all sides regarded as the heir, and in that
capacity properly respected.

With such a position and property assured, it is easy to
understand that the didactic young lawyer should have seemed
to Fanny's parents a very suitable match. To the girl herself
he became a being doubly impressive, possessing as he did
not only grave personal self-confidence, but also the status of
heir apparent to a considerable estate.

Of this status he was highly conscious. Although his
coming splendour did not check his enthusiasm for a barrister's
career, it stiffened his obstinate belief in his own judgment and
encouraged the love of speculation which, when dissatisfactions came, broke out disastrously.

During his engagement and for the first years of his married
life, Thomas Trollope was unremitting in his application to a
profession not ultimately vital to his livelihood. He impressed
his seniors and his colleagues by his knowledge and understanding of law and was regarded as among the most learned
of the junior Chancery barristers. But more than learning is
required to build and to maintain a legal practice. When
Thomas Trollope first began to realise that for all his toil and
reputation he was losing ground and not gaining it, the very
qualities which were causing failure blinded him to an understanding of it. On many men the sudden consciousness of
ill-success acts as a check and, by giving time for self-examina-
tion and for thought, turns them into the way of prosperity.
But Trollope was not of these. He had the intellect and the
application necessary to achievement, but of the even more
necessary humility, elasticity and readiness to see another
point of view, he had none at all. He was dour and un-
approachable, sullen under occasional defeat, arrogant in
victory. A barrister's practice—and indeed ordinary social
existence—conducted on the assumption that everybody else

is always wrong, is bound to wilt. Trollope offended his colleagues and, worse still, his clients. He was disputatious and opinionated, and the fact that in his many arguments he was usually in the right did not, in the eyes of others, justify his interpretation of a victor's bearing.

Respect without affection turns easily to dislike, and the unpopularity of Thomas Trollope grew steadily. From professional circles it spread to social ones. At the whist table, for example (and he loved the game), he scolded everybody so ceaselessly and provokingly that even old friends came to avoid his company. Fanny must early have found the need for patience and good humour in the adjustment of the casual contacts between society and a husband so tactless and so moody.

Naturally the man visited his secret disappointments on his family. He was incapable of pouring out his troubles to the wife who could have helped and consoled him. To admit that all was not going well would have been to admit himself at fault, and this (even though at times he may have longed to do it) was not possible to him. So he choked down his anger against fate and against himself, kept his head high with bitter pride and, in default of circumstance to dominate, ruled his children with a nagging despotism.

The timid restiveness of these young victims and even his wife's unfailing cheerfulness (for good temper in others sometimes increases bad temper in oneself) combined to aggravate Thomas Trollope's irritable dissatisfactions. He had a further trouble to endure in recurrent bilious headaches. This malady, to which he had always been liable, may well have been at the bottom of his discontents. As he grew older, his health grew worse and his headaches more regular and prostrating, so that it is not possible to follow his unhappy story very far before losing the power to criticise his faults in pity for his disabilities.

Bad health was the ostensible cause of the family's removal from Keppel Street. In 1816 Trollope took on a long lease and at a high rent from Lord Northwick a four-hundred-acre farm near Harrow. Here he built a big house (which he named "Julians" with, perhaps, impatient reference to that other Julians in Hertfordshire) and laid out a fine garden. His wife and children were established in the new home in 1817. He himself retained chambers in London, driving to town daily in his gig, moving his offices from one gloomy building to another in the hope of tempting the ever more elusive client. Law was to remain his profession, but farming should be the background of his life and its ultimate achievement.

If with all his knowledge he was failing as a barrister, it was not likely that with complete ignorance he would succeed at farming. Julians soon showed itself an expensive hobby. To his wife's protests he would reply that the heir to the Meetkerke thousands was dependent neither on advocacy nor agriculture; that his health and inclination had brought him to Harrow, where the latter was gratified and the former at least no worse than in London; that in the ordering of his household, as in everything else, he knew what should be done and meant to do it.

But when he had been a very short time in his new home a terrible thing happened. Mr. Meetkerke, now an old gentleman of over sixty, married a young wife and settled to the begetting of a large family of children.

Thomas Trollope, as his eldest son records, bore the blow with fine dignity; his pride, which brought him so often to catastrophe, was at least genuine. But as usual the poor man had been in part the architect of his own misfortune. During the time before the unexpected marriage, uncle and nephew had come to serious political disagreement. The former was a blustering illogical Tory of the old school, who "in his fine old hunting-field voice used to talk a great deal of nonsense," but certainly meant very little of the repressive violence that he professed. A wiser man than Thomas Trollope would have let the old man say his harmless say and changed the subject; but the disputatious arrogance which drove clients from his chambers also flayed the indignant uncle with closely argued, unanswerable Liberalism. So the rich man turned

from his nephew to the more conciliatory companionship of a
young wife, and the very foundation of the Trollope household
crumbled into sand.

For a while, however, life at the new Julians continued.
Thomas Trollope still believed he could make a success of
farming, and he had enough of private means to conceal from
the world (and unhappily from himself also) the seriousness of
the position. Not until 1827 did the real crisis come and the
intervening years at Julians, for all their false economics,
were happy and crowded. The sunny hospitality of Fanny
Trollope made her home a favourite place of gathering. She
was the ideal hostess—at once easy-going and practical,
thoughtful of her guests but careless of her own convenience.
During this time of busy entertaining and of frequent journeys
about England and abroad, she had great scope for her unfailing eagerness to hear new things and see new people. Also
she practised the ready observation which later gave racy
actuality to her novels. There were many encounters of
interest during these active years. It was at Julians that the
Merivale family first came to intimacy with the Trollopes,
Herman Merivale remaining Frances Trollope's closest friend,
while his sons and the Trollope children carried the friendship
further.[1] To Julians would come Auguste Hervieu, a French
artist, destined later to go with Fanny Trollope to America,
there to support her, and later still to illustrate several of her
books. Mary Russell Mitford, who as a girl of fifteen had met
Fanny Milton so long ago as 1802 (Heckfield was near both
to Reading and to Swallowfield, so that the Milton vicarage
was well within the Mitford orbit), was a frequent visitor. At
Julians George Hayter, the painter, persuaded Thomas
Trollope to sit for one of the lawyers in his much-engraved
picture of the trial of Lord Russell.

These friends and many others thronged the comfortable
house at Harrow, bringing with them talk of pictures, books
and social happenings, in which talk Frances Trollope joined

---

[1] The three sons were Herman (afterwards Under-Secretary for India);
Charles (afterwards Dean of Ely), and John, who became Anthony's special
friend (cf. below, pp. 120 and 141).

with all the ready interest of a cultivated, active-minded
woman. Intellectual interests were for her a pleasant adornment of a comfortable life. Never for a moment during this
time of apparent prosperity did she herself contemplate authorship. She would scribble charades and verses as would any
lady of her kind; but with professional writers she was content
to mingle, showing the kindly enthusiasm of an outsider,
applauding their triumphs, adjusting their quarrels and listening
to their ambitions with the genuine—if sometimes amused—
sincerity proper to the busy hostess of a handsome house, to
whom letters were an alleviation and not a livelihood.

In her actual neighbourhood also she made many friends.
The Milmans (from Pinner), Colonel Grant (whose family
helped so generously when bailiffs came to "Orley Farm"),
and others, were in and out of Julians day by day. But the
local intimacy which most influenced Frances Trollope was
that between her husband and the clan of Drury. Several
Drury brothers were on the staff of Harrow School, of whom
one was later to keep school in Brussels and employ Anthony
as an inefficient classical usher for a few months in 1834.
Another member of the same family—Arthur Drury—owned
the private seminary at Sunbury to which the young Anthony
was sent at one stage of his miserable boyhood. The connection between the Trollopes and the Drurys had the direct
effect of involving the former (and particularly Frances) in the
vexed local question of the Reverend J. W. Cunningham,
Vicar of Harrow.

Cunningham was a leading evangelical, whose controversial
book *The Velvet Cushion*, published in 1814, had created such
a furore that its author was nicknamed "Velvet" Cunningham
and became, as it were, a low church battering ram against the
fortress of aristocratic, hard-drinking Anglicanism. Although
he continued outwardly on terms with them, his tenets were
hateful to the clerical element of Harrow school. This body,
headed by the Rev. Henry Drury, formerly tutor and still
friend to Lord Byron, with the thoughtless cruelty of established social superiors at war with an aggressive interloper,
spread rumours, half humorous and half malicious, about the

base origin and private failings of the Vicar. The gossip had
enough of truth in it to hurt, enough of falsity to give retort
a chance. The neighbourhood split into pro- and anti-
Cunninghamites.

Actually the rights and wrongs of the two parties were fairly
matched. The incident of the funeral of Byron's natural
daughter Allegra showed not only a blend of rigidity and
flunkeyism in Cunningham, but also that his enemies were as
capable as himself of pharisaical prudery. Poor Allegra, the
child of Byron and Clare Clairemont, died at the age of five
and her body was sent home in 1822 to be buried in Harrow
Church. The vestry held a solemn meeting. Cunningham
and all the school-party were present, and it was decided that
the waif's grave should not be commemorated by any stone,
lest the perpetuation of her name should corrupt the morals
of the Harrow boys. Nevertheless after the meeting Cunningham, with the clumsy servility of a man over-conscious of his
inferiority, was foolish enough to ask Henry Drury to send
to Lord Byron on his behalf a message of fulsome compliment
on the recently published poem *Cain*. Drury, delighted with
this story against his enemy, spread it abroad. The anti-
Cunningham homes rejoiced and Fanny Trollope wrote a
long satirical poem on the theme, which fortunately enough
has disappeared.

This incident, discreditable enough to all concerned, is of
peculiar significance to the tale of Frances Trollope. In the
first place, the casual baiting of "Velvet" Cunningham, which
had been begun as an amusement, grew into an obsession. The
two were perpetually at odds. A story is told of a collision
between her and the Vicar which has the direct authority of
one of the Grant family. Frances Trollope was fond of giving
parties for young people, at which charades were a popular
amusement. Cunningham asked her one day if she considered
such play-acting a suitable diversion for young ladies. "Why
not, Mr. Cunningham?" demanded the lady. "Mrs. Cunningham has evening parties to which we are always glad to go to
hear your daughters play upon the piano." "Ah, yes" replied
the Vicar "but my daughters always have their backs to the

audience." By this and similar humbug Frances Trollope was provoked from an amused dislike of evangelicals into an obstinate detestation. Her novels contain numerous satires on the fire and brimstone school of clerics, and one—*The Vicar of Wrexhill*—was actually based on the character (as she was pleased to distort it) of Cunningham himself.

Her acceptance of the Drury attitude further shows that, with all her warm-heartedness and selfless desire to help her friends, she lacked that finer sympathy which shrinks from a conventional cruelty. The Drury vendetta against Cunningham was crude and foolish. Arrogating to themselves superiority of breeding, they yet acted with a bad taste which, could they but have realised it, betrayed their whole case. And Frances Trollope, unthinking or perhaps unconscious of the vulgarity of their behaviour, followed after them. A woman more subtle or more self-conscious would hardly have allowed herself to adopt, in imitation of her friends, a set prejudice against any sect or class. A woman less intelligent would have been unable to turn that prejudice to harmless, if clumsy, comedy. But Frances Trollope was very intelligent and rather insensitive. Over this particular matter, alike in her want of finer feeling and in her power of articulate humour, she was intensely herself. She was the ordinary Englishwoman, with certain elements carried to a higher power. Quick above the average and capable of great personal generosity, she had nevertheless the mass mind. She was prone to unreflecting generalised dislikes; stubborn alike toward ideas and in adversity; and lacking in that pride of individuality which throws persons of a different type into automatic opposition to herd-bias. All of these characteristics are plainly evident in her life story and in her books.

Something of the same easy acceptance of a conventional attitude, combined with a readiness to experiment in half-humorous extremism, marked her sojourns in Paris, and particularly her relationship with General Lafayette and with his wards Frances and Camilla Wright.

In 1824 she and her husband travelled to Paris, where,

through mutual friends and for the satisfaction of Thomas Trollope's ardent Liberalism, she contrived the acquaintance of the famous old revolutionary. The Trollopes visited the General's patriarchal home, and Fanny, once there, would naturally have thrown herself into the republican talk and advanced feminism of the household with the heedless enthusiasm of a suburban lady at a night club. It was all, to her laughing receptive mind, the greatest fun imaginable; but she was well aware that, next morning, so to speak, she would be in her own humdrum cheerful home again, and that to her ordinary existence the desperate extremism of her present company had no reference whatsoever. Thus she was able throughout her life to sample every kind of company. She could glow with the fervour of regicides and refugees, she could give warm welcome to proletarian conspirators, she could talk communism and trousers for women with Frances Wright, she could relish the opulent hospitality of archduchesses or gush over the newest books with blue-stockings —and all the time remain just Fanny Trollope.

Her eldest son in his memoirs and her daughter-in-law in her biography make much pother over her personal sympathy or otherwise with radical ideas. The point is a trivial one. Her political opinions were so subordinate to her temperament that their only importance to an understanding of her character lies in their very negligibility. Anthony, alone, read the matter aright, and set it down in his *Autobiography*. After making a little affectionate fun of his mother's penchant alike for parlour revolutionaries and for the *haute noblesse* (agreeable jesting for which he was solemnly taken to task by his brother Tom in the latter's subsequently published reminiscences), he says:—

With her, politics were always an affair of the heart—as indeed were all her convictions. Of reasoning from causes I think that she knew nothing. Her heart was in every way so perfect, her desire to do good to all around her so thorough, and her power of self-sacrifice so complete, that she generally got herself right in spite of her want of logic; but it must be acknowledged that she was emotional. I can remember now her books and can see her at her pursuits. She raved of him of whom all such ladies were raving then, and rejoiced in the popularity and wept over the persecution of Lord Byron.

The picture is surely a faithful one. Frances Trollope was feminine, impulsive, warm-hearted, but too busy with the bustling pleasures of a strenuous existence to go deeply into anything or to linger over the interests of yesterday when those of to-morrow called to her. Even when she had herself become an established authoress and her name stood high on the list of lending-library favourites, she remained an ordinary woman with no literary affectations or vanities, with no profundities either real or assumed. To the letters of flattery which poured in upon her she replied with genial unconcern; to reviewers' insults and the scurrilities of angry Americans she did not reply at all. She could not be lionised, having no sense of the leonine. She had measured herself too often against hostile reality to be cheated into attitude by phantom reputation. Daily life and the fortunes of her family had once been bitterly her burden; they remained her chief interest when the bad times were over.

All of this Anthony saw and set on record. He could divine his mother truly, because in this primary absorption in daily things he was so utterly her son.

III

IN SUCH A HOUSEHOLD as Julians, children had greater opportunity for precocity than for steadiness of mind. With a father alternately preoccupied and pedantically exigent; with a mother often absent on journey and, while at home, surrounded by visitors and in a whirl of parties, theatricals and intellectual small-talk; in a large, lavish but unstable home crowded with various and eccentric guests, the Trollope boys, apart from actual schooling (and that not of the most competent kind), had little enough of training, either in character or manners. They were not neglected—indeed both parents were fond and earnestly determined to do their duty by their children—but they were either bustled or ignored.

As time passed the father's gloomy and rigorous discipline, alternating with the busy mother's spasmodic tenderness, intensified the atmosphere of restlessness, and destroyed the serenity of home-background which is perhaps the most vital element in a child's upbringing. When to this restlessness was added a brooding sense of financial instability, conditions at Harrow were precisely such as might have been expected to throw up brilliant idlers or sullen rebels, but hardly lads destined to become men at once industrious and level-headed.

And yet of the three boys (for Arthur died when very young) only Henry gave even promise of instability, and he for the last years of his short life was under the deepening shadow of consumption. Both Thomas Adolphus and Anthony in their different ways developed characters remarkable for pertinacity and for good sense. Thomas Adolphus had over Henry the advantage of robust health, and over both Henry and Anthony (particularly over Anthony) the greater advantage of being closer to his mother than they. This greater intimacy, which in after years influenced not only the tenour but the actual circumstances of his life, in youth gave him an invaluable support. The years at Keppel Street were the only period of Frances Trollope's early married life when she had leisure of mind to be a real companion to her children; and, as Tom was the only one of those children old enough at Keppel Street to feel and to respond to his mother's friendship, he came inevitably to a fuller share of it, and greatly profited.

Henry, already suffering from the physical weakness which was to cut short his life, had the additional handicap of being his father's favourite. From his ruthless conception of boyish training Thomas Trollope excepted Henry. The lad was more sharply etched than his brothers and of more imperious manners; also he had the vivid quality which often accompanies a consumptive tendency. After two years at Winchester, where he was idle and wayward, he was brought home and allowed to trifle, first with this experimental training, then with that. From the time of his withdrawal from school to his death eight years later, Henry was the adored failure of the family.

Anthony remains, whose achievement was the most remarkable of all. Because he was younger by five years than Tom, his schooling was earlier subject to the father's bankruptcy and his share of the mother's undistracted affection considerably less. Entangled in the family distresses, his life as a small boy was harder and more cruelly solitary than that of either of his brothers. Nature and chance alike were against him. His clumsy stupidity provoked his father's most pitiless discipline; he had less social address than either of his elders, less money, clothes or family prestige to counterbalance awkward shyness. Bundled from one place to another, continually the victim of his parents' money troubles, supported only by the hurried moments of affection which were all his over-busy, harassed mother could afford to him, he grew from an unhappy little boy into a sullen youth and at eighteen was thrown into the pool of London loneliness to sink or swim.

Breeding and a large share of his mother's dogged pluck saved him from disaster. It may have seemed that little of the proud Englishry of generations of Trollopes survived in this untidy, ineffective lad. Indeed in his Autobiography, with characteristic and challenging dispraise of self, he blames his own lack of spirit for most of the troubles of his early life. But this lack of spirit was only a veneer of timidity, and not grained in the wood. Inherited pride was at the core of him, and in the real crisis of his existence held firm. Instinct told him that such as he neither surrendered to hostile circumstance nor ran away from life. He was usually idle; he was often insubordinate; sometimes, within the narrow limits of his purse, he sought a humble dissipation. But in those dreary London days he laid hold of courage and never again let go of it. Existence must more often have been intolerable than endurable, and pleasant more rarely still. But he stuck it out. He had his father's uprightness without the unpractical arrogance which transformed Thomas Trollope's best quality into his greatest handicap; he developed his mother's courage in the face of odds, and at the same time a genial humility of taste that could understand and relish the commonplace, and also make fun of it.

Anthony Trollope's own description of his childhood and schooldays is poignant as only truth can be. It treats from personal memory of the most squalid period of the family's existence; it portrays not only a little lonely boy, but the harsh uncomfortable home which was his only refuge from an unkind world.

My boyhood [he says] was, I think, as unhappy as that of a young gentleman could well be, my misfortunes arising from a mixture of poverty and gentle standing on the part of my father, and from an utter want on my own part of that juvenile manhood which enables some boys to hold up their heads even among the distresses which such a position is sure to produce.

My two elder brothers had been sent as day boarders to Harrow School and may have been received among the aristocratic crowd—not on equal terms because a day boarder at Harrow in those days was never so received—but at any rate as other day boarders. I do not suppose they were well treated, but I doubt whether they were subjected to the ignominy which I endured.

I was only seven, and I think that boys at seven are now spared among their more considerate seniors. I was never spared. I was not even allowed to run to and fro between our house and the school without a daily purgatory.

I was three years at Harrow and, as far as I can remember, I was the junior boy in the school when I left it.

Then I was sent to a private school at Sunbury kept by Arthur Drury. During the two years I was there, though I never had any pocket money and seldom had much in the way of clothes, I lived more nearly on terms of equality with other boys than at any other period during my very prolonged school-days.

When I was twelve there came the vacancy at Winchester College which I was destined to fill. It had been one of the great ambitions of my father's life that his three sons, who lived to go to Winchester, should all become fellows of New College. But that suffering man was never destined to have an ambition gratified. We all lost the prize which he struggled with infinite labour to put within our reach.

While Anthony was at Winchester, his father made a first unwilling concession to monetary embarrassment. The false prosperity of the years at Julians had run its course. In that large house the Trollopes had lived far beyond their means, and only a man blind to portents and deaf to commonsense could have endured, as Thomas Trollope endured, ten years of menacing collapse. But at last, early in 1827, he had to realise the hopelessness of his position. Unluckily his rash commitments left little scope for real retrenchment. His lease from Lord Northwick made impossible the complete abandonment of the Julians estate; the most that he could do was to reduce domestic liabilities. He compromised with circumstances by letting his large modern house to (of all people) the Reverend Mr. Cunningham, and himself rented another smaller farm in the neighbourhood, on which stood a smaller, shabbier, but more manageable house.

This new home was called " Julians Hill" and was confessedly the model for Anthony's later creation "Orley Farm."
To twentieth-century taste it looks, as Millais portrayed it, a
pleasant house enough, with just the quaintness now desired.
But it represented a sad decadence in 1827. In contrast to the
spacious modernity of Julians its small-scale shabbiness was
humiliating, so that outward loss of dignity and inward sense
of having failed of an ambition combined to sour still further
the unlucky lawyer's temper.

At Winchester the little Anthony was put, according to the
school custom, under his big brother Tom as a kind of pupil.
The mother wrote to Tom begging him to do his best for his
junior, and incidentally throwing a little light on the family's
estimate of this unattractive midget.

> I daresay you will often find him idle and plaguing enough.
> But remember, dear Tom, that in a family like ours, *every-*
> *thing* gained by one is felt personally and individually by all.
> He is a good-hearted fellow and clings so to the idea of
> being Tom's pupil and sleeping in Tom's chamber, that
> I think you will find advice and remonstrance better taken
> by him than by poor Henry. Greatly comforted am I to
> know that Tony has a prefect brother. I well remember
> what I used to suffer at the idea of what my little Tom
> was enduring.

The big brother interpreted his duties drastically. Indeed
Tony was mainly conscious of him as the most regular of
several disciplinarians.

> Since I began my manhood I and my brother Tom have
> been fast friends. Few brothers have had more of brother-
> hood. But at Winchester he was of all my foes the worst.
> As a part of his daily exercise he thrashed me with a big
> stick.

And yet, when Tom left school and shortly afterwards
accompanied his father to America, poor Anthony fell into
worse troubles still and may well have wished the thrashings

C

back again.   They at least reminded him that he had a background of a sort.

For something over three years Anthony endured a misery of neglect and outlawry—until, indeed, Thomas Trollope returned from the United States in 1830.   More sombre and dour than ever after his fruitless excursion into commerce, more terribly a martyr to sick headaches and their aftermath of irritation, he removed Anthony from Winchester on the ostensible ground that he had no chance of winning a scholarship at New College, and brought him to live at home again. If the boy expected that life was now to brighten, he was sadly disappointed.   Indeed the worst of all was yet to come.

The family fortunes were so shattered that even Julians Hill had become impossible.   Thomas Trollope moved house once again and this time sank almost to degradation.   Anthony vividly describes the new home (if home it could be called) and the supreme unhappiness that he himself endured there.

My father took himself to live at a wretched tumbledown farmhouse on the second farm he had hired!   And I was taken there with him.   It was nearly three miles from Harrow, at Harrow Weald, but in the parish; and from this house I was again sent to that school, as a day-boarder.

Perhaps the eighteen months which I passed in this condition, walking to and fro on those miserably dirty lanes, was the worst period of my life.   I was now over fifteen, and had come to an age at which I could appreciate at its full the misery of expulsion from all social intercourse.   I had not only no friends, but was despised by all my companions. It was the horror of those dreadful walks backwards and forwards which made my life so bad.   Here were the same lanes four times a-day, in wet and dry, in heat and summer, with all the accompanying mud and dust, and with disordered clothes.   I might have been known among the boys at a hundred yards' distance by my boots and trousers—and was conscious at all times that I was so known.

To this period belongs the only outside reminiscence on

record of Anthony Trollope as a schoolboy, and it tragically confirms what he himself has said of his solitude and his unhappiness.

Sir William Gregory, with whom later at Coole Park Trollope became a friendly intimate, writes thus in his autobiography:—

> It was when I was turned down that I became intimate with Anthony Trollope, who sat next to me. He was a big boy, older than the rest of the form, and without exception the most slovenly and dirty boy I ever met. He was not only slovenly in person and in dress, but his work was equally dirty. His exercises were a mass of blots and smudges. These peculiarities created a great prejudice against him, and the poor fellow was generally avoided.

> It is pitiable to read in his autobiography, just published, how bitter were his feelings at that time, and how he longed for the friendship and companionship of his comrades, but in vain. There was a story afloat, whether true or false I know not, that his father had been outlawed, and every boy believed it was the duty of a loyal subject of the crown to shoot or otherwise destroy "old Trollope" if possible. Fortunately, he never appeared among us.

> I had plenty of opportunities of judging Anthony, and I am bound to say, though my heart smites me sorely for my unkindness, that I did not like him. I avoided him, for he was rude and uncouth, but I thought him an honest, brave fellow. He was no sneak. His faults were external; all the rest of him was right enough. But the faults were of that character for which schoolboys would never make allowances, and so poor Trollope was tabooed, and had not, so far as I am aware, a single friend. He might have been a thoroughly bad young fellow, and yet have had plenty of associates. He gave no sign of promise whatsoever, was always in the lowest part of the form, and was regarded by masters and by boys as an incorrigible dunce.[1]

---

[1] *Sir William Gregory, K.C.M.G. An Autobiography.* Edited by Lady Gregory. (London, John Murray, 1894.)

Most boys have had brief periods of misery at school; a few never throw off the dread of "going back." But to nearly all of them home at least has been a refuge, and holidays a blessed interlude in adversity. Anthony Trollope, however, was as wretched in vacation as in term-time. Of one particular holiday he writes:—

I passed one set of holidays in my father's chambers at Lincoln's Inn. There was often a difficulty about the holidays, as to what should be done with me. On this occasion my amusement consisted in wandering about among those old deserted buildings and in reading Shakespeare out of a bi-columned edition. There was nothing else to read.

Even his evenings and his Sundays at home were miserable. He thus describes his father's dwelling and the life there:—

The farmhouse was not only no more than a farmhouse, but was one of those farmhouses which seem always to be in danger of falling into the neighbouring horse-pond. As it crept downwards from house to stables, from stables to barns, from barns to cowsheds, and from cowsheds to dung-heaps, one could hardly tell where one began and the other ended! There was a parlour in which my father lived, shut up among big books; but I passed my most jocund hours in the kitchen, making innocent love to the bailiff's daughter. The farm kitchen might be very well through the evening, when the horrors of school were over; but it all added to the cruelty of the days.

I wish I could give some adequate picture of the gloom of that farmhouse. Our table was poorer, I think, than that of the bailiff who still hung on to our shattered fortunes. The furniture was mean and scanty.

In the old house were the two first volumes of Cooper's novel called *The Prairie*, a relic—probably a dishonest relic —of some subscription to Hookham's library. Other books of the kind there were none. I wonder how many dozen times I read those two first volumes.

These eighteen months of purgatory were the culmination of Anthony Trollope's innocent suffering. He was to know other times of loneliness and danger, but he was never again to be so helpless in the grip of circumstance. When he left Harrow finally in 1834, his schooling had lasted for twelve whole years. Yet it may truthfully be said that he had no real education at all, save in the hazardous school of undeserved adversity.

It would be hard to parallel this record of wasted effort and useless suffering. No doubt the boy was difficult. A boy who did not grow sullen under such treatment and evade wherever evasion was possible, would not be human. Surely for Anthony's own shortcomings during those twelve miserable years, every excuse which may be needed can be found? What effect on a boy's after-life might not that so-called "education" have produced? Almost any degree of tragedy would be explicable. Yet there was no tragedy, nor even semi-failure. The lad built his own life more securely than do most of those for whom foundations have been lovingly and soundly laid. He built it of his own courage and his own industry. And therein lies the real greatness of the man, seeing that his many books are but expressions of himself and that the personality behind them was of his own fashioning.

"There ain't nowt a man can't bear if he'll only be dogged," says old Giles Hoggett to Mr. Crawley in *The Last Chronicle of Barset*. "It's dogged as does it. It ain't thinking about it."

IV

THE FRIENDSHIP OF FANNY TROLLOPE for Frances Wright was unique among the former's many transient enthusiasms in that it led directly to adventure and to influential change.

The sisters Wright, though of English birth, had gone to the United States about 1820 and had become even more American than their hosts. They were youngish women of large means, and Frances at least was very handsome. A person of strong character and almost fanatical idealism, this Frances had published in 1821 a volume of letters,[1] which derided the institutions of her native land and lauded those of her adopted one with a whole-heartedness very satisfying to the Americans and very offensive to a "Quarterly" reviewer. She had absorbed the teaching of Robert Owen, and blended the theory of his communist settlement in Indiana with a scheme of her own for bettering the conditions of the slaves in the Southern states. Despite her guardian's disapproval, she was determined to sink a large part of her fortune in buying a property in the Mississippi valley, freeing all the slaves upon it, and thereafter dwelling in their midst as a beneficent equal, enjoying with them the fruits of the earth.

It is possible to admire the unselfish enthusiasm of Frances Wright and at the same time to enjoy her absurdities more than her principles. The ludicrous lies terribly in wait for prophets of a better social order, and into its jaws poor Fanny Wright went headlong. Not content with anti-slavery as a cause for propaganda, she must tour England and America lecturing on political Utopias, rationalism and women's rights. She found adherents among the coteries, but, in England at least, her audiences came to smile and went to sleep. She was one of the earliest of that long line of earnest, noisy women

[1] *Views of Society and Manners in America during the years* 1818-19-20. London, 1821.

whose cacophonous reformism echoes down the nineteenth
century. She anticipated alike Amelia Bloomer and the
Reform-Kleidung of the German 'eighties. She preached both
free-love and contempt for men, with a fine disregard of con-
sistency and a numbing eloquence. In the end, poor soul,
she was beaten by the Nature that she worshipped and the
conventions she despised. Flooded out of her Eden in the
Mississippi valley, she transported all her freed slaves to Hayti,
where they were left (duly endowed) in the care of the President. She herself, at the end of a rousing series of lectures
against the slavery of wedlock, married a French teacher of
languages and died at Cincinnati in 1852, a respectable married
woman, washed up on the banks of her own extremism and
there stranded.

All this, to a detached posterity, seems comical enough.
But to Fanny Trollope the reformer's warm heart, loud genial
manner and daring opinions made immediate appeal. Here
was novelty; here was excitement; here, above all, was a
congenial acquaintance. Fanny Trollope, herself a brave and
generous woman, felt in her new friend a courage and a
generosity of another kind. The practicability or soundness
of the Wright gospel she would not trouble to test nor pause
to question. To her such theories were just "ideas" and, like
all ideas, of no real importance beside the cardinal fact of
personality. She liked Frances Wright, and that was sufficient.
The idealist was urged to visit Harrow and came, not once but
often. There was frequent discussion of America and its
possibilities. Fanny Trollope, pressed to help inaugurate
Nashoba—that Mississippi paradise of emancipated slaves—
laughed and replied carelessly that she would think about it.
And there normally the matter would have dropped, for Mrs.
Trollope was too busy and too happy in her English life to
cross the sea in search of an ideal. But unluckily Frances
Wright preached the perfection of America to Thomas
Trollope also, until in the obscure depths of that gloomy
gambler's mind an astounding idea took root.

There could have been no more propitious moment for
presenting to him the attractions of God's country. A year

earlier and he would have frowned even Miss Wright's insensitive loquacity into silence; now he was ripe for fresh
adventure. He was already conscious of a failing livelihood,
ashamed to find himself in an old-fashioned farm while the
mansion he had created-was in alien hands. To such a mood
America, as glowingly described by his wife's friend, smiled
irresistibly. The devil of speculation awoke and gripped him.
For him also should the new world redress the balance of the
old. So it happened that from the wild talk of Frances Wright
sprang Thomas Trollope's crowning lunacy—a scheme to
open a bazaar for fancy goods in Cincinnati. His unfortunate
wife was to do the pioneering. He would remain at home, buy
stock and later follow her. Success would be immediate;
profits immense. The family fortunes would be made. And
so, oddly enough, they were; but very much at the eleventh
hour and not at all as Thomas Trollope had anticipated.

2

On the fourth of November 1827 Frances Trollope and her
enthusiastic friend Frances Wright sailed from London for
New Orleans. With them went Henry Trollope, then a boy
of sixteen; his two sisters, Cecilia and Emily—little girls of
eleven and nine years of age—and the French painter Auguste
Hervieu.

They must have been a queer party. Frances Wright, aglow
with fervour at the now imminent achievement of her paradise
for slaves and, one cannot doubt, riding her hobby horse to
death; Mrs. Trollope outwardly gay, inwardly afraid, leading
a forlorn hope into the wilderness and torn between anxiety
for the children whom she had brought with her and those
whom she had left behind; Hervieu, voluble and eager for the
fine career of drawing-master to the Nashoba settlement which
Miss Wright had offered him and which he, poor rapturous
innocent, had joyfully accepted; the children running all over
the ship during the first days of the seven weeks' voyage, and,
for the rest, requiring most strenuously to be amused—they
formed of themselves a community of difficult and conflicting

qualities. Mrs. Trollope described the voyage as "favourable
though somewhat tedious." One may suspect that for her
it was also desperately tiring, seeing that she was the nodal
point of the whole party. She can hardly ever have been alone.
Into her ears and in pitiless succession must have been poured
the exaggerated idealism of Miss Wright, the broken English
of Hervieu, and the ceaseless clamour—joyous or petulant—
of the three children.

The plan of action was that from New Orleans the whole
party should travel up the Mississippi to Memphis, witness
Miss Wright's triumphal entry into Nashoba, and in that
perfect spot remain for several weeks. When the Trollopes
had fully appreciated the idyllic happiness of the settlement
and had seen Hervieu well established as prosperous arbiter
of Nashoba culture, they would proceed up the Mississippi
to St. Louis, passing thence to Cincinnati, where they would
decide the site and organisation of the department store that
was to make their fortune.

It was sixteen years after the river steamer bearing Frances
Trollope and her troupe had snorted away from New Orleans
on the voyage to Memphis, that Charles Dickens began the
writing of *Martin Chuzzlewit*. Yet the American chapters of
that enchanting tale might have been written from notes taken
on the tragi-comic journey of the earlier, obscurer novelist.
The adventures and observations of Frances Trollope antici-
pate those of Martin and Mark Tapley with a completeness so
amazing as virtually to prove the authenticity of both.

On board the boat Mrs. Trollope was unpleasantly struck
by "the total want of all the usual courtesies of the table; the
voracious rapidity with which the viands were seized and
devoured; the frightful manner of feeding with knives and the
still more frightful manner of cleaning the teeth afterwards with
a pocket-knife." She comments bitterly on the productive and
none too well-directed spitting of the many generals, colonels
and majors who, with the exception of a single judge, composed
the male contingent of the passengers. Told more briefly and
without any of Dickens' vivid and breathless humour, Frances

c*

Trollope's description of this voyage and her later descriptions
of hotels and boarding-houses at Memphis, Cincinnati and elsewhere foreshadow almost to the smallest detail Martin's journey
and his experiences at Mrs. Pawkins' boarding-house in New
York.

Mrs. Trollope's account of the squalid settlements along the
river banks—

> . . . One or two clusters of wooden houses, calling them-
> selves towns and borrowing some pompous name, generally
> from Greece and Rome; the sad huts of the woodcutters,
> nearly all of them inundated during the winter; and the best
> of them constructed on piles; their wretched inhabitants
> who are invariably the victims of ague, which they most
> recklessly sustain by the incessant use of spirits; the miser-
> able wives and children of these men, with complexions of
> a blueish white that suggests the idea of dropsy . . .

—and her conclusion that on the whole she "never witnessed
human nature reduced so low as it appeared on the unwhole-
some banks of the Mississippi"—are curiously prophetic of
the voyage to Eden and of the degradation that Mark and
Martin found there.

Perhaps the most striking parallel of all, and one that has no
misery to mar its rich absurdity, is that between the real
Frances Wright and the fictional Mrs. Hominy. Just as the
"mother of the Modern Gracchi" boomed over Martin and
deafened him with gloomy rhetoric as the steamer panted to
the foot of the mud-cliff on which stood New Thermopylæ, so
must Miss Wright in actual fact have towered over her luckless
fellow-travellers, stupefying them with loud praise of every
American institution not actually in sight and much unfavourable reminiscence of things observed in the Old World.

But Frances Wright had this disadvantage in comparison
with Mrs. Hominy, that, while the latter left her English
victims on the boat and thus escaped a testing for her boastful-
ness, the former must needs take them with her and in their
company behold the vaunted marvels of Nashoba. Fortunately she was so impenetrable in her self-confidence and so

well accustomed to a divorce of theory from practice, that
what to a normal being would have been the utter humiliation
of reality, provoked her only, after an embarrassed cough, to
rapture still more resonant on some other theme.

Nashoba was fifteen miles from Memphis and the way lay
through forest. Here, partly from her books, partly from
private notes, is Mrs. Trollope's story of the journey:—

We soon lost all trace of a road, for the stumps of the
trees which had been cut away to open a passage were left
standing three feet high. The forest became thicker and
more dreary looking every mile we advanced. The ever
grinning negro declared we should be sure to get to
Nashoba: and so we did. One glance sufficed to convince
me that every idea I had formed of the place was as far as
possible from the truth. Desolation was the only feeling.

When we arrived at Nashoba they were without milk,
without beverage of any kind except rain water. Wheaten
bread they used very sparingly and the Indian corn bread
was uneatable. They had no vegetables but rice and a few
potatoes we brought with us; no meat but pork; no
butter; no cheese.

I shared Frances Wright's bedroom. It had no ceiling,
and the floor consisted of planks laid loosely upon piles that
raised it some feet from the earth. The rain had access
through the wooden roof, and the chimney, which was of
logs slightly plastered with mud, caught fire a dozen times
a day.

As for poor M. Hervieu, as soon as he arrived he asked:
"Where is the school?" and was answered, "It is not yet
formed." I never saw a man in such a rage. He wept with
passion and grief mixed. He immediately determined to go
back to Memphis and try and get some employment there.

Fear of fever for her children decided Mrs. Trollope to quit
the swampy forest of Nashoba with as little delay as possible.
Within a fortnight she was on the Mississippi once again,
heading for St. Louis. Frances Wright remained awhile amid
the stagnant pools and rotting trees of her absurd philanthropy.

She soon recovered from the momentary shock of her guest's disillusionment. "I believe" writes Mrs. Trollope "that her mind was so exclusively occupied by her hope of raising the African to the level of the European intellect, that all things else were worthless or indifferent to her. I never heard or read of any enthusiasm approaching hers, except in some few instances in ages past of religious fanaticism."

After the troubles in which Miss Wright's enthusiasm had already involved her English friends, this comment seems good-natured enough, and it is hard to blame Fanny Trollope if, as time passed and her fortunes in America went from bad to worse, she became more caustic in her view of the apostle of feminism. She had come to know unkind reality too intimately to appreciate idealism, however beautiful; she had herself paid in the hard cash of suffering for the irresponsible vagaries of a visionary. She never again rose far enough above the world of actuality to free her mind from its worries, or to throw off the impatience which worry breeds against those more fortunate or less mundane souls who (either with the help of private means or at the expense of others) delight to consider the lilies of the field. To Anthony, among other legacies, she left this also—a contempt for cranks and a resentment against unpractical idealists. Both she and he were children of Martha, and to them the persistent prosperity of Mary's sons and daughters was of all mysteries the most infuriating.

3

If personal misfortune can excuse ill-temper, the bitterness of Frances Trollope, not only toward Miss Wright, but toward the whole of the United States, has excuse enough. She had not been long in Cincinnati before her money ran short. Owing to postal failures, no news was received from home. Repeated appeals to Thomas Trollope provoked neither draft nor letter. If Hervieu, who had found Memphis only less profitable a field for portrait painting than Nashoba, had not come on to Cincinnati and joined himself and his small savings to the Trollope party, it is difficult to say in what disaster the expedition might not have foundered. As it was, Hervieu saved them, and the gratitude which Mrs. Trollope showed to him in the years of her prosperity was fully his due.

But even with Hervieu as fellow-sufferer these months in Cincinnati were cruel enough. So sparse and difficult was life, that Frances Trollope, in her anxiety to spare one of her children at least from the rigours of poverty, forgot the lessons of Nashoba and, trusting once again to the promises of idealism, fell victim to the mirage of New Harmony.

A wealthy philanthropist named McClure, who, like Frances Wright, had thrilled to the teaching of Robert Owen, had founded a settlement at New Harmony at which pupils could be fed and educated, paying their way by pleasant intervals of manual labour. To this settlement, in the interests of health and training and to relieve his mother's purse, Henry Trollope was sent. He arrived to find that the philanthropist had tired of his project and departed elsewhere, leaving New Harmony in charge of a Frenchwoman of a highly practical nature, who discovered that, by dropping all pretence of education and doubling the periods of manual toil, she could herself live prosperously on the labours of the "pupils." Poor Henry, therefore, earned his bread by sowing, reaping and baking it, and his potatoes by digging them. He was never robust and the life was too hard for him. His French tyrant had neither use nor sympathy for weaklings. The boy, sinking into misery and sickness, appealed to his mother for rescue. Another raid was made on Hervieu's savings and the lad was fetched back to Cincinnati. The party then settled once again to endurance, and by every mail frantic appeals for help were posted home.

At last replies began to arrive. When they came, they not only brought money, but also the news that Thomas Trollope himself, accompanied by his eldest son, would arrive in Cincinnati in the late autumn of 1828 to make final arrangements for the establishment of the bazaar. Immediately— Fanny Trollope's temperament being what it was—despair gave way to excited optimism. The months of anxiety and discomfort slipped away; all the ill turns played on her by prophets of a new social order were forgotten. As full now of genial energy as, a few weeks earlier, she had been utterly . despondent, she set about preparing for her husband's arrival. With the money sent from England she hired a handsome house, and entered bravely into the social life of Cincinnati. This soon proved itself to be a provincial version of the life at Harrow. Parties, book-talks, theatricals and the preparation of a giant tableau, representing one of the "bolgias" of Dante's *Inferno*, occupied her time. When her husband and eldest son arrived and settled for a visit of four or five months, Mrs. Trollope was prepared for a winter of gaiety.

Her excitement had the unlucky effect of raising higher than before her husband's commercial ambition. He was now living wholly on capital; but the pleasure of having money in his pocket, and the airy enthusiasm with which he had been received by his wife and her friends, blew the last wisps of prudence from his mind. Where once he had contemplated adapting an existing shop or warehouse to his needs, he now determined to erect a special building. A site was purchased; grandiose designs were adopted. Already in his imagination the walls of the Trollope bazaar had risen from the soil of Cincinnati. Full of this rosy vision, he took leave once more of his wife, and, still accompanied by Tom, returned to England. Fanny Trollope was to superintend the building of the bazaar and he would forthwith ship stock across the sea. The grand opening need not for long be delayed.

It is only possible to give a general idea of the lines upon which this bazaar was planned. The chief attractions were to be an immense panorama of London painted by Hervieu and a kind of museum of English and European objects of interest; there was to be a lecture-hall; probably also a great globe. But the main source of revenue would be the retail counters, at which would be sold cutlery, leather goods, and a hundred other products of Old World enterprise, while in addition fancy work of all kinds was expected to be sent in for sale by such private citizens of Cincinnati as were eager to earn a little pin-money by the confection of pretty trifles to tempt idle shoppers.

The scheme, of course, was a tissue of follies and misjudgments. Disillusionment came quickly. The whole affair was a catastrophic failure. The bazaar was not yet finished when the goods arrived. The venture had been from the first resented in certain quarters of Cincinnati and many obstacles put subtly in its way. Now that the attractions it had to offer were unpacked and inspected, they were found in themselves to be wholly unsuitable. The workmen, their work still in progress, clamoured for pay; to satisfy them the stock from England must be sold for what little it would fetch. By November 1828 the goods had been dispersed and the final block of Thomas Trollope's capital had been engulfed.

So ended the madcap adventure of the great Trollope bazaar. The building was completed and became the unconfessed vanity of the city. Its astonishing architectural qualities made it one of the sights of Cincinnati. This physical prominence is evidenced by the references to its peculiarities which occur in the various diaries of travel in America published by English visitors during the decade following its erection. Captain Thomas Hamilton, who was in Cincinnati less than a year after Mrs. Trollope's departure, calls it:—

a large Graeco-Moresco-Gothic-Chinese looking building— an architectural compilation of prettinesses of all sorts, the effect of which is eminently grotesque. . . .

He continues:—

I had then never heard of Mrs. Trollope; but at New York I had afterwards the pleasure of becoming acquainted with her, and can bear testimony to her conversation being imbued with all that grace, spirit, and vivacity, which have since delighted the world in her writings. . . . Her claims to the gratitude of the Cincinnatians are undoubtedly very great. Her architectural talent has beautified their city; her literary powers have given it celebrity. But, strange to say, the market-place of Cincinnati is yet unadorned by the

statue of the great benefactress of the city! Has gratitude
utterly departed from the earth? [1]

Even Harriet Martineau, whose thoughts dwelt on subjects
more abstruse and less picturesque than architectural experiment, allowed herself a passing reference to the Trollope
memorial:—

> Before eight o'clock in the evening, the Cincinnati public
> was pouring into Mrs. Trollope's bazaar, to the first concert
> ever offered to them. This bazaar is the great deformity
> of the city. From my window at the boarding-house it was
> only too distinctly visible. It is built of brick, and has
> Gothic windows, Grecian pillars, and a Turkish dome, and
> it was originally ornamented with Egyptian devices, which
> have, however, all disappeared under the brush of the
> whitewasher. [2]

Finally, and a year after Miss Martineau, came Captain
Marryat to Cincinnati:—

> Mrs. Trollope's bazaar raises its head in a very imposing
> manner; it is composed of many varieties of architecture;
> but I think the order under which it must be classed is the
> *preposterous*. They call it "Trollope's Folly." [3]

Thus was the futile mark of Thomas Trollope set on a city
of the Middle West. For fifty years it lingered on—the city's
secret pride, the open sport of diarists. It has a place among
the classic "follies" of the world, for it was at once a fantastic
monument to a gambler's whim and a tragic tombstone,
marking the grave of a brave woman's hopes.

4

The crumbling of her ill-starred enterprise left Frances
Trollope penniless. In her extremity of misfortune she broke

[1] *Men and Manners in America*, by the author of *Cyril Thornton*. 1833.
[2] *Retrospect of Western Travel*. 1838.
[3] *Diary in America* (1st series). 1839.

down at last and lay on a sick bed in Cincinnati, hovering for weeks between life and death. When early in the spring of 1830 she crawled painfully back to health again, it was to find that Henry, who had recovered from the rigours of New Harmony, was once again ailing. The mother was literally without resources. But the boy was really ill and she did the only thing possible. She sold up her house and furniture, and, borrowing the balance of money necessary—partly from Hervieu, partly from American friends—she shipped him off to England. He reached Harrow at half-past midnight on April 19 1830 without a penny in his pocket and having walked from London. His father's greeting was a bitter grumble and a demand as to why he could not have stayed longer in America.

Thomas Trollope, after his last brief period of gambler's generosity, had sunk deeper than before into ill-health and into obtuse parsimony. He now took a pathetic pride in an exaggerated asceticism. It flattered his unhappy and twisted temper himself to live and to make his children live in squalor and almost in famine. Yet this extreme of penury was not really necessary. Certainly he had lost in Cincinnati almost all that remained of his once considerable capital; but for day to day expenses sufficient still remained, and he had house property in London which meant small annual rents incoming. A man more sound in mind and body could have kept his family at least in modest decency. But the twin devils of ill-health and wrongheadedness had now conquered Thomas Trollope, and drove him to stint and starve both himself and his sons, and to behave toward his wife and daughters with a lack of imagination that was almost callous.

That a man of his sensibility and training could leave a wife and two young girls in the middle of America with nothing to support them but occasional complaints against their extravagance is perhaps the culminating wonder of the whole preposterous story. There is, however, proof of the incredible, for there remains Frances Trollope's written description of the situation in which, and to her husband's knowledge, she found herself. During the wretched summer

that followed Henry's return to England she wrote to
Tom:—

> Everything from the time you left us went wrong, spite
> of exertions—nay, hard labour—on our part that would pain
> you to hear of. I suspect that poor Henry, suffering as he
> did in every way at Cincinnati, must have altogether avoided
> giving the painful details to your father, for by his letters it
> appears that he is still ignorant of nearly all the events.
>
> For instance, he says that he "cannot imagine why it was
> necessary for Henry to set off immediately," when the fact
> was *that every bed had been seized* and that we—your sisters
> and myself—were sleeping together in one small bed at a
> neighbour's and boarding there, while Henry and Hervieu
> both lay on the floor in the kitchen—*for the value of my
> parlour carpet!* And yet your father wonders why Henry
> did not stay the winter!
>
> Again your father writes: "How is it that you are de-
> pendent on Hervieu for your living when I have sent out
> goods to the amount of £2,000!"
>
> Is it not strange, Tom, that he does not yet know that
> these goods never brought *one penny* into my hands? The
> proceeds of those we sold went to the workmen and the
> servants and the *rest were seized*.

In her extremity she turned to an idea with which two years
ago she had played—the idea of writing a book.

> I amuse myself (she had said in a letter to Tom written
> in June 1828) by making notes and hope some day to
> manufacture them into a volume. I think that if Hervieu
> could find time to furnish sketches of scenery and groups
> a very taking little volume might be produced.

Now, in a grimmer emergency than any yet encountered,
the amusement of authorship has become a desperate resort.
In August 1830 she writes:—

> Poor Cecilia is literally without shoes, and I mean to
> sell one or two small articles tomorrow to procure some for

her and for Emily. I sit and write, write, write,—so old shoes last me a long time. As to other articles of dress, we should any of us as soon think of buying diamonds!

My eyes have greatly failed me since my illness. I can do nothing without spectacles and can no longer walk as I did. You must expect, my dear Tom, if Heaven indeed permits my safe return, to see a very old lady.

I wish with all my soul that you could see and hear poor Hervieu! He seems only to live in the hope of helping us. He has several good pupils and has just had a fifty dollar portrait ordered. He pays for our board here and has set his heart on getting us home without drawing on your father's diminished purse.

Sometimes my heart sinks when I think of our present dependence. But Hope tells me that it is just *possible* my book may succeed. It will have great advantages from Hervieu's drawings. If it *should* succeed, a second book would bring money.

Already then, and without certainty of publication, she had begun to fight want with her pen. In the meantime Hervieu stood nobly at her side. Through the winter of 1830 and the spring of 1831 he painted and taught and painted once again, securing from one day to another the existence of himself and of those who, by his own goodwill, were dependent on him. At last, with the help of a little money sent grudgingly from England and by sacrificing the painter's final resources, the unhappy party quitted the United States. They landed at Woolwich on August 5 1831. Frances Trollope was now fifty-one years of age.

V

FROM THE TOIL and anxiety and loneliness of America the indomitable woman had indeed escaped. But for what had she exchanged them? Her homecoming, to which she had so desperately looked, proved sombre enough. She found a husband worn by disappointment and persistent ill-health into a peevish invalid; she found, instead of Orley Farm with its modest comfort, a squalid ruin on Harrow Weald, which, even if she had heard tell of it, must have out-squalored her anticipation. Here, under a leaking roof, were the remains of the furniture and possessions she had once been proud to show. Tom, her eldest son, was away at Oxford; Henry, now struggling to read law in London, was in angry revolt against his father's refusal to grant him even a small allowance; Anthony was dragging miserably through the last stage of his protracted, useless education. In the midst of this unhappy family, at odds one with another and huddled in a tumbledown and meanly furnished farm, Frances Trollope could hardly hope for peace. But the money-need which had driven her to desperate writing in America was as urgent as ever. Because no respite was possible, she neither took nor asked for one. Uncomplaining she settled to the completion of her book.

It was soon finished and, with its suggested illustrations, sent for consideration to a publisher. The period of suspense before a book is taken or rejected is always an uneasy one; to Frances Trollope, for whom so much depended on her work's acceptability, it was distracting. To occupy her mind she began a novel of life in America, and busied herself in gathering up by correspondence the threads of many friendships broken by her absence. Her letters brought replies which (as so often in such cases) emphasised rather the sorrows and forebodings of their writers than their contentments. She had news of the Bristol Riots; of pestilence in London; of the stormy course of the Reform Bill, and of a dozen other reasons for disquiet. Between her private cares and the disasters that seemed to threaten her country and her friends, Fanny Trollope came near to lose her reason. Well might Hervieu write to Tom:—

> I have been for three weeks vexed beyond the power of any mild temper. First this cursed Reform Bill, then my illustrations to Billy Taylor, with all their merit, cannot bring me a single penny, then the lithographic stone from France is not yet here, your poor mamama floating about from incertitude to incertitude, cholera morbus and revolution spread their wings over everything we meet—yes, we must all go to the devil at last, that is my firm opinion!

At last the agreement for the book was signed; the proofs were received and passed; and on March 19 1832, just nine days after its author's fifty-second birthday, were published the two volumes *Domestic Manners of the Americans*.

2

It is difficult nowadays, reading this once-famous book, to understand the furore it caused. *Domestic Manners of the Americans* is a racy, often caustic account of society and ways of life in the New World, in which well-observed and humorous anecdotes of social happening alternate with conventionally overwrought descriptions of scenery and trite reflections on institutions and doctrines of government. But to the fashionable reading world of 1832 it became, a few days after its appearance, the mode of the moment. Just as two years later Ainsworth's *Rookwood*, with its exaggerated melodrama and its tedious display of "flash" doggerel caught the fancy of the town and turned every buck into a highwayman and every young lady of fashion into a Romany lass, so (and as inexplicably) did Mrs. Trollope's travel-diary set London gabbling Americanese.

> The Countess of Morley (she writes amusedly) told me that she was certain that if I drove through London proclaiming who I was, I should have the horse taken off and

be drawn in triumph from one end of the town to the other!
The Honourable Mr. Somebody declared that my thunder-
storm was the finest thing in prose or verse. Lady Charlotte
Lindsay *implored* me to go on writing—never was anything
so delightful. Lady Louisa Stewart told me that I had
quite put English out of fashion and that everyone was
talking Yankee talk.

Approbation more serious than that of idly cultured elegance
was given to Mrs. Trollope by the Lockharts, by Croker, by
Landor, by John Murray and, most practically of all, by
Captain Basil Hall, himself the author of a book on America
and an invaluable ally to his less experienced colleague in the
work of dealing with publishers and public. The generosity
and kindness of this sailor-author remained one of the most
agreeable elements in all Mrs. Trollope's writing life. He was
wholly unacquainted with her until, her manuscript having
been sent to him by Whittaker and Treacher for an opinion,
he took the trouble to seek her out and offer his services as
mediator with the publishers. During her struggle to establish
herself as a writer (for the overnight success of *Domestic
Manners* was not equivalent to a permanent livelihood), Basil
Hall was beside and behind her. His championship of her
work must have seemed, in American eyes at least, highly
suitable. When, shortly after English publication, a pirated
edition of *Domestic Manners* appeared in New York, there was
affixed an amusing preface by the "American Editor" declaring
that Basil Hall and Mrs. Trollope must be one and the same
person, as no English lady could write so grossly as had the
author of this vulgar and offensive book, and no other author
could so traduce America save Basil Hall.

In America, then, Mrs. Trollope was regarded either as
"Captain Basil 'All in petticoats" or as a disgrace to British
womanhood. In England she was applauded or attacked
according to the friendships or mentality of her critics. Because Hall was on her side, so also was Captain Hamilton.
Marryat was judicious but not enthusiastic. Harriet Martineau
was frankly hostile.

In this case there was a fundamental conflict of temperament. Harriet Martineau had the tenderness toward America proper to a philosophical radical. Being serious-minded and grave with duty to herself and to humanity, she found the hard frivolity of a woman who could throw out two volumes of quick sarcasm on a great subject like America galling and obnoxious. Consequently when she published *Society in America* in 1837 and in 1838 the sequel to that work, *Retrospect of Western Travel*, she pointedly ignored alike the personality and opinions of her predecessor, contenting herself with the sneer at "Trollope's Folly" already quoted and thus indirectly claiming virtue for the greater discretion of her own reminiscences. The contrast between the two women's books was noted by the critics. *Blackwood*, for example, in a review of *Society in America*, remarked that "Mrs. Trollope has to do battle for her views and statements with Miss Martineau." But it is improbable that Frances Trollope heeded (even if she read) this challenge, seeing that by 1837 she had forgotten America and all that appertained to it and was busy turning out novel after novel on quite different themes. When she wrote *Domestic Manners* she was wholly innocent of deliberate levity. She was a breadwinner, with her own pitiless work to do. America, like everything else, was marketable "copy," and with children dependent on her she had no leisure to respect the means that won them food. She could not take (nor did she ever come to take) herself seriously as an author. Her writing began in desperate necessity, continued as a good means to livelihood, ended as an agreeable habit. And if, in consequence, she never became a novelist of more than ephemeral significance, she at least kept her head clear of dangerous vanities during the urgent years of breadwinning.

It was this aloofness from any element of authorship save its earning power (an aloofness forced on her by cruel circumstance and not at all due to inherent greed for money) which saved Frances Trollope from too ready an acceptance of her first book's success. Titled ladies might gush and critics belaud or blame, but the publisher and his cheque were the real touchstone of achievement. She was too old a woman to be flattered by the adulation of literary parties; she was too anxious and worn a woman to set an artist's pride above a bookshop popularity. She let Basil Hall take her to this salon and to that; she wrote delightedly of compliments paid to her and of letters of congratulation that she had received; but all her comments on the triumph of *Domestic Manners* end on one note—the wistful note of hope. Perhaps she might now expect a success for her next book also; and after that for the next. . . .

As she stood in the drawing-room of the Misses Berry and smiled acknowledgment to all the fulsome chatter of the fashionable crowd, she was adding feverishly in her head the sums her publisher had that afternoon forecast. Behind the satin and gilding of London luxury, beyond the soft glare of the hundred candle-flames, she saw the squalid gloom of Harrow Weald with her embittered ageing husband, racked with sick headache, poring over his books. She saw also her children meanly clad; and the massed crowd of creditors, sullen and creeping slowly nearer.

The success of *Domestic Manners* was great; for a first book by an unknown author it was remarkable. But best-sellers did not in the 'thirties produce so large an immediate money profit as nowadays, and if Frances Trollope earned six hundred pounds by her book she earned more than her most sanguine friend could have foretold and far more than she herself had ever dared to hope. Never was money more greatly needed. Six hundred pounds, coming at that moment in her life, pulled weight with every penny of its value. The bulk of urgent debt was paid, and the immediate wants of the sons and daughters satisfied. Best of all, the family were taken from their wretched homestead on the Weald and once more installed at Orley Farm.

This achievement was more spectacular than prudent. The re-acquisition of Orley Farm involved a payment of eighty pounds for fixtures, as well as much refurnishing and the engagement of servants. But Mrs. Trollope was not a woman to practise economy unless she were compelled. She had earned unexpected money and she meant to enjoy it.

Unfortunately her problem was not merely the removal of a load of debt. Thomas Trollope had never got free of the original Julians, for which annually a sum quite out of proportion to his means had to be paid over to Lord Northwick. To make matters worse, and with his usual ill-luck, his London rents suddenly failed. Quite a short while after the publication of *Domestic Manners*, the book's earnings were all spent. A new crisis was threatening, and Fanny Trollope's second book and first novel was finished none too soon.

The Refugee in America, for twelve hundred copies of which she received four hundred pounds, was published late in 1832. Its success and the fierce attacks made upon it were alike provoked rather by its predecessor than by itself. The story is an artificial and stilted account of an English family in America, with much exaggerated sensibility and a priggish heroine. Its good qualities are (though somewhat diluted) precisely those of *Domestic Manners*, because the narrative only becomes real when it describes scenes and conditions in the United States which the author had herself observed. Its bad qualities are common to the fashionable fiction of the time. Such a book from any other pen would have faded into polite oblivion; but, as "Mrs. Trollope's new work," *The Refugee* gave an opportunity to her friends for active friendliness and (more important) to her enemies for virulent abuse. Basil Hall wrote to her:—

> You must be aware that, having written such a book as your travels, you necessarily raised an immense host of vindictive vulgar active enemies. . . . You have had the boldness to publish your opinions on America and having thereby incurred the risk of censure and ridicule you must not shrink from the endurance.

The warning was timely. Fanny Trollope, who had written without malice but merely with the amused high spirits of a quick-tempered, unmalignant observer and with a pen more bitter than she knew, shrank with surprised dismay from the savagery of some of the anonymous critics of her novel. Such critics, be it understood, were English and not American.

The indignation of the United States was loud and clamorous enough, but for American resentment she was well prepared. It was the personal spite of strangers at home which took her aback. She had not realised that America to the doctrinaire radicals of the period was almost sacrosanct. In their criticisms of the reaction and conservatism at home they referred continually to the United States in illustration of their idealism. For the most part they knew as little of real conditions in enlightened America as their antitypes in the seventeen-nineties had known of revolutionary France, or as their modern counterparts know of Soviet Russia. But reformist's zeal sets little store by facts; and the blasphemy of Mrs. Trollope did not go unreproved, because the defenders of the sacred cult of liberty had to rely on personal insult rather than on argument.

3

From any lasting pain at the hostility of her anonymous reviewers Frances Trollope was saved by the same need to go on earning which had kept her level-headed after the success of her first book. She had no time either for vanity or for depression. Also the high spirits of her children turned every literary happening to mirth. They called her "old Madam Vinegar," because some angry critic had used the word in his attack on her astringent prose. All egoisms are impossible in a house crowded with a loving but a disrespectful family.

Of Thomas Trollope's reaction to his wife's success there is unfortunately no evidence. He was himself deeply engaged on an immense Ecclesiastical Encyclopædia, which was to run to many volumes and be published through John Murray by subscription. He seems to have sunk latterly into a remote gloom, and to have become hardly conscious of what was going on about him. He worked untiringly at what his wife termed flippantly "his monks and nuns," until one of his terrible headaches came and laid him low; then he would lie up awhile and drug himself with calomel and groan and suffer.

It was soon after the publication of *The Refugee* that Frances
Trollope first had the idea of leaving England and settling her
household in some cheaper place abroad. Probably she realised
that her husband had finally relinquished any pretence of
managing his own affairs; perhaps she had a suspicion that
those affairs were worse than she was ever told. Her opportunity came with an event only recorded by E. A. Freeman in
an article written after Anthony's death. In 1833 Anthony
tried for a scholarship at Trinity College, Oxford, and (not
unnaturally) failed to win it. With this failure the problem
of a "gentleman's education" for the boys—an ambition very
near to Thomas Trollope's heart and cherished with a pathetic
obstinacy through these years of fading opportunity—had
solved itself. The University was not for Anthony, and he
was the youngest son. The last link holding the family to
England had been broken, and Frances Trollope, already
seeking a way of escape, would have been quick to recognise
the fact. Accordingly, and after a journey to Belgium and
Germany (which produced a travel book for Murray) and a
few months at Harrow (for finishing another novel [1]), she
canvassed her family on the subject of a sudden flight to
Bruges. She was shrewd enough to retain in a separate bank-
ing account some part of her own literary earnings, and when
in the spring of 1834 her brother Henry Milton helped her to
a full understanding of her husband's financial state, the precaution showed itself to be justified. Thomas Trollope had
literally no means at all. For some while he had not paid the
money due on Julians. The title to the house property in
London was insecure; even Fanny's own marriage settlement
was improperly registered. In short every possible legal
blunder had been made, and by a once competent lawyer to
his own destruction.

Fanny Trollope took her decision promptly. She must have
had wind of the impending catastrophe. Her husband,
bewildered but unprotesting, was packed off to Ostend on
April 18 1834; his wife and the children would follow four
days later. A few hours after Thomas Trollope had left his

[1] *The Abbess.*

Harrow home never to return, the house was in the charge of
sheriff's officers. Lord Northwick had put in an execution.

Anthony has characteristic paragraphs in his *Autobiography*
describing the collapse at Julians Hill:—

One day I was summoned very early in the morning to
drive my father up to London. He had been ill, and must
still have been very ill indeed when he submitted to be
driven by any one. It was not till we had started that he
told me that I was to put him on board the Ostend boat.
This I did, driving through the city down to the docks. . . .
When I got back with the gig, the house and furniture were
all in the charge of the sheriff's officers.

The gardener who had been with us in former days
stopped me as I drove up the road, and with gestures, signs,
and whispered words, gave me to understand that the whole
affair—horse, gig, and harness—would be made prize of if
I went but a few yards farther. Why they should not have
been made prize of I do not know. The little piece of dishonest business which I at once took in hand and carried
through successfully was of no special service to any of us.
I drove the gig into the village, and sold the entire equipage
to the ironmonger for £17, the exact sum which he claimed
as being due to himself. I was much complimented by the
gardener, who seemed to think that so much had been
rescued out of the fire. I fancy that the ironmonger was the
only gainer by my smartness.

When I got back to the house a scene of devastation was
in progress, which still was not without its amusement. My
mother, through her various troubles, had contrived to keep
a certain number of pretty-pretties which were dear to her
heart. . . . These things, and things like them, were being
carried down surreptitiously, through a gap between the two
gardens, on to the premises of our friend Colonel Grant.
My two sisters, then sixteen and seventeen, and the Grant
girls, who were just younger, were the chief marauders.
To such forces I was happy to add myself for any enterprise,
and between us we cheated the creditors to the extent of

our powers, amidst the anathemas, but good-humoured abstinence from personal violence, of the men in charge of the property. I still own a few books that were thus purloined.

It is likely that this detached and humorous view was shared by Frances Trollope. She was never unnecessarily serious, and on this occasion she had, even in the midst of the ruin, the satisfaction of knowing that her own money at least was safe. After a few days with the friendly Grants, she crossed to Belgium, taking with her Emily, Cecilia, Henry and Anthony, and leaving for the satisfaction of her husband's creditors the dismantled shell of Orley Farm.

4

But at Bruges, in the roomy bleakness of the Château d'Hondt, she was to be brought face to face with the most terrible crisis of her life. It came quite unexpectedly. The move from England was happily accomplished; she was in a cheap country, in a pleasant if barely furnished house, and had all her family (save Tom) about her. Another novel [1] was nearly finished; publishers were already on the bid for future work. That her husband should be unwell had become, alas, a pathetic commonplace; if Henry also had seemed out of sorts, she was accustomed to his languor after times of strain and, with her manifold distractions and all the business of her household on her hands, can be forgiven a rough and ready optimism in affairs of health.

Then, all at once, the situation changed. Henry fell defin- itely ill. The Belgian doctor without hesitation pronounced the verdict that Fanny Trollope, although at times she may have dreaded it, had always stifled among secret fears. The illness was consumption and in a dangerous form. Almost the next day Emily, the younger daughter, fell ailing and with disquieting symptoms. The mother's existence became sud- denly complicated by the dual problem of nursing the sick and

[1] *Tremordyn Cliff.*

isolating the healthy. She was in a foreign country with few friends and hardly any money save what she could earn from day to day by her own labours. Illness is costly; nursing is of all work the most ceaseless and wearying; consumptive patients are capricious of temper and, despite themselves, unreasonable. From her husband she could look for little sympathy and less of help. When he was not prostrate with his own pain, he would be sitting for hours in obstinate and useless industry over his ecclesiastical records. The only healthy members of the household beside herself were Anthony and Cecilia, of whom one was miserable with self-distrust and the other a timid girl of seventeen. Anthony describes himself at this time as "an idle, desolate hanger-on, that most hopeless of human beings, a hobbledehoy of nineteen without any idea of a career, a profession or a trade"; Cecilia, half a child as yet, had nothing but goodwill to fit her for her mother's place as household treasurer and executive. Everything, literally everything, fell on Frances Trollope. For the last six months of 1834 this woman of fifty-five was day and night nurse to two consumptive children; manager of a large and rambling house; provider of meals, not only for the invalids, but also for an ailing husband and (until Anthony and Cecilia went elsewhere) for two healthy adolescents; and solitary breadwinner, earning with her own hand and distracted brain the money necessary to keep the unwieldy home together. It is hard to say whether the departure—first of Anthony to his clerkship in the London Post Office, then of Cecilia to the disease-free Fulham home of her uncle, Henry Milton—lightened or increased the mother's burden. Although the material responsibilities of daily life were lessened, her sense of loneliness was intensified. Save for two Belgian maids she was now quite alone—with her uncanny, almost silent husband; with Emily, flushed and shaken by her cough; with, most terrible of all, the dying Henry. For there was now no doubt that he was dying. The sudden treacherous calms, so characteristic of advanced consumption, did not deceive the weary mother's eye. She could welcome "easy" days for her patient's sake; but for her own she dreaded them, knowing the reaction that

must follow, trying to gather up her strength, her patience and
her knowledge to meet the bad time which was sure to come.
Henry, who in health had always needed humouring, was still
more difficult in sickness. He had the wilfulness of his disease
—the sudden wants, the petulant insistence on some detail of
food or management. He resented anyone but his mother at
his bedside, and as the end drew near she hardly left his room,
save to snatch a few hours of sleep every alternate night. She
had a writing-table in the sickroom, and would sit the whole
night through, drugging herself awake with green tea, even
with laudanum, and writing, writing desperately.

Truly in those last weeks of 1834 Frances Trollope earned
her right to immortality. The heroism that can forget self to
keep a sick child at peace is a heroism peculiar to mothers; the
power to endure the unceasing strain of long and hopeless
nursing is by miracle given to many women; but, while
enduring thus heroically, to earn the next day's food or doctor's
bill by grinding out smart, racy fiction for the leisure hours of
fashionable idlers was the epic, surely the unique, achievement
of this battered but indomitable woman.

At last, on December 23, death came. She wrote at once
to Tom:—

It is over. My poor Henry breathed his last about nine
o'clock this morning. I wish Cecilia to return immediately
and I would wish you to bring her over. I need the comfort
of your presence. We want the comfort of seeing you and
Cecilia, dearest Tom. We have suffered greatly.

5

Although the death of Henry set Frances Trollope free from
the immediate slavery of sickroom service, it brought no
other alleviation. Poverty pressed more hardly than ever;
anxiety for Emily was no less; Thomas Trollope sank every
day a little deeper into eccentric gloom.

The mother, therefore, weary though she was and
stricken with her loss, must throw off sorrow and fatigue,

and in the early days of 1835 get once again about her business.

Partly with the idea of rousing her husband from his lethargy, partly to distract Emily's attention from dangerous dwelling on her brother's death, mainly to earn more money, she hurried to London and arranged with Bentley, the publisher, for a book on Paris and its people, to be written immediately and illustrated by Hervieu. In April she had transplanted her household from Bruges to the French capital. There she spent arduous months in talk and pertinacious questioning, arranged her notes, wrote them together, and in the autumn of the same year was reading the reviews which greeted the book's publication.

She was now back at Bruges and busy with an anti-slavery tale about the Southern States. This book—*Jonathan Jefferson Whitlaw*, which was published early in 1836 with spirited plates by Hervieu—is to the modern reader one of the most satisfying of her novels. Yet, like *Tremordyn Cliff*, it was written beside a death-bed, for September 1835 brought to the authoress another spell of nursing vigil.

The second autumn of sickness in the Château d'Hondt had not the agonising terrors of the first; but it was sad enough and, by its implications, more dramatic. Thomas Trollope throughout the summer months in Paris had been failing fast. He had hardly returned to Bruges before he fell really ill and in a kind of broken stupor was laid to bed. There, pathetically defiant, he waited silently on death. He had always been a proud man who met disaster with a tightening of the lips, and now at the last his bodily suffering could not shatter his control. But to the mental torture of those weeks of helplessness he finally surrendered. It seemed that all the bitterness and self-reproach, stored up during a lifetime of misfortune and obstinate folly, were now poured out to drown his anguished spirit. At the end, and literally, he turned his face to the wall. One afternoon in late October he was dead.

Frances Trollope, bowed by the bedside of her husband, sat in the fading autumn light and wept. On a table in the corner of the room were the piled papers of his Ecclesiastical Encyclo-

pædia. In Cincinnati he had left a grotesque unfinished
building to mark a failure in trade; now in the immense
desolation of the Château d'Hondt, he left a litter of useless
and unfinished manuscript, a second "Trollope's Folly," a
vague beginning of a book that no one wanted, a book which
by death's decree no one would possess.

The small tired figure by the bed knew well her husband's
life had been a failure. But he had loved her and she him; and
if he had caused her sorrow and anxiety and toil, he had also
given her much of delicious pleasure. She knew that it was
his imprudence which had brought her and her children to the
troubles they had so narrowly survived. She knew that his
warped temper had made not only his sons' lives unhappy, but
his own also. She knew that he had killed his own spirit,
withered his own charity, thwarted his own ambition by the
wrongheaded pride which was at once his fineness and his
infirmity. She knew that in his lifetime he had been, first a
continual danger to her peace of mind, then an inert and
suffering burden on her back. Yet now that he was dead—and
just because she had loved him, suffered for him, worked for
him and protected him—she wept, crouching beside him
under the high ceiling of the shadowy room.

They buried Thomas Trollope near to his son Henry in the
cemetery outside the Porte St. Catherine at Bruges. His wife
was done with Belgium. Before Christmas she was in England
once again and at home in a new house at Hadley in Hertfordshire. Here, only a few months after her husband's death, she
suffered yet another loss. The young Emily sank finally into
the long threatening consumption and died after a short illness.
The mother's grief for this her youngest child was crushing,
but was observed by none but her close intimates. The ageing
lady had now learnt from hard necessity to stifle sorrow in the
interests of her work. She had a duty to the living which no
personal affliction could be allowed to interrupt; wherefore,
for duty's sake and because others were dependent on her
courage, she sorrowed for Emily a little while in privacy,
then threw up her head and got to work again.

D

VI

BY COURAGE man can conquer fate, and Frances Trollope had won her victory. Three deathbeds and three deaths, tended and bravely met within the space of eighteen months, marked the final and most desperate stage of her long climb to happiness. Like John Masefield's hero Harker on his epic journey across the Sierra to the sea, she had been struggling up the bad side of a mountain range. She had traversed the stricken wilderness, had scaled the crags of rotten rock, had passed the final peril of the ice-cliffs; now she was over the ridge, and her path, stony and dangerous though it must remain for a while, lay downwards to the pinewoods and, beyond them, to the quays and seaboard of prosperity.

There was great comfort to her in her reunion with Tom. When this eldest son, with whom she had always been lovingly intimate, obeyed her order and brought Cecilia back to Bruges after Henry's death, he did more than pay a visit to his mother's house; he joined his life once more with hers. Brief intervals apart, they two were never again separated; and on Tom's strong shoulders the mother could henceforth lay some part of the burden of the family well-being which she had for so long a time borne alone.

Anthony also had crossed the threshold of the adult world. London was to try him as hardly as ever his schooldays had done, but he was on his feet and not far distant from the first building of his own solid fortunes. The pattern of the family was rearranged; its load more evenly distributed.

Because Frances Trollope had fought with fate and won the day, her remaining twenty-seven busy years of life were what she chose to make them—active, cheerful but monotonous. Before long the fortunes of the Trollopes split into three thriving parts. The mother became part of the household of her eldest son; Anthony, once away in Ireland, made his own home and buttressed it; Cecilia was quickly married. The foundations of these three lives Frances Trollope had with her own hands dug and laid; it was fitting that she should rest out her days beneath their shelter.

But because habits die hardly, and because she was not the person to content herself with idleness, the work of authorship and the eager busy interest in persons and events about her went on as briskly as when livelihood depended on them. Also with leisure and with solvency her restlessness and love of spending soon returned. She and Tom had several homes before even their first long visit to Florence in 1843; and in that city they lived in two houses before settling finally at the Villino Trollope. At intervals during the years between 1836 and 1845 Frances Trollope found herself over-spending, now on a foreign journey, now on the furnishing of a house, now actually on the building of one. At such crises she would rush to London, contract for a novel or a book of travels with a publisher, collect in cash such money as was offered on the spot, and rattle off again—heedless, tireless, living each moment of each crowded day. She was so inveterate a traveller and so unashamed a furnisher of travel-books, that her name became almost a household word for globe-trotting. A writer on Italy in *The New Monthly Magazine* for July 1847 remarks: "Of these abominable political turnpike gates no less than ten are to be met along the distance of scarcely as many miles between Sargano and Pontremoli . . . and if we recollect that no less than three of these irksome houses bear the cognisance of Este *we may easily conceive that the most enterprising tourist—a very Trollope—would give up the excursion in despair.*"

She handed on the travel-habit to her younger son. Some twenty-five years later Froude spoke bad-temperedly of "old Trollope banging about the world." The word (though peevish) was not badly chosen, for Anthony was a noisy man and bundled when he moved. But though his capacity as tourist may well have been inherited, he was never the travel-monger that his mother had been, who could make two octavo volumes from a month's holiday in Italy or from a few quite

ordinary trips through German towns. The most valuable
result of Mrs. Trollope's various wanderings is her novel *The
Robertses on their Travels*, in which she satirises the bad manners
of the English on the Continent with much point and humour.
Indeed that book (or an abridgement of it) might, when
European travel becomes possible again, be distributed by
tourist agencies in the interests of international amity. It
contains little, apart from costumes and methods of conveyance, that is really out of date.

2

If Frances Trollope as a traveller became proverbial, her
name as novelist and contributor to periodicals was even more
familiar. Between 1836 and 1856 she published without fail
a story every year and sometimes more than one. Library
subscribers came to count on her; she became one of the stock
fiction-writers of her period. Peter Priggins, the college-scout-
turned-author in Hewlett's extravaganza (edited by Theodore
Hook) reads, under the heading "Review of Current Periodicals," a notice of *The New Monthly* in which one of his own
reminiscences is printed. The review begins:—

> Paper by the editor—good as usual. By Mrs. Trollope
> —satirical as ever, with two engravings. Several others,
> all intended to please; Peter Priggins again . . .

and so forth. The appearance of Frances Trollope in this
context gives a definite indication of the place she occupied—
not in literature, but in contemporary letters. It is from
topical annotators of the type of Hook that one can detect the
vernacular of any period, and popular authors, popular taverns
or popular jokes are as much a part of the vernacular as is any
word of slang. Mrs. Trollope was, then, primarily famous as
a satirist, and certainly in this genre are her most remarkable
achievements. They were recognised by graver minds than
Hook's. Plumer Ward, discussing book-reviewers as a race,
takes as a type of them "the illustrious Marchmont, a jewel in

modern satire who can review a book without reading it." [1]
Mention such as this, from a man so seriously well-informed
as Plumer Ward, is proof sufficient of her status even among
the intellectuals.

But although in her day her reputation was mainly that of a
maker of astringent fiction for the libraries and as a skilled
assembler of travel-gossip, she may claim to hold a modest
place among the social reformers of the mid-nineteenth century.
She was by nature a woman of ready generosity, and her
sympathies toward misfortune or in cases of oppression were
easily aroused. Indeed, for the immediate effectiveness of her
protest, they were too easily aroused. She would fly to the
extremes of championship at the impulse of a sudden pity,
without pausing either to get up her subject or to consider the
best means of dealing with it. Her indignations were quick
and passionate, and throughout her life she made bitter
enemies by overstating her case or by hasty sarcasm.

Her first collision was, of course, with the Americans.
Domestic Manners, followed by the American scenes in *The
Refugee in America*, and capped by the fierce anti-slavery of
Jonathan Jefferson Whitlaw, roused the more nationalist citizens
of the United States to a frenzy of indignation. There can be
no doubt that some degree of anger was well justified. Catherine Maria Sedgwick, the well-known American authoress,
expressed the matter with moderation and good sense in a
letter to Mary Mitford:—

Mrs. Trollope must have been very unfortunate in her
associates in this country. There is undoubtedly a very
crude state of society in the new towns of our western states,
and in every part of our country in our best circles there
are persons to be met who have not been able to throw off
the coarse habits as they rose above the fortunes of their
early years. But Mrs. Trollope, though she has told some
disagreeable truths, has for the most part caricatured till the
resemblance is lost.

---

[1] *Memoirs of Robert Plumer Ward* (author of *Tremaine*, etc.). 2 vols. London,
1850. "Marchmont" is a character in *Charles Chesterfield*, a novel by Mrs.
Trollope published in 1841.

Such caricature arose from a too ready generalisation. Mrs.
Trollope was always breathless, always impulsive, always a
scrambler to conclusions. As Anthony says in his *Autobiography*:—

> She was neither clear-sighted nor accurate and in her
> attempts to describe morals, manners and even facts, was
> unable to avoid the pitfalls of exaggeration.

But with all her slapdash inexactitude, her main impressions
were usually correct. Dickens corroborates her picture of the
Mississippi valley; innumerable tales by other, later authors
show that her slave-trade novel was substantially within the
facts. Also she was regularly on the side of the angels.
Wherefore, when the dust had settled after a conflict between
her and critics of some book of hers, it was usually found that,
while both sides had shouted louder than they need, the lady's
battle-cry was of the two the more humane and honourable.

After *Jonathan Jefferson Whitlaw* she made no direct attack
on the Americans. But in 1843 she took the Widow Barnaby
to the United States. *The Barnabys in America* pictures very
amusingly the vulgarian of the Old World, who with a preposterous card-sharping husband (once O'Donagough; now
Major Allen Barnaby) outbluffs the bluffers and outswindles
the swindlers of the New. This story is indeed a kind of
portmanteau novel of all its author's favourite prejudices,
grotesqueries and jokes. She guys the English parvenu in the
Widow herself; she guys the adventurer, the company pro-
moter and the evangelical in the chameleon O'Donagough,
who is first a smooth swindling bully of London snobdom,
then a swaggering spitting bagman of American bar and
boarding-house whose only military quality is his name, and
last a canting minister, with one eye on heaven and the other
on the cash and prospects of his congregation. Finally, it is
more than likely that Mrs. Trollope meant to parody herself,
when she showed the Widow sitting down to write a book
upon America. Such baffling self-mockery came easily to one
of her ready laughing temper, and she was clever enough to
realise that no satire is more irritating or more impossible to

meet than that which, among other things, lashes the satirist himself.

Six years later America made its last considerable appearance in her work. *The Old World and the New* (1849) tells of an English family that travels to New York to seek its fortune. The book is sadly a machine-made fiction for the libraries, but it has flashes of the old spirit in its inquisitive Americans, and there is surely a memory of Nashoba in the backwoods settlement in which the Stormonts take despairing refuge. On the whole the tone is kindlier to the New World than in the past. Perhaps the author wished to make amends. More probably she was already touched by the indifference of age; for when the tale was written she was nearly seventy years old.

Readiness to criticise America did not blind her to abuses at home, and to hostility in the United States she added that of many of her fellow-countrymen. It was at the very dawning of the hungry 'forties that she came forward as a novelist-agitator, and published two important books written deliberately in the interests of English social reform. One, *Michael Armstrong*, is an attack on factory owners and particularly on their cruelty toward child labour; the other, *Jessie Phillips*, is an exposure of the workings of the New Poor Law. Both books are blows struck for the helpless and oppressed, and struck with something of the lusty, ill-directed violence of untrained indignation.

Michael Armstrong began publication in monthly numbers during 1839 and was issued in volume form with illustrations by Onwhyn and Hervieu in 1840. The tale was based on notes taken by the author and her son Tom on a special journey to Lancashire and Yorkshire, where they had letters of introduction from Lord Shaftesbury and were shown the evil realities of the remote moorland valleys. In Mrs. Trollope's tale horrors abound and virtue (in the person of a young heiress with a conscience) has no light task to triumph in the end. But the book has vigour and sincerity and—perhaps because conditions were so bad that exaggeration was almost impossible—the unabashed extremes of black and white are more con-

vincing than in some other novels from the same hand.
Indeed, according to the Hammonds' biography of Lord
Shaftesbury, the story may almost be taken literally.

No doubt there had been some improvement in the
Lancashire mills when Shaftesbury pressed for legislation;
no doubt there were Lancashire mill-owners who could have
pleaded financial embarrassments as serious as those which
Shaftesbury had inherited, and those in which he had involved himself by his errors. But the reader of the opening
chapters of Mr. George Edwards' autobiography, and the
reader of Mrs. Trollope's factory novel *Michael Armstrong*,
however much they allow for such difficulties and such
improvements, will feel that they do not qualify the terrible
truth of the picture before them.[1]

Further, the indictment as a whole went strongly home to its
contemporaries. The book was received with enthusiasm by
the Chartists and used as propaganda for their cause. Non-
party reviewers lauded its evident sincerity. "It is a great
mistake" wrote one "and a still greater injustice to suppose
that Mrs. Trollope offers *Michael Armstrong* as anything like a
pendant to the admirable works of Mr. Dickens. The leading
characteristic of those works is humour. But *Michael Armstrong* has a deeper design. . . . It is evidently intended to be a
deep moral satire, having a serious and even a solemn purpose
to accomplish—with *truth* alone as the means of its accomplishment and *good* alone as the ultimate end." From the side of
the enemy, the book was paid the compliment of a counter-
issue from the factory owners' point of view. In August 1839
(about five months after *Michael Armstrong* had begun to
appear) there was published the first of ten monthly numbers
of *Mary Ashley, or Facts upon Factories*, a work by "Frederic
Montagu," all advertisements of which were headed with the
legend "Mrs. Trollope refuted!"

It was on the last day of the year 1842 that was issued Part 1
of Mrs. Trollope's attack on the New Poor Law. *Jessie*

---

[1] *Lord Shaftesbury*, by J. L. and Barbara Hammond. London, 1923.

Phillips, illustrated by Leech and heralded by much competent advertisement of the typical Colburn kind, is less a book of horrors than of pathos. The tale itself shows a careless blend of momentary fervour for a cause and of trivial personal implication which is very characteristic of its author. It was written four years after Harriet Martineau had attacked *Oliver Twist* on the ground that Dickens had charged against the new Poor Law the evil consequences of the old. Frances Trollope admired Dickens and had made his acquaintance in 1838. She did not admire Miss Martineau and well remembered that lady's hostility to her own American opinions. It is not impossible, therefore, that *Jessie Phillips* was written to some small extent against Miss Martineau, and that the sidelong thrust was recognised at least by the reviewer of *Bell's Messenger*, who did not hesitate to say that "the dramatic force which Mrs. Trollope exhibits in painting the scenes of her work very far exceeds the powers of Miss Martineau."

But whatever feminine amenities may have contributed to the general tone of *Jessie Phillips*, the book's main impulse was its author's ready pity for unhappiness. A paragraph from her opening manifesto will illustrate the generous emotionalism that lay at the bottom of all her crusading, and serve to show the readiness with which, in matters of opinion and conduct, she would override material objections by appeals to moral conviction:—

The author is anxious to declare her detestation of the newly broached doctrine that the poor have no *right* to a sufficiency of necessary food to sustain the life that God has given them. She is far from denying that such a conclusion may be very logically deduced from the positions of dry, hard, utilitarianism and mere pounds-shillings-and-pence-counting political economy. But there is, it seems to her, an element in the question which is apparently not dreamt of in the philosophy of those who deny to the poor their *right* to a share in Nature's feast. She hopes and believes that there are still abundantly enough English hearts to join with her in scouting this doctrine as *Unchristian*.

D*

Like *Michael Armstrong*, the tale of *Jessie Phillips* provoked during part-issue a counterblast of wrath. But this time the opponent was one of her own party and his riposte was not a rival novel, but an open letter to the author, threatening to "curtail, if not altogether to confound, the circulation" of her work. The incident, in itself amusing, may be recorded as an early evidence of trouble caused by an author's inadvertent use in fiction of a real person's name.

The villain of *Jessie Phillips* is a brewer called Baxter, an important figure in the administration of the New Poor Law at the north-country village of Deepbrook. But in Wales dwelt another Baxter, a fierce opponent of the New Poor Law and, in his own view at least, a person of local eminence. For some reason at which one can only guess—and despite the fact that their Christian names, their occupations, their places of residence and their Poor Law opinions were entirely different—this gentleman considered Mrs. Trollope's brewer as a recognisable caricature of himself.

He could not—as did Captain Marryat a year or two earlier, when his surname was used by Frederick Denison Maurice for the villain of *Eustace Conway*—challenge the offending author to a duel, but he rushed into indignant print. His pronouncement, written with a ludicrous blend of personal vanity, verbosity and anti-Poor Law zeal, appeared as an inset leaf preceding text and illustration of the third of the ten monthly numbers in which *Jessie Phillips* was first published. This curious document was not preserved in the book issue of the novel.

Reading Mrs. Trollope's own statement of her belief in the right to live, realising the ferocity with which the vested interests countered her attacks upon their peace, and bearing in mind her early association with Frances Wright, one begins to understand her otherwise unaccountable reputation as a dangerous revolutionary and as a champion of downtrodden womanhood. "She used to be such a Radical" wrote Miss Mitford to a friend in 1852 "that her house in London was a perfect emporium of escaped state criminals"; while Lady Bulwer Lytton, whom Frances Trollope in an unlucky hour had met in Paris, hailed her as a pioneer of feminism, and (for a brief while) as her only friend.

Rosina Bulwer's novel *The Budget of the Bubble Family*, published in 1840, is dedicated to Frances Trollope, who, in a fulsome letter of praise, is told that: "While all admire your incorruptible honesty, which in you amounts to sublimity, some in detracting from your courage confess their own moral turpitude, by asserting that you stand too high and are too independent to suffer from being just and staunch *even to me*. You do indeed stand too high; not from the reasons they assign, but because your unflinching integrity approaches you on all occasions and under all circumstances to the divine service from which it emanates."

How the poor lady must have regretted the warm-hearted impulse which first led her to offer sympathy to this most pitiless of bores! The peevish vanity of Rosina Bulwer had already driven Tom Trollope half crazy, while he was doing her the none too easy service of finding a publisher for this very book. And then, when at last he and his mother had persuaded her to accept the generous terms which Bull (a publisher) had offered her, they found three volumes of illiterate and bad-tempered egoism tied to the Trollope tail by an unwelcome cord of fervent dedication.

Jessie Phillips was Mrs. Trollope's last excursion into politics or sociology. She was to write one or two further novels with a propagandist purpose (*Father Eustace*, an elaborate exposure of Jesuit intrigue, is perhaps the most noteworthy), but she had done with social reform. That she should ever have meddled with it shows one of the limitations of her capacity as novelist. It is good evidence of his better judgment and more genuine authorship that Anthony Trollope checked himself from following in his mother's steps, and only in his days of inexperience sought to gild reformist argument as fiction. In *The Warden* there is an element of propaganda that clogs and muddies the pure stream of character; in *Castle Richmond* there are facts and views about the Irish famine that show how strong was the temptation to pronounce a sermon on humanity's behalf.   But even on these occasions the wish to sermonise was not out of control, and Anthony pulled himself together. Later he became a master of the art of pure fiction.   He stuck to his tale and let the teaching go, with the result that all his novels are lessons in the art of life, but not one of them a preachment.

VII

FRANCES TROLLOPE DIED in her son's Florentine home on October 6 1863. She was in her eighty-fourth year, and the last illness was—as though in merciful tribute to her life's long gallantry—both short and painless. The end came too suddenly for Anthony to arrive from England. The news was telegraphed. On the day following the death he wrote a six-line note from Waltham Cross to Frederick Chapman:—

> My mother died at Florence yesterday morning. I tell you this that, if you are intending to go to Florence, you may delay your journey for a few days.

Shortly after, he sent a brief comment to a friend: "She ate and slept well and drank till the lamp went altogether out."

These letters' brevity, their practical good sense, their strict avoidance of all facile mournfulness are of the essence of the writer's character. Equally characteristic of their maker are the sentences in which Tom Trollope in his reminiscences records his mother's death:—

> If my mother had died a dozen years earlier, I should have felt the loss as the end of all things for me—as leaving me desolate and causing a void which nothing could ever fill. But when she died at eighty-three she had lived her life, upon the whole a very happy one, to the happiness of which I had (and have) the satisfaction of believing I largely contributed.
>
> It is very common for a mother and daughter to live during many years of life together in as close companionship as I lived with my mother, but it is not common for a son to do so. During many years and many, many journeyings and more tête-à-tête walks and yet more tête-à-tête home hours, we were inseparable companions and friends.

In these comments—the first two scribbles of a moment, the third written after thought, but all provoked by a single happening—are crystallised the diverse qualities of Anthony and T. Adolphus Trollope. The latter is at heart as oaken English as the former; but years of residence in Florence, the friendship of Landor, of Miss Isa Blagden and of Mrs. Browning have set a polish on the surface of the wood, have (maybe) inlaid a touch of Italian ornament, have softened ever so slightly and æsthetically the sturdy profile of the original joinery. One cannot but be conscious, throughout the tale of Anthony's life and ways, of this faint but intriguing clash between his uncompromising "Britishism" and the acquired Italianacy of his elder brother. The two were in fact so like, and yet, looked at from this distance of time, they fall into such different attitudes.

And both were sons of Frances Trollope. To the old lady, whose aged eyes had to within a few hours of her death looked with quiet content over the flowery garden of her home, whose aged mind had ranged in listless but contented retrospect over her years of fight and doubt and victory, these two huge writing men (for both were big, with bulk beyond their actual stature) owed life and more than life. They owed survival also and their chances of success. From her books came in reality the greater books of Anthony, and while his live, those that prepared their way should not be forgotten. At her knee in babyhood Tom Trollope learnt that honesty and toil make in the end for happiness, and the comfort he gave his mother in her latter days was but repayment of a debt.

A calm acceptance of whatsoever life might bring and a refusal at any stage to dramatise her own experience were among Mrs. Trollope's most characteristic qualities. She was almost without self-consciousness and wholly without vanity. Energy and courage were so much a part of her that she never thought to claim credit for displaying them; authorship was so candidly a means of livelihood as to bring with it no suggestion of intellectual superiority. Her lack of self-consciousness and of the portentous vanity to which female authorship is liable must have been very noticeable. Mrs. Lynn Linton, recording her memories of woman writers, remarks: "All of the women whom I remember in my early days were conscious of themselves and their achievements—all save Mrs. Trollope. She was in no sense a *poseuse*, but just a vulgar, brisk and good-natured kind of well-bred hen-wife, fond of a joke and not troubled with squeamishness." [1]

This genuine indifference to her own dramatic possibilities gives piquancy to the inevitable comparison between the life-story of Frances Trollope and that of Margaret Oliphant. They are an interesting pair—these gallant author bread-winners—who both fought poverty with the pen and kept their homes together by industrious scribbling. To a point they are as similar in character as in circumstance. Like Mrs. Trollope, Mrs. Oliphant was no "literary lady," but an ordinary woman with a taste for ordinary things; like Mrs. Trollope, she was a comfort-lover, spending her earnings quickly and with more pleasure than precaution; like Mrs. Trollope, she trained herself to write through every interruption and disquiet. Yet, when the two are in ultimate balance one against the other, Mrs. Oliphant is conscious of her own heroism but Mrs. Trollope is not. For all that her sorrows were so intimate and so abiding, Margaret Oliphant had yet the power and inclination to visualise her grief, to see herself bearing the grief, to record in words her miseries and her endurance.

Of such self-exposure Frances Trollope was utterly incapable. Her troubles were her own affair. She could take things as they came and think no better of herself for so doing; she shrank with an exaggerated diffidence from the self-betrayal of intimate reminiscence. She left no autobiography, and, even to her children, her letters have no tinge of wistful bravery. The point has not only a personal but also a racial significance. As Margaret Oliphant had the power of self-dramatisation characteristic of many a Scot, so Frances Trollope (and in this Anthony was very much her son) had the strange blend of shyness and imperturbability which is peculiar to the English. There is no doubt that she (and Anthony also in his

[1] *My Literary Life*, by Mrs. Lynn Linton. London, 1899.

turn) lost credit with an inquisitive and romantic posterity by
this close shrouding of their privacy. But they were very
English, and from their Englishry came at once the genius
of the son and the essential qualities of son and mother which
made them admirable.

2

Because she had not published a book for six years before
her death, and because in mind she was a daughter of the
'thirties and 'forties and not of the so different age which
followed 1851, the name of Frances Trollope—when her death
brought it once more into the papers—had almost faded from
the fickle memory of the public. There were memorial notices,
praising her industry, referring with a kind contempt to her
ephemeral popularity, recalling with a pleasant smile the huge
sensation of her *Domestic Manners*, back in the pre-Victorian
age, back in the early 'thirties. But they were mere newspaper-
mouthings—facile and perfunctory. Who would believe,
reading these pallid courtesies, that Frances Trollope in her
day provoked more anger and applause than almost any writer
of her time? Who would guess that books of hers once lashed
critics and public into furies of resentment, into rhapsodies
of praise?

Yet so it was. "No other author of the present day"
declared *The New Monthly Magazine* in 1839 "has been at once
so much read, so much admired and so much abused." The
article goes on to attribute these extremes of feeling to Mrs.
Trollope's "bold and uncompromising expression of her own
honestly formed convictions and opinions." To a point this
explanation is as likely as it is obvious. Books which im-
politely fall foul of the United States, of Evangelicism, of
factory-owners and of social climbers are bound to make
enemies in interested quarters. But why such bitter and
vindictive enemies?

To-day Mrs. Trollope's books, even her best books, seem to
lack the quality which stings, however lustily they may be-
labour. The good novels are racy, well observed and bright

with the glitter of life lived to the full and thoroughly enjoyed;
the bad ones are careless, angular and dull. All tend to diffuse-
ness, and many seem (as indeed they were) machine-made and
drawn out to a stipulated length. No hostility comparable to
that provoked by Frances Trollope greeted the satirical novels
of Maria Edgeworth; yet such a book as *Patronage* is every
bit as acid, shrewish, clear, clever and pitiless as the later
writer's most aggressive work.

Whence, then, Mrs. Trollope's power, fierce and undeniable,
to infuriate contemporaries? The question is not easily
answered. Some part of the hostility shown (especially that
which came from intellectual quarters) may have been due to
the dislike of the poetic temperament for the prosaic. This
fundamental conflict of taste (which shows itself at every period
and has more deeply affected literary reputations than is always
realised) appears markedly in the appraisement of Anthony
Trollope by his contemporaries and immediate successors, and
may well have been an element in the attacks on Mrs. Trollope
also. But the violence of her unpopularity must mainly be
accounted for by her reputation for vulgarity, and by an
assumption that there was a quality of provocation in her
manner which took readers between the joints of the harness.

At this latter quality we, who are of a different age and
squirm to different torture, can only guess—helped, perhaps,
by such direct reminiscences of the old lady's bearing as may
come our way. Here are three memories—the first and earliest
told to me personally; the second from an author's reminiscences, made posthumously public; the third communicated
by a near relative.

While this book was being written I spoke with a very old
lady whose grandfather was a first cousin of the Trollopes.
This old lady (with that peculiar memory of age which sees
the clearer for the distance of the scene remembered) could
recall, when she was a little girl of six or seven, that Mrs.
Trollope once sat opposite to her at luncheon. That was in
1841. She recalled the little woman—small and brown and
insignificant, with bright grey eyes and a sharp ironic voice—
as clearly as though the meal had taken place eight rather than

eighty years ago. She recalled further that during luncheon
the visitor made fun of the children (there were three present)
to their faces and that they never forgave her the discomfort
that they suffered.

This trifling memory is illuminating. No one could suspect
Mrs. Trollope of a wilful desire to distress or embarrass young
children; cruelty—even petty cruelty—was wholly foreign to
her genial bustling nature. But she often spoke without
thinking, or allowed herself little sarcastic jokes which had no
atom of ill-nature in them but nevertheless could give offence;
most important of all, she lacked an instinctive understanding
of the effect her words might have on other people.

Next comes a reminiscence of S. Baring-Gould, the novelist
of Devonshire and author of *Mehalah*, who also saw Mrs.
Trollope when he was still a child and during (probably) the
early 'fifties:—

> The winter we were at Pau, Mrs. Trollope, the authoress,
> was there as well, a good-humoured, clever, somewhat
> vulgar old lady. She took much notice of me. The English
> residents were not a little shy of her, fearing lest she should
> take stock of them and use them up in one of her novels;
> for she had the character of delineating members of her
> acquaintance, and that not to their advantage. Someone
> asked her whether this was not her practice. "Of course,"
> answered Mrs. Trollope, "I draw from life—but I always
> pulp my acquaintance before serving them up. You would
> never recognise a pig in a sausage." [1]

The final memory is of much the same epoch. During the
'fifties Mrs. Trollope was one of a party walking in the country
near Florence. She had fallen behind the main group, to
whom in much agitation the comparative stranger who had
been with her came running. "You must come at once!" he
gasped, seizing John Tilley, the old lady's son-in-law, by the
arm. "Mrs. Trollope has been taken ill! She has collapsed
into the ditch weeping!" The young man returned alone.

[1] From "Early Reminiscences," by S. Baring-Gould, published in the
Outlook, July 21 1923.

His mother-in-law was indeed in the ditch, but recognising him through her fingers, she showed a tearless face. "Oh, my dear John," she cried, "that man did bore me so!"

The blunt disregard of the elegance of social intercourse shown by this anecdote and by Baring-Gould's reminiscence was highly characteristic of her. It needs little familiarity with the conventions of Victorian deportment to realise how gravely such abrupt eccentricity of manner—especially in a woman—would have been generally regarded.

It was by this very impatience of the rigidities of polite behaviour that she earned the disrepute of vulgar-mindedness and—for that disrepute—paid heavily indeed. The vulgarity of Frances Trollope has been quoted as proof of her lack of feeling; it has been used to denigrate her personal courage in the face of disaster; and it has served as an excuse for the eviction of her books even from the hall of recollection.

The suggestion that in herself she lacked the sensibility that would, to a woman of a finer type, have made the ills she suffered unendurable, is cruelly unjust. Mrs. Trollope had the power of personal affection and the vehement sense of personal loss which in a woman so intensely womanly would be anticipated. But she was near to the primitive in type—a creature of strong individual attachments but little generalised affectibility. She was an emotional rather than an imaginative person. Where temperaments more complex and more nervous would magnify one trouble into a dozen more, or spoil an interlude of peace by fearful anticipation of the next catastrophe, she lived entirely in to-day, leaving to-morrow on the gods' knees. Doubtless hardship, working on a mind essentially practical, tended to circumscribe what was once at least a normal power of fancy. When she was a girl and in the first years of her marriage, she was an appreciative student alike of painting, music and letters. She would take the little Tom to see pictures in public galleries; with her friends she would discuss current literature—French and English—showing taste and knowledge. But anxiety came to crowd culture from her mind and slavery of work claimed leisure hours. Between reality and dream she chose reality, partly because she could not help it, but partly also from the profound instincts of her nature.

Of her preoccupations her books are evidence. They are chronicles of actuality where they are not earnest propaganda or blithe expression of personal prejudice. They have jollity, candour and friendliness, but they skim the surface of life only, with little of charm and less of beauty to stimulate a reader's thought. But preoccupation with material things is not of itself vulgarity. Searching for coarseness in her books—the undefined quality ascribed to her, alike by people of her own time and of the generation following—we are as little rewarded as in our quest for her astringency. She was a satirist of manners; a caustic observer of the trivial ambitions of those who hang about the outskirts of Society or, *faute de mieux*, strike intellectual attitudes with the coteries. But Mrs. Gore was all of these things, and who has termed Mrs. Gore vulgar? Why, then, poor Mrs. Trollope? Partly from snobbery, one fears. Her high society was not quite high enough; her salons were to the expert eye of critic-toadies a little tarnished, ever so little sordid. But her greater offence was that she was too truthful for the liking of the day. And with this statement of her second unforgivable transgression against the feeling of the mode, the indictment returns once more to her own brusque social manners, and the circle is complete.

*** *A Calendar of Events in the life of Frances Trollope and a Bibliography will be found in Appendix I.*

ANTHONY

I

THAT ANTHONY TROLLOPE all but became a cavalry officer in the Austrian army should be inscribed among historic might-have-beens! If only between 1834 and 1835 he had spent the allotted months in learning languages, he might in 1848 have ranged the north Italian—not the southern Irish—roads, with Piedmontese instead of postmasters for enemy; he might have fought side by side with Colonel Tom Silcote at Montebello; [1] he might even in the fatal year of 1866 have thundered short-sightedly to death at Königgrätz instead of bucketing harm-lessly over the pleasant Essex countryside near Waltham Cross.

But chance and his own indolence baulked Austria of her Prince Rupert. In order to equip himself for the cavalry commission which was mysteriously offered from Vienna, the young Anthony (no less mysteriously) took an usher's job, and went to teach classics to small boys at Brussels. He was a bad usher, and himself learnt as little French or German as he taught Latin to his pupils. When, therefore, a junior clerk-ship in the General Post Office was also offered, he resigned both schoolmastering and military fame and went to live in London on ninety pounds a year.

2

The date was 1834 and he was nineteen years of age. He remained in London and in the office in St. Martin's le Grand until 1841.

These seven years were the time of his final and severest testing. Their rigour so broke down his health that in 1840

[1] Cf. *Silcote of Silcotes*, by Henry Kingsley. Vol. III, chap. xii.

he nearly died; but while the body failed, the spirit toughened and became invincible. In 1841 he took to Ireland the character adversity had formed for him, and Ireland gave him health. So it was that the mature, triumphant Trollope was a product of a neglected childhood, of a young manhood turned adrift to sink or float in London, and of the Irish wind and rain.

Apart from two brief periods when his mother, pausing a moment in her ceaseless wandering, took a house in town or near at hand, young Anthony lived in cheap lodgings and alone. He had few friends and practically no money. His education had not been of the kind to prepare him either for the proprieties or improprieties of city life, and the London of the 'thirties, into which without advice or control he was thus rudely thrown, was a city as to one-sixth respectable or smart, as to five-sixths an outer darkness.

How, then, did he fare? The question can be answered by reference to his *Autobiography* and to the occasional novels which (admittedly or unadmittedly) make reference to this unhappy and probatory period of his life.

Now autobiography of any kind is rare in Trollope's novels. He was ready throughout his writing life to reproduce in fiction situations, scenes and even conversations which he himself had witnessed. But of self-portraiture he was very sparing. To a point this reticence was due to shyness. Behind his noisy self-assurance he was always a shy man with a characteristically English horror of self-betrayal. But the main reason for his reluctance to play a part in the imaginary dramas he created was a genuine modesty—a conviction that he was an ordinary being of no special quality, a cheerful, unresentful feeling that his private views and character could hardly be of interest to a world of strangers.

This unaffected lack of egoism, though it hampers the attempts of posterity to draw a portrait of Trollope the man, gives savour to the search for evidence.

The search is prolonged but not without reward. From this novel or from that can be pieced together something of all the Trollopes—the young and callow Trollope of the General

Post Office; the confident but still young Trollope of the years in Ireland; the prosperous, contented Trollope of the golden age at Waltham Cross; and the old and weary Trollope of the closing decade. Much of the reconstruction may be challengeable, but there is something to be said for every part of it.

To *Mr Anthony Trollope*

HIS MAJESTY's POSTMASTER GENERAL *has been pleased to appoint you* Junior Clerk on the Secretary's Office ———

in the room of Mr Diggle *Dismissed*

on the recommendation of myself ———

and you are, without loss of time, to furnish the Solicitor of this Office with the Names of two responsible Persons to become bound with you in the Sum of Two hundred ̄ *Pounds, for the due and faithful discharge of your Duty.*

GENERAL. POST OFFICE,
4 Nov² 1834

Entered,

Secretary.

The enclosed is the form of the Oath which you are to take to qualify you for your employment.

At first sight it may seem that the forlorn and solitary Trollope of the General Post Office requires no reconstruction, because in the pages of *The Three Clerks* and of the *Autobiography* he stands before us minutely sketched by his own later self. But when the Anthonys of 1857 and of 1876 combine to offer to posterity—all decently set out upon a tray—

the blemishes and misery and absurdities of the young lonely
Anthony of the late eighteen-thirties, those wise in Trollope's
ways will greet the gift with something of reserve. They will
not suspect a slurring over of shortcomings; on the contrary
they will question the blackness of the shadows, knowing the
sane, strong, genial being who evolved from the untidy junior
clerk, saying to themselves that Trollope, who loved to
unidealise himself, and probably liked to guy himself as well.

Let us examine the young Anthony as the older Anthony
has presented him, noting the details of his life.

His actual appointment to the Post Office was due to the
friendship between his mother and the then Secretary, Sir
Francis Freeling. The official document, with its agreeable
Dickensian reference to the defaulting Diggle, is reproduced
on the preceding page.

The manner of his subsequent entrance-examination is told
in *The Three Clerks*. We know from the *Autobiography* and
other sources how he fared as a junior Civil Servant; we
know that he ragged his immediate superiors, was late, idle,
disorderly and in perpetual danger of dismissal; that he played
cards with his fellows after lunch and smoked and drank with
resident clerks on such evenings as he was not up to graver
mischief in the London streets; that he splashed ink over the
august waistcoat of the Secretary himself; that he was tipped
half a crown by an aged German nobleman attending on the
Queen of Saxony; that duns pursued and money-lenders
swindled him; that an equivalent of breach of promise
threatened; and that the "Tramp Society" (composed of
Trollope, John Merivale and another) brought comic terror
to the farmers of the Home Counties.

Such details of incident, however, are not the whole story.
What manner of youth was he who lived so turbulent and yet
so drab a life? The answer must be read between the lines
(discreet for all their candour) of the *Autobiography*. In
summary of his adventures Trollope says:—

I wonder how many young men fall utterly to pieces
from being turned loose into London after the same fashion?

Mine was I think of all phases of such life the most dangerous. When I reached London no mode of life was prepared for me—no advice even given to me. I went into lodgings, and then had to dispose of my time. I belonged to no club, and knew very few friends who would receive me into their houses. . . . There was no house in which I could habitually see a lady's face and hear a lady's voice. No allurement to decent respectability came in my way. It seems to me that in such circumstances the temptations of loose life will almost certainly prevail with a young man. Of course if the mind be strong enough, and the general stuff knitted together of sufficiently stern material, the temptations will not prevail. But such minds and such material are, I think, uncommon. The temptation at any rate prevailed with me.

No one will deny that the risks to health and character of a sudden and friendless freedom such as Trollope experienced can hardly be exaggerated. He drifted from a dingy lodging-house to a ribald office, thence to a bar parlour, thence to his wretched lodging once again. And this went on day after day. He would have us believe that he lived "loosely." Certainly he had every opportunity of turning out a drunken waster; and whether he came within sight of such depravity, or was by nature too withdrawn from it to be in serious danger, he may claim credit for the sturdy self-respect which underlay his awkward rowdiness and brought him uncorrupted to a happier life.

But for the moment take him at his word. Suppose that indeed he slipped as deeply into the mire as his own memory of self implies. Could he, in such a case, even by strength of character have clambered out again? Would it have been possible for the Trollope of Waltham Cross—even the Irish Trollope—to have had behind him seven impressionable years of utter degradation?

The thing is inconceivable. Undoubtedly he was work-shy, unhappy and unattractive; probably he seemed, to those who knew him casually, to be a lad with no particular future.

When, however, in the *Autobiography* he speaks of himself as a profligate, we suspect a mid-Victorian exaggeration, a phraseology over-violent for what occurred, and reject the description as illogical and false.

This refusal to take Trollope at (so to speak) his own valuation raises another question. Why should he lay an unfair emphasis on his own youthful failings? Why, in writing of himself, should he use words so much stronger than their real significance? The answer is curiously illustrative of the differing standards of to-day and fifty years ago. The phrases used imply to modern ears licence rather than rowdy squalor, sensuality rather than mere loutish racket. But Trollope, writing in the eighteen-seventies, looked back at his own youth through glasses clouded with the reticence of his period, and therefore expressed with seeming violence a very mild reality.

The process is the reverse of hypocritical and should be observed by those who like to charge the mid-Victorians with cant and insincerity. The normal mid-Victorian mentality was not so much afraid of unpleasant truth as unaware of it. The standard of individual integrity was vastly higher either than it is to-day or was in the first decades of the nineteenth century; and those who (like Trollope) had that standard and cherished it, were frankly unable to conceive that any member of their class could fall considerably short of it. Therefore, when Trollope wrote the words quoted about his youthful ill-doings he was outspoken in his own way but not in ours. He was as innocent of overstatement as of a desire to palliate. He said what he meant, but what he meant would not to-day be similarly said.

Realise, therefore, that the libertinism of the young Trollope was rather pathetic than vicious. If his portrait is to be fairly drawn, it will require no violent colouring. The subject of it is as forlorn and unhappy as in his worst Harrow days. He has no means and many debts; now he is underfed for want of cash, now overdrunk for want of cheerfulness. Quite naturally he spends in his sour cheap lodgings as few evenings as possible, preferring a smoking party in the Post Office or the

warmth of a bar-parlour. Amid the sad greys of his bewilderment and loneliness are gleams of laughter and two warm
threads of friendship; but in the main the tone is sombre and
forlorn, befitting one who hated his work yet longed for more
to do, who hated his leisure, yet clung to it because it was spent
elsewhere than in the detested office.

Our portrait is progressing. We have distinguished the
essential details given in the *Autobiography* from the inessential.
We must now add some important touches from *The Three
Clerks*, for that, on Trollope's own admission, is in part the story
of his youth. Most notable of these are the money-lender
M'Ruen (who reappears as "Clarkson" in *Phineas Finn* and
holds the bill backed by Phineas for his friend Fitzgibbon);
the angry mother who invades the office corridors calling on
Charley Tudor to marry her daughter as he swore to do;
Charley Tudor himself sitting distracted in the bar-room of
the "Cat and Whistle" with pretty Norah Geraghty on his
knee and in his fuddled frightened brain twenty expedients
for escaping the consequence of a most genteel flirtation; and
little Katie Woodward, the novel's heroine, who lived at
Hampton and redeemed Charley from his evil ways, for—as
George Saintsbury says—"that 'buttercup' (the flapper of her
day) almost certainly had at least one model." [1]

There follow details from other books. Phineas Finn's
lodgings in Great Marlborough Street, with Bunce the copying
journeyman and Mrs. Bunce, who "did" for gentlemen, are,
no doubt, the lodgings in *Little* Marlborough Street where
Tom Trollope lived in 1834 and where the young Anthony
joined him when first he came to London. Maybe the Kneefit
passages in *Ralph the Heir* date from the author's knowledge
of the tailor's shop over which those first lodgings were
situated. The "touching in" process can, if you please, go
further still. A lodging can be brought from *Lady Anna*, a
street from *Ayala's Angel*, a walk in London from a third book,

---

[1] In the light of this perceptive comment, it may be noted that Trollope says
in his *Autobiography* : " *The Three Clerks* contains the first well-described love
scene that I ever wrote. The passage in which Katie Woodward, thinking that
she will die, tries to take leave of the lad she loves, still brings tears to my eyes
as I read it." The scene was well described because an eye-witness described it.

a game of cards from a fourth. But the picture is enough
advanced. Step back and judge of it. What do you see?
Surely this—a figure which, though it probably has a look and
more than a look of Trollope in his youth, is unmistakably a
likeness of one of Trollope's most debated characters—Lily
Dale's lover, Johnny Eames.

Is, then, the youthful Johnny Eames the author's youthful
self? I think he is. On investigation the parallel appears so
close and obvious that it is surprising it should not have been
earlier remarked. Mrs. Oliphant was conscious of it, but did
not pause to draw the moral. "Mr. Trollope's *Cæsar*" she
wrote to Miss Blackwood in 1874 "I cannot read without
laughing—it is so like Johnny Eames." George Saintsbury
is almost as "warm" as Mrs. Oliphant when he says: "Johnny
Eames himself is very good—an improved Charley Tudor,
décrotté to begin with, and supplied with a touch and not too
much of the hero of romance." [1] But even Saintsbury—and
despite his statement two pages earlier that Charley Tudor
was Trollope—does not round off his argument. Escott, in
his big book on Trollope,[2] also stops short. He identifies
Eames' love entanglement with Amelia Roper as, in part at
least, a reminiscence. But he goes no further.

Here are the words (from page nine of the first volume of
The Small House at Allington) which introduce John Eames to
the Trollopian stage. "Now John Eames was a young man
who had been appointed to the Income Tax Office with
eighty pounds a year." And about twenty pages further on,
this second, longer passage takes up the tale:—

> There is a class of young men who never get petted,
> though they may not be the less esteemed, or perhaps loved.
> They do not come forth to the world as Apollos, nor shine
> at all, keeping what light they may have for inward purposes.
> Such young men are often awkward, ungainly, and not yet
> formed in their gait; they struggle with their limbs, and

---

[1] "Trollope Revisited," in *Essays and Studies*, by Members of the English
Association. Oxford, 1920.
[2] *Anthony Trollope: His Work, Associates and Originals*, by T. H. S. Escott.
London, 1913.

are shy; words do not come to them with ease, when words are required, among any but their accustomed associates. Social meetings are periods of penance to them, and any appearance in public will unnerve them. They go much about alone, and blush when women speak to them. In truth, they are not as yet men, whatever the number may be of their years; and, as they are no longer boys, the world has found for them the ungraceful name of the hobbledehoy.

But the hobbledehoy, though he blushes when women address him, and is uneasy even when he is near them, though he is not master of his limbs in a ball-room, and is hardly master of his tongue at any time, is the most eloquent of beings, and especially eloquent among beautiful women. He enjoys all the triumphs of a Don Juan, without any of Don Juan's heartlessness, and is able to conquer in all encounters, through the force of his wit and the sweetness of his voice. But this eloquence is heard only by his own inner ears, and these triumphs are the triumphs of his imagination.

The true hobbledehoy is much alone, not being greatly given to social intercourse even with other hobbledehoys; he wanders about in solitude, taking long walks, in which he dreams of those successes which are so far removed from his powers of achievement. Out in the fields, with his stick in his hand, he is very eloquent, cutting off the heads of the springing summer weeds, as he practises his oratory with energy.

Such hobbledehoys receive but little petting, unless it be from a mother; and such a hobbledehoy was John Eames when he was sent away from Guestwick to begin his life in the big room of a public office in London.

At several points this passage anticipates almost word for word the Autobiography which Trollope was to write fourteen years later. Can there be any doubt that, just as Charley Tudor had been the author's self in circumstance but not in physical attributes or character, so Johnny Eames was Trollope's idea of the type of young man that he himself had been, but one whose history (with the considerable exception of Amelia Roper) was wholly imaginary?

Young Tudor's life in the Internal Navigation office, his pranks and shifts and money-borrowings, were, on his definite admission, Trollope's own. Trollope's own also (though this must be assumed without authority) were the embarrassing love affair with the pretty barmaid and the tenderness for Katie Woodward. But, though his *tale* is true, Charley Tudor is not young Anthony. It was one thing for a man of Trollope's innate shyness to turn into fiction distresses and amours long passed away; it was another to depict himself enduring or enjoying them. He could clothe Charley (an invented dummy) in his own memories, but when he came to draw himself he swerved from double truth. Consequently, when he undertook the creation of Johnny Eames—an act of unsparing self-analysis and a task of self-discovery—the result had to be smothered in unfamiliar incident, disguised by every trick of authorship. In fashioning Eames, Trollope partly defied, partly indulged, his own unconquerable diffidence. He wished to write himself down for his own shrinking self to read, but to write in such a way that others should not guess what he had done.[1]

Eames is an honest manly youth, but clumsy and a victim to his own awkwardness. By sheer ineptitude he blunders into an unmeant love affair with Amelia Roper, and years later into a not dissimilar entanglement—more sophisticated but no more intentional—with Madalina Desmolines. Both of these philanderings—and in the hands of a more experienced and deft Don Juan they would be mere philanderings—are in their way part of his abiding love for Lily Dale. He sees his Lily captivated by a face more handsome and manners smoother than his can ever be, and holds aloof, surrendering his hopes yet cherishing them. But when she is betrayed by her Apollo,

[1] Doctor Jeffrey Wortle, the central figure in *Dr. Wortle's School*, suggests self-portraiture of another kind. The Doctor's dilemma is not one in which Trollope ever found himself; perhaps the Doctor's character was not consciously modelled on that of his creator; but the former acts in certain circumstances as the latter would have acted, and the self-portrait of the mature Trollope—voluntarily or involuntarily—is a lifelike one. [Cf. below, pp. 394, 395.]

Johnny—no longer diffident—thrashes the scoundrel in a railway station.

Trollope himself may have performed no single action of the many attributed to Eames. But had he loved a Lily and had she treated him as Lily treated Johnny, Trollope and Johnny would have borne themselves with the same blend of dignity and diffidence, with the same fickle constancy and sudden righteous rage. Trollope, like Johnny, would have continued to worship Lily from afar; like Johnny, he would have taken his bruised vanity to be anointed by a Madalina, but left his heart behind; as zestfully as Johnny would he have beaten a Crosbie into pulp. Of all the villains who in Trollope's books come to be thrashed, Crosbie receives the fullest measure for his sin. Perhaps the joy of describing Crosbie's fall was Trollope's recompense for his own self-analysis. No one will grudge him his reward.

"Know thyself" was a command which Trollope—much as he may have wished to do so—could not ignore. Experience taught him to have few illusions about others; he taught himself to cherish none about himself. It was his pride to stand foursquare before the world and show unashamed each detail of each of his embattled walls; but he sought to hide the secrets of the castle keep from all eyes save his own. They were not shameful secrets—indeed they were pleasant and lovable, if a little crude—but they were his, and it was his humour to keep them close. Part of the process was the delineation of this cryptogram of self. Once Johnny Eames had been made alive and set to move through the long pages of two long novels, the callow Trollope of the 'thirties had been sized up and with a wry smile accepted by the mature Trollope of the 'sixties, as a fact regrettable and rather comic, but satisfactorily undisclosed.

With this conviction of the essential identity of Eames and Trollope, it is easy to resolve the question long debated among Trollopians as to whether or no the former was a "gentleman." To modern minds the problem may seem an academic one, but in the view of mid and late Victorianism it was essential.

Trollope's "nose for gentility" was notoriously keen. Would he have fumbled in a matter so important over a character so carefully worked out as Eames—even if that character were not *au fond* a piece of self-portraiture? He could draw a "half sir" as shrewdly and perceptively as he could draw a gentleman; and if Eames be a doubtful quantity, there is, one hazards, special reason for the doubt. For there is—and always has been—conflict of opinion. Trollope himself would always evade the question whether or no Eames was a gentleman, and in the circumstances such evasion was an affirmative. Others have expressed (and not by implication only) a contrary view. Professor Elton, for example, speaks of "Johnny Eames whose heart belies his bodily envelope and his breeding." [1] "Q" is more emphatic still:

> Trollope adds to his strain of coarseness, a strain—or at least an intimate understanding—of cheapness. . . . Those who understand this will understand why he could not bring himself to mate his "dear Lily Dale" with that faithful, most helpful little bounder Johnny Eames. [2]

One hesitates to differ from a critic so authoritative, but his argument, for all its ingenuity, is unconvincing. Is not the persistent denial to Johnny Eames of the Lily he so faithfully desired rather self-laceration on the author's part than judgment on poor Eames?

As *The Last Chronicle of Barset* progressed through its long series of weekly numbers, Trollope received letters from all parts begging him at last to give poor Johnny his lady, urging the fidelity he had shown, calling on Lily's creator to make her change her mind. But Trollope was stubborn, and when Lily disappeared for ever she was still Lily Dale. This obstinacy of Trollope's is significant. He was sensitive to the wishes of his public; we have his own word for the fact that, when he began to write a book, he never knew how it would finish. Why, then, could not he have melted Lily at the end?

[1] *A Survey of English Literature* 1830-1880, by Oliver Elton. London, 1920.
[2] *Charles Dickens and Other Victorians*, by Sir Arthur Quiller-Couch. Cambridge, 1925.

Clearly because, in the queer thwarted love affair of Eames and Lily Dale, he saw himself pursuing his ideal—loving her, fighting for her, serving her faithfully, but finally grasping empty air.

There is nothing fanciful in thus attributing to Trollope a wistful vision of his own youthful woman-worship. During his later schooldays, and even after he entered the Post Office, he "was always going about with some castle in the air firmly built within my mind. For weeks, for months from year to year I would carry on the same tale. . . . I myself was, of course, my own hero. I never became a king or a duke—much less, when my height and personal appearance were fixed, could I be an Antinous, or six feet high. But I was a very clever person, and beautiful young women used to be fond of me."

The tale of Eames and Lily Dale is but a prolongation of this rueful whimsicality. By the time it came to be written, Trollope had trained himself to mock at his own vanities and, for his own good, to do them violence.

3

The Trollope who in 1841 applied for and obtained a Surveyor's Clerkship in the far west of Ireland, owed more to his seven years in London than, perhaps, was apparent at the time, certainly more than he himself would have admitted. In appearance he was little changed from the sulky youth who had first entered the office in St. Martin's le Grand; in his private brooding he was still diffident, bored, unhopeful of the future. But, like a chrysalis on the verge of breaking, he was, though still a chrysalis, ready for a transformation. In other words, the potentialities of the young man of twenty-six, who seven years earlier had been an ungainly boy, gave the measure of London's teaching more truly than the young man himself.

Trollope had always been lonely and often neglected. But not until he found himself faced with the immense indifference of London, had he a chance to learn that friendlessness can

E

be a healing privacy. After his school experience and the
vague idleness of Bruges, he was in real danger of accepting
ostracism as an inevitable fate. He was coming to regard
himself as different from his kind, as—for some reason that
in his sullen bewilderment he took no pains to understand—a
being destined to slouch along the roads of life, despised and
solitary. This he himself admits. "I fear" he says in the
Autobiography "that my mode of telling of the first twenty-six
years of my life will have left an idea simply of their absurdities; but in truth I was wretched—sometimes almost unto
death. There had clung to me a feeling that I had been looked
upon always as an evil, an encumbrance, a useless thing—as
a creature of whom those connected with me had to be
ashamed." This state of mind would have been one of
extreme danger to a youth less tenacious in the face of misfortune or—let it candidly be said—more keenly imaginative.
From the outset London seemed to promise a mere dreary
repetition of the old sufferings. His first experience of the
Post Office was as galling as any he had ever had. He
was received with an impatient disgust, and made to feel
that, though other clerks might in the past have been un-
promising, he was of all Government scullions the most
contemptible. But before long he began to find that his
forlorn incompetence was of no interest to anyone but his
immediate superiors. The people in the shops, his landlady,
the barmen and barmaids whom he came to know, only
asked that he should say a friendly word, pay for what
he had, and go about his business. If he defaulted, the
persons concerned made life a hell until their claims were
met; but after settlement they forgot all about him. His
solitude was no longer that of an unhappy cur baited by
cruel boys, but one of the million solitudes which go to make
the bustle of a city.

Trollope's first gain from London therefore was self-confidence. When no one cares how a man behaves, he soon
ceases to care very much himself; and this drift toward heed-
lessness—in many cases catastrophic—was in Trollope's case
the tendency most needed. Behind the screen of a now

welcome isolation, he learnt to contemplate his own character and behaviour as problems of his own private concern and without reference to other people. Once he was able to criticise himself by the standard of his own ideals and not by that of others' mockery, he had dispelled his inferiority complex and won his first and most essential battle with existence.

After self-confidence came observation. He surveyed the teeming London scene and saw how London lived. Undoubtedly his power of gauging the quality and mind of any company in which he found himself grew from the experience of these metropolitan years. He would sit in the corner of a bar and watch and listen; he would walk the streets and idle at street corners, and note the little trivial things that distinguish one class from another—one kind of man from another. His various love affairs taught him the ways of girlhood; occasional visits to the few "comfortable" families of his acquaintance gave him an opportunity of contrasting the manners, reserves and outlook of the upper bourgeoisie with those of the less fastidious and less conventional persons who thronged the parks and public places. In the Post Office—where he soon won something of a name for insubordination and made the interesting discovery that defiance of authority can bring repute as well as disesteem—he studied the characters of his fellow-clerks, and gauged the varying powers of discipline among his superiors. In short, wherever he went he studied the reactions of personality to circumstance, and—without thought of authorship but because humanity in its daily life was his instinctive interest—came to an understanding of the normal English scene.

From this persistent scrutiny of class and individual developed one of the most emphatic of his later mental attitudes— an amused dislike of the professional castes in English life. Reading his novels, one is struck again and again with his resentful interest in those groups of citizens who, sharing a common privilege or speciality of work, form of themselves an "order" within the framework of society. The Church, the Civil Service, the legal and medical professions, politicians,

the peerage—each of these in its way intrigued Trollope by its
separateness, and fascinated or enraged him by its contacts
with the rest of the world. His life in the Post Office was his
first experience of the caste-tradition, and the Civil Servant was
the first type of caste-mind with which he grew familiar. The
experience was a fruitful one. From it sprang his reluctant
absorption in all the closed domains which are scattered,
gracious but arrogant, about the social landscape, and to that
absorption the world owes many of the finest passages in
his novels.

Two other qualities of Trollope's mature work may be
attributed to his life in London. The first is his tolerance of
frailty. Perhaps the indifference of others towards his own
shortcomings, which had given him the chance of self-
discovery, claimed a direct return. Certainly he never developed any tendency to "watch committee" discipline or to
uncharitable judgment. In his *Autobiography* he speaks of the
moral purpose of his fiction; but no modern reader can take
this statement very seriously. It is merely another example
of the influence of his period on his method of self-expression.
At heart he was of all men the most tolerant of others' failings;
and of this tolerance his books are full. There are certain
sins he cannot forgive (though even these he understands),
but toward most of the lapses that a conventional society
condemns he shows a humorous sympathy which is almost
cynicism.

But if Londoners' forbearance made him forbearing, their
rare but ready harshness accustomed him to rigorous treatment
of the unforgivable. Hence the relish with which in his books
he inflicts physical chastisement on the characters whose failings
may not be condoned. London in the 'thirties was a city of
knockabout. Fists and broken crowns were everyday events,
so that Trollope (in whom a definite pugnacity was inherent)
came to regard a thrashing as, in certain circumstances, a
proper squaring of accounts.

In short, he learnt in the unrivalled school of London life,
to smile at neighbourly vagaries and to bear normal jostling
with good humour. He also learnt, when the limits of his

tolerance were overstepped, to choose the moment for a blow and the best way of giving it.

These lessons, however (and others less directly influential on his later work), were in the main unconsciously absorbed and always below the surface of his present discontent. He could not yet disentangle from his day-to-day unhappiness the new interests and the new self-respect that were to become foundations of a prosperous life. He felt himself trapped in the sour cellars of the Civil Service, a creature with no prospects of advancement and yet—because he had no other livelihood—desperately fearful of dismissal. His health grew worse. Under-nourishment and irregular habits were breaking down his physique. Early in 1840 came collapse. The *Autobiography* (curiously enough) makes no mention of the serious illness which he so narrowly survived. But Tom Trollope records the family anxiety, and two letters from Frances Trollope to Lady Bulwer Lytton show her feelings while nursing him in London:—

> How your kind heart would pity me could you witness the anxious misery I am enduring! My poor darling lies in a state that defies the views of his physicians as effectually as it puzzles my ignorance. It is asthma from which he chiefly suffers now; but they say this can only be a symptom, and not the disease. He is frightfully reduced in size and strength. Day by day I lose hope and so, I am quite sure, do his physicians.

Then two or three weeks later:—

> My poor Anthony is so very nearly in the same state as when I last wrote that I have not a word to say that can help to give you information of our future movements.

But the disease had spent itself. Anthony's constitution outlasted it and by the autumn of 1840 he was about again. Perhaps the lingering remains of sickness strengthened his longing to be free of London and the Post Office; perhaps his

mother used her influence to make a change possible. He himself records that in August 1841, from weariness of his work
at St. Martin's le Grand and of his debt-ridden life in town, he
applied for a vacant clerkship in a Surveyor's office in the
wilds of Ireland. The job was so unattractive that there was
hardly another candidate, and his superiors in London were
glad of a chance to be rid of him. The appointment was
confirmed.

II

TROLLOPE LIVED IN IRELAND more or less continuously for the ten years from 1841 to 1851. During this time he came to know gaiety and good-fellowship; and if in later years he gave to Ireland all credit for his discovery of happiness and none at all to the formative London years which had pointed the way thither, the bias was a natural one.

The work that awaited him at Banagher on the Shannon—a small town near the centre of Ireland and on the Galway boundary of King's County—was the direct opposite of that assigned to him in St. Martin's le Grand. Instead of sitting at a desk in a stuffy room and copying letters, he had to make incessant tours of the post offices in his district, inspect the postmasters' accounts, listen to civilian grievances, and in his ungainly, townbred, ignorant but energetic person to unite the qualities of avenging superior and obliging public servant.

Readers of Somerville and Ross will recall the post office in Mrs. Coolahan's public house on the coast of Connemara; [1] and, although that description was written more than fifty years after Trollope's first Irish journeyings, it may be taken substantially to represent the sort of problem and the sort of people with which, in his capacity of deputy inspector, he was confronted. After a frenzied search for the official pen, which Katty Ann is thought to have taken for some unusual purpose to the cow-house:—

> "Only that some was praying for me" declared Mrs. Coolahan "it might as well be the Inspector that came in the office, asking for the pin, an' if that was the way we might all go under the sod. Sich a me-aw!"
> "Musha! Musha!" breathed prayerfully one of the shawled women.

---

[1] *All on the Irish Shore*, London, 1903, p. 226 *seq.*

The task of controlling yet appreciating such folk as the Coolahan family required precisely the quality of humorous sympathy which Trollope now possessed. By sheer good fortune he had found work he could do, and the Post Office had stumbled on an Englishman able and willing to be on terms with Irish character. Rapidly Trollope's nascent self-confidence benefited from a sense of being, for once, the right man in the right place, although the place was of the most obscure and the man a very junior official. From the outset of his life at Banagher he liked the Irish, and this liking grew into one of the most stable of his loves. The Irish returned his liking; for though in many ways he was a most English Englishman and every bit as aggressive in argument as they themselves, he had none of the starchy dignity which more mercurial races regard as an English speciality, and he shared at least this characteristic with the folk around him that a joke against himself was a better joke than any other.

His dealings with the private individuals who had a grievance against the postal administration were no less congenial than those with his subordinates. He tells in the *Autobiography* the story of the indignant country gentleman who wrote so furiously to complain of postal inefficiency that Trollope was despatched in snowy mid-winter to investigate the case. He arrived at the distant house in County Cavan to find the injured gentleman so ready with hospitality, so concerned at the deputy inspector's weather-beaten plight and so delighted to have company, that all thought of Post Office shortcomings was drowned in hot brandy and water and the grievance hardly mentioned during an overnight visit of music and cheerful conversation. Other stories—not dissimilar—might be told. All go to prove how utterly different life's aspect had become; how far away seemed London's dragging squalor.

And if the pleasant sense of liking his fellow-men and being liked by them healed Trollope's ailing mind, his long days on horseback, riding the lonely roads from little town to little town, restored his body. Living out-of-doors and in all weathers, he was equally happy in wind or rain or mist or sunshine. Also he began to hunt. He had learnt to ride in boyhood and had even, on rare occasions, followed hounds; but now for the first time he began to go out regularly. The surveyor under whom he worked was a master of fox-hounds. Trollope, with some of the money borrowed from a friend in London but not entirely used in paying debts, bought himself a horse and ventured boldly into the hunting field.

In this way he discovered the greatest of all the pleasures of his life:—

> I have ever since been constant to the sport [he says] having learnt to love it with an affection which I cannot myself fathom or understand. . . . I have written on very many subjects and on most of them with pleasure; but on no subject with such delight as on that of hunting.

He was quick to realise the connection between this new-found hobby and the successful conduct of his work. The latter depended on popularity rather than on technical ability and knowledge, and there was no surer path to Irish friendship than that of enthusiasm for the favourite Irish sport. Trollope learnt to adjust his official tours of inspection to the arrangements of local hunts. He became known (and liked the better) for his habit of appearing at a post office in full hunting kit, counting the cash, checking the ledgers and then hurrying off to the near-by meet. In the field he was soon popular for his pluck and good humour. In Essex, later on, his short sight would land him in trouble, but his ready sense of the ridiculous turn his own ill-luck into noisy laughter and persistence regain his place among the leaders of the field. Similarly in Ireland he would crash his way over the rotten banks and loose stone walls of Connaught, heavy and reckless of results, but fearless, boisterous and keen through all the phases of a long and tiring day.

His horsemanship was typical of his character and mental quality. From the point of view of style and actual technique he was a bad rider—clumsy and wasteful of his own energy. But he had "hands." And there can be no better way of expressing his peculiar genius as a novelist than by this phrase from the vocabulary of horsemanship. His work is often

E*

diffuse, straggling, wanting in elegance and finish; but when
—as constantly—it is concerned to portray character, it shows
a sort of second sense, an instinctive power of judging motive,
a prescience of human inclination. Trollope on horseback
could exercise that super-sensitive control which certain horse-
men use and others cannot learn; and it was the same with
Trollope the novelist of character.

2

Marriage is an event in the life of any man, and in the life
of an author the beginning of his first work is often no less
significant. Both of these adventures came to Trollope during
his three years at Banagher. Both were important to him,
but the one influenced his career materially as much as spiritu-
ally, and the other was so completely a false start as to have
virtually no influence at all.

His engagement to Rose Heseltine twelve months after his
arrival in Ireland and his marriage to her two years later are
good evidence of his new sturdiness and self-confidence. In
London he had been barely equal to the responsibility of
managing himself; after a year of Banagher he could undertake
to control not only his own life, but that of a young woman
also. In this direction, therefore, the Irish cure worked
rapidly.

As the world judges marriages this one was a success. From
June 11 1844 until his death in December 1882 Anthony and
his wife lived in untroubled amity. She bore him two sons;
helped him in the ordering of his work; entertained his
friends; travelled in his company; and provided just that
background of calm, well-managed comfort which was
essential to so hard a worker. Indeed it may be said that her
devoted competence made possible his prolonged and successful prosecution of two wholly different livelihoods, and this
service—to a man of Trollope's arrogant energy—would of
itself have been cause for lifelong gratitude. Another element
in their mutual contentment was a community of domestic
taste. The Victorian conception of a wife's duty came as

acceptably to him as it came naturally to her, and as the one desired what the other had to give, the two lived happily.

So much for Trollope's marriage, which may without offence be termed a well-managed settling down. As much cannot be said of his first fumblings after authorship.

When in the autumn of 1843 he wrote the first chapters of his first story, *The Macdermots of Ballycloran*, he did indeed begin a novel, but not a novelist's career. Not until ten years later in an English cathedral city did he conceive the tale which marks his début into literature. The intervening decade saw three novels, a play, some essays and a trial section of a guide-book; but each and all of these were unproductive—not only of material profit, but also of a realisation of his own power of authorship.

In other words, Trollope the writer was, during his Irish period, as much a square peg in a round hole as had been Trollope the man during the years in London. He had ambitions toward literature, but only discovered by the painful process of elimination the way to their achievement.

What was the origin of these ambitions? Looking back on his own life from the standpoint of autobiographer, he claimed that the idea of becoming himself a novelist had been conceived almost in adolescence. But although the possession of a novel-writing mother would naturally have influenced his youthful aspirations, those aspirations could hardly have been so definite as he implies.

In London he had studied and enjoyed much poetry and had taught himself to read Latin and French with ease. It is even probable that for a short period he was involved in a project for a *revue des jeunes*, and that the incidents of *The Panjandrum* [1] were gleams of memory. But these occupations had been a hobby for spare time, his real and absorbing task having been that of adjusting an uneasy self to an unconciliatory world. The whole tendency of his existence had been toward finding his equilibrium as member of a community. His desires were

---

[1] Cf. *An Editor's Tales.*

not for writing fame or writing skill; they were for fellowship, and for an easy bearing among others of his kind.

The literary ambition is either something more remote than this—an impulse to withdraw into an ivory tower beside the sea of contemplation—or else a fierce determination to impose one's individual view upon the market-place. Now Trollope had none of the instincts of the recluse. His talent and his tastes were for the rough and tumble of the human scene, his every craving was for the freedom of the crowded street. But this he sought as a boon companion, not as an orator. To teach one's fellows demands at least some basis of self-confidence. Every writer, however inexperienced, thinks that what he has to say will interest or improve a handful of his fellowmen, and therefore possesses a modicum of self-esteem. But Trollope, until he had spent some months in Ireland, was hardly aware that he was capable of self-esteem. It is not credible that a young man in his state of bitter apathy should seriously have had the idea of writing tales for other folk to read. He claims in the *Autobiography* that his youthful habit of keeping a private journal taught him the rudiments of self-expression, and that this training turned his mind to authorship. But diary-writing, however valuable as drill, cannot create the novelist's mentality, which waits on circumstances exterior to the individual—on, in fact, contacts between the individual and the world.

The birth of Trollope's novelist-ambition was undoubtedly a direct outcome of his Irish health and happiness. In London he had learnt to observe; in Ireland he learnt, having observed, to savour and to criticise. To this lesson he was helped by being half a foreigner. Surrounded by the so different Irish, he became conscious of his own Englishry. Listening to their persistent talk of Ireland's wrongs, and hearing—amused but argumentative—their comments on his own people, he was impelled—almost despite himself—to mental counter-comment from the English point of view. At once the whole basis of his outlook changed. He was no longer an outcast, pleading for entrance to the club of ordinary men; he had become an ambassador of England, living in disputatious amity with one of the most race-conscious nations in the world. And from the sense of being—however humbly—an envoy of his country, his literary ambition and his love of politics grew rapidly and side by side. It was a short step from verbal discussions of the Anglo-Irish problem to written pronouncements on this and allied themes; it needed only the atmosphere of political declamation and good-humoured wrangling in which his Irish friends perpetually lived to rouse his own potential enthusiasm for politics, which—once it was roused —remained keenly awake throughout his life.

North of Banagher and just south of Carrick-on-Shannon is the little town of Drumsna. Here, in September 1843, Trollope and his friend John Merivale took an aimless walk. In a village called Headfort they happened on the abandoned ruins of a country house, and the description of that house is the first chapter of *The Macdermots of Ballycloran*. It is interesting to contrast the naïve, over-detailed presentation of Ballycloran House with Trollope's later mastery of *mise-en-scène*. But it is more than interesting—because it gives a revelation of his personality—to note how he reacted to a scene of desolation, with all its implications of mystery and melancholy and withered hopes. His reaction is inventive, ingenious and genuinely felt—but it is not imaginative. He ignores the dramatic possibilities of the past and present of Ballycloran House. Not until he gets to grips with the actual characters of his story does he seem to realise the pathos and fascination of collapse. Thady Macdermot is vividly realised and movingly portrayed; Pheemy, his luckless sister, and a crowd of minor characters are already quick with genuine Trollopian vitality. But when the author strays beyond the actual thoughts and doings of his men and women, he is bleakly unpoetical, and lapses readily into either sociology or politics. The magic fades. The novelist has given place to a close-thinking, honest, but rather tedious lecturer.

The two chief blemishes of *The Macdermots of Ballycloran* are lack of imagination and excess of instructional zeal. The book may be negligible to an estimate of Trollope's literary fame;

but for its very faults' sake it is important to a knowledge of his character, revealing as it does the bias of his mind at the present stage of his career and also his chief (and abiding) mental limitation.   He was not really an imaginative man. In the finer forms of fancy he was deficient, inheriting from his mother, not only many of her admirable qualities, but this imperfection also.   In consequence his novels, from first to last, are inventive, sympathetic and amazingly perceptive, but rarely—very rarely—novels of imagination.   They leap and run and glide and linger in the shade; they do not soar.

3

The instructional element in *The Macdermots* has interest of a different kind.   Although his best English work is distinctively free from them, interpolations of historical or economic fact persist throughout the Irish novels.   Not only *The Macdermots* and *The Kellys and the O'Kellys* (both 'prentice works and, as such, in part immune from criticism), but *Castle Richmond* also and *The Landleaguers* have, though in slightly different form and varying degree, this same insistence on actual political happening.

The explanation may be found in the experiences and pre-occupations of those first influential years at Banagher.   It is a part of the queer contradictory effect on Trollope of his life in Ireland—an effect half stimulating and half deadening, a bringing alive and forthwith a strangulation.

If, as they say, Ireland takes pride in contradictiousness, she may find satisfaction in her influence on Trollope, than which none could be more paradoxical.

So immense were the effects of Irish residence on his character and capacity for life that it would seem natural also to give to Ireland the credit for his novel-writing fame.   Yet she can not—save indirectly—claim even a share of it.

Ireland produced the man; but it was left to England to inspire the novelist.   Indeed one may go further.   Ireland, having by friendliness, sport and open air saved Trollope from himself, all but choked the very genius that she had vitalised by her insane absorption in her own wrongs and thwarted hopes.

Trollope, as has been said, came to self-knowledge in the midst of folk who talked of politics and argued politics; who took an interval for horse-dealing, another interval for whisky punch, then fell to politics again. He heard his companions trace each present grievance of their country back to English tyranny as surely as they traced their lineage to Irish kings. He liked them the better for the vivid humour of their grumbling, but could not let the challenge pass. He must defend his countrymen; explain their policy. The heady but interminable tale of Irish misery had in it enough of provocation to rouse his lust for argument, and enough of truth—painfully visible truth—to move his ready sympathy. He could not let the clamour of grievance pass and England's reputation go by default; he could not look about him and deny that there was ground for grievance and to spare.

As it happened, he could hardly have had a better opportunity of realising how justifiable were Irish anger and lamentation. He lived through the terrible famines of 1846 and 1847 with their attendant pestilence; he saw the stricken wretches littering the desolate roads; he went in daily expectation of encounters with the bands of marauders who, homeless and foodless, ranged the countryside. But his stubborn faith in English good intentions (no Englishman will admit an evil motive in his countrymen, however bitterly he may blame them for mismanagement) would not permit him to cry guilty to the reckless charge of Saxon perfidy. He knew and declared that many things were wrong; but he was convinced that English knavery was not the explanation for their wrongness. To find this explanation it became necessary to study the subject, to marshal the facts, to equip himself for controversy. With characteristic thoroughness he set about the task.

He read all the principal novels of Irish life which had appeared during the preceding thirty years. He read Banim's *O'Hara Tales* and *The Collegians* by Griffin; he read Lady Morgan, Maturin and the early books of Mrs. Hall; he read Maria Edgeworth; most effectually and eagerly of all he read and re-read the works of William Carleton. Then at Sir William Gregory's house, Coole Park, whither he had gone to exchange Harrow memories with his old schoolfellow, he met Charles Lever. *Charles O'Malley* had just appeared to swell the chorus of delight which had greeted *Harry Lorrequer*, and Lever's charm and reputation sent Trollope the more eagerly to his researches into Irish history. He no longer confined himself to fiction. Such statistical and other records of Irish governance and Anglo-Irish dealings as the Coole Park library possessed, or as he could contrive to borrow elsewhere or afford to buy, were rapidly absorbed. He became in a few years a compendium of facts relative to Ireland and her uneasy partnership with Britain.

This state of mind had two direct results. The first was that Trollope's interest in Ireland became inextricably involved with political happening and political contention, so that he never learnt to disentangle Irish individuals from the sorrows and aspirations of their native land. In the second place, his new wish to write took naturally the form of a desire to write of Irish conditions and, in his honest laborious English way, at once to prick the bubbles of exaggeration and to show scrupulous fairness to the facts.

Thus Trollope was stirred to authorship by Irish influence. But the same influence, and simultaneously, set him on a path of authorship which led no-whither. His entire work was nearly blighted by this first impulse to devote to politics a mind and pen whose proper genius was humanity. Had it not been for his own discouragement and a chance transfer to the English provinces, he might have spent a lifetime over books which, like *Castle Richmond*, are documented essays on distress or, like *The Landleaguers*, sad accounts of wretched actuality in which characterisation is submerged in floods of almost literal fact. It was a narrow escape.

4

Trollope's official reputation mounted steadily during his years in Ireland. He rose in the hierarchy of the Post Office, from deputy surveyor to surveyor, from surveyor to special commissioner charged with the planning of a rural postal service. His ugly-duckling days were done; he was now an established public servant, maybe not too popular at headquarters, but valued for his good sense and industry.

He did not, of course, spend all of his Irish years at Banagher. In 1844 he had been moved to Clonmel in the south, where in furnished lodgings his two sons [1] were born. Thence the family was transferred to Mallow, a town in County Cork in the centre of good hunting country. In Mallow, and in the first house of his own that he had ever rented, Trollope lived happily until 1851.

In melancholy contrast to his steady purposeful rise in the ranks and estimation of his profession was his restless search after a proper outlet for his literary inclination.

The Macdermots of Ballycloran, begun in 1843, was not completed until early in 1845. It was accepted (a little torpidly and at the special urging of the author's mother) by a minor publisher in 1846 and issued, still-born, in 1847. The author proceeded immediately to a second Irish novel. *The Kellys and the O'Kellys* is as much a pamphlet in fictional guise as its predecessor, being equally a product of Trollope's absorption in the Irish question. To pass on from such a work to a series of letters (written for *The Examiner*) on the state of the Irish poor was a natural development. The letters appeared during 1848 and 1849, and while they were publishing, the European upheavals of '48 (which had a certain intimate interest because of Frances Trollope's foreign residence) sent a faint tremor into the heart of Ireland and directed Anthony's attention still more closely to political events. He sent his mother a shrewd opinion on the prospects of revolution in Ireland and even (arguing from his innate sense of his countrymen's character) in England also. The letter has a brusque, sceptical humour that is very typical:—

Everybody now magnifies the rows at a distance from him. You write of tranquillity in Tuscany, where we

---

[1] Henry Merivale and Frederick Anthony.

expected to hear of revolt, provisional governments, and military occupation. And I get letters from England, asking me whether I am not afraid to have my wife and children in this country, whereas all I hear or see of Irish rows is in the columns of the *Times* newspaper. . . . Here in Ireland the meaning of the word Communism—or even social revolution—is not understood. The people have not the remotest notion of attempting to improve their worldly condition by making the difference between the employer and the employed less marked. Revolution here means a row. Some like a row, having little or nothing to lose. These are revolutionists, and call for pikes. Others are anti-revolutionists, having something to lose and dreading a row. These condemn the pikes, and demand more soldiers and police. There is no notion of anything beyond this;—no conception of any theory such as that of Louis Blanc. My own idea is that there is no ground to fear any general rising either in England or Ireland. I think there is too much intelligence in England for any large body of men to look for any sudden improvement; and not enough intelligence in Ireland for any body of men at all to conceive the possibility of social improvement.

The events of '48 sent Trollope to the histories of France, and in particular to that of the French Revolution. Chance took him at the same time into those parts of Galway where lived descendants of refugees from the Terror of 1793. Falling into talk with them, he conceived the idea of a novel of revolutionary France. The book was to be based on his own reading, but coloured by these Galway memories of parents' tales and even, here and there, by the actual reminiscence of survivors. With such an origin it is not surprising that *La Vendée*, though historical in theme, is in essence purely a novel of political argument. Trollope had views on tyranny, and these views he used his story to express. The result is a work of unexampled dreariness, which, coming at a time when costume novels were already in decline, met with a failure which is easily understood. One thing at least *La Vendée* shows—that the man who wrote it was still far from conceiving novel-writing as a presentation of an imaginary society, still far from understanding that fiction of the highest type must exclude both an author's private prejudice and recognisable contemporary events. Trollope was still a gatherer of distressful facts, which, whether made palatable by a sugar-coat of fiction or served as undisguised physic, represented his real preoccupation and showed his own idea of the subjects best suited to his talents.

5

In July 1849 Anthony's mother, now in her seventieth year and just recovered from a bad attack of bronchitis, crossed over to Ireland on a visit to the home at Mallow. She brought with her her son-in-law, John Tilley, who had lost his wife (Anthony's sister Cecilia) three months before. Change of scene did much to restore the old lady from the illness which had been brought on by this last ordeal of nursing. Her son and daughter-in-law drove her about the countryside.[1] All was contentment. "Anthony and his excellent little wife," she wrote, "are as happy as possible."

The weeks spent in the house of her younger son constituted the first protracted encounter between Frances and Anthony since his departure from Brussels fifteen years before. They had, of course, in the interval corresponded regularly, and on occasions had seen one another. During Mrs. Trollope's brief and expensive trial of the Lake Country as a place of residence Anthony had stayed with her; he had met her in London once or twice. But these contacts had been brief. Now they were thrown, over a period of several weeks, into the intimacy of a small house in a small Irish town. Without doubt they talked of novel-writing and in particular of the son's two unsuccessful efforts.

Anthony tries to defend his application of fiction to didactic purposes. Frances waves such ponderosity aside. The libraries, she explains, want tales of love and of contemporary

[1] She made use of this Irish experience in her novel *Uncle Walter* (published 1852).

life, not three lugubrious volumes big with Irish melancholy.
Beyond everything, no more Ireland! She recalls what Newby
said of *The Macdermots*; [1] she points to Colburn's letter to
Anthony in which, after announcing the failure of the *Kellys*,
he said: "It is evident that readers do not like novels on Irish
subjects as well as on others. Thus you will perceive it is
impossible for me to give any encouragement to you to
proceed in novel-writing." "Colburn knows his business,"
she says. "Do not despise the expert, even though he be only
a publisher." Anthony declares that his new book is without
tinge of Ireland and reads her in manuscript the partially
finished story of *La Vendée*. She throws up her hands in mock
despair. A costume novel—and an instructive one into the
bargain! The boy must be crazy! Does he not know that
Mrs. Bray killed the costume novel years ago; that even
Ainsworth is a fading glory? Whereupon Anthony shrugs his
shoulders and laughs, agreeing that he is a sad blockhead and
his mother, as always, in the right.

Anthony's next literary venture may safely be attributed to
Frances' visit. He had learnt this much of his lesson—that
love and satire were the public taste, that historical fact and
crying contemporary injustice should be left to the professors,
that entertainers should entertain and let reform go hang.
But with characteristic clumsiness instead of trying his hand
once more at fiction and in the light of his mother's advice,
he ventured on a play. *The Noble Jilt*, a comedy in five acts,
written partly in prose, partly in blank verse, was composed
in 1850 after the publication of *La Vendée*. It was at once an
attempt to substitute romance and comedy for undeniable but
painful fact and—being staged in Bruges in the year 1792—a
by-product of the author's study of the French revolutionary
period. How the manuscript was sent for an opinion to
Frances Trollope's old actor friend, George Bartley; what

[1] " I have seen Newby about Anthony's book," Frances Trollope had written
to Cecilia Tilley in August 1846. " He, like everybody else, gives a most
wretched account of the novel-market. He has offered to print the book at
half profits, but declares that he has no hope that there will be anything above
expenses. He says that he thinks it very cleverly written, but that Irish stories
are very unpopular."

George Bartley thought of it, and how his kindly but un-disguised discouragement checked Trollope from further dramatic experiment, is related in the preface to the first pub-lished issue of the play itself, which was discovered twenty years ago in MS. and printed for the Trollopian enthusiast.[1] The comedy came back to Mallow labelled in huge letters "failure preordained." Even the sturdy Trollope winced.

> As my old friend warmed to the subject [he writes in the *Autobiography*, describing Bartley's candid letter of advice] the criticism became stronger and stronger till my ears tingled. . . . The neglect of a book is a disagreeable fact which grows upon an author by degrees. There is no special moment of agony, no stunning violence of con-demnation. But a piece of criticism such as this, from a friend and from a man undoubtedly capable of forming an opinion, was a blow in the face. But I accepted the judg-ment loyally and said not a word on the subject to anyone. I merely showed the letter to my wife, declaring my con-viction that it must be taken as gospel, and as critical gospel it has since been accepted.

After this fresh set-back Anthony might have been expected either to abandon writing or, by hazard, to hit on some genre more suited to his real but undiscovered genius. He was, however, still under the obsession of Ireland and of the urge to set the Irish scene before the English reader. The ill wind still blew, and bore him this time in a very strange direction.

He visited London late in 1850 and proposed to John Murray a guide-book to Ireland. The publisher asked for a specimen section of the work, and Trollope spent many weeks in drafting the chapters describing Dublin and the county of Kerry. The manuscript was sent to Albemarle Street and there engulfed. After nine months of silence Trollope, im-patient for news, demanded a decision. His bundle of papers was returned without a word.

---

[1] *The Noble Jilt.* A Comedy by Anthony Trollope. Edited with a preface by Michael Sadleir. London, 1923. The preface is reprinted in *Things Past*, 1944.

Posterity should be as grateful to John Murray for his sublime neglect of this unlucky manuscript as to George Bartley for his firm disapprobation of *The Noble Jilt*. "Had he been less dilatory" says the *Autobiography* "John Murray would have got a very good guide-book at a cheap rate." No doubt. But the world might have paid dearly for the bargain. Trollope would, very likely have gone from guide-book to political philosophy, and thence maybe to economic theory, and be to-day a long-forgotten publicist instead of the undying creator of the society of Barset and of the Dukes of Omnium.

In this way, first the bluntness of an English actor, then the inspired incompetence of an English publisher, defeated the influence of years of Irish stimulus. From the intoxication of Irish talk and Irish charm, which had set him running heavily along the paths of publicism, Trollope was jarred to sudden sobriety and, for a year or two, to self-distrust again. He began to ask himself whether his dream of authorship had been indeed only a dream. He plunged into new and absorbing work. Not until 1853 did he attempt to write another book. By then he had spent two years in travelling Gloucestershire and Somerset; by then he had fallen, wholly and finally, beneath the slow, wise, soothing spell of rural England; by then (though he was not immediately aware of it) his feet were on their proper road.

The incidents of Trollope's Irish sojourn can now be viewed in sequence. Thanks to Ireland he becomes a personality; then a political personality. Nearly he hardens in this mould —so nearly that it leaves its trace on every handling of an Irish theme. His mother takes a hand at reformation. On her advice he tries romantic comedy, but shackles himself with fetters of dramatic form. Fortunately a candid friend is found to disabuse him of complacency. The play is locked into a drawer, and Trollope drifts again to tabulation of Irish actuality. He becomes the fortunate (though angry) victim of a publisher's indolence. He hesitates. Perhaps he has no bent to authorship? And at this vital moment the third and happiest chance of all befalls him; the Irish influence—once a stimulus, now an induration—is withdrawn.

After two years' experience of the English countryside he writes *The Warden*, which is the first Trollopian novel. Those which preceded it can, in the light of what we know now, be appraised here and there by the standard of his maturer work; but they were in fact the products of a wholly different mental attitude alike to life and to authorship. That is why the starting of *The Macdermots* was no significant event in Trollope's life. It did not mark the rising of the Trollopian sun; it was a false dawn.

III

TROLLOPE WAS SO HAPPY at Mallow with his wife, his small boys, his hunting and his pleasant share in pleasant Irish life that he was at first inclined to resent the official order which removed him to England and gave him the intricate task of planning rural postal deliveries over the wide areas of the south-western counties.

But the conditions of the new life proved so exactly to his taste—he almost lived on horseback and found opportunities more frequent even than in Ireland of combining work and hunting—that he was soon comforted, and could later describe the years spent in touring western England as two of the happiest of his life.

But Trollope the novelist owed to these years a greater thing than happiness. They supplied the very foundation upon which his genius could build. They taught him the lie of English countryside; the disposition, appearance, and relative dignities of English country houses; the influence in a county of the county town, and in that town the subtle grading of the citizens. They taught him that the leading townsmen regarded the surrounding gentry with a blend of servility and jealousy peculiar to provincial life; that the landed magnates—with one eye on election times, the other on their social dignity—adopted toward the notables of their county capital an attitude of patronising geniality. Above all, this fine-combing of English country life revealed to Trollope the immense strategic strength of the social position of the upper clergy.

Where there was a cathedral city these important clerics, many of whom had relationships of blood or marriage with the landowners of the hinterland, could play the town's game in the country house or, conversely, influence from their strongholds in the Close such municipal happenings as were of interest to the mansions round about. Further, because the patronage of many country livings was in their hands, they were able, by planting here and there about the country their special nominees to vicarage or curacy, to do a service to the local squire or, if they so desired, to set a spy upon him.

The interest which Trollope always felt in the varied and intricate contacts of society received its first powerful impulse from his observation, during these years, of the small intrigues, jealousies and *quid pro quos* which went to compose the life of a prosperous English county. With amused detachment he listened to gossip, noted the evidence of trivial plot and counterplot, and remarked that in nearly every grouping or entanglement of individuals or of classes the clergy played a part. Because he had a keen eye for human foible, a tolerant smile for human scheming and an instinctive sense of the influence of rank and precedence on the actions of the time, he came to sense a social drama where no drama was evident, and so, by practice in his trade of authorship, to tell a tale of almost breathless interest without the help either of sudden incident or of striking misadventure.

These two years of English interlude played a vital part in deciding the manner no less than the matter of his story-telling. Trollope emerged from them with the two distinct attitudes toward individuals and toward social groups which characterised him throughout his life. These attitudes—the first affectionate, the second hostile or contemptuous—were, of course, an extension of his reluctant interest in the influence of any caste on the individuality of its members. Just as he loved to point the difference between the individual parson and the tribe of clerics, between the individual lawyer and the legal sect, so, in his studies of ordinary men and women, he distinguished between their impulses as human beings and their actions as members of the community or of some sub-section of it.

His novels are almost without exception novels of a conflict between individual decencies and social disingenuities. This is because he regarded private persons with a friendly optimism but society with cynical distrust. He believed that the ordinary man or woman is at heart an honourable, kindly creature; that only when he or she sets out to scale a social height or to defend a social fortress meanness and cruelty come to tarnish the natural brightness, or cloud the natural transparency. Sometimes an individual candour can resist, can defeat, can even transform social ambition; and such rare triumphs gave Trollope keen satisfaction. More often the personality yields to the pressure or to the temptations of convention; and such frequent tragedies had for him an unwilling but an irresistible fascination.

It is not easy to express without over-emphasis this dual strain in Trollope's outlook on the social scene. He was not in the accepted sense an "individualist," for theories of social science were, like all other theories, distasteful to him; nor was he in his dislike of society-tyranny wholly a cynic, seeing that he judged all things from a practical standpoint and admitted that many conventions have at least the sanction of commonsense. But the contrasted attitudes were there and utterly a part of him. On the one hand, he was in his heart of hearts profoundly critical of the established order (greatly more critical than at first sight appears); on the other, his patience with most individual shortcomings was inexhaustible.

If this is true of Trollope the established novelist, it is true because Trollope the man was thus moulded by his English experience of the early 'fifties. Note the parallel between the author and the books. In manner boisterous and in his zest for life insatiable, Trollope seemed a man content to take and to enjoy existence as he found it. Precisely this same impression is at first glance given by his novels. No comment on Trollope as a novelist is more frequently made than one which assumes, usually disparagingly, his complacent acceptance of things as they are. Yet after more careful study his books reveal qualities very different from those of mere uncritical geniality. Beneath their apparent acquiescence they reveal a preparedness for human shifts and weaknesses of which only the very wise are capable, while at the heart of them lies an amused disgust at the contrast between the practice of their characters and the professions of the society to which those characters belong. In the same way, under the surface of his own easy-going jollity, the mature Trollope gauged—and with

abnormal shrewdness—the conventional virtues of his time.
He weighed society against the sum of its individual members
and, more often than not, found the former wanting. But
having no itch to set the world to rights, having in its place
a sense of humour beyond the ordinary, he very seldom
worked himself into a passion of indignation. Ordinarily he
shrugged his shoulders, smiled and passed on in search of
further comfortable hypocrisies.

He was a sceptic with a twinkle in his eye; a spectator at
the game of life, excited but non-partisan, eager to applaud a
brilliant piece of play or to shout against a blunder, but more
or less indifferent as to which side won, provided that the
match were keen and clean and that no vainglory went with
victory.

2

From the final months in Ireland and from the time spent
touring in the west of England, phrases and incidents may be
taken to illustrate the final stage in the maturing of Trollope's
character.

Fragments from letters written to his mother just before
leaving Ireland show alike the high spirits which had become
his normal mood and his instinctive recoil from the parrotings
of mob enthusiasm. The preparations for the Great Exhibition of 1851 were already filling the newspapers with columns
of grandiloquent rubbish. A generation only too familiar
with the bombast of "Exhibitionitis" can appreciate the tone of
complacent self-advertisement with which the England of
1850 heralded Prince Albert's huge venture in commercialism.
Trollope, well aware of the profit-seeking which lay behind
the pious ejaculations of an inspired Press, treated with sceptical amusement an undertaking of which the moral significance
was solemnly trumpeted but the financial purpose carefully
concealed. Characteristically his satire took the form of self-
mockery. He wrote: "God send that we may all meet in
1851 under the shadow of some huge, newly-invented machine.
I mean to exhibit four three-volume novels—all failures—
which I look on as a great proof of industry."

In 1851, a joint visit to Hyde Park with Frances Trollope and with Tom having been perforce abandoned, he writes:—

We intend going to see the furriners in June. As for the Exhibition itself, I would not give a straw for it, except the building itself and my wife's piece of work which is in it. . . . We are all agog about going to London. Rose is looking up her silk dresses and I am meditating a new hat.

Hats, and particularly his own, were a favourite source of fun to Trollope. Certainly he looked very odd in some which he possessed. The illustrations to *How the "Mastiffs" went to Iceland* should be endeared to all Trollopians for the fidelity with which they show him with a melon-shaped bowler of enormous size, perched entrancingly on the very top of his head. In his book on the West Indies he describes the purchase at Panama of "a light straw hat with an amazing brim," the whole of which he covered with white calico. He wrote from South Africa to his son in 1877, describing his adventures in Bloemfontein, and on the blank reverse of the letter is written:—

> I have bought a coat
> > a waistcoat
> > trousers
> > three pairs of socks
> > > and
> > a hat
> all ready made.

The reaction from any herd absorption which led him to make mock of the Great Exhibition showed itself again after the death of the Duke of Wellington. As may be imagined, the papers were full of sycophantic platitude. Trollope writes:—

We are getting dreadfully sick of the Duke of Wellington. He is administered at all hours and in every shape. Oh that he was well buried and there an end! I have heard fifty anecdotes of him in the last five days—all equally applicable to any one else.

It is from casual self-expressions such as these that one comes to a knowledge of the real Trollope and to a realisation of the genial mockery which underlies the demure sobriety of his many novels. The time for such knowledge is ripe. The genuine début of the novelist is not far away.

3

In 1850, shortly before Anthony was sent to England, Frances Trollope's novel *Petticoat Government* was published. This book, duly read at Mallow, must be numbered among the moulding influences of a crucial period. Later developments suggest that the portions of it which lingered most vividly in the memory of the author's son were the opening chapter (where Frances Trollope shows an unusual terseness in her management of *mise-en-scène*) and the passages describing life in the Close at "Westhampton" (Exeter) and the part played therein by the worldly, genial, comfort-loving Prebendary Dr. Wroughtley. *Petticoat Government* has been suggested on other grounds as part-impulse to the Barchester novels. I have heard one of the woman-characters declared to be the prototype of Mrs. Proudie. Such precision is perhaps an overtax on what may have been the most indirect of influences. But Mrs. Trollope's book has certainly enough in it suggestive in a general way of Anthony's skill in setting a stage for fiction and of his numerous excursions into clerical psychology to earn a special mention in any story of his writing life.

If the reading of this novel of his mother's were one preliminary to fresh adventures of his own, the reading early in 1851 of Carlyle's *Latter-Day Pamphlets* was (strangely enough) another. His opinion of this book was most unfavourable. He wrote to his mother:—

I have read—nay, I have bought!—Carlyle's *Latter-Day Pamphlets*, and look on my eight shillings as very much thrown away. To me it appears that the grain of sense is so smothered up in a sack of the sheerest trash, that the

former is valueless. He does not himself know what he
wants. He has one idea—a hatred of spoken and acted
falsehood; and on that he harps through the whole eight
pamphlets. I look on him as a man who was always in
danger of going mad in literature and who has now done so.

Lack of sympathy between such a man as Trollope and the
Carlyle of *Latter-Day Pamphlets* is not surprising, but there is
irony in the novelist's sweeping condemnation in view of
what was to follow, after the writing of *The Warden*.

As for *The Warden*, its conception and slow achievement may
be best told in the words of the *Autobiography*:—

> Wandering one mid-summer evening [in May or June
> 1851] round the purlieus of Salisbury Cathedral I conceived
> the story of *The Warden*, from whence came the series of
> novels of which Barchester, with its bishops, deans and
> archdeacons was the central site. . . . On July 29 1852 I
> began *The Warden* at Tenbury in Worcestershire. It was
> then more than twelve months since I had stood for an
> hour on the little bridge in Salisbury and had made out to
> my own satisfaction the spot on which Hiram's Hospital
> should stand. . . . The work of taking up a new district was
> too heavy to allow of my going on with my book at once.
> It was not until the end of 1852 that I recommenced it and
> it was in the autumn of 1853 that I finished the work.

It has been assumed—and not unnaturally—that because
Trollope here declares the story of *The Warden* to have been
"conceived" at Salisbury, that city was the model for Barchester. Nevertheless his inspiration was much more com-
posite. As will be seen, the idea of a cathedral city as stage for
his drama did not arise spontaneously, but followed on his
desire—which desire was the real impulse of the tale—to
construct a fiction round the administration of an almshouse.
Now he had been at school at Winchester, and in Winchester
the actual case of the hospital of St. Cross had for long occupied
legal minds (it was finally settled in the Court of Queen's
Bench in 1857) and was frequently mentioned in the papers

during the early 'fifties. Was not Winchester rather than Salisbury the starting point for his invention?

Indeed it was; and Trollope himself bore witness to the fact only a few weeks before his death. In October 1882 he paid a visit to E. A. Freeman in the West Country and was closely questioned as to the geography of Barsetshire. Freeman tells the story well:—

It was perhaps fitting that, in the short time that Mr. Trollope was with me, the only people we had a chance of introducing him to were two bishops, of different branches of the vineyard. In company with one of them, Bishop Clifford of Clifton, I took him over part of the range of hills between Wells and Wedmore, that he might look out on the land of Barset, if Barset it was to be. It is a land that Mr. Trollope knew well in his post-office days; but he was well pleased to take a bird's-eye view of it again. He enjoyed our scenery; but he did not enjoy either our mud or our stiles, and it was pleasant to see the way in which the Bishop, more active than I was, helped him over all difficulties. For then Mr. Trollope was clearly not in his full strength, though there was no sign that serious sickness was at all near. This was on October 25th; the next day he was shown Wells and Glastonbury in due order. He allowed Barset to be Somerset, though certainly Gatherum Castle has been brought to us from some other land. But he denied that Barchester was Wells. Barchester was Winchester, where he was at school, and the notion of Hiram's Hospital was taken from Saint Cross. But I argued with him that, if Barchester was not Wells, at any rate Wells, perhaps along with other places, had helped to supply ideas for Barchester. The constitution of the church of Barchester, not exactly like either an old or a new foundation, and where the precentor has the singular duty of chanting the litany, seemed to imply that ideas from more than one place were mixed together. The little church over the gate could not come from Wells; but it might come from Canterbury as well as from Winchester, or even from Langport without the bounds of Barset. And was it not "Barchester *Towers*"? and towers are a feature much more conspicuous at Wells than at Winchester. And did not the general idea of Hiram's Hospital come from Wells, where a foundation for wool-combers with a becoming inscription is still to be seen? But no; Barset was Somerset, but Barchester was Winchester, not Wells. He had not even taken any ideas from Wells; he had never heard of the Wells woolcombers.[1]

---

[1] *Macmillan's Magazine*, January 1883.

TROLLOPE'S BARSETSHIRE

"As I wrote *Framley Parsonage*," says Trollope in his *Autobiography*, "I became more closely than ever acquainted with the new shire which I had added to the English counties. . . . This was the fourth novel of which I had placed the scene in Barsetshire, and, as I wrote it, I made a map of the dear county."

For a generation Trollopians wondered where—if indeed it was ever made—that map was hidden. Pending its discovery two enthusiasts—Mr. Spencer van Bokkelen Nichols in America, and Father Ronald Knox (as he then was) in England—tried their hand at a reconstruction of the county as Trollope conceived it. They worked from such (often contradictory) details as are given in the various chronicles of Barsetshire.

Overleaf—and by courtesy of their designers—these reconstructions are reproduced. Opposite to them— redrawn in the interests of clear reproduction—is Trollope's *own* map, which was drawn as he declared and was found, while this book was being written, among some papers.

Mr. Nichols published his map in a form more elaborate than can here be given, as frontispiece to *The Significance of Anthony Trollope* (New York 1925), a book of notes and observations designed to the glory of the novelist. At the end of this book is an atlas-index of Barsetshire which gives, alphabetically and with comments, a valuable list of the towns, villages, country houses, etc., within the boundaries of the shire.

Father Knox published his map in *The London Mercury* (February 1922), as illustration to an amusing article on Trollope's imaginary geography, with special reference to his self-contradictions.

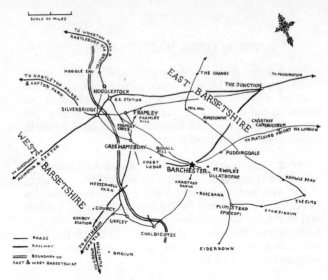

MR. NICHOLS' RECONSTRUCTION OF BARSETSHIRE

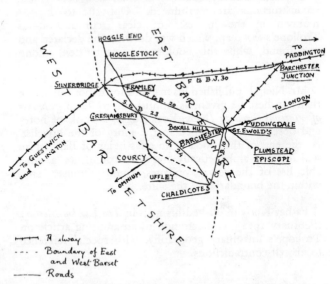

FATHER RONALD KNOX'S RECONSTRUCTION OF BARSETSHIRE

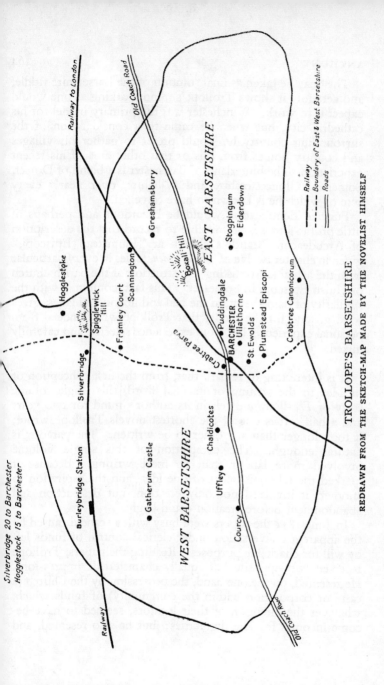

TROLLOPE'S BARSETSHIRE

REDRAWN FROM THE SKETCH-MAP MADE BY THE NOVELIST HIMSELF

EAST BARSETSHIRE

WEST BARSETSHIRE

Railway to London

Old Coach Road

• Greshamsbury

Goxall Hill

• Stogpingum
• Eiderdown

• Hogglestoke

Spigglewick
Hill

Scannington

• Framley Court

Silverbridge

Puddingdale

Crabtree Parva

BARCHESTER
Ullathorne
• St Ewolds
• Plumstead Episcopi

Crabtree Canonicorum

Burleybridge Station

• Gatherum Castle

• Chaldicotes

• Uffley

Courcy

Old Coach Road

Railway

——— Railway
– – – Boundary of East & West Barsetshire
═══ Roads

Silverbridge 20 to Barchester
Hogglestock 15 to Barchester

This may be taken as final solution of the Barsetshire riddle, and certainly it shows Trollope's mind working as one would expect it to work. Winchester was the primary model for his cathedral city, but when he came to a consideration of the surrounding country he would prefer to gather his villages and country homes from this or that other area of his recent experience. The hinterland of Barchester is a blend of Dorset, Somerset, Gloucestershire and Wiltshire, over nearly every acre of which he is known to have travelled.

Further identification would be hazardous and perhaps of little profit; but it is permissible to record that the description of Archdeacon Grantly's church at "Plumstead Episcopi," given in chapter twelve of *The Warden*, tallies in every particular with the actual (and existing) construction of the parish church of Huish Episcopi in Somerset. This fact, combined with the similarity of name between the real and fictional villages, gives solid ground for the theory that Trollope wrote indeed from personal experience, but from experience selected and carefully mixed.

It is interesting to remark that, from the first conception of its idea to the writing of its final word, this single-volume story of *The Warden* dwelt in its author's mind for two years and a half. It is one of the shortest novels Trollope wrote; it took longer than any other to be written. The paradox is natural enough. The completion of this single volume involved more labour than its mere writing. Because it marked the relinquishment of one ideal and the aspiration to another, it involved not only creation, but destruction and abandonment before creation could begin.

In June 1851 the papers were busy with a scandal caused by the apparent malversation under clerical control of funds left by will for charitable purposes. Reading the papers, Trollope received two opposite but equally characteristic impressions. He resented, on the one hand, the possession by the Church (a caste or corporation within the community) of funds which, whatever the intention of their legators, seemed to have become incomes for idle dignitaries; but he also resented, and simultaneously, the virtuous indignation of the Press towards the recipients of these incomes, who were not directly to blame for enjoying monies to which in equity they were not entitled.

These simultaneous but inconsistent reactions to a topical scandal reflect exactly Trollope's divergent and contrasted attitudes toward social cliques and toward individuals. He was distrustful of group-morality and jealous of caste-arrogance; therefore he was ready to attack the Church *as a caste* for misapplication of funds. But he was even more distrustful of Press-clamour (another and an aggressive form of caste-assertion) and at the same time unwilling to think ill of individuals; wherefore, he wished to defend Church dignitaries *as individuals* from the very charge which he was himself ready to bring against them as members of a corporate body. Later on, when writing the *Autobiography*, he saw the impossibility of the contradictory task that he had set himself, and described with humour the dilemma of the novelist who wishes to be an advocate but cannot help disliking both sides in any quarrel he espouses. In 1851, however, warmed with the double indignation and thinking rather to profit by the agility of his conscience than to trip over it, he rushed headlong into the fray, only to succeed in boxing his own ears.

Fortunately for him the instructed taste of the day saw little harm in propagandist fiction, even of a self-contradictory kind, and as matters turned out, *The Warden* pleased most by the very qualities which in a modern view are least commendable.

By the time the manuscript was complete Trollope had finished his work in England and was back in Ireland again. He had taken a house for eighteen months in Belfast, whence on October 8 1854 he posted *The Precentor* (as the story was originally entitled) to the publishing firm of Longman, Brown, Green and Longmans. His own narrative of the acceptance and publication of the book is bleak and brief; but by great good fortune the early correspondence between Trollope and William Longman has survived, and with it the reader's reports—not only on *The Warden*, but on the books that followed it. These most valuable documents clothe the bare bones of the *Autobiography* with flesh, and even—if such anatomical enterprise be tolerable—add a limb or two.

Longman's reader reported on the manuscript with commendable promptitude. This is what he said:—

In re *The Precentor*

Oct. 13 1854.

This story takes its rise from the recent exposé of the abuses that have crept into Cathedral and Hospital Trusts. Not a very promising subject, one might infer at first sight! But such is the skill of the author that he has contrived to weave out of his materials a very interesting and amusing tale. The scene is laid in a cathedral town; and the chief characters consist of the precentor, a good-natured conscientious clergyman who is at the same time warden of an adjoining hospital; his son-in-law, the archdeacon, a keen and ardent churchman; the Bishop—easy indolent and benevolent; and an eager reformer of Church abuses who is in love with the warden's younger daughter and in whose internal conflict between love and duty lies the main interest of the story.

How the story ends I will not tell you, as I hope you will read it for yourself. The characters are well drawn and happily distinguished; and the whole story is pervaded by a vein of quiet humour and (good-natured) satire, which will make the work acceptable to all Low Churchmen and dissenters.

The description of the *Times*, under the nom de guerre of *Mount Olympus*, I will back against anything of the kind that was ever written for geniality and truth. In one word, the work ought to have a large sale. *Roderick Random* has made me cautious, and therefore I think it right to say that there is a passage at page 23 which might be too strong for men and women of strong imaginations. To me it is quite fair.

This generous but quaint report is so characteristic of its period that it has an interest beyond the merely Trollopian. Its value as a frank expression of opinion—and therefore as a

revelation of a cultured mentality of the day—is exceptional.
Observe, first of all, that the selling quality of the tale is judged
to be in its appeal to persons of an evangelical or dissenting
frame of mind. Trollope, whatever his gratitude for critical
approval, would have shaken his head in disgust at the thought
that he of all people (and his mother's son) should come before
the public as a novelist for Low-Church leisure hours! Clearly,
of the two indignations which provoked the book, that against
indolent and greedy clergy struck the reader the more forcibly.
Probably this particular advocacy chimed with his own in-
clinations. But from another point of view the critic's reference to a Low-Church public is of interest to dwellers in a
later age. How many publishers' readers nowadays judge
fiction by its appeal to this denomination or to that? If tabloid
evidence were needed of the immense influence of religious
forms over the ordinary life of England in the early 'fifties,
that evidence this report supplies.

Observe, further, that the passages most pleasing to the
critic are the very passages which, in the view of a lover of
Trollope to-day, almost spoil the book. The heavy-handed
playfulness in chapters fourteen and fifteen, where *The Times*,
Carlyle and Dickens are in turn put through the primitive
mangle of Trollope's satire, strike the reader of the 'fifties as
genial and true (as perhaps they are), but not as extraneous to
the story's theme, or as in direct conflict with the story's spirit,
or as foreign to the story's very purpose. Novels were not
mere literature in 1854; they were—or were expected to be—
pulpits or lecture-desks or foghorns of private prejudice. If
since then they have advanced in critical estimation, the credit
is as much Trollope's own as anyone's. He realised quickly
and thoroughly that he had made a mistake, and devoted the
rest of a busy life to proving that the genuine novel-writer
should be an artist, and not a governess, a parson or an
agitator.

The Precentor was promptly accepted for publication and,
with its title changed at the publisher's suggestion, appeared in
January 1855. Trollope had left Belfast and taken a house at
Donnybrook near Dublin, where he was to live for several

years. It was numbered 6 Seaview Terrace, was a substantial house with a fine garden, and stood off the Ailesbury Road in Donnybrook. On February 17 (a little impatiently) he wrote to Longmans to ask for a report on sales. He explained that he had planned a second part to the story—had, indeed, already written a third of it—and desired to know whether or not to go further with the work. The reply was discouraging; the sequel to *The Warden* was abandoned.

Then followed that singular literary venture which was forecasted at the time of Trollope's reading of *Latter-Day Pamphlets*—a venture not mentioned in the *Autobiography*. He had worked off his spleen against Carlyle in an unlucky passage of *The Warden*. But after spleen came a queer desire to emulate. He, Anthony Trollope, would set the world to rights; from Ireland should arise the doom of Anti-cant.

Wherefore he wrote to William Longman:—

Dublin, 27 *March* 1855.

I send you the MS. of which I spoke to you when in London and will be obliged if you will see if it will suit you and let me know as soon as you conveniently can. There are some reasons incident to the MS. itself which will make it desirable that it should be published soon. It is called *The New Zealander*.

The publishers sent the book to the same reader, who, prompt as ever, reported as follows on April 2:—

If you had not told me that this work was by the author of *The Warden* I could not have believed it. Such a contrast between two works by the same pen was hardly ever before witnessed. The object of the work is to show how England may be saved from the ruin that now threatens her!! And how the realisation of Macaulay's famous prophecy of the "New Zealander standing on the ruins of London Bridge" may be indefinitely postponed.

With this view the author goes through all the leading influences and institutions of the State and pours out the vial of his wrath upon them. This he does in such a loose,

illogical and rhapsodical way that I regret to say I would
advise you not to publish the work on any terms.

All the good points in the work have already been treated
of by Mr. Carlyle, of whose *Latter-Day Pamphlets* this work,
both in style and matter, is a most feeble imitation.

This unlucky experiment in philosophical pamphleteering
marked the last flicker of the old reformist Trollope; it marked
also the final defeat of Irish at the hands of English influence.
Messrs. Longman, like John Murray, did the world good
service when they rejected *The New Zealander*, for their rejection
exorcised from Trollope's mind for ever the devil of reformism.

The eighteen months between the refusal of *The New
Zealander* and November 1856 were spent over a story destined
to become one of the classic novels of the nineteenth century.
Barchester Towers (such from the first was its superb title)
reached Longmans during the first week in November. The
same reader was consulted. His opinion and the correspondence that arose from it are of absorbing interest, so vividly do
they show the differing standards of those days and of our own,
so utterly has the skilled judgment of the middle 'fifties been
falsified by time.

The report read as follows:—

Dec. 8 1856.

It is very difficult for me to convey to you a distinct
impression of my opinion of this work, since my own
impressions of it are themselves very indistinct. And no
wonder; for the execution is so unequal, that while there
are parts of it that I would be disposed to place on a level
with the best morsels by contemporary novelists, there are
others—and unfortunately these preponderate—the vulgarity and exaggeration of which, if they do not unfit them
for publication, are at least likely to be repulsive to the
reader.

Viewed as a whole the work is inferior to *The Warden*, to
which it is a sequel. You have the old characters again in
action, with the addition of a weak bishop and his managing

F*

wife, Mr. Slope, the bishop's chaplain (a low-minded Low Churchman), an Oxford don, some rural grandees and their dependents, besides the dean and chapter and all the other odds and ends of a Cathedral town, in which High and Low Church are struggling for mastery.

Plot there is none, the main part of the story turning upon the [? giving] [1] up of the office of Warden and the intrigues arising out of it. These give full scope for a display of the author's best powers and his subtle analysis of the motives that actuate his dramatis personæ, while the style is easy and natural and correct (not so the orthography). The grand defect of the work, I think, as a work of art is the low-mindedness and vulgarity of the chief actors. There is hardly a "lady" or "gentleman" among them. Such a bishop and his wife as Dr. and Mrs. Proudie have certainly not appeared in our time, and prebendary doctor Stanhope's lovely daughter, who is separated from her husband—an Italian brute who has crippled her for life—is a most repulsive, exaggerated and unnatural character. A good deal of the progress of the tale depends upon this lady, whose beauteous countenance makes sad havoc of the virtuous feelings of the clergymen and others who come in contact with her. The character is a great blot on the work.

But in noticing these defects I am far from saying that it is uninteresting. On the contrary, there is a fatal facility in the execution that makes you fancy that the author is playing with his reader, showing how easy it is for him to write a novel in three volumes, very much in the same way as [? Aytoun] [1] proved how easy it was to [? rival] [1] the "spasmodic poets." It would be quite possible to compress the three volumes into one without much detriment to the whole. If you will read Vol. 2, chapters 1, 2 and 3, you will discover specimens of the author's merits, and if you wish to have a notion of what I consider his defects you will find a specimen in Vol. 1, page 177 seq.—"Mrs. Proudie's Reception"—and Vol. 2, page 173 seq.—"A Love Scene."

---

[1] Words illegible owing to the original document having been damaged by fire.

Longmans forwarded to Trollope their reader's criticisms, and he replied from Derry on December 20 1856:—

> I am sorry that I am such a distance from you. Were I in London we might more easily settle as to what you would wish to have withdrawn from *Barchester Towers* and as to what I would not object to withdraw. I beg at any rate to assure you that nothing would be more painful to me than to be considered as an indecent writer.
>
> I shall have no objection to altering any scene open to objection on this score, but I do object to reducing the book to two volumes—not because I am particularly wedded to three, but from a conviction that no book originally written in three can be judiciously so reduced. . . . But I do not think that I can in utter ignorance have committed a volume of indecencies. I do not now remember what can be the sin of the special scene to which you allude. Of course the woman is intended to [? appear] [1] as indifferent to all moralities and decent behaviour—but such a character may, I think, be drawn without offence if her vice be not made attractive.
>
> But I do not now write in my own defence. I propose to get my friend Mr. Tilley to call on you. You will find him a sufficiently rigid censor. If you can explain to him to what you object or can show him the passages marked, they will either be altered or else the MS. withdrawn. I do not think I should be disposed to make other changes than those suggested on the score of delicacy. Mr. Tilley will, however, have *carte blanche* to act for me in any way.

He wrote again from Dublin on January 10 1857:—

> I have just heard from Mr. Tilley that he has seen you respecting *Barchester Towers*, and I am led by what he says to fear that you do not think well enough of the MS. to publish it on terms to which I could agree. If this be so, it will be useless for me to give you further trouble by making arrangements as to any alterations.

---

[1] Word illegible owing to the original document having been damaged by fire.

It appears that you think £100 too high a sum to pay in advance for the book. It seems to me that if a three-vol. novel be worth anything it must be worth that; and that it is vain for an author to publish such a work with any view to profit if he is to consider such a sum as this excessive. Indeed, were it to be regarded as full payment of the work it would be wholly inadequate.

Of course there is no reason why you should pay so much, or half so much, if you do not judge the article to be worth so much of your money. But it is a reason why we should not deal. You allege very truly and with great kindness that a change of publisher will be prejudicial to my interests as an author. I feel that this is true. But I also feel that if a novel of mine in three vols. is not worth to a publisher £100, I have no interest to prejudice, and that I cannot depreciate in value that which is already so valueless.

If therefore you are of opinion that you cannot afford to pay in advance so moderate a price as £100, I think it will be better for me to withdraw my MS. In such case I shall be very sorry to be deprived of the value of your name on my title-page.

The publishers reconsidered their position and decided to yield the advance payment demanded. They also invited suggestions from their reader for the improvement of the story, which suggestions were in due course despatched to Ireland.

After consideration of the proposed changes Trollope, on February 1, wrote from Donnybrook:—

I now send your reader's list with my observations, and I feel inclined to think that you will be contented with what I have done. I have complied completely with by far the greater number of his suggestions and have done so in part with all but three. I have *de bon* [*cœur*] changed all the passages marked as being too warm. And I believe in every case have struck out the whole of what was considered objection-able. I have complied with all the objections to short passages, whether I agreed or no in the [. . . . .] [1] of the

---

[1] Word illegible owing to the original letter having been damaged by fire.

objections, being wishful to give way wherever I could do so. In the longer passages marked as "ineffective" I have, with two exceptions, either omitted or re-written them. In these two cases objection is made to two whole chapters that they are tedious. I will not praise myself by saying that they are not so, but I must profess that I cannot make them less so. Were I to withdraw these chapters I must write others, and I am quite sure that such patchwork would not be an improvement on the original composition.

This is a patient letter which few authors, faced with so destructive a schedule of detailed depreciation, would have had the good temper or the humility to write. But Trollope could endure any kind of criticism save that which challenged the design or proportions of his work. The suggested alteration in *Barchester Towers* which made the deepest impression on him was that which charged the book with over-length and asked that his three volumes be reduced to two. Not only was this proposal sturdily rejected, but it was never forgotten.

I declared [he records in the *Autobiography*] that no consideration should induce me to put out a third of my work. I am at a loss to know how such a task could be performed. I could burn the MS., no doubt, and write another book on the same story; but how two words out of six are to be withdrawn from a written novel I cannot conceive.

Years later the point still rankled. In January 1878 he was writing to John Blackwood about the novel *John Caldigate*, the MS. of which had been sent home from South Africa and as to which Blackwood hinted at some desired alteration:—

What about the novel? [asked Trollope]. In writing to Henry you suggested some alterations. What are they? I am a reasonable man and up to anything short of re-writing the second volume, which poor William Longman once proposed that I should do.

Certainly in the matter of his own work Trollope was always both reasonable and free from vanity; but he had his obstinacies, and against one of these the serious and well intentioned reader of *Barchester Towers* had stubbed his toe.

When the story was at last regarded as satisfactorily altered, the manuscript was despatched to the printer. But even now trouble was not quite over nor the proprieties sufficiently observed. Trollope writes on March 3 1857:—

> At page 93 by all means put out "foul breathing"; and page 97 alter "fat stomach" to "deep chest," if the printing will now allow it. But I should have thought the sheets had been taken off long ago. I do not like a second title nor the one you name. I do not wish the bishop—male or female—to be considered the chief character in the book. I was puzzled for a title, but the one I took at last is at least inoffensive and easy of pronunciation.
>
> I write in a great hurry in boots and breeches, just as I am going to hunt, but I don't like to delay answering your very kind letter. I am very thankful to Longmans for the interest they feel in the book.

Here the correspondence ceases. It provides an admirable gloss on the brief description given in the *Autobiography* of the negotiations that preceded the acceptance and publication of the now famous novel. But it does more than that. In the first place, it reveals to an almost horrific degree the perturbations of the squeamish 'fifties. Even when reporting on *The Warden* the reader has fears of one passage, regarding it as no less distasteful to propriety than parts of *Roderick Random*. This passage may be assumed to be the scene in chapter two showing the archdeacon—swathed in bedclothes, it is true, but none the less in a night-shirt—declaiming to his wife (equally undressed) the vices of John Bold. But when he comes to *Barchester Towers*, the delicacy of the critic is shocked beyond control. There is something deliciously pathetic in Trollope's solemn abjuration of indecency, and we must sigh over the disappearance of the uncensored text of *Barchester Towers*, which clearly differed greatly from the published version. Let us be thankful, however, that the author's submissiveness did not extend to the elimination of the Signora

Neroni. To save her from suppression we gleefully accept the sacrifice of "foul breathing" and of "fat stomach," although the former would have invigorated the first presentment of the revolting Slope and the latter is but poorly substituted by "deep chest."

The Longman–Trollope letters do more than illuminate the conventional morality of their time; they mark the awakening of a new element in the personality of Trollope himself. In them appears for the first time his sturdy conviction that the labourer—even the author-labourer—is worthy of his hire. Although posterity has tended to overstress the material strain in Trollope's literary ambition, such a strain was definitely and proudly present. The *Autobiography* is impregnated with the author's stolid determination to do good work and to receive good wages; and it is during his discussion of *Barchester Towers* that Trollope first professes this firmly held faith:—

I am well aware that there are many who think that an author in his authorship should not regard money,—nor a painter, or sculptor, or composer in his art. I do not know that this unnatural self-sacrifice is supposed to extend itself further. A barrister, a clergyman, a doctor, an engineer, and even actors and architects, may without disgrace follow the bent of human nature, and endeavour to fill their bellies and clothe their backs, and also those of their wives and children, as comfortably as they can by the exercise of their abilities and their crafts. They may be as rationally realistic as may the butchers and the bakers; but the artist and the author forget the high glories of their calling if they condescend to make a money return a first object. They who preach this doctrine will be much offended by my theory, and by this book of mine, if my theory and my book come beneath their notice. They require the practice of a so-called virtue which is contrary to nature, and which, in my eyes, would be no virtue if it were practised. . . .

. It is a mistake to suppose that a man is a better man because he despises money. Few do so, and those few in doing so suffer a defeat. Who does not desire to be hospitable to his friends, generous to the poor, liberal to all, munificent to his children, and to be himself free from the carking fear which poverty creates? The subject will not stand an argument;—and yet authors are told that they should disregard payment for their work, and be content to devote their unbought brains to the welfare of the public. Brains that are unbought will never serve the public much. Take away from English authors their copyrights, and you would very soon take away from England her authors.

Trollope chose the right moment for this declaration of his work-pride. Doubtless he remembered that *Barchester Towers* provoked it and gave it first expression. Thanks to the survival of the Longman letters, the actual words of that expression are preserved.

4

The publication of *Barchester Towers* in May 1857 confirmed Trollope once and for all in his novelist's ambition. He had won, not a large public, but a public of the kind which encourages a writer to go further, which flatters ambition but checks complacency. He says of *The Warden*: "I soon felt that it had not failed as the others had failed. I could discover that people around me knew that I had written a book." And of *Barchester Towers*: "It was one of the novels which novel-readers were called upon to read." These phrases well express that curious intuition of potential success, combined with an eager wish to try again and differently, which comes to an artist when he has roused the anticipations of the perceptive few but not as yet the uncritical enthusiasm of the crowd. Trollope felt the spur to future effort, but no temptation either to repeat himself or to regard his race with fortune as already won. It did not as yet occur to him to regard novel-writing as other than a spare-time occupation nor to boast himself other than a spare-time novelist. He accepted authorship as a career simultaneous with that of an official, trusting to the latter for his bread and butter, looking to the former for a share of the world's jam.

Spare-times were more than odd-times to Trollope. Every

hour that was free from post-office work was divided scrupulously between hunting (when available) and an industrious pursuit of literary reputation. His great power of exploiting leisure moments—which had hitherto, for lack of direction, caused him to blunder ineffectively from genre to writing genre —could now be concentrated where was the best prospect of success. Nevertheless there was to be one more ill-judged experiment, one more almost blatant expression of the queer obtuseness which was as much a part of his character as his sturdy honesty. In July 1857—less than three months after *Barchester Towers* had appeared and after informing Longmans that another three-volume novel was almost complete—he wrote:—

> I shall be glad to know whether you would approve of publishing at Christmas one volume—say about two-thirds the size of *The Warden*—to be called *The Struggles of Brown, Jones and Robinson*; *by one of the Firm.* It will be intended as a hit at the present system of advertising, but will, of course, be in the guise of a tale. Publisher's advertisements are not reflected on.

Richard Doyle's *Foreign Tour of Messrs. Brown, Jones and Robinson* had been published two years earlier; numerous skits on advertising enterprise provoked by the Great Exhibition had cluttered the bookstalls since 1852. Yet Trollope could in all seriousness conceive as a "follow" to the spontaneous novelty of *Barchester Towers* a facetious variation on a theme already stale and under a title notoriously secondhand! Was ever man of genius more liable to misconception of his own powers and interests? It is remarkable that, hand in hand with his peculiar genius, should have gone this queer incapacity to criticise, alike his own work and that of other people. The *Autobiography* contains a number of judgments on novels, and whether they be self-judgments or judgments passed upon contemporaries, they are mostly trite or unconvincing. The fact merits observation, because it helps to isolate and to distinguish the real quality of his achievement. Being absolutely honest with himself, he could be honest in appreciation of other people. He possessed an intuitive understanding of individual human nature which no other English novelist can rival, and a command of easy flexible language exactly suited to the expression of ever-changing human moods. But he was uncertain as a reasoner and insensitive to ideas, and made a number of mistaken decisions because in default of critical instinct he relied on practical good sense.

It generally happened that he was as ready as anyone else later to recognise his own errors of judgment and to admit them. Occasionally, however, he clung with a pathetic fidelity to the ugly ducklings of his numerous brood, and the unlucky *Brown, Jones and Robinson* was at once the ugliest and the most cherished of these failures. Longmans showed no interest whatever in the projected satire; but the idea of it was not—like the manuscript of *The New Zealander*—abandoned altogether, nor like *The Noble Jilt* pigeon-holed and taken out from time to time to be regarded with an affectionate but disillusioned melancholy. *Brown, Jones and Robinson* was intended to be written and should, come what may, be not only written but printed. And so indeed it was, but not at all for its own sake.

Its first revival was in 1858. Very soon after Chapman & Hall had published *Doctor Thorne* (they had paid the author's price without demur, and got something worth having for their money) Trollope, eager to exploit the amiability of these promptly generous publishers, proposed his work of humour for the coming Christmas season. If necessary, the work should appear anonymously; he would make this sacrifice on its behalf. Edward Chapman's letter of rejection is a skilful piece of tactful obliquity.

193 *Piccadilly.*
June 16 1858.

I think on the whole that I had better hold to my resolve to decline B., J. and R. I should not like to do it without your name, and at the same time I feel convinced that it is better that your name should be withheld, for there is a strong impression abroad that you are writing too rapidly for your permanent fame.

Two and a half years later it was the turn of Smith, Elder. This time—in January 1861—the ill-starred manuscript scored its first success. George Smith, full of a publisher's enthusiasm for the man who had done so much to win success for the *Cornhill* by his novel *Framley Parsonage*, consented to serialise the tale in that magazine. Smith never did anything by halves. If he liked an author or an author's work, he would not turn him away for an occasional failure nor even seek to buy the failure on easy terms. He treated *Brown, Jones and Robinson* (a tale of which he had the very lowest opinion) as though it were Trollope of standard quality, buying the copyright at standard rate, and even securing—at the author's definite request—an undertaking from Thackeray that the tale should suffer no editorial revision.

In this Smith proved himself a good publisher; for if he lost three-quarters of what he paid for this particular book, he repaid himself tenfold from *The Small House at Allington*, *The Claverings* and *The Last Chronicle of Barset*, no one of which three novels might have come his way had he shown toward *Brown, Jones and Robinson* the indifference or the parsimony which the wretched thing deserved.

But even George Smith, having paid his author and carried out his promise of a serial, was not disposed to lose more than was necessary. He flinched to see the lowering influence on his magazine of this unlucky narrative,[1] and when the serial had run its course, he withheld the usual reincarnation in book form, letting the dead instalments lie. The years passed, and at last, either because Trollope urged him to do so or because the novelist's reputation was now so great that even a bad book might be hoped to pay its way, he relented and set the ill-starred waggery between cloth covers. At last in 1870 *Brown, Jones and Robinson* made an appearance in one volume, only to stand forlornly like a tombstone at the grave of failure.[2]

---

[1] Contemporary reviews were instantly unfavourable. The *Illustrated London News*, in a review of periodicals, said on August 10 1861 : " Mr. Trollope's newly devised comic epic gives but modified satisfaction to the readers of the *Cornhill*. The complaint is that nobody can understand what Mr. Trollope means."

[2] An unauthorised book-edition was printed from the serial and published in America in 1862. History does not record whether Trollope was aware of this or, if so, what he felt about it.

A sorry book and with a sorry history! Twice rejected in advance—once in 1857, again in 1858; an unpopular serial in 1861; an unwanted book in 1870, it never lived yet would not die. Nevertheless Trollope could write of it in the *Auto-biography* with a quaint if misapprehending satisfaction: "It was meant to be funny . . . I still think that there is some good fun in it, but I have heard no one else express such an opinion. I do not know that I ever heard any opinion expressed on it, except by the publisher, who kindly remarked that he did not think it was equal to my usual work. . . . I do not know that [in book form] it was ever criticised or ever read. I received £600 for it. I think that *Brown, Jones and Robinson* was the hardest bargain I ever sold to a publisher."

In that last sentence lies at once the satisfaction and the mis-apprehension, for though Trollope could relish six hundred pounds, he failed to realise that they did not represent a bargain shrewdly struck, but a wise publisher's gamble on favours yet to come.

When Longmans declined even to consider the satire on advertisement, Trollope returned doggedly to the question of his new three-volume novel. It is possible at once to admire his courageous determination to get progressive payment for this work, and to sympathise with the publishers who received his pertinacious letters. These are here quoted because they show Trollope's now abundant self-confidence (and it needed self-confidence to risk at this early stage of his writing career a breach with a firm of Longmans' eminence and reputation), and as illustrating aspects of the eternal struggle between author and publisher.

On August 21 1857, Trollope writes from Donnybrook:—

I have finished the three-vol. novel. Though it is ready I do not want it to be published now or sooner than you approve. What I do want is to know on what terms you would be willing to publish it. While you were from town I got a letter from your firm not saying much about the sale of *Barchester Towers*, while the letter just received,

though it gives no bad news, gives none that are good.
From this I suppose I may imagine that you do not consider
the sale satisfactory. If this be so to such a degree as to
make your firm unwilling to deal with me on such terms as
are usual for works of fiction of fair success, perhaps I may
be giving you useless trouble by sending you my MS. I
am strongly advised not to publish without getting a price
that may be regarded as in some way remunerative. If
therefore you think your firm will decline to purchase from
me at some such price perhaps you will say so.

The publishers' reply may be inferred from Trollope's next
letter, written a week later:—

August 29 1857.

I certainly did mean you to understand by my last letter
that I should want a better price for another novel. Indeed
I may say at once that I would not under any circumstances
take less than double what I received before, viz: two
hundred pounds in advance, and as you seem to think that
your firm will not give more than £100 I fear it will hardly
be worth while for you to have the MS. read.

I am sure you do not regard £100 as adequate payment
for a three-vol. novel. Of course an unsuccessful novel may
be worth much less—worth indeed less than nothing. And
it may very likely be that I cannot write a successful novel.
But if I cannot obtain moderate success I will give over,
and leave the business alone. I certainly will not willingly
go on working at such a rate of pay.

The final stage is reached in October.

I promised [Trollope writes on October 18] to let you
know what I did about the MS. of my new novel. I disposed of it yesterday to Mr. Bentley, who acceded to my
own terms. The sum I asked was indeed higher than that
I suggested to you. I know, however, that this will not
break any bones between you and me.

The breach had taken place and proved complete.   As

matters turned out the publishers were the sufferers, for Trollope became a best seller and never returned to Paternoster Row. But one may doubt whether, even if Longmans had been allowed a sight of *The Three Clerks*—for this was the book that they were asked to buy—they would have paid his price. Their reader's report on it can be imagined, and modern taste can agree with its disfavour, if not with the arguments which would have supported it.

The *Autobiography* gives further facts as to the publishing history of *The Three Clerks* and, incidentally, shows that Trollope—usually so clear-headed in matters of the kind—did in this case confuse an advance payment and an outright purchase. Longmans having refused to pay £200 in advance of half profits, the author visited Hurst & Blackett, the successors to Henry Colburn and, suitably enough, the fiction-manufacturers of London. One of the partners (perhaps Henry Blackett, who, as Mrs. Oliphant records, knew nothing about books, but had business instinct enough to contrive in 1855 to bribe Dinah Maria Mulock away from Chapman & Hall and, as reward, to get for his firm the immensely popular *John Halifax, Gentleman*) broke an appointment. Trollope waited an hour with *The Three Clerks* under his arm. An apologetic foreman made conversation with him. "I hope it's not historical, Mr. Trollope," this worthy man remarked. "Whatever you do, don't be historical. Your historical novel is not worth a damn." Trollope, cured of *La Vendée* and remembering his mother's pungent criticism, laughed good-naturedly. No, it was not historical; but neither could it waste time waiting on peccant publishers. He walked out into Great Marlborough Street and round to Richard Bentley, who bought the story's copyright on the spot for two hundred and fifty pounds, cash down.

Thus Hurst & Blackett, by losing an appointment, lost a star-novelist also; for Trollope never returned to them any more than to Longmans, and the only two books of his which bear their imprint are books of which the copyright had been sold already to other firms and by them sub-let.

IV

THE YEARS FROM 1857 TO 1859 unexpectedly developed into years of travel. Although the first journey was one of personal duty and of pleasure—a visit to Frances and to Tom Trollope in the villa at Florence—this was quickly followed by a series of official missions, to Egypt, to Scotland and to the West Indies.

The influence of these thirty-odd months of globe-trotting was strong on Trollope, whom they infected with the third and last to be acquired of his three most cherished tastes. All who knew him, or even by hearsay came into contact with him, testify to the triple absorption of work, hunting and travel, which held his attention and occupied his time to a notorious degree, leaving a mere fringe of leisure for friendship, whist or politics and less still for literary society.

Trollope on tour was very thoroughly Trollope. The banging, jolting, bustling adventure of train, steamer, diligence and mule-back travel, so far from tiring or fretting him, set him banging and jolting in response; spurred him to greater energies; strengthened his determination to triumph over petty obstacles. Further, once he had been tested by the Post Office as missioner and found to be an envoy of forceful competence, he had as many opportunities as he cared to take of indulging his endless curiosity about life, and his peculiar love of doing business and of taking pleasure at the same time. This love had led him to perfect in Ireland and whilst touring western England the art of dovetailing surveyorship and hunting; this love had taught him to write in trains; this love now lured him to a new and more elaborate experiment—that of using an official journey as a means to sightseeing, and sightseeing as a means to authorship. Thus each one of Trollope's interests went to strengthen the rest. The Post Office was his overlord, and almost ferociously he served it.

But the service had by-products, one of which was opportunity for his adored sport of hunting, another a varied and continual experience of men and things, a third travel. All these could be turned to the advantage of his private trade of authorship; and were so turned—with a thoroughness which earned him the affectionate ridicule of his contemporaries.

2

Frederic Harrison, in an essay first published in the *Fortnightly Review* and later issued in book form,[1] declares that Trollope, "though a great traveller, rarely uses his experiences in a novel, whereas Scott, Thackeray, Dickens, Bulwer, George Eliot fill their pages with foreign adventures and scenes of travel." In a limited sense this assertion is not without truth, but as a general reflection on the inspiration of the Trollopian novel it is false. Trollope, indeed, seldom staged a fiction—or even important isolated fictional scenes—against an exotic background. He had none of the vanity which occasionally tempted the authors mentioned to ostentatious use in novel-writing of their own "reading-up" or learned sightseeing. But there was not a hint of psychology—whether of English folk abroad or of non-English men and women—observed by him from a café-table on a square, in a frontier Customs house, on board a steamer or in a cosmopolitan hotel, which did not, sooner or later, go to the elucidation of some character in a tale. Are not Count Pateroff and Sophie Gordeloup in *The Claverings* memories of travel? And Lopez in *The Prime Minister*? And Melmotte in *The Way We Live Now*? And half the characters in *John Caldigate*? And the Americans in *Dr. Wortle's School*, *The American Senator*, *The Duke's Children* and other novels?

In his short stories Trollope makes still more thorough use of his globe-trotting experience. The stories are (and admittedly) largely composed of actual incidents of travel, and in several of them we are given a glimpse of their author as he appeared to himself.

[1] *Studies in Early Victorian Literature.* London, 1895.

Archibald Green in *The O'Conors of Castle Conor* [1] is certainly the young Trollope, fresh to Ireland and to Irish hospitality, the Trollope of the first months at Banagher. When Green reappears in *Father Giles of Ballymoy* [2] he is again Trollope, this time journeying on some Post Office business, and coming among the Irish populace to misadventure as ludicrous as that which, in the earlier story, befell him in an Irish country house. Of the European tales there are likewise a few which show their author laughing a little heavily at his own heaviness. John Pomfret of *John Bull on the Guadalquivir* [3] has confessedly the reactions to Spanish customs and to Spanish loveliness which Trollope himself had, when in 1858 he returned from Egypt by the way of Spain. The love story is, of course, imaginary; he would as readily have jumped the moon as frolicked with a maiden Daguilar, when on official journey and he a married man of forty-three. But he admits himself guilty of mistaking a duke for a *torero*; and the abrupt and rather wistful tributes to the easy, indolent beauty of Spanish sunlight, the reluctant "fine writing" of the descriptions of river, street and cool creeper-clad *patio* show us Trollope, massive, appreciative, inquisitive and amazingly English, on one of his many explorations of the world.

A similar interest have such other tales. In *A Ride Across Palestine* [4] the upstanding (but amused) virtue of Jones, when confronted with the fact that the "young man" with whom he has travelled for a week across the desert is really a runaway girl in disguise, is beautifully Trollopian. *Relics of General Chassé* [5] and *A Journey to Panama* [6] are both self-portrayals, though of unequal importance. The former is a foolish and laborious joke about trousers, staged in Antwerp and sadly reminiscent of Mrs. Trollope at her worst; while the latter stands high among Trollope's short stories, being not only the most courageously "unfinished" of them all, but also, with those included in the volume *Why Frau Frohmann Raised her*

[1] *Tales of All Countries*, 1st series.
[2] *Lotta Schmidt : and Other Stories.*
[3] *Tales of All Countries*, 1st series.
[4] *Ibid.*, 2nd series.   [5] *Ibid.*, 1st series.
[6] *Lotta Schmidt : and Other Stories.*

Prices, the most vital to an understanding of his full-length work.

Little in fact passed Trollope by while on his journeys round the world, and little remained unused at some stage of his story-telling. The true distinction between him and his contemporaries lay in this—that they could set out to write a tale of foreign lands and let characterisation wait on *mise en scène*, but Trollope, a characteriser first and all the time, believed that human beings were men and women before they were English, French or German, and that their basic impulses must be divined apart from nationality. When the moment came to put the finishing touch to them, then—if they were to be American or French or Slav or what you will—he was ready with knowledge of manners and of customs, ready to add the surface-tricks of bearing, ready to give that final twist of "foreignness" which the construction of his tale required. But such adornment (and indeed all of what is known as "local colour") was to Trollope the grease paint on the actor's face—a final touch to help illusion, but trivial beside the personality of the actor himself, a mere subsidiary to his skill in rendering the part.

3

As Trollope's taste for travel chimed with his other tastes and swelled the chorus of his resonant personality, so were his interests when abroad in perfect harmony with his character. He toured foreign countries as he toured the English country-side, watching for character, noting each fresh expression of the human soul, and retaining in his memory just so much of the houses and the background as seemed to him contributory to a true understanding of the people. He loved the unfamiliar scene of daily life abroad; the little comedies of travel; the glimpses—under the surface of a non-English community—of emotions, ambitions and perplexities common to a humanity which knows no nationality.

But to the ordinary thrills of tourism his response was conventional, almost automatic. Although he visited cathedrals

and points of view and picture galleries, collecting knowledge
and appreciation in the orderly, efficient manner that one
would expect from a person so acquiescent in the normal
machinery of experience, he was not profoundly moved, either
by natural loveliness or by the beauty of man's handiwork.
This accusation he would himself hotly have denied. Every
educated British tourist who has done his serious duty by the
Louvre, the Prado, the Brera and the Uffizi, has gazed at
Chartres, stood on the terrace at Fiesole and wandered through
the alleys of old Heidelberg, violently resents any suggestion
that the beauty seen and even appreciated has not, in the true
sense of the word, been "felt." Yet such is with sad frequency
the case; and the charge can be brought home to Trollope,
because in some dozen million words of fiction he wrote himself down for posterity to read. Indeed on this score, no less
than on the score of calm in love, his novels rise in witness
against him. They show that art and landscape were an
essential element in his view or his enjoyment of life only in
so far as they had direct bearing on the actions or characters
of men and women.

There is no denying that in his work he shows a noticeable
reluctance to elaborate descriptive detail and to set beauty
down in words, and this reluctance must to a point be attributed to want of understanding. But only to a point. There
were two further elements in his abstention from æsthetics,
both highly characteristic of him and one especially important
to the survival of his novels' popularity. The first was
humility; the second an uncanny instinct for the essence of a
novelist's duty.

His humility toward art, combined with a quaint and rather
irritating materialism in its appraisement, is demonstrated by
an essay on "The National Gallery," contributed to Mrs. S. C.
Hall's magazine St. James's for September 1861. In this
article he reveals himself as in every respect the type of man
who "does not pretend to know about pictures, but knows
what he likes." Appreciation from such a source irritates the
genuine student, and certainly—in so far as the man who
"knows what he likes" has often a facility for names and dates

and generalities of attribution—the irritation is forgivable. Nevertheless there is often more diffidence than crude complacency in the attitude of these amateur art-lovers, and Trollope's article, pawky and drab and materialistic though it is, has yet its pathos. It is the article of a man too proud to shirk a theme which is conventionally a part of culture, too shy and too honest to pretend to knowledge he does not possess. There are flashes of understanding. Thus: "Raphael's grace has the grace of fiction, not the grace of nature. . . . After him came ruin and decay." Such a realisation of the overripeness of Raphael's beauty was more remarkable in 1860 than it would be to-day, and that it was a genuine realisation and not mere word-spinning is shown by the reassertion of it five years later in a *Pall Mall* essay on "The Art Tourist."[1]

> The art tourist will come gradually to perceive how the long visaged virgins of Botticelli grew out of the first attempts by Cimabue and how they progressed into the unnatural grace of Raphael and then descended into the meretricious inanities, of which Raphael's power and Raphael's falseness were the forerunners.

But perceptive comment such as this is rare in the earlier *St. James's* article. Each tiny jewel is embedded in a mass of commonplace. Trollope cannot refrain from quoting the price paid for this picture or for that, and then declares that picture-seeing in a public gallery is a "cheap amusement," and that the cheapness is the more gratifying when the amateur considers what sums have gone to the provision of his entertainment! The article concludes: "I have been looking at pictures for many years till I have grown to be fond of them. I do not aspire to be a connoisseur."

It was instinct rather than humility which kept his novels virtually free from comment on art. He realised that the novelist parades at his peril his personal and ephemeral tastes. So it was rare for him even to attempt a "correct" description

[1] Later published with other essays under the title *Travelling Sketches*. London, 1866.

of architectural detail and rarer still to express an opinion as to
relative comeliness. It is one of his glories that in comparison
with his contemporaries he seldom "dates," and this distinction he owes as much to his disregard of topical prejudices
as to any other cause.

Apart from a laboured criticism of the pre-Raphaelites in
The Warden, an incidental sneer at Nash's Regent Street in
Castle Richmond, and an unfortunate comment on Framley
church ("It was but a mean and ugly building, having been
erected about a hundred years since [*i.e.* about 1760], when all
churches were made to be mean and ugly"), his novels are
mercifully free from the æsthetic "viewiness" which offends
the altered taste of later generations. They have a broad
serenity suited to the age-long human impulses with which
they deal.

To call Trollope "a philistine" is both right and wrong.
"Like other sporting men" says Frederic Harrison in the
essay already quoted "who imagine that their love of 'sport'
is a love of nature when it is merely a pleasure in physical
exercise, Trollope cared little for the poetic aspect of nature.
His books, like Thackeray's, hardly contain a single fine
picture of the country, of the sea, of mountains or of rivers.
Compared with Fielding, Scott, Charlotte Brontë, Dickens,
George Eliot, he is a man blind to the loveliness of nature."

This, the second of Frederic Harrison's pronouncements, is
like the first. From one point of view it is truly said, and might
have been extended to include Trollope's attitude alike to
architecture, to painting and to music. But in the sweeping
sense of the writer's intention it is misleading. Trollope was
not incapable of seeing natural beauty or of expressing it in
words; he was merely uninterested in it as a conception
detached from human life.

The analogy is perfect between this indifference and his
indifference to ideas and to ideals. Art and philosophy, as
things of independent spiritual significance, lay beyond his
mental reach; but set him to appraise or to unravel the working of an idea or of an aspiration which has direct bearing
on the existence and behaviour of ordinary people, and he

shows a subtlety and judgment rivalled by one other novelist only.

For it is in this aspect of his work that may most clearly be discerned his spiritual kinship with Charles Dickens. When George Santayana wrote of Dickens the words which follow, he might with equal truth have been writing of Trollope:—

> It is remarkable, in spite of his ardent simplicity and openness of heart, how insensible Dickens was to the greater themes of the human imagination—religion, science, politics, art. . . . Perhaps, properly speaking, he had no *ideas* on any subject; what he had was a vast sympathetic participation in the daily life of mankind.[1]

This is no fanciful parallel between Dickens and Trollope. Each had his sphere of understanding; Dickens is as uncertain a creator of persons of the upper and upper-middle class as Trollope is of humbler folk; but the two had a common inspiration and a common instinct—the inspiration of humanity and the instinct for its interpretation. Both lacked a lively sense for fine art, for the power of spiritual principle or for natural beauty; but both, where dramatic force in landscape or in the handiwork of man could help to illustrate a character, called it to their aid and worked it dexterously.

Consider from this point of view some of Trollope's actual books. Perhaps one's first impulse is to declare that in these novels the descriptions of country town or country house, of garden or of field and lane are strangely few and perfunctory. But on second thoughts they appear not so infrequent, and the most vivid—for Trollope can, when he so desires, present a scene both clearly and unforgettably—are those which, being in themselves bleak or pretentious, squalid or complacent, reflect or help to express those of his characters who have concern with them. From this it follows that scenes unusual or unhappy or exaggerated are better visualised than those of mere prettiness, the former being as they are because their owners make them so, the latter owing their charm to age, to

---

[1] *Soliloquies in England*, by George Santayana. London, 1922.

floweriness, or to the fine conception of some long dead architect.

The Castle and town of Courcy—being the Courcy family in terms of bricks and mortar—are vividly presented in *Doctor Thorne*; and the same novel gives a three-paragraph picture of Gatherum Castle, so complete and so unmistakable that it can stand as representative of all the baronial monstrosities of that mid-Victorian feudalism to which the old Duke of Omnium conspicuously belonged. But, in comparison, the presentation of Greshamsbury House—"in some sense the finest specimen of Tudor architecture of which the country can boast"—is perfunctory and unpictorial. Why? Because Trollope, faced with a building which had its own perfection and interpreted the canons of good architecture rather than the family of Gresham, felt no profound interest in it and was content to parrot a text-book appreciation.

Again and again the novels reveal this contrast between the artistic and the personal approach to buildings and to landscape. In *The Claverings* Ongar Park, supposed to have every charm and elegance that a modest but wealthy country house can have, is described, indeed, but barely realised; on the other hand, Clavering itself—cold, square and hard as the bitter man who owns it—is set for ever in the reader's memory as the inevitable home of Sir Hugh Clavering, as the ordained scene of his poor wife's trampled misery, as the superbly ironic background to the love tale of Julia Ongar and young Harry Clavering. In *The Small House at Allington* Mrs. Dale's cottage and the Squire's home are taken so nearly for granted, that one can almost imagine Trollope glancing at any Victorian wood-engraving of the houses in a conventional English village of the time and telling himself that everyone would know the kind of cottage and the kind of manor house that Lily and her uncle must naturally inhabit. But when Crosbie and the Lady Alexandrina set up house in London, they must be given a dwelling suited to their own jerry-built arrogance, and such a dwelling to perfection is the new house in the terrace northward from the park. *Framley Parsonage*, where all the backgrounds are of the type of "English antique charm," is without such descriptions as linger in the mind. Who is there that can claim really to *see* Framley Court or Chaldicotes, though both are detailed and with a certain care? *The Belton Estate*, on the other hand, is rich in pictures, and for the good reason that all its houses are, in the author's intention, expressions of their owner's character. Belton Castle, Plaistow Hall, Mrs. Winterfield's house in Perivale, Aylmer Park—each one of these is as distinctly featured and as real as are the folk who dwell in them.

It would be possible to extend almost indefinitely this survey of Trollope's use and neglect of architecture and of landscape. The method is continuous right down to the novels of the final period. Manor Cross, Lord Brotherton's house in *Is He Popenjoy?*, is, like the town of Brotherton itself, hardly sketched at all, again because both mansion and town are of a different epoch from that of the tale so that their qualities have no bearing on the characters presented. But in *An Eye for an Eye*, Ardkill Cottage, where Kate O'Hara lives, and the gloomy immensity of Scroope Manor, whence her seducer comes, are painted with unusual care, being designed—by pointing a once the contrast and the similarity between the untidy, reckless tedium of western Ireland and the portentous, stately tedium of feudal Dorset—to account for Nevill's love-piracy and for Kate's surrender. Both seek escape; but for the man escape means forfeiture, and he goes back to prison—where at least are dignity and comfort—leaving his fellow-fugitive to her tragic fate. *Mr. Scarborough's Family* and *Sir Harry Hotspur of Humblethwaite* are another such pair as *Is He Popenjoy?* and *An Eye for an Eye*. What reader can imagine Tretton, where old Scarborough planned his horrible jest, whither from the very graveside of his father the duns gave chase to Mountjoy? The house and grounds are left almost unpictured, for the very practical reason that their importance to the tale is as a mere mass of property, a conglomerate wealth to be left in a will, something to be inherited, to serve as security for debt, to set a family against itself. It does not matter how they looked, it only matters that they are *property*; for *Mr. Scarborough's Family* is a novel of property.

Sir Harry Hotspur, on the other hand, is a tragedy of love

unworthily bestowed. For the full realisation of Emily
Hotspur's constancy and courage, it was essential that the
Hotspur dignity be vivid and unmistakable. Hence the fine
description of Humblethwaite Hall—the longest and most
arresting description of a big country house in the whole of
Trollope's work—skilfully set against a background of moorland and of scattered rocks. One cannot read *Sir Harry
Hotspur* without mentally contrasting it with its forerunner,
Can You Forgive Her?—a longer novel, not dissimilar in theme,
inferior in quality—and remarking that not the least element
in the contrast is the neglect of landscape and architecture in
the earlier book, their brilliant realisation in the later.

From all of this, it follows logically that churches and other
monuments to the idealisms of the past should fare worse with
Trollope than do dwelling-houses. He does not excel—he has
no temptation to excel—as a painter of cathedrals, of town
halls, or of public edifices generally. Such things, being of
communal inspiration and utility, cannot express the personality of any individual; cannot, in consequence, rouse the real
interest of this exclusive enthusiast for individual life. Barchester Cathedral does not emerge from all his chronicles of
its clergy and its worshippers. Hiram's Hospital is to him less
of an architectural relic or a piece of pious history than a cause
of nineteenth-century dispute, a thorn in a tender individual
conscience, a provocation to an individual's reformist zeal.
Just as his clerical types are men uniquely realised, but men as
non-religious as if they were agnostic schoolmasters, so is
Barchester a town of real and living people, but not—save in
narrative statement—a town containing a cathedral and many
traces of the loveliness of mediæval England.

4

It is necessary to interpret Trollope the traveller in terms of
Trollope the novelist, because all of the knowledge and experience which he gained went to the building of his novels, and
because that experience was by its very nature of a kind to be
unadventurously won. To Trollope on journey little that was

G

spectacular befell, and his travels have of themselves little of narrative interest.

It was shortly after the sale to Richard Bentley of the copyright of *The Three Clerks* that Trollope and his wife left London for Florence. They moved slowly through Switzerland and over the Alps, visiting Milan, Verona and other towns before arriving finally at their destination. They found the aged Frances already sinking into the remote indifference of old age. Although she was destined to live for six more years, she had finished her work. Her battles were over; the pen was laid finally aside. Her happiness was now in that of her children and her grandchildren, in the flowers beyond the loggia, in the small daily gossip of Anglo-Florentine society.

To this society—to Landor, to the Brownings, to Isa Blagden and the rest—Tom Trollope was eager to introduce his brother. Tom had already contrived, with a skill Anthony could never have possessed, to adjust his bulky commonsense to the frail intellectualism of the English colony. As time passed he became one of its leading figures. He had, of course, the advantage of an education such as Anthony had never had; even more importantly his first wife, Theodosia (to whom, among so many others, Landor wrote a poem), was of the type to prosper and to rule in the exquisite futility of Italianate exile. But it remains a striking and an intriguing fact that a genuine Trollope—for Tom was in himself as burly, noisy and uncomplicated as was Anthony—could have so thriven in that rarefied atmosphere as to become a salon holder and even to be nicknamed "Aristides" by Mrs. Browning.

It may be suggested, without undue ill-nature, that the beauty and comfort of the Villino Trollope helped Tom and Theodosia Trollope to the attainment and maintenance of their supremacy. Even persons of genius appreciate good food and luxurious hospitality, and certainly the Trollopes offered both of these. Kate Field—the lovely young American, who was to become so intimate with Anthony—thus gushingly described the Villino Trollope and its owners:—

Ah, this Villino Trollope is quaintly fascinating, with its

marble pillars, its grim men in armour, starting like sentinels from the walls, and its curiosities greeting you at every step. The antiquary revels in its majolica, its old bridal chests and carved furniture, its beautiful terra-cotta of the Virgin and Child by Orcagna, its hundred *oggetti* of the Cinque Cento. The bibliophile grows silently ecstatic as he sinks quietly into a mediæval chair and feasts his eyes on a model library, bubbling over with five thousand rare books, many wonderfully illuminated and enriched by costly engravings. . . .

It is late in spring. Soft winds kiss the budding foliage and warm it into bloom; the beautiful terrace of Villino Trollope is transformed into a reception-room. Opening upon a garden, with its lofty pillars, its tessellated marble floor, its walls inlaid with terra-cotta, bas-reliefs, inscriptions, and coats of arms, with here and there a niche devoted to some antique Madonna, the terrace has all the charm of a *campo santo* without the chill of the grave upon it; or, were a few cowled monks to walk with folded arms along its space, one might fancy it the cloister of a monastery. On this warm spring night there is laughter and the buzz of many tongues. No lights but the stars are burning, and men and women, talking in almost every civilised tongue, are sipping iced lemonade—one of the specialities of Villino Trollope.

And in another place: "Mr. Trollope is such a fine man— half Socrates and half Galileo. His wife is promiscuously talented, writes for the *Athenæum*, composes music, translates but does not go very far in any one thing." [1]

It is amusing to imagine Anthony in such a setting, watching with earnest admiration his brother's Britishness muted to suave and dignified Italianacy, and making, under the personal guidance of "Aristides," his uneasy tour of Anglo-Florence! Unfortunately no details survive of his adventures.

Although he was little suited to this denationalised society, Anthony contrived, in the first flush of Tom's sponsorial

[1] *Kate Field.* A Record by Lilian Whiting. Boston & London, 1899.

eagerness, a brief and rather combative acquaintanceship with
Mrs. Browning, which developed quaintly in 1858. When
The Three Clerks appeared, a copy found its way into the
Browning household, and they, like Thackeray, read it entranced. "We both agree with you" Elizabeth Browning
wrote to Tom Trollope's wife "in considering it the best of
his three clever novels. My husband, who can seldom get a
novel to hold him, has been held by all three and by this the
strongest. It has qualities of which the others gave no sign.
I was wrung to tears by the third volume. What a thoroughly
man's book it is! I much admire it, only wishing away, with
a vehemence that proves the veracity of my general admiration, the contributions to the *Daily Delight*—may I dare to
say it?"

This letter could hardly have been phrased more skilfully to
point the difference between the so English Anthony and the
so Italianate Elizabeth. The blend of sweetness and condescension; the archness of "What a thoroughly *man's* book it
is . . ."; the false humility of the final criticism—all these
must have combined to set the novelist growling into his
beard. When early in the career of the *Cornhill* Mrs. Browning's poem *A Musical Instrument* ("What was he doing, the
great God Pan?") was published, Anthony took his revenge.
He wrote a long letter of criticism to his brother, in the course
of which, carefully sandwiched between words of compliment,
he said: "I am inclined to think she is illustrating an allegory
by a thought rather than a thought by an allegory. . . . I can
hardly believe that she herself believes in the doctrine which
her fancy has led her to illustrate." The letter came round at
third hand to the poetess. As indirectly she replied to it: and
in her reply, behind the gaiety and wit and ingenuity, one hears
the jangle of nerves, jarred and dismayed by the presumption
of a beef-fed philistine.

But if Trollope took away with him from Florence only
a tepid liking for its shrewdly gracious femininity, he had a
double profit from the time spent actually in his brother's
house. He always liked Tom's company and admired his
qualities; and from this visit he returned the richer by more

than friendship, for Tom it was who invented the plot of *Doctor Thorne*.

Anthony had not for long been back in Dublin and *Doctor Thorne* was only a volume written, when the Post Office authorities, desirous of concluding a postal treaty with the Egyptian Government for the conveyance of British mails from Alexandria to Suez, had the idea of sending their chief Irish Surveyor to do the business. In January 1858, therefore, Trollope was in London, attending St. Martin's le Grand for his instructions, buying his clothes and tickets, enjoying each moment of each bustling day. He tells in the *Autobiography* of his last-minute dash from Bentley's office to that of Chapman & Hall, and how Edward Chapman, confronted with a tempestuous stranger demanding £400 for a novel half completed, fingered the poker but agreed to pay the price. It was a rough voyage to Alexandria, but Trollope wrote his novel day by day. There is something tremendous in the thought that *Doctor Thorne*—so smooth, so delicate—was partly written between actual bouts of sea-sickness on board an uncomfortable boat and during the miseries of a stormy February. Nor, when he reached Egypt, was he the least exhausted by his toil. Indeed the Armenian Excellency, with whom his business must be done, found him assertive and peremptory. Years later the Pasha spoke amusedly of Trollope's method as negotiator, describing his manner as "having about it less of the diplomatist than of the author who meditates scolding his publisher if he will not come round to his terms, and even carrying his literary wares elsewhere."

Whatever its crudity, the method was effective. Seldom had Government negotiation been accomplished with such blunt efficiency. His treaty made with modern Egypt, Trollope turned on antiquity and "did it" thoroughly. He showed the fierce determination of a man who had come out to do a job, to see a foreign land and to write a book, and meant to realise each part of his design. His opinion of Egypt as a tourist's playground and his own method of exploring it are beautifully expressed in a letter written to Edmund Yates (also an official in the Post Office), who had announced himself as on his way

to Egypt and expected to find Trollope waiting for him.
Instead he was handed the following admirable product of
tabloid tourism:—

Alexandria.
11 *March* 1858.

MY DEAR YATES,

It is matter of great regret to me that I should miss you.
But were I to stay now I should lose my only opportunity
of going to Jerusalem. I had hoped to have got there and
back before you came out, and it has been impossible for
me to start till today. I shall probably still see you on 22nd.
At Cairo see (above all) the newly-opened catacombs of
Sakhara—by taking a horse and mounted guide you may
see that and the Pyramids of Ghizeh in one day. Hear the
howling dervishes of Cairo at one on Friday. They howl
but once a week. Go to the citadel of Cairo, and mosque
of Sultan Hassan. See, also, the tombs of the Caliphs.
Heliopolis is a humbug, so also is the petrified forest. At
Alexandria see the new Greek church they have just ex-
cavated. Go to the Oriental Hotel at Alexandria, and
Shepheard's at Cairo.

Yours ever,

ANTHONY TROLLOPE.

While Yates was profiting by the very practical instructions
of his vanished colleague, that insatiable being was travelling
the Holy Land, finishing *Doctor Thorne*, beginning *The Bertrams*
and arranging to return home by Malta and Gibraltar, in
which places he proposed to inspect the Post Offices. This
done, he journeyed to London through Spain and France and
reported at headquarters about May 20.

St. Martin's le Grand was enchanted at the energy of its
missioner. Four days after his arrival he was despatched on an
official errand to Scotland (and particularly to Glasgow), which
occupied him for two months. It was the end of July before
he reached Dublin once again.

There is a paragraph in the *Autobiography* referring to his
Glasgow visit, which illustrates at once the astonishing

thoroughness of his official work and the dogged industry with which he stuck to spare-time authorship. One of the problems before an inspector of the Glasgow posts was the fair adjustment of deliveries. The men declared that climbing to the top flats of apartment houses was not allowed for in their schedules of work and pay. In order to test this claim, Trollope—now a high official and a visiting official into the bargain—himself trudged each postman's round, dragging through midsummer heat his very considerable bulk up flights and flights of stairs. Here is his quaint comment on the experience: "Wearier work I never performed. The men would grumble, and then I would think how it would be with them if they had to go home afterwards and write a love scene. But the love scenes written in Glasgow, all belonging to *The Bertrams*, are not good."

From travelling he was to have little respite. The Post Office now had him labelled "missioner" and, when there arose an urgent need for someone to visit the West Indies and there reorganise a decrepit postal system, Trollope was instantly selected for the work. By November 1 he was in London making his preparations; on November 17 he sailed.

The West Indian journey—its itinerary is given both in the *Autobiography* and in the book *The West Indies and the Spanish Main*—lasted until the summer. It included extensive journeys in Central America and British Guiana, which are described racily and with unfailing humour. One incident, however, was not narrated in the published version of the tour. Trollope was determined to prove that a certain distance could be covered on mule-back in two days. The local postal authorities declared that the journey would take three, and to support their claim purposely provided the troublesome visitor with an uncomfortable saddle. In consequence the first day's ride reduced the missioner to the extremes of raw discomfort. The morrow (if he were to carry his point) must be another, equally fatiguing day. Only one remedy was possible, and that a drastic one. He ordered two bottles of brandy, poured them into a wash-basin, and sat in it.

Quite shortly after Trollope's return home came his trans-

ference from Ireland to the eastern district of England. This
was an event in his life of the very greatest importance. It
established him within easy reach of London; it made possible club-life and all this was to mean to him; it gave him
friends and a home in which with ease and dignity he could
entertain them; it ushered in the golden age of his prosperity;
it cleared the way to that supremacy among contemporary
novelists which he was to hold for nearly twenty years.

V

WALTHAM HOUSE, at Waltham Cross in Hertfordshire, where Trollope settled in the winter of 1859, was a fine Georgian house of weathered brick, which had in those days a large garden, good stabling and surroundings of great rural beauty. The house still stood in the period between wars; but encroaching London, and the haphazard disfigurement of factories and market-gardens, had destroyed much of the solitude and cleanliness which for twelve crowded years were Trollope's balm after toil, and his stimulus to further labours.

Trollope at Waltham Cross was the most thriving and content of all the Trollopes. He had his hunters in his stable, and about him his wife, his children and his friends; he had the excitement of the dawn of real success, followed by the delicious glow of a sustained and splendid popularity; he had health and growing wealth; he had the warm consciousness of his continual and fecund industry. "Early in the year" notes Anne Thackeray in her journal for 1865 "to Waltham Cross to stay at the Trollopes. It was a sweet old prim chill house wrapped in snow." [1] Another memory, this time of Waltham in high summer, comes from a review in "Maga" [2] of the *Autobiography*:—

At Waltham House amongst his cows and rows of strawberries Trollope delighted to welcome at his dinner table some half-dozen intimate friends. Those who were occasional guests there remember how in the warm summer evenings the party would adjourn after dinner to the lawn, where wines and fruit were laid out under the fine old cedar tree, and good stories were told, while the tobacco smoke went curling up into the twilight.

---

[1] *Letters of Anne Thackeray Ritchie.* London, 1924.
[2] *Blackwood's Magazine.* November 1883.

For children, no less than for adults, the house was the scene of many joyful gatherings. One of Trollope's nephews records that the children's parties at Waltham were so like those at Noningsby in *Orley Farm*—with blind-man's buff and snap-dragon by candlelight at Christmas time, and "Commerce" on any and every occasion—that he has only to re-read that novel to live again those childhood days. Trollope would join in all the games, contriving with great ingenuity that at "Commerce" the children got the winning cards.

He himself is characteristically bleak in his references to this prosperous and happy home. "I settled myself at a residence about twelve miles from London, which was somewhat too grandly called Waltham House. This I took on lease and subsequently bought, after I had spent about £1000 on improvements." Again: ". . . A house in which I could entertain a few friends modestly, where we grew our cabbages and strawberries, made our own butter, killed our own pigs." Again: "It was a rickety old place, requiring much repair and not as weather-tight as it should be. But for strawberries, asparagus, green peas, out-of-door peaches, for roses and such everyday luxuries, no place was ever more excellent." The final, the valedictory reference is perhaps the most charming of all. After explaining that in 1871 a voyage to Australia and other considerations made the abandonment of Waltham advisable if not essential, he remarks: "The house had been a success and the scene of much happiness. . . . As must take place on such an occasion, there was some heartfelt grief. But the thing was done and orders were given for the letting or sale of the house. It never was let, and remained unoccupied for two years before it was sold. I lost by the transaction about £800. As I continually hear that other men make money by buying and selling houses, I presume I am not well adapted for transactions of that sort."

His private grief at giving up this much-loved home became traditional among his intimates; it was typical that he should smother that grief within himself, and in his message to posterity merely deplore the incident—a little jauntily—as a financial loss.

2

The move to England and the discharge of a high postal office (he was now Chairman of Surveyors at a salary of £800 a year) within a dozen miles of the General Post Office itself naturally involved Trollope much more intimately than hitherto with the internal politics of St. Martin's le Grand. He was not, as may easily be imagined, a very docile Civil Servant. Indeed he contrived within a surprisingly short time of his settlement at Waltham to get at loggerheads with his superiors and to revitalise the old tradition of his incompatibility, which had lingered on during the Irish years, a legacy from the unruly, idle, squalid junior days when first he "got across" authority. The situation had, of course, radically changed. Trollope was now too valuable an official to be dealt with as harshly as, now and again, the Secretary may secretly have wished. Also, his brother-in-law, John Tilley, was Assistant Secretary and an assiduous and skilful peace-maker. But there was intermittent strife, and between secretarial sarcasm and Trollopian bluster the private workings of Her Majesty's postal services suffered recurrent shocks.

Trollope himself is candid (as one can trust him to be) in his admission that official life was not a perfect harmony. He shows also a definite and characteristic relish for dissension:—

At this time [he says] I did not stand very well with the dominant interest at the General Post Office. My old friend Colonel Maberley had been, some time since, squeezed out, and his place was filled by Rowland Hill, the originator of the Penny Post. With him I never had any sympathy, nor he with me.[1] . . . I was always an anti-Hillite, acknowledging indeed the great thing which Sir Rowland Hill had done for the country, but believing him to be entirely unfit to manage men or to arrange labour. It was a pleasure to me

---

[1] One reason for this lack of sympathy (a reason implied in the very words "squeezed out") was that Hill was an importation to the Post Office. He had been appointed Secretary from outside, in recognition of his work for Penny Postage and in deference to the public wish.

to differ from him on all occasions; and, looking back now, I think that in all differences I was right.

I had not, from my position, anything to do with the management of affairs; but from time to time I found myself mixed up in it. . . . I was very fond of the department and, when matters came to be considered, I generally had an opinion of my own. I have no doubt that I often made myself very disagreeable. I know that I sometimes tried to do so. But I could hold my own, because I knew my business and was useful.

He goes on to explain the manner in which he most provoked authority. *The Three Clerks* had already given offence; a lecture delivered to the staff on the right of the Civil Servant to freedom of political opinion gave offence still greater; [1] as a writer of official reports in unconventional and rather flippant language he became a continual and a cumulative irritation.

An amusing picture of Trollope in the Post Office at this period is given by Edmund Yates in his reminiscences. Allowance must be made for the writer's inherent shrewishness. Yates was jealous of Trollope, both as an official more competent and as a writer more successful than himself. Inside the Post Office he was a creature of Sir Rowland Hill's, and was not unwilling to play upon the chief's dislike of Trollope, or to bait Trollope to rebelliousness.

There were incidents, as well as incompatibilities, which helped to embroil these uncongenial colleagues.

In the first place, they collided angrily in one of the numerous little whirlpools of ill-feeling which followed on the splash of Yates' expulsion from the Garrick Club. Trollope, as an idolater of Thackeray, out-partisaned his party; Yates, snarling and biting in the aftermath of his humiliation and not venturing to turn on Thackeray himself, vented his anger on the most outspoken of his lesser enemies.

The second "brush" between the rivals took place in the

[1] This lecture, somewhat rewritten, was later printed in the *Cornhill Magazine* for March 1861.

early part of 1861, when Trollope (foolishly, as will be seen) reposed in Yates a casual confidence and Yates exploited it, to gratify indirectly his lingering grudge against the Thackeray he dared not openly attack.

The third incident was a curious one and, though flattering to Trollope, must have served to intensify the jealousy of Yates. In August 1861, just before he was sailing for America and when *Framley Parsonage* was drawing near the end of its triumphant serial career in the *Cornhill*, Trollope received through a third party the following strange proposal from John Maxwell (a publisher and the future husband of Miss Braddon), who in December 1860 had started the monthly magazine *Temple Bar* in admitted imitation of the *Cornhill*:

> Mr. Maxwell has asked me to offer you £1000 a year for three or five years, with the ostensible editorship of *Temple Bar*, if you will undertake to supply a novel and fill the position that Mr. Sala now occupies.
>
> All the real work of editorship will be performed—as heretofore—by Mr. Edmund Yates, who would act with you as sub-editor.

Trollope might have been forgiven had he lost his normal sense of proportion at this somewhat unscrupulous but very lavish offer. Not to many novelists is it given to earn with their first best-selling story not only reputation and money from the book itself, but also an editorial sinecure at one thousand pounds a year. But his good sense held firm; a stocky pride in standing on his own feet and in being neither figure-head nor log-rollers' darling made him reject the offer without hesitation. His "hands were full" he wrote, and in any case he "would not undertake a mock-editorship." To Yates, on the other hand, there must have been bitterness in his proprietor's attempt at editorial change, for Maxwell's intention was obviously known to him.

Finally, in 1867, Yates was chosen to be personal and confidential underling to Scudamore, the Post Office librarian, when this man was promoted Assistant Secretary over Trollope's head. Trollope threw in a blusterous resignation, and drew the obvious conclusion that he had been passed over thanks (in part, at least) to a Yates intrigue.

It should be repeated, therefore, that Yates on Trollope must be read with caution and his veiled implications taken with a pinch of salt. Nevertheless, dislike apart, his picture of Trollope is too recognisable to be dismissed for caricature.

> Rowland Hill and Anthony Trollope cordially hated each other. Trollope admits it in his *Autobiography*.
>
> Sir Rowland Hill was far too cautious and reserved ever to put his likes or dislikes into print. But he hated Trollope very cordially, and could not avoid showing it when they were brought into contact. Trollope would bluster and rave and roar, blowing and spluttering like a grampus; while the pale old gentleman opposite him, sitting back in his armchair and regarding his antagonist furtively under his spectacles, would remain perfectly quiet until he saw his chance, and then deliver himself of the most unpleasant speech he could frame in the hardest possible tone.
>
> . . . It is scarcely possible to imagine a greater contrast to Rowland Hill than Anthony Trollope, physically—save that both were bald and spectacled—and mentally. One small, pale, and, with the exception of a small scrap of whisker, closely shaven; the other big, broad, fresh-coloured, and bushy-bearded: one calm and freezing, the other bluff and boisterous; one cautious and calculating, weighing well every word before utterance, and then only choosing phrases which would convey his opinion, but would give no warmth to its expression; the other scarcely giving himself time to think, but spluttering and roaring out an instantly-formed opinion couched in the very strongest of terms.

The paragraph concludes with this two-line anecdote.

> "I differ from you entirely!" Trollope roared out once to the speaker who preceded him at a discussion-meeting of Surveyors. "What was it you said?" [1]

---

[1] *Edmund Yates : His Recollections and Experiences.* 2 vols. London, 1884.

3

From August to November 1859 (between the finding of
Waltham House and its actual occupation) Trollope did not
relax his writer's industry, even though he had a new home in
prospect, new work and new responsibilities. Partly in Ireland, partly on a holiday in the Pyrenees, he began a new novel
(*Castle Richmond*) and wrote several stories from the stock of
experience collected on his travels.

There came to him, during October, news of the preparations for the *Cornhill Magazine*, which had already announced
itself as due to start publication on the first day of 1860 under
Thackeray's editorship. Perhaps determination to leave un-
tried no single opening for authorship, perhaps from enthusiasm for *Esmond* (published in 1852, read and re-read, and
later pronounced to be "the greatest novel in the English
language"); perhaps from the instinct which forewarns a man
of the approach of some all-powerful influence in his life—
for any of these reasons or for all of them Trollope, on October
23 1859, wrote to Thackeray (whom he had never seen)
offering short stories for the forthcoming magazine. He gives
the answer verbatim in his *Autobiography*, and, with its neat
phrasing and its pleasant compliment to *The Three Clerks*, it is
an answer such as Thackeray, a prince of letter-courtesy, well
knew how to write. Certainly the first links in the chain of
adoration—for Trollope's love and respect for Thackeray
developed almost into worship—which was to bind the gruff,
undemonstrative novelist-Surveyor to Titmarsh chariot wheels
were forged in the fire of that so sympathetic letter.

But a charming letter was by no means the only result of
his spontaneous approach to the *Cornhill*. With Thackeray's
answer came an offer from the *Cornhill's* publishers of £1000
for a three-volume novel, to start when the magazine started
and to run serially. The price was nearly double that already
agreed with Chapman for the unfinished *Castle Richmond*; the
opportunity of starring throughout the first year of the new
magazine was a dazzling one. But there were only six weeks

allowed before a considerable portion of the book must be
ready for the printer, and during that six weeks the Trollope
household must remove to Waltham Cross. A man less
trained to work, and one less accustomed to taking clear and
rapid thought, might have shrunk from the test or missed its
true significance. Trollope, however, realised instantly that
his chance had come; he knew also that he had strength and
power of concentration sufficient for the task. Without a
moment's hesitation he hurried to England, and having
listened to the specification of the kind of tale Smith, Elder
wanted for their magazine, made his agreement with them.
Travelling back from London to Ireland on the night of
November 4 1859, he wrote the first few pages of his book;
seven weeks later there appeared in the first number of the
Cornhill the first instalment of *Framley Parsonage*. From the
opening words the novel found instant and enormous popularity. The *Cornhill* prospered, the publishers smiled, Thackeray
glittered with self-forgetful glee. As for Trollope, his name
and fortune were made. But in his later references to this
brave taking-at-the-flood of Fortune's tide he shows no trace
of vanity, giving, indeed, all the credit for his and the magazine's success to Thackeray's name and keeping for himself
only a few words of the self-mockery he loved.

I will not say that the story was good, but it was received
with greater favour than any I had written before or
have written since. I think that almost anything would
have been then accepted coming under Thackeray's editorship. . . .
The service of almost any English novelist might have
been obtained if asked for in due time. It was my readiness
that was needed rather than any other gift. . . . Thackeray
had himself intended to begin with one of his own great
novels, but had put it off till it was too late. *Lovel the
Widower* was not substantial enough to appear as the principal joint at the banquet. Though your guests will undoubtedly dine off the little delicacies you provide for them,
there must be a heavy saddle of mutton among the viands.

I was the saddle of mutton. My fitness lay in my capacity for quick roasting.[1]

Thackeray acted towards his new contributor with characteristic generosity. In the first of the *Roundabout Papers*, which served as declaration of faith in the first number of the magazine, he made the following charming reference to Trollope:—

> Novels having been previously compared to jellies—here are two (one perhaps not entirely saccharine and flavoured with an *amari aliquid* very distasteful to some palates)—two novels under two flags, the one that ancient ensign which has hung before the well-known booth of *Vanity Fair*; the other that fresh and handsome standard which has lately been hoisted on Barchester Towers. Pray, sir or madam, to which dish will you be helped?

It has been said that his establishment at Waltham Cross brought Trollope for the first time into the society of persons of his kind. Hitherto his exile in Ireland, broken only by brief stays in London when going or coming from abroad, had kept him to an unusual degree apart, not only from literary persons, but from the men and women of every kind who, belonging to his social world, would normally have been his intimates. Now, however, he had easy access to London and, by the hazard of his early connection with the *Cornhill*, ideal sponsors for his introduction to that group of writers, artists, thinkers and dilettanti who ruled one part at least of the intellectual roost of 1860. That no time was lost in turning the social opportunity to good account was mainly due to the generous kindness of George Smith.

This remarkable man, for over fifty years the despot of the great publishing house of Smith, Elder & Co., entered his father's office in 1843 at the age of nineteen. He began almost immediately to make his mark on the list of the firm's publications. The very first book he secured was R. H. Horne's curious compilation *The New Spirit of the Age*. He passed on to a

---

[1] *Thackeray.* (" English Men of Letters.") London, 1879.

publishing connection with Leigh Hunt; to an issue of the
collected novels of G. P. R. James; to friendship (private and
practical) with G. H. Lewes, Dr. Mahony, Ruskin, Thackeray
and Mrs. Gaskell; to the excited discovery of *Jane Eyre* in
manuscript; and so to the invention and launching of the
Cornhill. He died in 1901, having lived to see the realisation
of his last and greatest project the *Dictionary of National
Biography*.

George Smith was supreme among the great Victorian
publishers for his uncanny skill in contriving at the same time
personal friendship and smooth business relations with the
authors and artists in whose work he dealt. His reminiscences
(in part published in a volume prepared for the firm of Smith,
Elder and issued privately) [1] form a fascinating record of the
life, struggles and achievements of a man who was a real
publisher, and who lived through the now fabulous years of
nineteenth-century England. He was, of course, immensely
helped in the building up of his position by the fact that he had
great wealth from other sources than from publishing. With
this money at his command he entertained lavishly, paid high
prices for work which took his fancy, and never haggled. But
he knew how to use wealth wisely, and no money-power could
have secured—as did his personal judgment, taste and generosity—the continuing friendship of the large group of writers
and of painters who collected round him.

To be accepted by George Smith so soon after his establishment in England was for Trollope a rare piece of good fortune.
From the very first the publisher showed his genius for management of men by engaging J. E. Millais to illustrate (from its
third instalment onward) his new author's serial. Trollope
had a great admiration for Millais. [2] This admiration he happened to express to Smith, but not until after *Framley Parsonage*
had pledged its first two numbers to appear unillustrated in the
magazine. Smith, without a word, arranged with Millais for

---

[1] *The House of Smith, Elder*. London. Privately Printed, 1923.
[2] The admiration had developed from what had been originally a rather
critical appreciation of the artist's talent. In Chapter XIV of *The Warden* there is
reference to " a singularly long figure of a female devotee by Millais."

a series of wood-engravings to accompany the later portions of the story. Tact had its reward; Trollope was entranced, and never forgot the dexterous thoughtfulness which at once embellished his story, gratified a secret ambition, and won for him one of the dearest of his personal friends. Here are two short letters written by him to Smith, the first sent in ignorance of the identity of a just-promised illustrator, the second showing his pleasure when that identity had been revealed:—

> *Waltham Cross.*
> *20 Jan.* 1860.

I think the scene most suited to an illustration in part 3 of *Framley Parsonage* would be a little interview between Lord Boanerges and Miss Dunstable. The lord is teaching the lady the philosophy of soap bubbles, and the lady is quoting to the lord certain popular verses of a virtuous nature. The lord should be made very old, and the lady not very young. I am afraid the artist would have to take the description of the lady from another novel I wrote called *Doctor Thorne*.

And then, three weeks later:—

> *Cambridge.   Feb.* 12 1860.

Should I live to see my story illustrated by Millais nobody would be able to hold me.

The publisher's next contribution to the advantage of his new and ardent author was to invite him to a *Cornhill* dinner.

It was in January 1860 [says Trollope in the *Autobiography*] that Mr. George Smith gave a sumptuous dinner to his contributors. It was a memorable banquet in many ways, but chiefly so to me, because on that occasion I first met many men who afterwards became my most intimate associates. . . . It was at that table and on that day that I first saw Thackeray, Sir Charles Taylor—than whom in later life I have loved no man better—Robert Bell, G. H. Lewes and John Everett Millais. . . . Also Albert Smith, for the first and indeed for the last time, as he died soon after;

Higgins, whom all the world knew as "Jacob Omnium";
Dallas, who for a time was literary critic to *The Times*;
George Augustus Sala and FitzJames Stephen.

George Smith has also left a record of this same evening's
entertainment, which adds — and so noticeably that one
wonders whether it was not done on purpose—a flavour
of astringency to Trollope's own uncritical enthusiasm. It is
certainly possible that Trollope—always a little aggressive in
his desire to conquer shyness and, maybe, at this moment
excited by his recent triumphs into a more than normal self-
assertiveness—bore himself at this first introduction into the
inner ring of Thackeray intimates with a bounce and a noisiness
that caused a momentary offence. It is equally possible that
the host, a little ruffled by the stranger's boisterous *sans gêne*,
was not reluctant to observe and memorise an incident which
seemed a snub, which was in fact only an unfortunate coincidence. In any case, here is the anecdote, which calls up so
vividly the embarrassment of poor Trollope that it is hard to
read it, even long after the event, without a squirm of sympathy:—

> We lightened our labours in the service of the *Cornhill*
> by monthly dinners. The principal contributors used to
> assemble at my table in Gloucester Square every month
> while we were in London; and these "*Cornhill* dinners"
> were very delightful and interesting. Thackeray always
> attended, though he was often in an indifferent state of
> health.
> At one of these dinners Trollope was to meet Thackeray
> for the first time and was greatly looking forward to an
> introduction to him. Just before dinner I took him up to
> Thackeray and introduced him with all the suitable *empresse-
> ment*. Thackeray curtly said, "How do?" and, to my
> wonder and Trollope's anger, turned on his heel! He was
> suffering at the time from a malady which at that particular
> moment caused him a sudden spasm of pain; though we,
> of course, could not know this.
> I well remember the expression on Trollope's face at that

moment, and no one who knew Trollope will doubt that he *could* look furious on an adequate—and sometimes on an inadequate—occasion! He came to me the next morning in a very wrathful mood, and said that had it not been that he was in my house for the first time, he would have walked out of it. He vowed he would never speak to Thackeray again, etc. etc. I did my best to soothe him; and, though rather violent and irritable, he had a fine nature with a substratum of great kindliness, and I believe he left my room in a happier frame of mind than when he entered it. He and Thackeray became after close friends.

George Smith's reminiscences pass to another incident connected with the *Cornhill* dinners, in which Trollope is concerned less pitiably than blamefully. This incident has already been referred to as an element in the quarrel between Trollope and Edmund Yates.

There appeared in a New York paper an article signed by Edmund Yates disparaging the *Cornhill Magazine*, declaring it a failing property and telling (inaccurately) an anecdote of one of the private dinners at Smith's house. This anecdote was so related as to throw ridicule alike on Thackeray and on Smith. The *Saturday Review* took up both article and anecdote and, mainly out of hostility to Smith, enlarged so cruelly upon them as to give real pain to several of the persons concerned. Thackeray's *Roundabout Paper*: "On Screens in Dining Rooms" [1] was written as the *Cornhill* response to the *Saturday's* attack, and the *Pall Mall Gazette* (when later it came into existence) took up the quarrel on its proprietors' behalf.[2]

Smith concludes his story thus:—

Shortly after the *Saturday Review* article appeared Trollope walked into my room and said that he had come to confess that *he* had given Yates the information on which his article was founded. He expressed the deepest regret. I am afraid I answered him rather angrily. Trollope, however, took it

---

[1] "Roundabout Papers." No. VI. *Cornhill*, August 1860.
[2] There was published in the *Pall Mall Gazette* during February 1865 a bitter attack on Yates under the name of "Neddy Yapp."

very meekly, and said: "I know I have done wrong, and you may say anything you like to me."

This disagreeable incident is of real significance to an understanding of Trollope's at that time innocent worldliness. He knew more than the average person of his age and kind of the technique of daily life about the world; but of the unwritten laws of polite society—having for so long lived outside of it— he was strangely ignorant. To talk at random of incidents that took place at a private dinner was of itself of dubious discretion; to talk of them to a journalist was dangerous; to talk of them to such a journalist as Yates, whose bitter enmity to Thackeray was common knowledge, was sheer insanity. Why, then, did Trollope do it? The deed can be explained, though not excused. That he committed an error of judgment and of taste cannot be denied. Flushed with the wine of his own natural vanity (for to be invited to the *Cornhill* table was no trivial matter), he let his tongue wag and, as it proved, disastrously. On the other hand (and here appears the naïveté of inexperience), he did not realise the implications of such seemingly casual entertainments as the *Cornhill* dinners. He never conceived it possible that a man of his own kind could so cherish a personal jealousy as to sacrifice to it the loyalties of friendly conversation and to betray in print the pleasant informalities of a dinner party in a private house.

Poor Trollope! He had a rude awakening. His social ignorance had led him into a ditch wider and wetter than ever lurked for him beyond an Essex fence.

In the end good came out of evil. Smith liked and respected him the more for his sturdy acknowledgment of guilt; Thackeray bore no malice; and he himself learnt two new lessons from life—that even "fellows like oneself" can still be Yateses, and that by London usage a friendly gathering of men of intellect is like a club, in that it imposes a duty of discretion upon all its members.

VI

TROLLOPE AT WALTHAM throve equally in authorship and in personal contentment. Indeed the one was consequent upon the other, seeing that hard work was his road to happiness and, therefore, work well done a happiness achieved. By 1860 he had got into his stride, and through the prosperous, ardent 'sixties went (as one critic has ingeniously said) "trolloping" along from day to strenuous day. The years to 1869 were not, perhaps, busier than many of their predecessors; but they were more rhythmically productive. No more time was wasted over tasks unsuited to his talents; not a story was written, not a novel planned and finished, not a journey taken, enjoyed and used for copy, but went to strengthen and to amplify the solid, profit-bearing body of his literary work.

Until the end of 1860, he was writing *Castle Richmond* and *Framley Parsonage* concurrently. In July he began *Orley Farm* and, while this long novel was in the making, found time also for short-story writing, for planning future undertakings, for putting his new house in order and (one presumes) for surveying the postal arrangements of the Eastern counties.

A series of letters to George Smith reveal many of his literary preoccupations. The first refers to a proof of *Framley Parsonage*:—

Waltham. 2 *April* 1860.

Look at page 18—and chapter 15 in the revise, and see what the printer has done for me by changing a word in one line instead of in the one below. Utterly destroyed the whole character of my own interesting personage! If he don't put the word back I shall resign.

Then follows a proposal to which Smith showed no favour. Perhaps the rash hint of an analogy to *Brown, Jones and Robinson* was of itself enough to prevent a realisation of the Italian story:—

Garland's Hotel,
Suffolk Street.
8 *May* 1860.

Touching the story for the *C[ornhill]* *M[agazine]* wanted for six numbers, I think I could do one that would not be known as mine by intrinsic evidence. I have the story— that is to say the plot; but the scene is laid in Italy. In such case it would be indispensable that I should know at once, as I shall myself be going to Florence this month, if this committee be brought to an end. I fancy the Italian story would be less easily recognised than *Jones, Brown &* R. [sic]. My belief, however, is that these things always get abroad. If you really think of either let me know at once.

The story was never written, nor did Trollope go to Italy until October. He was still at home in June, wrestling with the proofs of *Framley Parsonage* and considering a proposal that he should visit India and write such a book as that already produced on the West Indies.

Smith, who had proposed the Indian book, had suggested that he call on Trollope and discuss the project. Trollope writes:—

Waltham.
28 *June* 1860.

I will be at the Post Office at any time at which you will say that you will call. Let me have a line to say when—— Make your man ring at the private door (? private!)— nearest to the gates at the South end, *i.e.* the end of Newgate Street. I hang out within that door.

The results of the interview are tabulated by Trollope a few days later. He sets forth the terms agreed upon and says:—

G.P.O.
Private.
3 *July* 1860.

C. & H. have accepted all my terms as to the serial. I

therefore am not in a position to accept your proposal on that head.[1]

On the other two matters—the India question and the short story for the Magazine—I would accede to your propositions, if it would suit you to carry them out without the serial.

I should certainly like to do the India book, but will not break my heart if the plan falls to the ground. *Per se* going to India is a bore,—but it would suit me professionally.

Even should you accede, the matter must still remain partly undecided till I learn whether or no I get the leave. I do not think I should have any difficulty.

The Indian project proved abortive. Whether the price offered was not sufficiently attractive or whether (as is more probable) there was opposition to his nine months' absence from the Post Office, the plan was abandoned. Trollope, as he had promised, did not break his heart. The correspondence about *Framley Parsonage* and various minor writings went on its way.

Waltham. 21 *July* 1860.

Many thanks for the Magazine. The Crawley family is very good,[2] and I will now consent to forget the flounced dress.[3] I saw the *very pattern of that dress* some time after the picture came out.

There is a scene which would do well for an illustration. It is a meeting between Lady Lufton and the Duke of Omnium at the top of Miss Dunstable's staircase. I cannot say the number or chapter, as you have all the proofs. But I think it would come in at the second vol. If Mr. Millais

---

[1] Smith had clearly expressed an interest in *Orley Farm*, inquiring whether Chapman & Hall were able to give the story the serial publicity that the *Cornhill* could offer. Indeed the next paragraph suggests that he wished to make the Indian commission conditional on his securing the new long novel. But Trollope, having put the point to Chapman, had been offered publication in monthly numbers prior to book-issue and had accepted.

[2] The illustration appearing as frontispiece to Vol. II of the book-issue.

[3] The illustration facing p. 333 of Vol. I of the book-issue—Lucy Robarts lying on her bed.

would look at it I think he would find that it would answer.[1]
If so I would send him the vol. of *Dr. Thorne* in which there
is a personal description of the Duke of O.

The R. Paper is not so severe as I thought it would be—
but it is better so.[2]

I will sign a dozen of such receipts if your accountant wishes
it—altho' I was told in London last week that a lady denies
that I wrote *F. P.*, claiming to be the author herself. I don't
know what better compliment she could pay to the book.[3]

I have a story, written within the last ten days, about the
Holy Land. I suppose it would not be wanted by you for
the Magazine. It would run to 30 pages and have to be
divided into two—or three if you preferred. But, as I said,
I do not presume it would be wanted, and therefore ask the
question almost idly.

The name is: *The Banks of Jordan.* If you see it or hear
of it elsewhere don't mention it as being mine. Not that I
have any idea of publishing it immediately.[4]

2

At the beginning of October Trollope was in Italy. The
journey proved an eventful one, for it brought him for the first
time face to face with the American girl Kate Field, his affection
for whom glistens like a golden thread—almost the only golden
thread—through the staunch but monotonous pattern of his
mature manhood and his middle age.

---

[1] The suggestion was adopted. The illustration faces p. 254 of Vol. II of
the book-issue.

[2] The paper in which Thackeray commented on Yates' satire on the *Cornhill*
dinner (see above, p. 213).

[3] To this curious incident George Smith refers in his reminiscences. The
case interested Trollope, who made further investigation and found that the
culprit was a hysterical girl in a country town, who conceived the fantastic idea
of gaining local notoriety by claiming to be the author of *Framley Parsonage*,
which story was appearing anonymously in the *Cornhill*. The real writer dealt
very gently with the pretender.

[4] The story ultimately appeared in the *London Review* for January 1861,
entitled: " The Banks of the Jordan." It was republished in the Second Series
of *Tales of All Countries* (1863) under the title " A Ride Across Palestine "
(see above, p. 185).

He never made love to her; he was not that kind of man. But in love with her he certainly was. The result was both curious and interesting. Her beauty and her intelligence provoked him to a heedless gaiety such as normally his great shyness held in check. Writing or talking to Kate Field he forgot embarrassment, so that such evidence of their friendship as remains shows us a Trollope who rarely appears elsewhere.

Kate Field, at the time of her meeting with Trollope, was a girl of twenty. She was the daughter of Joseph M. Field, an actor of some reputation in America and a friend of Edgar Allan Poe. A precocious child, she grew into a schoolgirl of unusual intelligence. Provoking a somewhat overheated affection from a younger sister of her mother's, who had married a rich man and lived in Boston, Kate was introduced during her impressionable 'teens into the literary and artistic society that her adoring aunt collected round her. That from such beginnings she should have developed first into a *Schwärmerin* for all the arts, then into a blue-stocking, and finally into a champion of woman's rights was well-nigh inevitable. Her achievement lay in the retention—despite her somewhat grim preoccupations—of an allurement and freshness which impressed all and enslaved not a few of those who made her acquaintance.

It is in itself proof of her amazing charm that, possessing as she did all that Anthony Trollope most disliked in the way of feminine enthusiasms, she could yet make a conquest of him. She it was to whom he referred, when in his *Autobiography* he wrote:—

There is a woman, of whom not to speak in a work purporting to be a memoir of my own life would be to omit all allusion to one of the chief pleasures which has graced my later years. In the last fifteen years she has been, out of my family, my most chosen friend. She is a ray of light to me, from which I can always strike a spark by thinking of her. I do not know that I should please her or do any good by naming her. But not to allude to her in these pages would amount almost to a falsehood. I could not write truly of myself without saying that such a friend had been vouchsafed to me. I trust she may live to read the words I have now written, and to wipe away a tear as she thinks of my feeling while I write them.

Also, it may be suspected, he had Kate Field and himself in mind when in old age he wrote that short (and wrongly disregarded) tale *An Old Man's Love*, which tells of the fondness —half protective and half passionate—of a man of fifty for a girl some thirty years his junior.

In January 1859 Kate Field had sailed from the United States to Italy to study music and art in Rome and in Florence. Her uncle and aunt came with her (they were later replaced by her mother), and it was not long before she was friendly with all the leading English and American settlers in Italy—among whom, naturally, were Tom Trollope and his cultivated wife.[1] She made the tour of Florentine reception rooms as Anthony had done two years before; but, unlike Anthony, she had the enthusiasms, the pliability and above all the youthful beauty to make her at once and permanently a welcome guest. The Brownings, Isa Blagden, and of course Landor (she earned her poem from that foolish sage within a short year of her arrival in Italy) fussed and fêted her; but no amount of flattery nor the companionship of literary and artistic eminence could make her other than she was—an eager, candid, clever girl, interested in everything and everybody, natural and vigorous. One night in October 1860 Theodosia Trollope gave one of her agreeable parties, at which her brother-in-law was present. A few days later Kate wrote a letter home:—

> Mr. Anthony Trollope is a very delightful companion. I see a great deal of him. He has promised to send me a copy of the *Arabian Nights* in which he intends to write, "Kate Field from the Author," and to write me a four-page letter on condition that I answer it.

---

[1] It is curious, seeing how often Kate Field refers to the Tom Trollopes in her letters and diaries and how regularly she frequented their house, that Tom Trollope himself hardly mentions her in his reminiscences.

He fulfilled his promises. A letter to George Smith shows how the *Arabian Nights* was secured, and reveals Trollope as an unofficial literary agent for his brother's friends in Florence:—

> *Waltham.*
> *Nov. 10 1860.*

MY DEAR SMITH,

I shall be in London on Tuesday and will call to settle the important question as to the young lady's copy of the *A. Nights.* Will you kindly send in to Milroy telling him not to pack the box till I call?

Thanks for the letter about Miss Blagden's book. I do not suppose you will make a fortune by it; nor, I suppose, will she. Can you say when it will be published? And also can I tell her that she may have the sum which the American publisher will give for sheets? Do not forget that she wants to describe the novel as by IVORY BERYL.

I have completed *Mrs. Talboys.* My wife, criticising it, says that it is ill-natured. I would propose you should call it: *Mrs. General Talboys.* I hope and trust that there is not and never has been any real General of that name. If so, we must alter it.[1]

The four-page letter to Kate Field (apart from a slight and regrettable mutilation) was as follows:—

> *Waltham Cross.*
> *November 15 1860.*

MY DEAR MISS FIELD,

I have fulfilled my promise as far as the *Arabian Nights* are concerned, having seen a copy put into the box which is to take out to Beatrice [2] her saddle. I hope it will do you

---

[1] This story, which was rejected for the *Cornhill* and published in February 1861 in the *London Review*, Trollope describes in another letter as " among the most inward of my inward things, no one being privy to it but my wife." Presumably it contained an element of portraiture and from models recently observed. Nevertheless it was published three years later in book form and over its author's name, in the Second Series of *Tales of All Countries*.

[2] Daughter of Tom and Theodosia Trollope. She later married Charles Stuart-Wortley (Lord Stuart of Wortley) and died in 1881 leaving one daughter.

good mentally and morally. (I saw yesterday over a little school this announcement put up—"In this establishment morals and mentals are inculcated"; and if your education be not completed, I would recommend you to try a term or two. The mentals may be unnecessary, but the morals might do you good.) Don't attempt to read them—the A^n N^{ts}—through at a burst, but take them slowly and with deliberation and you will find them salutary.

I am beginning to feel towards you and your whereabouts as did your high-flown American correspondent. Undying art, Italian skies, the warmth of southern, sunny love, the poetry of the Arno and the cloud-topt Apennines, are beginning again to have all the charm which distance gives. I enjoy these delicacies in England—when I am in Italy in the flesh, my mind runs chiefly on grapes, roast chestnuts, cigars, and lemonade. Nevertheless let me counsel you in earnest not to throw away time that is precious. If in some few years time you shall hear and read of precious things in Florence which then you do not know, you will not readily forgive yourself in that you did not learn to know them when the opportunity was at your hand.

Give my love to Miss Blagden. I shall write to her as soon as I can answer her letter.

Remember me most kindly to "Cleopatra"—to whom, by the bye, I propose to send a very highly bred asp, warranted of unadulterated poison. Recommend her to that picture of Guido's with reference to the elegant use of the animal. Tell her also and tell yourself that I shall be delighted to see you both here when homesickness takes you away from Florence. Not that it is homesickness with you in the least. [Letter cut away.]

I do not in the least know your address—so send this to the care of my brother. "Kate Field, near the Pitti" might not reach you.

Here, for the time being, the nascent intimacy paused. It was to revive and progress during 1861, when Trollope himself visited America; in the interval he resumed his writing, his Surveyorship, his hunting and his steady exploration of the London social scene.

It was during the first six months of 1861 that he became a member of the Garrick Club. His election and his rapid acceptance by the club's governing clique was a direct consequence of his *Cornhill* success and of Thackeray's friendship. After the Yates–Thackeray quarrel and the secession of the Dickens party, the author of *Esmond* and his two friends, Sir Charles Taylor and Henry de Bathe, became club autocrats. All three met the new member with welcoming kindness, and Trollope came very quickly to regard the Garrick as a place where awaited him that comradeship and easy friendliness of men which throughout his life he had plaintively desired. "The Garrick Club" he says "was the first assemblage of men at which I felt myself to be popular." This fact alone would explain his continuing fondness for its hospitality. He became, as time went on, a faithful and contented member of several clubs; he developed the "club" talent—a casual jollity, a certain self-assurance and that species of uncritical good-humour which allows a man to exchange platitudes unblushingly with his fellows; but no club, either as a social meeting place or as a congenial card-table, ever rivalled the Garrick in his affections. It is fitting that his portrait—painted by his friend Henry O'Neil and presented to the club—should hang on one side of the fireplace in the little smoking-room in Garrick Street, while on the other hangs that of his friend and mentor Thackeray.

In the meantime, and without interruption, his unpicturesque but highly practical correspondence with George Smith continued briskly.

The letters which compose this correspondence may be individually trivial, but the abrupt spatter of their succession —they assail the office in Cornhill from every corner of the Eastern Counties—gives a vivid impression of Anthony's machine-gun methods of dealing with the rapid production and marketing of literary work.

On November 25 he writes his opinion on a new number of

the magazine: "Ariadne began finely, but waxes sloppy and commonplace towards the end. Maria has watched for her lover with red eyes almost once too often."

On Jan. 26 1861: "Thank you for your check" [for an occasional article in a recent issue]. "For such a subject the payment is more than liberal. Indeed I consider it so high for 'padding' that I ought to make it known to the *Saturday*. You have *three novels* this time!" [running concurrently in the *Cornhill*]. "Very depressing for the padding trade."

On February 8 1861 he refers to his lecture on the Civil Service which was so unpopular with the authorities at St. Martin's: "The *Civil Service Gazette*, I think I may say, did *not* report the lecture . . . I shall probably call to-morrow between one and two; but you are always eating little plates of cold meat or pork pies at that time."

On March 31, after unsuccessful attempts to see George Smith, he says: "It is not your holidays that make you difficult of access, but that double counting-house [at 65 Cornhill and at 45 Pall Mall]—at each of which you spend ten minutes ten times a day, living the best part of your life in cabs."

On June 26, in response to a suggestion for a new long novel for the *Cornhill* (the negotiation ended in the writing of *The Small House at Allington*), he writes:—

> I should like to have a little chat with you about your proposition. There are two drawbacks to your offer. In the first place you want the copyright. And in the second place, you will, I presume, wish to extend the publication over a considerable time.
>
> Presuming the novel to be intended for the magazine— which would be the manner of publication which I should prefer—it would extend over 20 months. The money stretched over that time, with an interdict against other writing of a similar class, would, as you will see, not come to so much as it looks.
>
> Also you will get your quid piecemeal. But I will have my quo in a lump when it is finished.

The negotiation, completed on July 6, met Trollope's re-

quirements in full. He was to receive his payment in instalments as each section of the story made its serial appearance,
and no mention was made of an interdict on other writing
during a stipulated period.

3

On June 15 Trollope had finished *Orley Farm*; on June 23 he
had resumed work on the long-abandoned initial fragment of
Brown, Jones and Robinson. On August 3 he wrote the last
words of that extravaganza; and on August 24 he sailed for
the United States in the "Arabia." He explains in the *Autobiography* that interest in the Civil War revived an old project
for a journey to America which would enable him to write a
book as his mother had done, but a book more judicious and
less provocative. "My mother had seen what was distasteful
in the manners of a young people" he says "but had hardly
recognised their energy." With the laudable desire to redress
the balance in the favour of "our cousins over the water" (the
cliché is his own) he applied to the Postmaster-General for nine
months' leave of absence. " 'Is it on the plea of ill-health?'
he asked, looking into my face, which was then that of a very
robust man. I told him I was very well, but that I wanted to
write a book." The leave was granted.

' Trollope made his agreement with Chapman & Hall and set
out on his journey. His wife accompanied him. One of the
first American women she encountered, noting the name upon
her bag, asked if she had altered her opinion of God's Country.
Mrs. Trollope explained that, having been ten years of age at
the time that *Domestic Manners* was written, she could not be
held guilty of the book's discourtesy. But the lady insisted.
"I guess you wrote that book" was all she said.

Of the itinerary and actual happenings of the American trip
the two huge volumes of *North America* give an entertaining
account; [1] of Trollope's views on the causes and progress of

---

[1] Especially worthy of notice are the passages which reveal with humorous
good sense the author's likes and dislikes when travelling, and the chapter
on American hotels.

H

the war, these volumes (and the *Autobiography*) equally remain as evidence.

But from the months of touring survive also the letters written to Kate Field. Just before starting for America he had written to her in Florence. She had replied that her return home was imminent. With the half-hearted prudence of one who longed to see her in America, he urges her to remain in Italy till things become more settled:—

Waltham Cross.
Aug. 9 1861.

MY DEAR KATE,

The great distance, added to my bald head, may perhaps justify me in so writing to you. I thank you heartily for your letters, one of which I have already sent off in a note from myself begging that rooms may be kept for us in the Tremont House.

Has not this battle been terrible? The worst of it is, that by no event could a stronger presage of long bloodshed be given. Had the Southerners been thrashed it would have led to some compromise; but victory on the part of the Southerners can lead to none. It is very sad, and one cannot but feel that the beginning of the end has not yet come.

You were thinking of returning. But as you say nothing about it, and as I hear nothing of it from others, I suppose your plans are altered. I can not but think that Florence is at present the better residence for you.

But the Fields held to their plan and by October were in Boston. Kate wrote to Anthony, announcing their arrival. He replied:—

New York.
November 5 1861.

MY DEAR KATE,

I am amused by the audacity of your letter. Ever since we have been here we have been abusing you for not keeping your word. You told us that we should find you in

the neighbourhood of New York. That you would let us
know your address there or thereabouts. And that we were
to trust to you to meet us—not at Boston, but New York.
Now you turn upon us as tho' we were to blame.

However, we will forgive you on condition that you
remain at the address named till next Tuesday—this day
week. We shall reach Boston that evening, and will seek
you out very soon. I suppose you could not come up to
us that evening?

You write about not sending my wife home as tho' she
were as free from impediments in this world as your happy
self. She has a house, and children and cows and horses and
dogs and pigs—and all the stern necessities of an English
home. How could a woman knock about in winter, as we
have both done during the autumn? But we shall be a
fortnight in Boston and I do hope we may have a good time
of it. I can assure you that in looking forward to it, I do
count not a little on you. I have been real angry with you
this week for not turning up.

The travellers spent their fortnight in Boston, travelled New
England, crossed the border into Canada and back again, and
were in Washington by mid-December. Trollope sends Kate
Field a letter highly typical of his love of self-caricature.

> 305 *I Street*
> *Washington.*
> *Dec.* 17 1861.

MY DEAR KATE,

You will be surprised to hear from me again so soon,
but I want to know whether that lecture which we heard
from Everett at Roxbury has been published; and if so I
want to get it. Can you let me know?

I am in a lamentable position. I have an anthrax on my
forehead and can not get out of the house. I have been to
see no one since I came here and am all alone in my lodgings.
A doctor has chopped it across twice, as you see in the
following picture.

The cross chops. But the healing and the collected itself come out. To-be chopped chops contused healing.  means the two chops will keep thing which has inside will not morrow it is to again and the to prevent them All this is unpleasant, especially as I am anxious to get out and see the people before war is declared.[1] I wish you were here to condole with me and get yourself scolded.

MY FOREHEAD.

There will be war if those two horrid men are not given up.[1] I wish Wilkes and his whole cargo had gone to the bottom. I am no lawyer, but I felt from the first that England would not submit to have her ships stopped and her passengers hauled about and taken off. The common-sense of the thing is plain, let all the wigged fogies of the Admiralty courts say what they will. Because you quarrel with your wife nobody else is to be allowed to walk the streets quietly.

I expect we shall be in Boston before long, shaking hands with you and embracing and crying, as I get on board the Cunard boat with my head tied up in a huge linseed poultice —as it is now.

Tell me about the lecture.

At the turn of the year Mrs. Trollope went home. It had always been intended that she should return to England about Christmas; her husband wished for his book's sake to venture into districts too remote and dangerous to offer suitable winter-travelling for a woman. When, therefore, Anthony next writes to Kate Field, he is alone in Washington.

The letters which follow mark a new stage in their relationship. Hitherto he has been progressing slowly from playful

[1] Trollope refers to war between the United States and England which at that time seemed inevitable. " Those two horrid men " are Slidell and Mason, the Southern envoys who were taken off a British ship on the high seas by Commodore Wilkes, acting on Lincoln's orders.

friendliness to real intimacy. Now he is aware that he is as fond of this girl as though she were his own daughter, and with the extra element of fondness that non-relationship can give. He can have a care for her future and ambitions for her success with, at the same time, the romantic thrill of watching and guiding the career of a young woman, whose only claim on him is a claim on the affections.

His letters now assume a tone of loving discipline. She has naturally confided her plans for authorship; he, as naturally, offers the guidance of his own convictions and experience. He takes her literary aspirations seriously, partly for themselves, but even more because he is beginning to dread the influence of lectures and of the idle canvassing of advanced ideas on her young enthusiasms. He sees, with characteristic shrewdness, that she is in danger of becoming an automatic idealist, and tries by a word in season to save the girl he loves from the 'isms and the 'ologies that he abhors.

The attempt was vain. Circumstances made it impossible for his influence to persist. Though Kate Field undertook and achieved much writing of her own, it was never more than mediocre; and with the passing of the years she slid away from the toil of it, becoming the rather tragic figure—talked of, widely known, but with more promise than performance— presented in the last chapters of Miss Whiting's sympathetic memoir. To posterity Kate Field appears as a woman whose devotion to idealism, whose response to nobility of purpose, whose generalised humanity were acknowledged by admirers of two hemispheres. But she sacrificed too much of her feminine personality to become a professional intellectual, and in consequence left behind her little of permanent achievement. That she was in danger of so doing, Trollope foresaw Perhaps, if matters had fallen out differently, he might in his prevision have saved her. But the odds were too much against him; not even his forcefulness could contrive a lifelong cure in a few weeks of daily intercourse and a few years of desultory correspondence.

Early in 1862 began his fight for her salvation:—

Washington.
Jan. 4 1862.

MY DEAR KATE,

All manner of happy new years to you and to your mother.

Why no story? I fear you are idle—that you spend your time in running after false gods—Wendell Phillips,[1] the woman Doten [2] and so on, seeking the excitement of "ultra" ideas and theoretical progress, while you begrudge the work of your brain, and the harder work of your fingers and backbone.

Those lectures are but an intellectual idleness, an apology for sitting without a book to read or a skirt to hem or a sheet to fell instead of with them. You want to go ahead of other folk—you know you do; but you wish to do it lazily; or rather you are lazy in your mode of wishing it. You would whistle for a storm like a witch; but storms now a days will not come for whistling. You must sit down with a trumpet and blow at it till your cheeks would split. If you'll do that, something of a puff of wind will come at last. Now I hope you will find yourself well rated, and will send me your story off hand.

So Slidell and Mason are gone. I will not argue with you about them in a letter. To do so fairly would take hours and pages. Cobden is no statesman—never even tried his hand at statecraft. As for Bright—of course, if he or any other man will re-echo American ideas and American desires, Americans—and you as one—will return the echo again. But he has been alone in England. He did not even dare to make that speech in a large city. But the men are gone, and, thank God, we shall have no war. Do not think that I triumph because they are gone. I only triumph because I need not quarrel with you and yours.

The blaze on my forehead has gone out and I have been starring it about with all my accustomed personal attrac-

---

[1] The prominent Boston abolitionist and lecturer on women's rights.
[2] Lizzie Doten, a New England lady who published several volumes of poems which, she declared, had been dictated to her by spirits.

tions. I have seen most of the bigwigs here except the President, but have not as yet been to the White House. I spent four days in the camp (without washing), and had quite enough of it. I think of leaving this for Harrisburg and Cincinnati on the 12th or 14th.

> Yours always, dear Kate,
> Very affectionately,
>
> A. T.

My love to your mother.

I presume you will have heard from Rose. She was very unhappy on her voyage, having resolved that she would be so. But now is at peace with her cows and pigs. Write to her.

This letter crossed one from Kate Field, enclosing some verses upon which an opinion is asked. That opinion (given in his next letter) reveals an interest in, and a deep respect for, poetry which, coming from Trollope, may be unexpected.

> *Washington.*
> *Jan.* 6 1862.

DEAREST KATE,

I am afraid my verdict about the enclosed will pain you. The lines are not manipulated—not cared for and worked out with patience and long thought as should, I think, be done with poetry. Fine poetry is not, I think, written by flashes.

Poetry should be very slow work—slow, patient, and careless of quick result. That is not your character. Philanthropical ratiocination is your line, not philandering amatory poetising. I will not say that poetry will not come. As you grow older and calmer, and as you learn to think closer and with less of individual blood in your thought, the gift of poetry may come to you. But I doubt that it is to be desired.

Ah me! It gives me such pain to write this. I still believe in you as strongly as ever. I still think that if you will work, you will succeed. But I should have said, *a priori*, that you would do better as a writer of prose than of poetry. I still think so—and advise you accordingly.

I know how bitter this is. You'll say that it isn't, and you'll be good, and then you'll go about for a day or two with a heavy feeling of ill-treatment at your heart:—ill-treatment not from me, but from the world. I know from *much* experience how bitter are the sapient criticisms of our elders on the effusions of one's youth! I too have written verses, and have been told that they were nought. I am very fond of you, and it grieves me to pain you. But that will be no consolation!

You will have understood that my late "jorbation" letter [1] was written before yours came with the pieces of poetry. Take courage, dear Kate, and stick to the story. If you don't like it, do it again. It is a great profession, that of writing, but you must spoil much paper and undergo many doubting, weary, wretched hours. But I do think that you can write good, nervous, readable prose,—and I know that you have a mind capable of putting something into that vehicle.

A week later he writes again:—

Washington.
12 *Jan.* 1862.

MY DEAR KATE,

I have put off your letter and have only one moment to tell you that my address will be St. Louis. I shall be there 23rd of this month, but shall not remain there. You had better now keep your story, as I shall be in a state of turmoil, and heaven knows where in regard to post offices. You speak of causes which prevent your working. Do you mean your health? But you may have troubles and sorrows by the score of which I know nothing. It is so with our dearest friends. But God has been good to me and gives me no grievance of which I cannot speak—unless it might be thought unmannerly to say that I have another horrible carbuncle on the small of my back (if my back has a small).

Your letter to me was written after receipt of my first, but before the receipt of my last. I fear I shall have pained you.

---

[1] See above, the letter of January 4.

The upshot of my criticism was meant to be this—that good work will require hard toil.

Rose writes me in most lachrymose spirits, all my letters from the west having gone astray. I hope they have amused the Post-office officials.

Yours always—just now in great trouble of haste.

A day or two later Trollope left Washington for St. Louis and the West. The letter that follows is the last one to survive of those written during his first American journey and, with another long letter despatched from Waltham soon after the appearance of the book on North America, concludes the first period of the Kate Field correspondence.

Cairo [*Kentucky*]
Feb. 4 1862.

MY DEAR KATE,

I was very glad to get your letter—and your pardon for my criticisms. As I hope to be in Boston by the end of this month, or quite early in March, I will not now say any more about the story. Miss Crow says that you are not well. Is this so? I know that you are not a female Hercules. None but Englishwomen are. But I hope you are not really ill,—or, which is almost worse,—really ailing. If so, I will not bully you again about writing.

I do not like the West. It is well to say it out at once. Boston I do like, and New York. I do not dislike the people at Washington, tho' the town itself is bad. At Philadelphia I could get on very well. But I do not love the Westerners. They are dry, dirty and unamusing. Till I came here I thought St. Louis the dirtiest place in the world; but this place certainly bears the palm.

The discussion of my military adventures I must put off till I see you. I am deep in guns, bombs, shells, mortars and questions of gunpowder generally. Oh, what thieving, swindling, and lying there has been in the management of this war! How your unfortunate country has been plundered! Gunpowder that won't explode—shells that won't

H*

burst. Blankets rotten as tinder. Water put up in oil casks. Ships sent to sea that can hardly hold their planks together! There have been crimes in the North worse even than the sin of Buchanan & Floyd.

If you only want money to go to St. Louis I will not pity your poverty. You are better at Boston. But if it was wanted to carry you to England I would negotiate a loan for you under Mr. Chase's wing among the Crœsuses of Wall Street.

Write me a line, saying how you are, to Niagara Falls Post-office. My kind love to your mother.

Yours affectionately,   A. T.

I had some talk with Elliott [1] about you. "Let her marry a husband," said he. "It is the best career for a woman." I agreed with him—and therefore bid you, in his name as well as my own, to go marry a husband.

How the postscript was received is not recorded. Probably the young lady wrinkled her pretty nose over the fogeyism of her bluff English mentor. Certainly the advice was never taken.

The last, longest, and in some ways most important letter of the series, though at some sacrifice of regular chronology, shall here be transcribed:—

Waltham House,
Waltham Cross.
August 23 1862.

MY VERY DEAR KATE,

I forget when I wrote to you last, but I hope it was not very long ago, and that in writing now I display my own great merit rather than satisfy any just claim of yours. However, I have a very nice long letter from you to answer, and therefore acknowledge that you are a fit *object* for my generosity.

You will not be glad to hear me declare that your dear friend (and my dear friend also) Miss Blagden is a plague.

---

[1] Charles Wyllys Elliott, merchant, author and philanthropist, who founded the Children's Aid Society of New York and was one of the Commissioners for the laying out of Central Park.

She has no idea of business, and in her [word illegible] greatly perplexes those who want to befriend her. She got me to sell a MS. of hers—and then bargained about it with some one else, because she did not get from me a letter by return of post,—she having given me no address! So I have to go back from my word with the publisher! Don't tell her that I grumble, for I don't want to make her unhappy. But she is a plague.

Yes! I was mean not to give you my book [*North America*]. I wrote to you about it before you wrote to me, —blowing me up—which you did with a vengeance——! I *was* mean. I had to buy all the copies I gave, and did not think your beaux—— (I cannot remember how to spell the word) worth 24/-. There! I have owned the fact, and you may make the most of it. But, dear Kate, I would give you ten times twenty-four shillings ten times over in any more pleasant way, fitting for yourself. One gives presentation copies to old fogies and such like. When you write a book, you will of course give one to me. But you are a young lady.—A ring, a lock of my hair, or a rosebud would be the proper present for you, not two huge volumes weighing no end of pounds. Believe me, I should have been wrong to send it to you.

Your criticisms are in part just, in part unjust—in great part biassed by your personal (may I say love?) for the author. The book *is* vague. But remember, I had to write a book of travels, not a book of political essays—and yet was anxious so to write my travels, as to introduce, on the sly, my political opinions. The attempt has not been altogether successful. The book is regarded as readable, and that is saying as much for it as I can say honestly.[1] Your injustice regards chiefly abolition ideals, freedom and such like; on which matters we are poles asunder.

---

[1] The contemporary reviews were many and voluminous, for the theme of the book was a contentious one and the American war in everyone's mind. But whether the critics (as in *Blackwood* for September 1862) attacked Trollope fiercely for his support of the North, or (as in the *Cornhill* for July 1862) repeated with relish his good-humoured sarcasms at American expense, they all agreed that his book was fresh, dexterous and readable as a novel.

What am I to say about your present state? I am not myself so despondent, as it seems to me are many of you Yankees. Things will go worse before you gain your object than I thought they would;—but still you will ultimately gain it.

This conscription is very bad. Was it absolutely necessary? My feeling is that a man should die rather than be made a soldier against his will. One's country has no right to demand everything. There is much that is higher and better and greater than one's country. One is patriotic only because one is too small and too weak to be cosmopolitan. If a country cannot get along without a military conscription, it had better give up—and let its children seek other ties. But I do not on this account despair. It was not to be supposed that in doing so much all should be done without a mistake.

Thanks for your newspapers. They are, however, very bad. I thank you as a friend of mine once thanked his God. "I thanked God" he said "for a quiet night. But he did not give me one wink of sleep!" I say as much to you for the newspapers; but I never can learn anything from them.

We are not going to Italy this autumn, but in the spring. We are building a house,—or making ours larger, and it does not suit to be away. The bricklayers would run away with the forks.

I was thinking to-day that nature intended me for an American rather than an Englishman. I think I should have made a better American. Yet I hold it higher to be a bad Englishman, as I am, than a good American—as I am not. If that makes you angry, see if you would not say the reverse of yourself.

Tell me whom you see, socially, and what you are doing socially and as regards work. I didn't at all understand how you are living, where—with whom—or on what terms. But I don't know that it matters. How little we often know in such respects of those we love dearest. Of what I am at home, you can have no idea;—not that I mean to imply that I am of those you love dearest. And yet I hope I am.

I am not writing at home, or Rose would send her love. I send mine to your mother and my kind regards to your aunt. To yourself—full assurance of true friendship and love. A. T.

Write often.

This letter is full of its writer's characteristic humour. Also it rounds off the American journey, and at the same time closes the first encounter of Trollope with the Anglo-Florentines.

It has also a profound significance to an appreciation of the real Trollope. His remarks on war and patriotism seem tragically apt to a generation which is now, for the second time in thirty years, enduring the evil consequences of ruthless racial ambition. When it is said that Trollope had no loftiness of mind and never wrote or spoke words of majesty, let it be counter-claimed that in a letter written in 1862 he set the truly cosmopolitan mentality at the summit of man's endeavour, declaring a raucous nationalism to be the refuge of the weak. Nor was this attitude really in conflict with what follows in the same letter—namely, that he would himself rather be a bad Englishman than a good American. In daily things Trollope would always insist that a man should be as much himself as is compatible with letting his fellows live as they prefer. He believed in an obstinate individualism, but one subordinate to the general calm of the community. His insistence on sturdy self-sufficiency, joined to his preference for a life without fuss or hysteria, made him an Englishman, and an aggressive Englishman. Nevertheless, even as an Englishman, he clung to the ultimate liberty of the individual, insisted that in no circumstances should government deprive a man of the captaincy of his soul.

FOOTNOTE (1944) TO CHAPTER VI

Brief reference must be made to a curious incident which, in the summer of 1942, caused a slight flutter in Trollopian circles. There was offered in a sale at Sothebys on August 12 the following letter written by Trollope from Waltham Cross in March 1861 :—

MY DEAREST DOROTHEA SANKEY,

My affectionate and most excellent wife is as you are aware still living—

and I am proud to say that her health is good. Nevertheless, it is always well to take time by the forelock and be prepared for all events. Should anything happen to her, will you supply her place—as soon as the proper period for decent mourning is over ? Till then, I am your devoted Servant,

ANTHONY TROLLOPE.

As the date of this letter is almost exactly contemporary with the beginnings of the writer's correspondence with Kate Field, this seems the suitable place for such comment as the matter requires.

My first reaction, after having examined the letter and found it to be undoubtedly genuine, was to regard it either as a sham solemnity addressed to a child or as part of some adult joke to which the key was lost. These suggestions, in support of a letter written by the novelist's grand-daughter, I sent to *The Times*. I added that more details should, if possible, be obtained of the provenance of the letter and the nature of the Album from which, according to the auctioneers, it had been torn.

During the next few weeks attempts were made to obtain these details ; but enquiries were baulked in a way which can only be regarded as suspicious. No identification of Dorothea Sankey was forthcoming ; no description of the Album ; no statement as to how the seller had become possessed of the letter. The affair smelt strongly of a shabby commercialism, as though the explanation could have been quite simple, but that to give it would have destroyed the " scandal-appeal " of the letter and consequently lessened its market price.

Now, two years later, I am sure that one of my original alternative solutions is the true one, and that the former is the more likely. A letter of the kind, written in jest to amuse a little girl, would come quite naturally from a man in his middle forties and from such a man as Trollope.

The other possibility—that the letter was part of a joke—is further-fetched, but nevertheless conceivable. Suppose that Miss Sankey kept an Album, and had the idea of collecting for it as many offers of marriage as she could get her friends to make. Is not this letter just the kind of formal absurdity which, invited to join in the game, Trollope would have written? There is something analogous in his promise of an *Arabian Nights* to Kate Field inscribed " from the Author "—a gay little joke from a mature man of letters to a young girl.

It is in connection with this theory that some knowledge of the other contents of the Album is essential. That knowledge was denied to us.

One thing is certain—the letter was not written seriously and reveals no hidden romance in Trollope's life. The phraseology—a deliberate blend of affectionate address, formal leave-taking and emphatic practicality—is manifestly humorous, and hardly calculated to provoke in a young woman any feeling save amusement.

VII

IT WAS LATE IN APRIL 1862 that Trollope reached home again from the United States. He had completed his book before sailing and despatched the manuscript to Chapman, so that the actual publication almost coincided with his reappearance in England. A book completed was to him a book finally disposed of; he wasted no time either on final polishings or on second thoughts, but left his publisher to launch the craft upon its voyage, and turned his own mind instantly and relentlessly to the designing of another one.[1]

It is certain that a little longer spent on manuscript or on proof would have secured for Trollope a more continuing reputation than he has actually enjoyed. His carelessness in proof-reading has become proverbial, and an author with a greater sense of "craftsmanship" would, on re-reading, have removed much of the prolixity and awkwardness which some-times—though with surprising infrequency considering the conditions of their production—mar his books. But a man can only be himself, and a scrupulous revising Trollope would have been a different Trollope altogether. It is with his books as it was with the man. To appreciate fully the richness of his generosity, the tenderness of his strength, his courage and shrewd sympathy, it was necessary to endure his brusqueness, his loud raillery, his occasional asperity. Similarly, the reader of the novels whose interest can be distracted by clumsiness of fashioning or by garrulity, will never penetrate beneath the rather commonplace surface of the work to the astonishing divination of human nature, to the genial sanity and to the unfailing sympathy that constitute its real quality. Trollope

[1] One of the letters to George Smith provides a good example of this readiness to pass on. In February 1863 he sends the completed MS. of *The Small House at Allington* and adds: "If it quite suits you to let me have the *quid pro quo* I shall be very much obliged." Then, four days later: "Many thanks. All *my* interest in the *S.H. of A.* is now over; you fellows are beginning."

was no Flaubert to fashion patiently a perfect elegance; he was rather, as Nathaniel Hawthorne implied, an urgent, beef and ale-fed giant, hewing raw lumps of England at his generous will and setting them—one after another, all ragged and un-fashioned as they were—under glass cases for the world to see.[1]

But with this ceaseless rough-and-ready productivity went a queer pride in his work's integrity. As the history of *Barchester Towers* has already shown, he would tolerate any criticism of the perfection of his books, but none whatever that charged him with shirking or dishonesty. Thoroughness, punctuality to engagements and reliance on himself were his chief vanities, and he hit out at any one who impugned them. He had written to Edward Chapman from Washington, on New Year's Day 1862, a letter expressing with much force his hatred of one particular form of critical impertinence:—

> You sent me an article on "Mr. Trollope," out of some paper. From what paper was it cut? The author of it criticises my writings, pointing out their weakness, and in so doing follows the proper line of his profession.
>
> But he goes beyond that when he takes upon himself to analyse my motives in writing. His charge is that I write for money. Of course I do;—as does he also. It is for money that we all work, lawyers, publishers, authors and the rest of us. If we do bad work we shall not get paid for it, and I, like others, must feel myself to be governed by that law or else shall fall to the ground. If my work be bad, let him so tell his readers and there his work should end.
>
> But I have worse to say of this critic than that. He insinuates that I have published under my name, the writings of other people. He does not dare to say this; but he said that which is intended to make his readers so believe. This is in every way unfair and cowardly. No man should insinuate

---

[1] Nathaniel Hawthorne wrote, on February 11 1860, to Fields, the Boston publisher: "Have you ever read the novels of Anthony Trollope? They precisely suit my taste; solid, substantial, written on strength of beef and through the inspiration of ale, and just as real as if some giant had hewn a great lump out of the earth and put it under a glass case, with all its inhabitants going about their daily business, and not suspecting that they were made a show of."

such a charge, unless he has strong ground to believe it to be true. This man can have no such ground. To those who know me I need make no assurance that such a charge is false.

Independence and pride in his own integrity had prompted this letter to Chapman; independence and a sense of his duty to contractual engagements sent him, immediately on his return to Waltham, into correspondence with George Smith regarding the long novel for the *Cornhill* agreed upon before he left for the United States. One passage in a letter dated May 2nd 1862 is as follows:—

> I called this morning, but I was a little too early. I *will* change the name, though I cannot as yet say what the name shall be. I will change it as you don't like it, as I myself do not feel strongly in its favour. But I must say that your reason against it as touching Mrs. B. Stowe's novel would not have much weight with me. Am I to eschew pearls because she has got one? Not if I know it.

This paragraph is not without significance. Clearly Trollope had already conceived the main features of the story of Lily Dale and had announced his intention to Smith of calling it "The Pearl of Allington," or perhaps "The Two Pearls of Allington," which remains the title of the second chapter. Clearly the publisher had demurred to the title because Mrs. Beecher Stowe's novel *The Pearl of Orr's Island* was then running serially in England. In his reply Trollope shows himself little pleased that he should yield to a mere woman from America (eight years later, and in circumstances not dissimilar, he is resentful at the dislocation of one of his serials in favour of that "pretentious Frenchman," Victor Hugo), but nevertheless not obstinate beyond the point of commonsense. It is sensible to give way; therefore he gives way. But he will have his grumble first.

With the autumn of 1862 hunting invades already crowded days, and thrusts its way into his business correspondence with George Smith. "I have been very busy. I have been trying to hunt three days a week. I find it must be only two. Mortal man cannot write novels, do the Post Office and go out three days." (November 21) "I have just returned from a hunting campaign in Oxfordshire and have five days to write a Christmas story for *Good Words*." [1] (December 1) "Many thanks for the *Cornhill*. I did make your wife a promise to go down to Brighton, and I am a beast not to keep a promise, the keeping of which would be so pleasurable; but the fact is I have become a slave to hunting;—as men who hunt must do at this time of the year. It is not that I would not willingly give up my hunting for the Wednesday—or even the Wednesday and Saturday—but that engagements get themselves made which will not have themselves broken. As it is I have people here on the Wednesday, and indeed up to I don't know what day—Xmas, I believe—who are all more or less in the boots and breeches line. Mrs. Trollope bids me say that no further persuasion than your own would have been necessary—had she been a free agent. But she is not. A good wife always does head groom on such occasions." (December 4.)

In February he is ill, touched in the liver by that east wind to which in his books he often bitterly refers:—"*The Small House at Allington* is finished. I wish you had my liver just for to-day!" (February 11 1863.) The next letter is subscribed as "given from my bed at Waltham on St. Valentine's Day." Four days later: "Ah me! If I could only have one of those spitted nests of oysters to remind me of what you are doing! For myself, I had a bit of boiled mutton at three, and my wife remarked that she didn't think half a glass of sherry would do me any harm." (February 18.)

Rose Trollope would have had her hands full, nursing this far from docile patient.

2

While he lay abed there came this letter from his friend, Norman Macleod, one of the chaplains to Queen Victoria and editor of the young, though well-established periodical *Good Words*.

[1] It is to be feared that he was late. *The Widow's Mite*, his first tale to be published in *Good Words*, appeared in January 1863.

Adelaide Place,
Glasgow.
Friday.
[*February* 1863]

MY DEAR SIR,

As the Editor of a humble sixpenny Monthly—*Good Words*—I approach you with the respect and reverence becoming a beggar seeking crumbs from a rich man's table. But as Chaplain of the Gaiters, I knock at your door with the boldness of one having authority. Be so good, my son, as to hear your Revd. Father!

You will be waited upon by my publisher Mr. Strahan, as sensible a fellow as I know—truthful, honourable, generous —and with enterprise fit to cement again the American Union.

He wants a story, *i.e.* a novel from you for *Good Words* for 1863. Now please read on and don't pitch this into the fire.

You never perhaps heard of *Good Words*? But Strahan will tell you all about it. Enough, that our circulation is now 70,000—and that *I* am Editor!

You fancy we won't pay up to the mark? Well, name your price to Strahan and hear what he says. As to matters of detail we have time enough to consider these.

Seriously, you and Kingsley are the only men whom I should like to have a story from—and I should feel proud to have you—and one of your best—in my pages. I think you could let out the *best* side of your soul in *Good Words*— better far than ever in *Cornhill*.

Trollope may have smiled or (being liverish) have growled at the final sentence. Only a Scottish divine could without flinching recommend a magazine to Trollope because it offered scope for ventilation of the soul! But with bland righteousness went practical good sense, and Macleod could trail with equal skill the nets of Mammon. His comforting reference to terms caught the attention of the desired contributor.

Trollope had already had one short story published by *Good*

Words [1]; he was acquainted with the editor and not exclusive in his choice of media for publication. An author of a different kind might, in his place, have let a *Cornhill* vanity arm him against this evangelical temptation, for *Good Words* had but a meagre reputation with the intellectuals. Mrs. Oliphant, writing to Blackwood in 1865 about an offer for a serial made to her by Macleod, said: "If you have any dislike to see the name of your contributors [to *Blackwood's Magazine*] in Dr. Macleod's somewhat ragged regiment, I will not think of it further." But Trollope owned no allegiance either to individual publisher or to a private conception of his writer's dignity. He boasted himself a workman, taking such work as came to hand. Wherefore he "named his price" and, the publisher of *Good Words* agreeing, struck the bargain.

On March 3rd he began the story *Rachel Ray*, which was to gratify the admirable Strahan and brighten seventy thousand Sunday afternoons.

But his enrolment in the "ragged regiment" soon led to trouble. *Good Words* blazoned abroad their forthcoming attraction. Instantly their even stricter rival, the *Record*, came on them heavily for a heathen sheet, which published godless works by godless men. Thus:—

> *Good Words* professes to be a journal for every day in the week; that is to say, it professedly contains reading adapted for the Sabbath, and no reading not so adapted. We suppose very few even of its warmest friends and admirers would say that all the contents of the magazine are suitable for Sabbath reading. . . . We doubt if the addition of the names of Messrs. Kingsley and Davies, and Dr. Stanley and Anthony Trollope, will cause very many to buy and read the able papers of such writers as Arnot, Guthrie, and McDuff. That is at the least doubtful. But there is no doubt of this, that under the sanction of the names of these latter, and on their wings, so to speak, the writings of the former are carried home to hearts and minds which without such effective help they never could have reached.   (*Record*. April 1 1863)

---

[1] See p. 242, note.

And a fortnight later:—

> We cannot dilate on the sensation novels of *Good Words*, as we would fain have tried to do at the close of a series of reviews which has already dragged itself out to too great a length. . . . But we have a word or two for Mr. Anthony Trollope, this year's chief sensation writer. To think of the conjunction of names—Anthony Trollope and Dr. Guthrie; John Hollingshead and Dr. David Brown; Drs. Robert Lee and James Hamilton; Adelaide Ann Procter and ——, but we have already gone too far. In some of these trashy tales the most ungodly sentiments are uttered and left to work their evil effects upon the young mind.
>
> (Record. April 13 1863)

Finally on April 20 the attack was pushed home and, in a leading article, *Good Words* roundly accused of serving two masters:—

> We have remarked on what Hooker calls the mingle-mangle which an excellent West End incumbent long ago described as applicable to Dr. Macleod's periodical. We have called attention to the unseemly appearance of such a man as Dr. Guthrie retained to write in concert with a secular novelist such as Mr. Anthony Trollope; to the anomaly of seeing Prof. David Brown, so well known for his writings on Revivals, linked with John Hollingshead, another of the novel writers of the day. The chief of these names have been lately placarded all over London, evidently intended to produce the impression that between men thus co-operating there can be no such impassable gulf as Holy Scripture points out. Does this recall the spirit of the Apostolic times? It would seem as if by means of high retaining fees (largely boasted of and sometimes exaggerated by common fame) the spirited publishers had at last bridged over the impassable gulf, and so united the servants of opposite masters, that the sword which Christ came to unsheath has been put up into its scabbard; that the fire which he came to kindle has been extinguished; that the

offence of the Cross had ceased; that God and Mammon, God and the world, were all reconciled in the Utopian harmony of the genial gospel proclaimed in *Good Words*.

(*Record*.   April 20 1863)

Reading these diatribes Trollope chuckled, hoping for more. That his name in an advertisement should thus embroil the "unco' guid" was agreeable to him.   It was amusing to be cursed for a sensation novelist; he judged it a shrewd thrust on the *Record's* part to charge Macleod with serving God and Mammon.   He worked on busily at his story, and even discussed its illustration with J. E. Millais, who was also a *Good Words* contributor and at that very time doing his famous drawings of the Parables.

But very soon Trollope's detached enjoyment of a quarrel in which he had no direct concern gave place to the indignation of a man disastrously involved.   Macleod, having read the greater part of *Rachel Ray*, woke suddenly to its worldliness. He declined to publish it in his paper, and declared that Strahan should make good all pecuniary loss arising from the breach of contract.   Trollope was torn between disgust at an eleventh-hour morality and satisfaction that the nonconformist conscience should thus admirably have come up to scratch. He wrote to Millais, echoing the *Record's* leading article:—

X (a Sunday magazine) has thrown me over.   They write me word that I am too wicked.   I tell you at once because of the projected and now not to be accomplished drawings.[1] They have tried to serve God and the devil together, and finding that goodness pays best, have thrown over me and the devil.   I won't try to set you against them because you can do parables and other fish for their net; but I am altogether unsuited to the regenerated!   It is a pity they did not find it out before, but I think they are right now.   I *am* unfit for the regenerated and trust I may remain so, wishing to preserve a character for honest intentions.

---

[1] The collaboration was not wholly abandoned.   The first cheap edition of *Rachel Ray* (1864) was furnished with an admirable frontispiece by Millais.

To Strahan the publisher he was severely businesslike:—

Waltham Cross.
June 10 1863.

DEAR SIR,

I am sorry that you and Dr. Macleod have been forced to the conclusion at which you have arrived with reference to my story. I claim for myself, however, to say that the fault in the matter is yours, and not mine. I have written for you such a story as you had a right to expect from me, judging, as you of course did judge, by my former works. If that does not now suit your publication I can only be sorry that you should have been driven to change your views.

I have, as I take it, an undoubted right to claim from you the payment of £1,000 for the story. I do not, however, desire to call upon you for a greater sacrifice than must be made to place me in a position as good as that which would be mine if you performed your agreement and published my story during the next six months. If I publish that story in another form during the autumn,—as I shall do under the circumstances I am now contemplating—I shall get for it £500 less than the sum which I should receive were you to publish it in *Good Words*. That sum of £500 I am willing to accept from you. But you will, of course, understand that in making this offer I reserve my legal right to demand the £1000 should you not accept the proposed compromise.

His protest to the editor has not survived, but two days later (and evidently in reply to a communication of his own) he received Macleod's apology. This is presumably the "letter full of wailing and repentance" to which he refers in the *Autobiography*. But the description is not a very happy one. The minister is vastly self-righteous behind the veil of his facetiousness, and presumes to lecture the author whom he has thrown over. His definition and defence of "fair and reasonable Evangelicalism" deserve to be printed in full. There is especial tartness in the reference to the *Record* and to "God and Mammon."

Glasgow. June 11 1863.

MY DEAR TROLLOPE,

I presume you and Strahan have to-day met, settled accounts, and parted—friends? I resolved, for many reasons, not to write to you until that part of the unpleasant business was over.

As it is now past 12 o'clock it is full time for me to settle, as far as possible, my accounts with you, should I be able to pay only 6*d.* in the pound.

Let me begin my letter by most cordially reciprocating the kind wish with which yours ends, that after this you and I may be as we were. Thank you, my boy, for that! It has removed a burthen from me.

And now a few (?) words in explanation of what induced me with so much reluctance to give up *Rachel Ray. You* are not wrong; nor have you wronged me or my publishers in any way. I frankly admit this. But neither am I wrong! This "by your leave" I deny, and will "stick to my bundle" if my bundle will stick by me. The point is that I misunderstood you, and you me—tho' I more than you have been the cause of the misunderstanding.

What I tried to explain and wished you to see when we met here, was the peculiar place which *Good Words aimed* at occupying in the field of cheap Christian literature. I have always endeavoured to avoid on the one hand the exclusively narrow religious ground—narrow in its choice of subjects and in its manner of treating them—hitherto occupied by our "Religious" Periodicals; and on the other hand to avoid altogether what was either antagonistic to the truths or spirit of Christianity, and also as much as possible whatever was calculated to offend the prejudices, far more the sincere convictions and feelings of fair and reasonable Evangelical men. Within these extremes it seemed to me that a sufficiently extensive field existed in which any novelist might roam and find an endless variety of life and manners to describe with profit to all and without giving offence to any. This problem which I wished to solve did not and does not seem to me a very difficult one, unless for very one-sided "Evangelicals" or anti-evangelical writers. At all events, being a clergyman as well as an Editor—the one from deepest convictions, tho' the other, I fear, from the deepest mistake —I could not be else than sensitive lest anything should appear in *Good Words* out of harmony with my convictions and my Profession. Well then, was I wrong in assuming that you as a Christian worshipper were an honest believer in Revealed Christian truth? I was not! Was I wrong in believing and hoping that there were many truly Christian aspects of life as well as the *canting* and *humbug* ones with which you heartily sympathised and which you were able and disposed to delineate? I was not! Was I wrong in thinking that *Good Words* was a periodical which from its aims and objects afforded you perhaps freer scope for this kind of writing than even *Cornhill*? Perhaps I was wrong in my judgment, and had no ground for hoping that you would give me a different *kind* of story than those you had hitherto published. If so, forgive me this wrong. Possibly the wish was father to the thought. But the thought did not imply that any of your former novels had been false either to your own world within or to the big world without—false to truth or to nature—it assumed only that you could with your whole heart produce another novel which, instead of showing up what was weak, false, disgusting in professing Christians, might also bring out, as has never yet been done, that Christianity as a living power derived from faith in a living Saviour working in and through living men and women, does, has done, and will do what no other known power can accomplish in the world for the good of the individual or of mankind. If no such power exists, neither Christ nor Christianity exist—and if it does, I must confess that most of our great novelists are, to say the least of it, marvellously modest in acknowledging it. The weaknesses —shams—hypocrisies—gloom—of some species of professing Christians are all described and magnified, but what of the genuine human-born Christian element? Why, when one reads of the good men in most novels it can hardly be discovered where they got their goodness. But let a Parson, a Deacon, a church member be introduced, and at once we guess where they have had their badness from! They were *professing* Christians.

Now all this and much more was the substance of my sermon to you at Arran and here—and I thought you would either bring out more fully the positive good side of the Christian life than you had hitherto done, or avoid at least saying anything to pinch, fret, annoy, or pain those Evangelicals who are *not* Recordites.

Now, my good Trollope, you have been, in my humble opinion, guilty of committing this fault—or, as you might say, praiseworthy in doing this good—in *Rachel Ray*. You hit right and left—a wipe (?) here, a sneer there, thrust a nasty *prong* into another place, cast a gloom over Dorcas Societies, a glory over balls till 4 in the morning,—in short, it is the old story—the shadow over the Church is broad and deep, and over every other quarter (?) sunshine reigns— that is the *general impression* which the story gives, so far as it goes. There is nothing, of course, bad or vicious in it— that *could* not be, from you—but quite enough (and that without any necessity from your hand or heart) to keep *Good Words* and its Editor in boiling water until either were boiled to death. I feel pretty certain that you either do not comprehend my difficulties, or laugh in pity at my bigotry. But I cannot help it.

You do me, however, wrong in thinking—as you seem to do—that apart from the structure of your story, merely because of your name I have sacrificed you to the vile *Record* and to the cry it and its followers have raised against you, as well as against me. Before I read your story, I and Strahan had taken a decided stand against such "Evangelical" tyranny and bigotry. As some proof of this I send you a printed copy of a letter written weeks ago to Professor Balfour in Edinburgh, but sent only a few days since. My only pain is that the *Record* will suppose that its attack has bullied me into the rejection of your story!

What you mean by my attempt to serve God and Mammon, I do not understand—for I presume neither you nor the *Record* represent either Deity! I know well that my position is difficult, and that too because I do *not* wish to please both parties, but simply because I wish to produce if possible a Magazine which, tho' too wide for the Evangelicals and too narrow for the anti-Evangelicals, and therefore disliked by both cliques, may nevertheless rally round it in the long run the sympathies of all who occupy the middle ground of a decided, sincere and manly Evangelical Christianity.

I wish I could *say* all this, with such comments as would prevent my words or my spirit being misinterpreted. Please *take* a kindly meaning out of it, and don't give a Recordite meaning to it. But you have had enough of this kind of extempore (out of season?) preaching, and I suppose my sermon, like many others, will leave preacher and hearer very much where they were.

I look forward with sincere pleasure to the Pipe & Baccy with "summ'at to cheer the heart"—for mine is rather sad and heavy after a hard winter's work. I probably intend going to Iceland with George in August. Will you come and light your pipe at Heckler (*sic*) or make your toddy from the Geysers? Let us dispute on the voyage. It will enliven it. There is no chance of your giving in to me. I'll be hanged if I give in to you! So farewell, and light your pipe with my epistle to make it legible and luminous.

Yours sincerely,

N. MACLEOD.

P.S. This letter will keep cold till you are at peace with all the world, with a pipe well filled and drawing well. Read it then—or a bit each day for a month.

The incident was closed. Strahan paid £500; Trollope finished the rejected story by the end of June and it was published in book form during October. The book (as he says) "remains now to speak for itself. It is not brilliant, but it certainly is not very wicked. There is some dancing in one of the early chapters and it was this to which my friend demurred."

Fortunately the friendship survived. Trollope, whose angers never lasted very long, bore no malice, and his contributions to *Good Words* were numerous during the remainder of his writing life. As he would have said, the affair "moulted no feather" between him and Macleod. They saw each other frequently and toured the Scottish hills together. It was perhaps not unfitting that the disagreement should have been thus happily concluded. After all, *The Warden* had been accepted for publication because of its appeal to a dissenting public. . . .

3

The autumn of 1863 saw two deaths—the one of Trollope's mother; the other of Thackeray, his mentor, his literary idol and his friend.

The little letter to Chapman already quoted shows that Frances Trollope's death on October 6 came too suddenly for her younger son to be at her side when the end came. But in itself the death could not have been a staggering blow. She was so old and had for so long been visibly failing, that the passing of her tired and life-scarred spirit came rather as a wistful fulfilment of her sons' expectations than as a sudden grief.

Thackeray's death, on the other hand, which shocked two hemispheres, struck Trollope with peculiar poignancy. He had worshipped the genius for so many years, had come to know and love the man so recently.

> I was going to write to you on another matter [he wrote to George Smith on Christmas day], but have been stopped in that, as in everything, by Thackeray's death.
>
> You will, of course, insert in the next *Cornhill* some short notice of him. Who will do it for you? If you have no one better I will do it gladly. Of course you will know that what I offer is a work of love.
>
> I have not the heart to wish anyone a Merry Christmas.

When Smith accepted the offer of the brief obituary, Trollope wrote:—

Jan. 17 1864

I received together at Norwich on Friday your letters of the 13th and 14th. In the former you propose to insert my paper with papers and verses from Dickens and Lord Houghton, and in the latter you suggest a longer memoir for the March number.

I prefer the former plan. I do not feel up to writing a memoir. I do not personally know enough, and though I might possibly borrow all that can be said from Hannay's excellent article, I do not care to borrow in that way. More of criticism than what I have attempted would, I think, be almost out of place. I have said nothing that I do not think and believe, but if I were to say more, I should perhaps run into rhodomontade or else cool down into ordinary eulogy.

In February 1864 the article appeared:—

It is not so much [it said] that he who has left us was known, admired and valued, as that he was *loved*. He who knew Thackeray will have a vacancy in his heart's inmost casket, which must remain vacant till he dies. One loved him almost as one loves a woman, tenderly and with thoughtfulness. One loved him thus because his heart was tender, as is the heart of a woman.

When in 1879 appeared Trollope's little book on Thackeray —the book which so unhappily, to the modern reader so mysteriously, and (this much is certain) by its author so unwittingly gave offence to Thackeray's family—a further tender and heartfelt tribute was paid to the memory of a dead friend and to a spirit whose surpassing fineness only a being of Trollope's blunt humility could so generously have acknowledged.

The first chapter of this book is biographical and gives a character sketch of the man as he had lingered on in the writer's memory. It contains one passage, characteristic alike of its subject and its author:—

His charity was overflowing. His generosity was excessive. I heard once a story of woe from a man who was a dear friend of both of us. The gentleman wanted something under two thousand pounds instantly; had no natural friends who could provide it, must go utterly to the wall without it. I met Thackeray between the two mounted heroes at the Horse Guards and told him the story. "Do you mean to say that I am to find the £2000?" he said angrily. I explained that I had not even suggested the doing of anything, only that we might discuss the matter. There came over his face a peculiar smile and he whispered his suggestion, as though half ashamed of his meanness: "I'll go half," he said, "if anybody will do the rest."—And he did go half at a day or two's notice.

Such is a typical paragraph of Trollope's essay, written to the glory of Thackeray. He does not say who paid the other half. That too is like him.

At the very end of the chapter are these words:—

Such is my idea of the man whom many call a cynic, but whom I regard as one of the most soft-hearted of human beings, sweet as Charity itself, who went about the world dropping pearls, doing good, and never wilfully inflicting a wound.

When, four years after this monograph was published, Trollope himself died, his old friend John Blackwood turned these words, written for Thackeray, to the honour of the man who wrote them. As Trollope wrote of Thackeray, so was another to write of Trollope.

VIII

GRIEVOUS THOUGH IT WAS, Thackeray's death did Trollope one great service. It gave him the opportunity of "rounding off" at once his personality and his literary position. While Thackeray lived, and however successful or popular a novelist Trollope might have become, he would always have been—and proudly have declared himself to be—only a second in command, only a disciple to a man he venerated.

But with Thackeray's sudden vanishing, there opened several vacancies, to fill which Trollope chanced to be the most likely candidate. There was a vacancy at the Garrick Club; a vacancy in Smith, Elder's list of leading novelists; a vacancy in the hierarchy of living writers as conceived by critics and by public. Trollope succeeded imperceptibly but without challenge to these several thrones. He had now "arrived," and more than arrived. He was no longer a promising youngster, no longer even "in the front rank of our contemporary novelists"; he was "Trollope," and entitled to the uncritical adoration, the contented approval, the jealousy or the contempt which are the reward of fiction writers with a huge and faithful public. "To be known as somebody—to be Anthony Trollope if it be no more—is to me much," he says in the *Autobiography*; and to this eminence he had now attained. He had entered on the final phase of any living literary reputation—the phase when output is regular, prosperous and suavely standardised, when criticism becomes either perfunctory praise for an established master or restless denigration from the rebellious young.

The chronicle of Trollope's life now tends, therefore, to become a mere rhythm of smoothly rolling wheels. The steady calendar of his books lengthens and gains in dignity; he becomes Chairman of the committee of the Garrick Club;

under Rule Two [1] he is elected member of the Athenæum; he visits Millais in the Highlands, Sir Henry James (later Lord James of Hereford) in Kent and Wiltshire, Lord Lytton at Knebworth, Lord Houghton at Fryston. He hunts in winter, travels in Switzerland and Italy in summer and early autumn, lectures about the country, plays his games of whist, and lives untiring, diligent, almost legendary days. He has become the noisy, thriving Trollope of amused, affectionate tradition.

Extracts from letters to George Smith, made somewhat at random, will serve to lighten and reveal his life's industrious monotony.

In the early summer, at his publisher's request, Trollope sat for his portrait to Samuel Laurence. It was one of George Smith's best judged and most appreciated habits as a publisher to cause his leading authors to be pictured at his instigation and expense. In Trollope's case the result was doubly satisfactory, for the experiment produced a delighted novelist and an attractive portrait.[2] It will further be observed from the letters that follow that Smith also presented Trollope with a portrait of Thackeray.

Waltham.
July 1st 1864.

Laurence seemed to think the black ground of the frame too dark; but I daresay he is wrong. *Pray do not have it altered.* I thought it very nice.

Such a week as I have had in sitting! Only that he is personally such a nice fellow and has so much to say for himself, I should have been worn out. I have been six times, or seven, I think,—and am to go again. He compliments me by telling me that I am a subject very difficult to

---

[1] " It being essential to the maintenance of the Athenæum, in conformity with the principles on which it was originally founded, that the annual introduction of a certain number of persons of distinguished eminence in science, literature or the arts or for public services should be secured, a limited number of persons of such qualifications shall be elected by the Committee. The number of persons so elected shall not exceed nine in each year.

[2] Two drawings of Trollope by Laurence survive—one in the possession of the family and reproduced as frontispiece to Escott's book, the other in the National Portrait Gallery.

draw. He has taken infinite pains with it. Of course I
myself am no judge of what he has done.

Waltham.
July 6 1864

This morning we hung Thackeray up in our library, and
we are very much obliged to you for the present,—not only
in that it is in itself so valuable, but more especially because
it is so suited to our feelings. To-day we go into the [new [1]]
Garrick Club and have an initiatory dinner at which as
Chairman I shall propose his memory. I heard yesterday
from Shirley B[rooks] that the Dean of Westminster has
consented to put up a memorial (whether bust or statue is
not yet decided) and the subscription list is now opened. I
have been nervous about this lest the time should slip away.
The next thing will be to have a perfect edition of his works,
—for which we must look to you.

Windermere.
July 16 1864

I'm here, by no means having a holiday,—but working
harder than I ever worked before,—making up for the time
that I was being drawn. I did not tell you, I think, that my
wife liked the portrait *very much indeed*. She seemed to have
a fuller respect for me when she had seen it than ever before.

Freshwater, I. of W.
10 Oct. 1864

I suppose you are back from your Italian wanderings, and
I write a line to thank you—in my wife's name chiefly, but
also in my own—for your glorious present to us of myself,
—done to the life in a wonderfully vigorous manner. When
I look at the portrait I find myself to be a wonderfully solid
old fellow. The picture is certainly a very good picture, and
my wife declares it to be very like, and not a bit more solid

---

[1] Trollope intended a reference to the installation of the club in its new
building (that now occupied) in Garrick Street.

I

than the original. For your munificence we both thank you very heartily, and hope you and your wife will soon come to see it—and the other—in their places.

P.S. Mrs. Macquoid [1] has written to me to ask to dedicate her novel to me. I have written to decline, as I hate such trash.

Early in November the Archbishop of York preached a sermon against "sensation-novelists," and his remarks, which amounted to a general attack on novel reading as a practice pernicious to the young, became the subject of a leader in *The Times*. Trollope, with memories of the *Record* prompting his pugnacity, asked if he might argue in the *Cornhill* that modern fiction of good quality had taken the place of poetry in the cultivation of the mind and was able to teach—though by means less lofty—many of the lessons about life that were formerly learnt from a reading of poetry.

The article was begun but unfortunately never completed. One page of the *Autobiography* (in Chapter XII) summarises his point of view; a lecture entitled "On English Prose Fiction as a Rational Amusement," written about 1870 and privately printed for his own convenience, develops more fully what he calls "an apology for my profession." But a *Cornhill* essay would have given better scope and publicity than either of these to a defence of his craft, which defence would not have lacked application at any time.

The year 1865 saw George Smith's second great periodical venture. Thackeray had used to speak of an imaginary paper called the *Pall Mall Gazette*, and under this title, with Frederick Greenwood as editor, a paper now appeared. Trollope was of the inner ring of its promoters. He had finished *The Claverings* for *Cornhill* serial at the end of December 1864, and set to work at once on a series of hunting sketches for publication at frequent but irregular intervals in the new paper, which was

---

[1] Katherine Macquoid, a prolific library novelist. The book she wished to dedicate was *Hester Kirton*.

at first published twice daily. The hunting sketches grew tedious to him. On March 12 he writes:—

> I send back the proof of "The Master of Hounds" and I send a paper on "How to Ride to Hounds." That shall be the last of the set, and I don't think I'll write another word about hunting. I had given you credit for ordering the "Sportswoman's" letter.

The final words refer to a letter contributed to the *Pall Mall* in praise of one of Trollope's articles; in this trivial matter, as in so much else, he shows the scepticism of his genuine humility. Yet three days later the pride which partnered his self-depreciation asserts itself:—

> Will you kindly ask your assistants in Salisbury Street *not* to alter my MS.? Let them send back or omit to use any paper that is unsatisfactory, and I will not even ask the reason. But don't let one be altered.

On March 31 he makes a characteristic comment on a suggested illustration for *The Claverings*:—

> The drawing, which I return, is very spirited, pretty and good. But the horse is faulty. He is too long. Look at the quarters behind the girl's seat. And your artist has made the usual mistake of supposing that a horse goes at his fence in the full stride of his gallop. He does not do this, but gathers himself for his jump exactly as a man does. This horse could only have gone through the paling,—could not possibly have jumped it.

The experience related in the *Autobiography* of his attendance at a May Revivalist meeting in Exeter Hall provoked the following letter of protest to George Smith:—

> I went to a May meeting to-day at 11 a.m. punctual, and would not go to another to be made Editor of the *Pall Mall Gazette*! You do not know what you have asked. Go to one yourself and try. You sit for four hours and listen to six sermons;—and the sermons are to me (and would be to

you) of such a nature that, tho' they are in their nature odious and so tedious that human nature cannot listen to them, still they do not fall into a category at which you would wish to throw your ridicule.

I will to-morrow morning write you an article ("A Zulu at a May Meeting"), for which the materials arranged themselves not unhappily; but *I can do no more*. Suicide would intervene after the third or fourth.

I had thought perhaps my boy Harry might have done the attendance for me, but he—having accompanied me to-day—found so ready a resource in somnolence, that to him a May meeting would simply mean sleep for the future.

The actual article, in the form of a letter written supposedly by "A Zulu in London," appeared in the *Pall Mall* for May 10 1865. It is not a very good article. Trollope had not the talent for emergency journalism, and came to recognise his own lack of it. "I found myself unfit for work on a newspaper," he writes in the *Autobiography*. "I was fidgety when any word was altered in accordance with the judgment of the editor, who, of course, was responsible for what appeared. I wanted to select my own subjects—not to have them selected for me; to write when I pleased—and not when it suited others. As a permanent member of a staff I was no use, and after two or three years I dropped out of the work."

But during his two or three years he was assiduous. To the early volumes of the *Pall Mall Gazette* he contributed many articles on many subjects. In addition to his "Hunting Sketches," the essays later published as "Travelling Sketches" and "Clergymen of the Church of England" all appeared in the pages of Smith's paper, and this style of writing had a curious revival at the very end of his life, when, from July to September 1880, he contributed an interesting series of little articles (also to the *Pall Mall Gazette*) on London Tradesmen.[1]

He wrote also on the American War, Napoleon III, the Civil Service, Lord Brougham and many other subjects. To

---

[1] These were published in 1927 with an Introduction by the present writer. That Introduction is reprinted in *Things Past*.

one of his contributions attaches a particular interest. He wrote an article about Lord Westbury, who resigned the Lord Chancellorship in the early summer of 1865 as a result of the public outcry caused by "The Edmunds Scandal." [1] To this article he refers in the *Autobiography*. He mentions no names, but describes the circumstances which led to his intervention in the *cause célèbre* and the sad effect of its pungency on his old and valued friendship with the man principally concerned.[2] In letters to George Smith are two brief allusions to the incident, the second of which shows once again the writer's instinctive appreciation of the English mentality—this time in the conduct of public affairs:—

June 27 1865

·I have sent to the P.M.G. office a letter about Lord Westbury—which I hope you may find yourself able to use....

Touching Lord Westbury, his fault (in my judgment) has been this:—that he has taught himself to think that intellect would do without moral conduct in English public life. He certainly ought to go, as no one can doubt that he has disgraced his position.

The *Pall Mall* like the *Cornhill*, had its dinners, at which Trollope made new and lasting friends. Prominent among them was Richard Monckton Milnes, afterwards Lord Houghton. Through friendship with Houghton Trollope became also intimate with William E. Forster—so intimate, indeed, that their continuous rivalry at whist has become one of the minor traditions of the Athenæum Club.

Of both Houghton and Forster, Henry Adams gives a living description which shows why, although of contrasted types, both were congenial to Trollope and he to them:—

Monckton Milnes was a social power in London—possibly greater than Londoners themselves quite understood, for in London society, as elsewhere, the dull and the

---

[1] For details of this case, as related by a contemporary observer, cf. *The Letters and Memoirs of Sir William Hardman* (London, 1925), pp. 278-80.

[2] *Autobiography*, Chapter XI.

ignorant made a large majority, and dull men always laughed at Monckton Milnes. Every bore was used to talk familiarly about "Dicky Milnes," the "cool of the evening"; and, of course, he himself affected social eccentricity, challenging ridicule with the indifference of one who knew himself to be the first wit in London, and a maker of men—of a great many men. Behind his almost Falstaffian mask and laugh of Silenus, he carried a fine, broad, and high intelligence which no one questioned. . . .

He was a voracious reader, a strong critic, an art connoisseur in certain directions, a collector of books, but above all he was a man of the world by profession, and loved the contacts—perhaps the collisions—of society. . . . Milnes was the good-nature of London; the Gargantuan type of its refinement and coarseness; the most universal figure of May Fair.

William E. Forster stood in a different class. Forster had nothing whatever to do with May Fair. Except in being a Yorkshireman he was quite the opposite of Milnes. He had at that time no social or political position; he never had a vestige of Milnes's wit or variety; he was a tall, rough, ungainly figure, affecting the singular form of self-defense which the Yorkshiremen and Lancashiremen seem to hold dear—the exterior roughness assumed to cover an internal, emotional, almost sentimental nature. Sentimental and emotional he must have been or he could never have persuaded a daughter of Dr. Arnold to marry him. Pure gold, without a trace of base metal; honest, unselfish, practical; he took up the Union cause and made himself its champion, as a true Yorkshireman was sure to do.

With two such men Trollope would have instinctive sympathy. There was something of the "mask and laugh of Silenus" about the novelist himself, and no "exterior roughness" ever covered a more emotional, honest, unselfish, practical nature. Whenever Houghton invited Forster and Trollope for a simultaneous visit, Fryston was noisy with debate and merriment.

2

Simultaneously with his active share in the publishing ventures of George Smith, Trollope was making and fulfilling contracts with the firm of Chapman & Hall. While during 1864 and 1865 they were issuing the monthly numbers of *Can You Forgive Her?* he was writing *Miss Mackenzie*, which appeared in March 1865. No sooner was *Miss Mackenzie* finished than he began *The Belton Estate*, a novel destined to appear as the first serial of a new periodical for the launching of which he was directly responsible.

The foundation in May 1865 of the *Fortnightly Review*—an adventure to which the *Autobiography* gives several pages of queerly rueful comment—opened a turbulent chapter in Trollope's writing life. He was not the man to foresee unhappy consequence from any momentary enthusiasm, and therefore rubbed his bruises in bewildered indignation when, after some months' experience of the *Fortnightly*, he found that he had lost a lot of money and, into the bargain, run his head against an unanticipated and most uncongenial wall.

Always impulsive, he plunged thunderously (and to the practical extent of £1250) into the creation of a paper vowed to freedom of speech and to the personal responsibility of contributors for their views. G. H. Lewes was editor and Trollope himself Chairman of the Finance Committee. From the very first the scheme went awry. A fortnightly review proved distasteful to the wholesale newsagents; wherefore the paper became a monthly but retained its original name. That a review so serious, so earnest in its aim of improving all and everything, should carry a misnomer was an offence to Trollope's idea of suitability; but he was soon face to face with a more serious contradiction—the inevitable clash between eclectic precept and partisan practice. Shrewdly he says:—

> Liberalism, free-thinking and open inquiry will never object to appear in company with their opposites, because they have the conceit to think that they can quell their opposites; but the opposites will not appear in conjunction

with liberalism, free-thinking and open inquiry. As a natural consequence our publication became an organ of liberalism, free-thinking and open inquiry.

But this wise reflection after the event was the result of sad experience. At the time, it was a shock to find that he could not for long take an intimate and active share in the organ from which he had hoped so much, without coming into fierce conflict with many of his fellow-contributors. He awoke, as it were, to find himself in a cranks' kitchen. The original co-operative financial scheme had failed. The paper went bankrupt, and Chapman & Hall bought it cheaply and floated it as a venture of their own. Lewes retired for reasons of health and was succeeded by John Morley, in whose wake flocked the brilliant group of writers who gave to the *Fortnightly* the reputation for thoughtful (if astringent) liberalism which it has never wholly lost. Trollope among the Morley intellectuals was a mastiff among lurchers. All were tempersome; but he was large and rough and incoherent, while they, though often ill-conditioned and peevish, were nimbly articulate.

Trouble was due and trouble came. There is pleasant irony in the thought that, while *The Belton Estate*—that smooth, enchanting, but most unprovocative story—was completing its gentle serialisation in the magazine, its author was growling uneasily behind the scenes in the centre of a crowd of contemptuous doctrinaires, who thought his novel a lump of spongy commonplace, and—for all their great personal liking for him—said as much.

Nor was the growling all behind the scenes. The most emphatic public manifestation of Trollope's discomfort was his famous dispute with E. A. Freeman over the cruelty of field sports and particularly of hunting. Never were antagonists more hopelessly at variance; seldom were controversialists more angry. And yet, despite their irritation, each felt behind the other's heterodoxy a personality appealing and congenial. When years afterwards they met and became friends, their intimacy gave keen pleasure to them both; but during 1865 feeling ran high, and Trollope must have thumped a dozen tables, declaiming against the sentimental don who dared blaspheme against the hallowed sport of gentlemen.

Frederic Harrison (one of the Morley breed who, like the rest, loved Trollope as a man although misprizing him for an incarnate platitude) records a memory:—

> I cannot forget the comical rage which Trollope felt at Professor Freeman's attack on fox-hunting. It chanced that as a young man I had been charged with the duty of escorting a certain young lady to a "meet" of fox-hounds in Essex. A fox was found; but what happened I hardly remember; save this, that, in the middle of a hot burst, I found myself alongside Anthony Trollope, who was shouting and roaring out "What!—what are you doing here?"
>
> He was never tired of holding me up to the scorn of the "Universe" club as a deserter from the principles of Professor Freeman and John Morley. I had taken no part in the controversy, but it gave him huge delight to have detected such backsliding in one of the school he detested.

Freeman himself, in the memorial essay on Trollope from which quotation has already been made, writes more agreeably of the once virulent dispute:—

> I saw Mr. Trollope in Rome for the first time on March 29th 1881. I had long wished to see him. Some may remember that, about a dozen years before that time, I had a controversy with him on the question of the "Morality of Field Sports."
>
> One who was by described the meeting—"They took to one another in a moment." I certainly took to Mr. Trollope, and I have every reason to think that Mr. Trollope took to me. He told me that before that time he had hated me for two reasons. One was that in the controversy about field sports I had, with special reference to the last moments of the fox, asked the question which Cicero asks about the *venationes* of his time: "Quæ potest homini polito esse delectatio?" I was a little proud of this ground of hatred,

I*

as I took it for a sign that I might fairly cry "Habet." [1]   The
other ground I thought was less reasonable.   When one of
the last meetings on South-eastern affairs was held, as late
as 1878 [2] while I was away at Palermo, I was asked, as I
could not be there, to write something, and what I wrote
was read at the meeting.   Mr. Trollope hated me because
time was spent in reading my letter, which would have been
better spent in hearing a living speech—perhaps from Mr.
Trollope.   I have no doubt that Mr. Trollope was quite
right in so thinking; but he should surely have hated those
who asked me to write, not me who simply did what I was
asked.   But these, I fancy, were feelings of a past time.   I
certainly never hated Mr. Trollope at any time, neither do
I think that Mr. Trollope hated me after that pleasant
March 29th.

The arguments used during the dispute itself need not be
recorded.   They were the inevitable arguments of idealism in
conflict with practical commonsense, of anti-vivisectionist at
grips with vivisectionist, of visionary at war with realist.
Freeman's first article appeared in the *Fortnightly* for October 1
1869; Trollope's reply in the issue for December 1; Freeman
had the "last word" (by editorial favour), and Trollope resented almost more than anything that he was not allowed the
final rejoinder which logically was due to him.

Five years later (May 1874) Freeman contributed to the
Fortnightly an essay on "Field Sports and Vivisection," in
which he made reference to the earlier dispute.   But the
challenge was not taken up; the quarrel was really over.

[1] The quotation from Cicero certainly rankled.   It was bitter to Trollope to
have words of the adored Tully used against him.   He says in his *Autobiography* :
" ' Was it possible,' asked Mr. Freeman, quoting from Cicero, ' that any educated man should find delight in so coarse a pursuit ? '   The absurdity of the
charge as to the general brutality of hunting and its consequent unfitness for an
educated man is to be attributed to Mr. Freeman's ignorance of what is really
done and said in the hunting field—perhaps to his misunderstanding of Cicero's
words."

[2] Lord Bryce records (*Studies in Critical Biography*, London, 1903) that Trollope
appeared on the platform of a public meeting at St. James's Hall in December
1876 and made a powerful speech on the South-eastern question.   The fact
explains Freeman's reference.

Again seven years and it had become a friendship. On the hill where once stood the white streets of Tusculum, Trollope and Freeman stood side by side, talking of Octavius Mamilius and of Marcus Tullius Cicero. Then, in the gold of the Italian sunset, they turned and went together down the slope of the *arx* to their hotel.

3

The effect of success upon such a mentality as Trollope's was to create a new dissatisfaction—not dissatisfaction with the extent of the success, but uneasiness lest it had not been deserved.

For all his noisy jollity, he was the least self-complacent of men and, though dogged in misfortune, became easily despondent when life ran smoothly.

From the commencement of my success as a writer [he says] I had always felt an injustice in literary affairs which had never afflicted me or even suggested itself to me while I was unsuccessful. It seemed to me that a name once earned carried with it too much favour. I indeed had never reached a height to which praise was awarded as a matter of course; but there were others who sat on higher seats, to whom the critics brought unmeasured incense and adulation, even when they wrote, as they sometimes did write, trash which from a beginner would not have been thought worthy of the slightest notice. I hope no one will think that in saying this I am actuated by jealousy of others. Though I never reached that height, still I had so far progressed that that which I wrote was received with too much favour. The injustice which struck me did not consist in that which was withheld from me, but in that which was given to me. I felt that aspirants coming up below me might do work as good as mine and probably much better work, and yet fail to have it appreciated. In order to test this, I determined to be such an aspirant myself, and to begin a course of novels anonymously, in order that I might see whether I could obtain a second identity,—whether as I had made one

mark by such literary ability as I possessed, I might succeed
in doing so again.

It is a common thing for a writer to use two or more personalities for different types of work, and pseudonyms are
frequent as methods of disguise where disguise is for some
reason desirable or necessary. But it is rare for an established
author deliberately to throw away the advantage of a well-
known name and, as a test of self, to start again a race already
run.

A week after finishing *The Belton Estate* (in September 1865)
Trollope began the story of *Nina Balatka*. By the end of the
year it was complete and its author took George Smith into his
confidence. The publisher hesitated. He liked the little book,
but . . . At last Trollope wrote:—

9 March 1866

If you like to publish N[*ina*] B[*alatka*] in the *Cornhill* for
£300 you shall do so. If you like to publish 1500 copies for
£300 you shall do so. If you like to buy the copyright
for £500 (undertaking not to declare the name without my
permission) you shall do so.

Smith looked the proposition up and down and decided
against it. He had already a contract for a new long novel
from Trollope and felt (perhaps once more the spectre of
Brown, Jones and Robinson haunted his mind) little disposed to
minor anonymities. Trollope took the rejection with his
usual good humour:—

21 March 1866

All right about *N. B.* Would you kindly send her back
—to Waltham? She won't mind travelling alone. Whether
I shall put her by, or try another venture with her I don't
quite know. At any rate you are too much the gent to claim
acquaintance if you meet her in the street.

But *Nina* was dear to her creator and he could not bring
himself to let her lie. Being intimate at the Garrick Club with
J. M. Langford, the London manager of the Edinburgh publishing firm of Blackwood, he proposed the issue of the tale in

Blackwood's Magazine and its subsequent anonymous appearance in book form. Hitherto Trollope had had no publishing relations with the Blackwoods, who gladly took this opportunity of making contact with the most popular novelist of the day. John Blackwood was wise in his decision. The acquaintance made over *Nina* ripened into close friendship, and the little book proved the first of several novels to appear serially in the firm's magazine.

The identity of the author of *Nina Balatka* was widely canvassed. Trollope himself declares that the secret was guessed by R. H. Hutton, who caught a trick of style which reminded him of earlier Trollopian books. And yet it is doubtful whether the secret had not leaked out earlier. The novel appeared in book form on February 1 1867; on May 25 Mrs. Oliphant wrote to Blackwood from Prague:—

> I am here for three quarters of a day and am just going to look for Nina Balatka's bridge—a pilgrimage which Mr. Trollope (I beg your pardon, I forgot he was anonymous) should take as a compliment from a veteran novel-reader like myself.

It is evident from this letter that the writer had known for some little while the identity of *Nina's* creator; it is suggested by the note of coy conspiracy that the information had come to her from the publisher. And yet in a letter of April 3 1867 John Blackwood himself reports to Langford that Laurence Oliphant has written: "I am much questioned as to the authorship of *Nina Balatka*. Is it Trollope?" and that he (Blackwood) had replied that the author's name was secret and might even be Disraeli! So perhaps Laurence Oliphant had also written to his cousin and she had jumped to a conclusion.[1]

It is sad to record that Trollope's scepticism as to the popularity of work published without his name—the popularity

---

[1] Nevertheless, that the authorship was (and remained) unknown to the great majority of the reading public was amusingly proved during the original printing of the present work. In July 1926 was published a dramatic version of *Nina Balatka*, declared by its author to be "founded on an anonymous tale with the same name which came out in *Blackwood's Magazine* in 1866." (*Oliver and Nina Balatka*: Two Plays by Col. T. Walter Harding. Cambridge, 1926.)

of its inherent quality as opposed to the popularity of its label —proved to be justified. *Nina Balatka*, though it became the gossip of the coteries, did not sell. But Blackwood was tolerant of one more venture of the same kind.

> I am pleased to hear [he wrote to Langford] of Trollope's disposition for further relations. When you see him, give him my compliments and say I am quite inclined.

Linda Tressel, the companion story to *Nina Balatka*, occupied six weeks of Trollope's time in the summer of 1867. As the moment for serial opening approached, Blackwood had qualms. *Nina* had certainly sold badly; was it perhaps a folly to repeat the experiment? [1] Trollope, as always, wished a publisher to share his own faith in any literary venture. He was never the man to hold another to an unwilling bargain. He wrote on September 16 1867:—

> I will return the proofs of *Linda Tressel* to-day or to-morrow, but I write a line at once to say that you are quite at liberty to give up the story if you do not mind the expense of having put it into type. Do not consider yourself to be in the least bound by your offer; only let me have the MS. back at once without going to the printers. What has been with them must, of course, be re-copied.
>
> Feel quite sure that your returning it to me will moult no feather between you and me.

But Blackwood, recovering confidence or judging that a stalwart spirit now might be rewarded by later novels over Trollope's name, held to his undertaking. As the serial drew to an end, he informed the writer that "Linda excites much interest. . . . She is, I think, more talked of than *Nina* and will I hope find a wider audience than her predecessor." Yet, when in May 1868 *Linda Tressel* was published as a two-volume story "by the author of *Nina Balatka*," she made no mark upon the Circulating Libraries. Trollope's worst fears were realised;

---

[1] On July 16 1867, Blackwood informed the author that less than 500 copies of *Nina* had been sold—and this in the first five and a half months after publication.

the public chose their favourite novels by the name upon the title-page, and cared little whether a book be good or bad, provided it bore the guarantee of an accepted author's signature.

The realisation of this fact, though more or less expected, was a disappointment.

> Both stories [says Trollope in his *Autobiography*] were written with a considerable amount of labour and after visits to the towns in which the scenes are laid—Prague and Nuremberg. . . . There was more of romance proper than had been usual with me, and I made an attempt at local colouring—at descriptions of scenes and places—which has not been usual with me. In all this I am confident that I was in a measure successful. In the loves and fears and hatreds, both of Nina and of Linda, there is much that is pathetic. Prague is Prague, and Nuremberg is Nuremberg. I know that the stories are good, but they missed the object with which they had been written. Of course there is not in this any evidence that I might not have succeeded a second time as I succeeded before, had I gone on with the same dogged perseverance. Another ten years of unpaid, un-flagging labour might have built up a second reputation. But this at any rate did seem clear to me, that with all the increased advantages which practice in my art must have given me, I could not at once induce English readers to read what I gave to them, unless I gave it with my name.

Linda Tressel was Trollope's last experiment in anonymity. He had, immediately on that book's completion, written a third short novel on romantic lines and with full complement of foreign and picturesque scenery—*The Golden Lion of Gran-père*, a story of the Vosges—which it was his intention to issue as a third volume of the *Nina* series. But the idea withered in the cold wind of failure. All thought of anonymity was abandoned and *The Golden Lion* offered to Blackwood early in 1871.

> Will you purchase of me for your magazine [Trollope

wrote on February 20] a third story after the manner of
"Linda" and "Nina" to run through any eight numbers
you please of 1872 and to be republished in 1872? I shall
have no other work published entire in that year. I would
propose that it should come out with my name and that you
should then have my permission to publish my name with
the other two should it suit you to do so. The story in
question does not end unhappily as do *L. T.* and *N. B.*,
but it is otherwise of the same class.

But Blackwood declined and the tale (five years after it had
been written) was ultimately published serially in *Good Words*
during 1872 and in book form later in the same year. Both
serial and book issues bore the author's name.

4

It has been said that, when George Smith decided against
the inclusion of the anonymous *Nina Balatka* in the *Cornhill*,
he had already contracted with Trollope for a new full-
length novel. This was the tale which some consider the
greatest he ever wrote. It is certainly in words the second
longest.[1] He began the writing of *The Last Chronicle of Barset*
on January 20 1866 and at first planned to give to this monumental work, in which are tragic dignity and love-despairs and
comedy and friendship and the last rout of Mrs. Proudie, a
title wholly trivial and one foolishly suggestive of the conventional fiction of its time. The epic tale of Mr. Crawley was
nearly called: "The Story of a Cheque for Twenty Pounds
and of the Mischief which it did." Perhaps George Smith
deserves the credit of averting this catastrophe. If so, he made
amends for his earlier disservice to *The Last Chronicle*—the
rejection of Millais' offer of illustration.

Millais was talking to me about certain illustrations
[wrote Trollope in August 1866] and I said: "You know

[1] *The Way We Live Now* about 425,000 words; *The Last Chronicle* about
378,000.

you will not do any more." He replied: "If you like it, I'll do another of yours." Shall I write and ask him?

But Smith declined. He had engaged a certain G. H. Thomas for the work.

The Thomas pictures to *The Last Chronicle* are not so desperately bad as those in some of Trollope's later novels, but they are bad enough. Even the author was but temperately appreciative. He had asked for copies of *Framley Parsonage* and of *The Small House at Allington* to be sent to Thomas, "so that he can see the personages as Millais has made them"; but the results were not wholly satisfactory.

I sent back the proofs with the lettering [he wrote on November 10]. It is always well if possible to select a subject for which the lettering can be taken from the dialogue. Because this cannot be done as to No. 1, the lettering is poor.[1] As to Nos. 2 and 4 it is all right. In No. 3 the scene is sufficiently distinct to dispense with the rule. The best figure is that of Miss Prettyman in No. 2.[2] Grace is not good. She has fat cheeks, and is not Grace Crawley. Crawley before the magistrates is very good.[3] So is the bishop. Mrs. Proudie is not quite my Mrs. Proudie.[4]

Sadly enough, the comparative failure of G. H. Thomas to interpret the characters as their creator saw them, helped to kill Trollope's interest in his illustrators. The ultimate decadence,[5] and such pitiful embellishments as those which disfigure *The Vicar of Bullhampton*, *Ralph the Heir* and, worst of all, *The Way We Live Now*, were partly due to an indifference on the author's part. And yet only partly—for Trollope's interest, even while it lasted, was not always of the most instructed. Left to himself and with Millais unavailable, he could select a picture-maker of a calamitous incompetence. That the first volume of *Can*

---

[1] "Mr. and Mrs. Crawley," facing p. 6, Vol. 1 of first book issue.
[2] Facing p. 46, Vol. 1 of first book issue.
[3] Frontispiece to Vol. 1 of first book issue.
[4] Facing p. 90, Vol. 1 of first book issue.
[5] Only relieved by Marcus Stone's beautiful drawings for *He Knew He Was Right*.

You Forgive Her? was illustrated by "Phiz" and the second by a woman of the tamest mediocrity was due entirely to Trollope's dislike of the school of illustrators to which Hablot K. Browne belonged. George Smith once suggested the engaging of "Phiz" for *The Claverings*.

> I think [replied Trollope] you would possibly find no worse illustrator than H. Browne; and I think he is almost as bad in one kind as in another. He will take no pains to ascertain the thing to be illustrated. I cannot think that his work can add any value at all to any book. I can never express satisfaction at being illustrated in any way by H. Browne.

> I am having the ten last numbers of *Can You Forgive Her?* illustrated by a lady. She has as yet done two drawings on wood. They are both excellent, and the cutter says that they will come out very well. She had £5: 5:- a drawing for them. Why not employ her? She is a Miss Taylor of St. Leonards.

We may, therefore, be thankful that, in admiring Millais, he admired at least one illustrator who was also an artist. With Millais as collaborator, he was all keenness and delight. And never were author and artist in greater sympathy. They worked, each in his genre, along identical lines. "Each creative or inventive stroke" said Millais of his own method as illustrator "is inspired and stimulated or corrected by mental reference to the unseen models of memory." And Trollope: "The art practised by Millais and myself is the effective combination of details which observation has collected for us from every quarter." With such community of method, it is not surprising that their joint production should have a harmony and completeness unusual in work part written and part pictured.

Even an enemy of them both admits that artist and author chime agreeably together. In one of the bitter attacks on Trollope's work that came periodically from Grub Street is reference to his partnership with Millais. A miscellaneous writer named J. Hain Friswell issued in 1870 a book of essays

entitled *Modern Men of Letters Honestly Criticised*, in which he
did his worst with the reputation of a score of his contemporaries. Trollope was pungently included. That the book
came to grief and was hastily withdrawn under a threat from
—of all the victims of Friswell's "honesty"—George Augustus
Sala is pleasantly ironical; but in fact Sala was less a sufferer
than some of the others—less so, certainly, than Trollope, who
is treated with much uncivil condescension. What Friswell
has to say of Trollope is for the most part negligible; but his
comments on Trollope illustrators are shrewd enough, and
into the disapprobation felt for Trollope's work in general
Millais is thus pitilessly (if ungrammatically) swept:—

> Trollope's pictures of an age very poor and weak in its
> nature . . . have found an excellent illustrator in a man who
> has great merit, but which the age persists in accepting as an
> illustrative artist—you might as well call him a balloonist
> —John Everett Millais. He is as well fitted to Trollope
> as Phiz is to Dickens. When Phiz tried to illustrate our
> author, as he did in *Can You Forgive Her?*, he failed miser-
> ably; he actually put life and humour into some of the
> figures under which Trollope had written descriptions.
> dry as old nuts, but singularly descriptive of the author
> and his mind.

Even Friswell, then, may have resented the intrusion of this
G. 1I. Thomas into the Close of Barchester; even Friswell may
have felt regret at the separation of Trollope and Millais. For
separation it was. Although Millais did indeed fully illustrate
one more of Trollope's novels (*Phineas Finn*) and draw a
frontispiece for yet a further one (*Kept in the Dark*), the continuity of their alliance was broken when *The Last Chronicle*
went to other hands, and, having been broken, was never
really re-established.

The Last Chronicle was finished at the Athenæum on September 15 1866. One of the best known of all anecdotes of
Trollope tells how he overheard two members of the club

declaring their weariness of his recurrent characters, and particularly of Mrs. Proudie. He walked across the room, admitted his identity and said: "As to Mrs. Proudie, I will go home and kill her before the week is over." And so he did.

Trollope came to regret the impulsive murder of his classic shrew, and we can go further. It is likely that his involuntary eavesdropping ended not only Mrs. Proudie but the whole Barset saga also. But for the peevish small talk of two strangers in their club armchairs, the world might have had more of Barchester. Perhaps the children of Frank Gresham and Mary Thorne would have grown old enough to fill a novel with their loves and chatter; perhaps more would have been told of Bertie Stanhope and his sister Madeline; more of Johnny Eames; more even of Lily, Pearl of Allington, who passes homeward to the Small House in a late chapter of *The Last Chronicle of Barset*, vowed to spinsterhood. But the two Athenæum grumblers made all of this impossible. Trollope, always too sensitive to what the public thought and said, abandoned Barset as an outworn theme, passing to Phineas Finn, the Duke of Omnium and the new series of political novels.

Years later—in August 1881—a distinguished American wrote and begged him to write one more chronicle of Barsetshire. His refusal has the weariness of old age and reads pathetically from a man once so undismayed and work-loving:—

> I am nearly seventy years of age and cannot hope to do what you propose. Though I still go on writing, the new characters are much less troublesome than old ones, and can be done without the infinite labour of reading back again and again my old works.

5

Trollope had been preparing the way for *Phineas Finn* and its political sequels by a season of close reading. One of the few mysteries of an otherwise clearly tabulated life is that of his achievement as a reader. When he read, and how in the crowded programme of his days he found time to annotate his reading and to use his annotations, can barely be imagined. Yet now and again he produced a book which—whether it be a good book or a bad one—could not have been written at all without much preparatory reading (such is his Life of Cicero and his edition of Cæsar's Commentaries; such are his books on North America, Australia and South Africa), and this reading he indubitably did.

Phineas Finn was preceded, then, by a thorough examination of contemporary political philosophy and papers, which examination had two by-products—the one his own unfortunate desire to become Member of Parliament for Beverley, the other his little monograph on Lord Palmerston. The Beverley election did not take place until 1868; *Palmerston* was not published until 1881; but both ventures had their origin in 1866, during the months of exploration into politics which equipped him for the second of his two great novel-series.

And during 1866 also, he began the writing of a History of English Prose Fiction. According to the *Autobiography*, this undertaking proved frankly too heavy to be borne. "I broke down because I could not endure the labour in addition to the other labours of my life." The few pages of introduction that were actually written are now printed as a curiosity in an appendix to this book. Attached to the manuscript is a list of novels which, according to the scheme, were to be read and criticised. The list begins with *Arcadia*, the works of Aphra Behn, and *Roscoe's Novelists' Library*. Also included are the obvious and famous eighteenth-century novels, together with less "accepted" works such as *The Monk*, *Caleb Williams*, *Udolpho* and *A Simple Story*. The nineteenth-century selection shows three books by Sir Walter Scott, *Pride and Prejudice* (the *Autobiography* declares that as a young man "I made up my mind that *Pride and Prejudice* was the best novel in the language—a palm which I only partially withdraw after a second reading of *Ivanhoe* and did not completely bestow elsewhere till *Esmond* was written"), *Peter Simple*, *Jane Eyre*, three books of Thackeray's, and—most unexpected of all—*Granby* by T. H. Lister and *Richelieu* by

G. P. R. James. Apart from the few pages of introduction and some annotations at the end of his own copies of several of the books, only one written relic of this history of fiction remains —an essay on *Clarissa Harlowe*, composed about this time but not published until November 1868. It appeared in *St. Paul's*, the magazine that had by then been founded for his editorship by the firm of Virtue.

The inception of *St. Paul's Magazine* was the final event of 1866. James Virtue was an important printer and block-maker to whom—as to so many important printers—had come the hazardous ambition to become a publisher. Since about 1860 he had been issuing a few art and illustrated books; but he now wished to build up a general list. This, by the custom of the time, could most rapidly be done if the aspiring publisher possessed a monthly magazine. One by one publishers were thus arming themselves for competitive battle. There had for long existed *Fraser's*; *Bentley's Miscellany* had come and gone; *Macmillan's Magazine* was founded in 1859. But the new florescence began with Smith, Elder's *Cornhill*, which created Maxwell's *Temple Bar*. This was soon bought by Bentley, leaving Maxwell to the creation of *Belgravia* in its place. Then had come *Once a Week* (Bradbury & Evans), *The Argosy*, *Tinsley's Magazine*, and others. Now Virtue in his turn had set his heart upon a magazine and came (as Maxwell had done earlier) to ask Trollope if he would edit it. According to the *Autobiography* Trollope did all in his power to dissuade Virtue from his project. But the publisher was obdurate. If Trollope would not become his editor, some other man of letters would be more amenable. Virtue's first idea was to buy the *Argosy*. This monthly paper had been announced by Sampson Low & Co. in November 1865, had at the last moment been transferred to Strahan (publisher of *Good Words*) and was by December 1866 already so far gone in failure as to be cheaply purchasable.[1] But there were difficulties; and Virtue, growing each day more eagerly ambitious, determined that an entirely new magazine should be launched. The essence of

---

[1] The *Argosy* was in fact bought early in 1867 by Mrs. Henry Wood, author of *East Lynne*, and continued under her editorship for many years.

the scheme being that Trollope should contribute a long novel for serial issue, it was decided not to begin publication till October 1 1867, so that the editor could prepare his novel and collect about him the desired contributors for the early numbers of the paper. In the matter of title, publisher and editor were at friendly variance. Virtue wanted "Trollope's Monthly"; Trollope replied with "The Monthly Westminster" and "The Monthly Liberal." "My own name would be objectionable" he wrote. "It would mean nothing when the connection between the magazine and the editor had been dissolved." But Virtue, a discerning and a friendly man, never let the temperamental growling of his distinguished friend depress or startle him. Throughout their connection he acted with calm geniality, so that Trollope grew as fond of him as he ever was of any publisher and gave him in the *Autobiography* this charming testimonial:

> If the use of large capital, combined with wide liberality and absolute confidence on the part of the proprietor and perpetual good humour, could have produced success, our magazine certainly would have succeeded.

The name "St. Paul's" was finally selected. Trollope claims (and rightly) no great originality for this invention. "If we were to make ourselves in any way peculiar" he says "it was not by our name that we were desirous of doing so." At least they took no risks.

The terms of contract gave to the editor a fee of £1,000 a year for two years; complete freedom of editorial control; the right to pay contributors (including himself) at the rate of twenty shillings per page; and the sum of £3,200 for the copyright of *Phineas Finn*. He set to work at once to engage an assistant editor, and offered the job to Robert Bell.

This man, whose acquaintance Trollope had made at his first *Cornhill* dinner, was a scholar and a man of letters, for whom fate seemed to reserve all the misfortune and ill-health that can befall a single individual. Implicated in nearly every literary venture of importance, Bell never achieved either the reputation or the success his qualities deserved.[1] He had fallen into real distress not very long before the definite inception of *St. Paul's*, through the reckless investment of a large part of his capital in the "English and Foreign Library Company, Ltd."—a company floated to develop Hookham's Lending Library along what was considered to be modern lines. The early 'sixties were years of wild speculation in lending-library flotations. Many were the bankruptcies, and not the least that in which Bell had rashly and without experience involved himself.

Trollope counted Bell one of his dearest friends, and to be Trollope's friend was to have Trollope's loyal help to the extremes of generosity. The offer of the assistant editorship of *St. Paul's*, with a salary of £250 per annum to be paid out of the editor's own pocket, was a gesture of pure friendliness. Bell was no longer a young man; he was broken in health and spirits and, though his capacities were great, they were too fine in quality to fit him for the work of devilling on a monthly magazine. Trollope knew all this, and that the toil of assistant editorship must, if Bell accepted his proposal, fall largely on himself. The offer came when Bell was too ill even to write a letter of thanks with his own hand. His wife writes to express his gratitude; perhaps when he is rather stronger . . . Three months later he was dead.

> You know probably [wrote Trollope to George Smith in April 1867] that dear old Robert Bell died this morning. I send a notice of him which I hope you may find yourself justified in inserting in the *P.M.G.* to-morrow. He was a very manly fellow. I loved him well. And I should be sorry that he should pass away without a word of record.

The tribute was published in the *Pall Mall Gazette* on April 13 1867. It was Trollope's public monument to his dead friend. His private monument was raised soon after. The

[1] Among the works of Robert Bell were an edition of Chaucer; an anthology of Ancient Poems and Ballads; a Life of Canning; and two novels: *The Ladder of Gold* (1850) and *Hearts and Altars* (1852). He was also editor of *The Story Teller*.

widow was in penury, and the dead man's library was advertised for sale by Willis and Sotheran. Trollope went secretly to the executors and bought the whole collection at his own generous valuation. "We all know the difference between buying and selling books" he explained a little awkwardly, when after the event some friend discovered what had been done. Into Bell's books were pasted the Trollope book-plate. Now and again volumes presented by their authors to Robert Bell and bearing the blue-paper crest and the name "Anthony Trollope" are offered in the antiquarian shops. Such volumes are not only books which once were Trollope's; they are the little children of his generosity.

IX

IN THE AUTUMN OF 1867—when the first publication of *St. Paul's* was drawing near—Trollope resigned the Post Office. To his chagrin at the promotion of a junior over his head the *Autobiography* bears candid witness. Other reasons are given also—weariness of harness, weariness of the crushing burden of work which, in the pursuit of two exigent occupations, he had bound upon his shoulders.

The decision brought relief, but also sadness. He loved the Post Office; the lecture printed in the *Cornhill* expresses his love, and with an emotion foreign to his usual mode of speech. He had served it more faithfully than many a man with no rival interest would have done. Yet were there (and still are) persons ready to hint that, in the interests of novel-writing or of travel, he so neglected his official work as to make resignation, if not unavoidable, at least desirable. Such a suggestion, to anyone who has a moderate familiarity with Trollope's character, is almost too silly to create offence; but the rumour that men spoke thus of him angered Trollope and caused him such suffering as comes from mean and anonymous slander.

As a kind of parting compliment, the Post Office entrusted him, immediately after his resignation, with a postal mission to the United States. To this mission was joined another from the Foreign Office—a charge to achieve, if possible, that visionary bliss (it dances down the decades like a marsh-fire, beckoning writers and publishers to illimitable swamps) an international copyright between Great Britain and America. Trollope made his postal treaty; but of international copyright he achieved nothing. The two or three powerful American publishers who made their livelihood from piracy defended the continuance of non-copyright on the ground of public advantage. They claimed that the American people wanted cheap books and that under the existing system English books in America could be published very cheaply indeed. But Trollope was not impressed by talk of popular opinion. "It is the man who wants to make money, not he who fears that he may be called upon to spend it, who controls such matters as this in the United States," he said.

His work for Post Office or for author's rights was, however, a less important feature of this second sojourn in America than the reappearance of Kate Field in the near foregound of his life.

Kate Field had now a certain reputation in America; also she was a little farther gone in authorship than formerly. But she was still not too proud—maybe, in Trollope's view, still neophyte enough—to receive advice from an old friend who was (incidentally) also an editor. She asked his counsel, sent him manuscripts for criticism. As on the earlier journey he wrote her long and interesting letters. Several express his considered views on authorship and were written straight from the heart and out of his—by this time—great experience.

Washington. 24 May 1868.

DEAR KATE,

I got your letter on my return to W. from Richmond, whither I have been to look after memorials of Davis & Lee and the other great heroes of Secession. The ms. of which your letter speaks has not reached me. The printed story, "Love and War" (which I return as you may want it), I have read. It has two faults. It wants a plot, and is too egoistic. Touching the second fault first, it is always dangerous to write from the point of "I." The reader is unconsciously taught to feel that the writer is glorifying himself, and rebels against the self-praise. Or otherwise the "I" is pretentiously humble, and offends from exactly the other point of view. In telling a tale it is, I think, always well to sink the personal pronoun. The old way, "Once upon a time," with slight modifications is the best way of telling a story.

Now as to the plot—it is there that you fail and are like

to fail. In "Love and War" there is absolutely no plot—
no contrived arrangement of incidents by which interest is
excited. You simply say that a girl was unhappy in such
and such circumstances, and was helped by such and such
(improbable) virtues and intelligences. You must work
more out of your imagination than this before you can be
a story-teller for the public. And I think you could do it.
In spite of Dogberry, the thing is to be done by cudgelling.
But you must exercise your mind upon it, and not sit down
simply to write the details of a picture which is conveyed to
you, not by your imagination, but by your sympathies.
Both sympathy and imagination must be at work—and must
work in unison—before you can attract.

Your narration as regards language and ease of diction is
excellent. I am sure that you can write without difficulty,
but I am nearly equally sure that you must train your mind
to work, before you can deal with combinations of incidents.
And yet I fully believe that it is in you to do it.

If I give you pain, pray excuse me. I would so fain see
you step out and become one of the profession in which
women can work at par alongside of men. You have already
learned so much of the art—and then you are so young.

Most affectionately yours,

A. T.

The end of your story should have been the beginning.

The next letter shows how thoroughly he had himself arrived
at the true conception of a novelist's duty, although less than
a decade had elapsed since he had written *Castle Richmond.*

MY DEAR KATE,   *Washington.   May* 28 1868.

I have read your ms. and return it. Of course, as it is
a fragment, I cannot tell how far the plot might be successful. It is much more pretentious than the printed story,
and is for that reason worse;—but I should say of it that
the author ought to be able to write a good story.

As a rule young writers—(I speak, of course, as writers

of fiction)—should be very chary of giving vent to their
own feelings on what I may call public matters. If you are
writing an essay, you have to convey, of course, your own
ideas and convictions to another mind. You will, of course,
desire to do so in fiction also, and may ultimately do so
(when your audience is made) more successfully than by
any essay writing. But your first object must be to charm
and not to teach. You should avoid the "I" not only in
the absolute expressed form of the pronoun, but even in
regard to the reader's appreciation of your motives. Your
reader should not be made to think that *you* are trying to
teach, or to preach, or to convince. Teach, and preach,
and convince if you can;—but first learn the art of doing so
without seeming to do it. We are very jealous of preachers.
We admit them at certain hours and places for certain
reasons. We take up a story for recreation, and the mind,
desirous of recreation, revolts from being entertained with
a sermon. Your story about the Artist is intended to convey
your teaching as to what Americans and Americanesses
should have done during the war. You will hardly win
your way in that fashion. Tell some simple plot or story
of more or less involved, but still common life, adventure,
and try first to tell that in such form that idle minds may
find some gentle sentiment and recreation in your work.
Afterwards, when you have learned the knack of story
telling, go on to greater objects.

There's a sermon for you.

The sermon over, he turns to his more normal gaiety, to
mockery of himself and teasing comment on the intellectual
ardour of his correspondent.

[*From Washington*]   3 *June* 1868

MY DEAR KATE,

I don't seem to care much about Planchette.[1] However,
I am mild and submit to be taken to Planchettes and Humes

---

[1] Kate had just plunged with her usual enthusiasm into this—the latest craze
of the intellectual coteries. She published a small book of " results " under the
title *Planchette's Diary* (New York, 1868), the contents of which were reprinted
in the Third Series of *The World Beautiful*.

and Dotens—(was that the name of the Boston preaching and poetising woman?).[1] I should like of all things to see a ghost, and if one would come and have it out with me on the square I think it would add vastly to my interest in life. Undoubtedly one would prefer half an hour with Washington or Hamilton to any amount of intercourse with even Butler or Charles Sumner. But when tables rap and boards write, and dead young women come and tickle my knee under a big table, I find the manifestation to be unworthy of the previous grand ceremony of death. Your visitor from above or below should be majestical, should stalk in all panoplied from head to foot—at least with a white sheet, and should not condescend to catechetical and alphabetical puzzles.

I enclose a note for your great friend, Mr. Elliott.[2] He writes (apparently) from No. 44 Bible Bower. But as I cannot believe that there is as yet in New York any so near approach to the Elysian Fields, I think it better to send my note to you, than to trust it so addressed to the post. I do not know when I shall be in N.Y. I won't say that I might not be there to-morrow. This place is so awful to me, that I doubt whether I can stand it much longer. To make matters worse a democratic senator who is stone deaf, and who lives in the same house with me, has proposed to dine with me every day. I refused three times, but he did not hear me, and ordered that our dinners should be served together. I had not the courage to fight it any further, and can see no alternative but to run away.

If you are going out of town, let me know when you go, and whither. I have half a mind to take a run to Niagara for the sake of getting cool in the spray.

Washington.   10 *June* 1868

DEAR KATE,

I got a telegram on yesterday (Wednesday) morning which took me away from N.Y. at 10—instead of 12—and so I do not know whether that horrid little Silenus sent the

---

[1] It was. Cf. above, p. 230.   [2] C. W. Elliott (see above, p. 234).

photographs or no. I guess he didn't. At any rate he was bound to send them before and I hope he may be drowned in Burgundy and that his deputy with the dirty sleeves will photograph him in his laſt gasp—piteously. If they ever reach you, tell me whether they are good for anything. I should like one of you ſtanding up, facing full front, with your hat. I think it would have your natural look, and you can't conceive how little I shall think of the detrimental skirt of which our Silenus complained.

I have got letters from England, and such letters. My wife says in reference to her projeĉted journey over here— "Don't I wish I may get it." Had I told her not to come, woman-like she would have been here by the firſt boat. However, she is quite right, as Washington would kill her.[1]

For myself shall write my epitaph before I go to bed to-night.

> Washington has slain this man,
>   By politics and heat together.
> Sumner alone he might have stood *
>   But not the Summer weather.
>
>   * Very doubtful.

My letters tell me that I should have received a telegram from England before I got them, which will enable (or would have enabled me) really to begin my work. But no telegram has come. As I muſt remain, I shall run for the V.-Presidency on the ſtricteſt Democratic ticket—which I take to be repudiation of the debt and return to slavery. I shall pass the next two months in reading Mr. Elliott's various mss. which have arrived in a cheſt.

Washington.
July 8 1868

MY DEAR KATE,

I have put off answering your note of the 2nd till I could say certainly what my movements would be—but even now I can say nothing of the kind. The P.M.G. is away, eleĉting

---

[1] Rose Trollope did, however, join her husband in New York. Kate records in her diary that she secured rooms for them, and that during June Mrs. Trollope arrived.

a democratic candidate for the White House, and consequently I am still in suspense. Oh, Lord! what a night I
spent—the last as ever was—among the mosquitoes, trying
to burn them with a candle inside the net! I could not get
at one, but was more successful with the netting. I didn't
have a wink of sleep, and another such night will put me
into a fever hospital.

I still hope to leave here in time for the boat home on
this day week. As I do not know where you are or where
Mrs. Homans is, I do not think I shall go on to Boston
at all. If I had a day or two I would either run to Niagara
or to Lake George. I am killed by the heat, and want to
get out of a town. If you will go down close to the sea, and
near enough for me to get at you, I would then go to you.

I don't quite understand about the photographs, but I'll
do as you bid me, pay the bill (including the drink) and
send you one of the two. I have got your section framed
down to the mere hat and eyes and nose. It is all I have
of you except a smudged (but originally very pretty)
portrait taken from a picture.

Thanks for the account of myself taken from the two
papers, which describes me as being like a mimic bull with
gloves on. If I saw the writer I should be apt to go off
and let him know that I never wear gloves. What fools
people are! I saw in some paper an account of you amidst
other strong-minded women—Janet L. Tozer, Annie B.
Slocum, Martha M. Mumpers, Violet Q. Fitzpopam, etc.—
I observed that every one except you had an intermediate
initial—I really think that with a view to the feelings of the
country you should insist on one. It is manifestly necessary
to success. Kate X. Field would do very well.

Of course I will do what you ask me about the proofs of
the Dickens paper. You must send them to the Brevoort
House. If you could have got Dickens to do it for you in
London it would have been better.[1]

---

[1] Dickens had been in New York in January 1868 and had given readings
from *David Copperfield* and other works. Kate Field made his acquaintance and
became friendly with him. She promptly began work on her *Pen Photographs*

What do you think your friend Elliott has proposed? That I should have his novel published in England with my name on the title-page—and with any slight alterations in the vol. which I might be pleased to make!!! That I call cool—and peculiarly honest. So clever too, as no two people were ever more unlike each other in language, manner, thought, and style of narrative! [1]

Give my kindest love to your mother. The same to yourself, dear Kate,—if I do not see you again—with a kiss that shall be semi-parental, one-third brotherly, and as regards the small remainder, as loving as you please.

> *Brevoort House, N.Y.*
> 13 *July* 1868   *Monday*

MY DEAR KATE,

Here I am, and I start for England on Wednesday. Last night, I came from Washington. To-night I go to Boston. Tuesday night I come back here. I shall therefore be within 12 miles of you but shall not see you. I could not possibly get back to you, as you will see from the above programme. I wish I could have seen your dear old face once more (before the Gray Nuns come, on the wings of which you will arrive in Heaven)—but I do not see how it is to be.

I have got the photographs and have paid for them—$11.50. I wish I could have paid for yours at the same time.

Your friend who lives in the Bible hotel has written me a most polite letter to say that my answer to him was just what he expected.[2]

Touching the story for the *Saint Paul's*—remember that it is to go into one number and be not more than from

---

of Charles Dickens' Readings (under this rather foolish title the collection of brief essays was published in Boston in 1868) and was anxious that the proofs should be seen by Dickens himself with a view to the publication in England of one or all of the papers. As a later letter shows (see below, p. 290) Dickens would not consent to their issue in his own country.

[1] The book in question was probably *Wind and Whirlwind*, published in New York in 1868 under the pseudonym "Thom Whyte."

[2] C. W. Elliott again.

K

14 to 16 pages—each page 520 words.[1] I say this because
Tom writes to ask me whether you are not going to write a
longer kind of story. I should have no room now for a
longer story.

God bless you, dear. I wish I thought I might see your
clever laughing eyes again before the days of the spectacles
—but I suppose not. My love to your mother.

As on the earlier occasion, one final letter from Waltham
closed the correspondence :—

> *Waltham House,*
> *Waltham Cross.*
> 30 *Sept.* 1868.

MY DEAR KATE,

I have just got your letter. I thought you had one of
the photographs. You had said something of taking one
from the intoxicated little party. However, I now enclose
one, as I understand from your letter that I am scolded
for going away without leaving it.

And now about your ms.—as to which I should doubtless have written with more alacrity had I had good news
to send. I lost not a moment in applying to Dickens after
my return home, but I found that he was opposed to the
publication altogether;—and I also found, as I was sure
would be the case, that without his co-operation the publication with any good results would be altogether impossible.
You may take it for granted that he would not like it. I
greatly grieve that you should have had so much fruitless
labour in preparing the paper for publication here.[2]

On that Tuesday Mrs. Homans told me that she expected
you. I had gathered that you were already too far from
Boston to make it possible that you should be there. It
was a melancholy day, as I felt quite sure that it would be

---

[1] Kate Field's diary shows that Trollope had invited her to write a story for
his magazine : " June 6 (1868) : Mr. Trollope came and remained an hour or
two. Asked me to write a story for his *St. Paul's* magazine. If I can, it will be
a feather in my cap. If I can't—well, we shall see."

[2] It is sad to have to record that, after Dickens's death, Kate Field acted
contrary to his expressed desire. *Pen Photographs* was published in London in
a " new and revised edition " in 1871.

my last day in America. But I was better pleased to spend
it in Boston than elsewhere. Whether I shall ever see again
you or her must depend on your coming here. I am becoming an infirm old man, too fat to travel so far.

Let me have the story when it is ready, I will do the best
I can with it—for indeed I would willingly see myself in
some little way helping you in a profession which I regard
as being the finest in the world.

God bless you—my kindest love to your mother.

There have survived two or three more letters from Trollope
to Kate Field, written at intervals during the remaining years
of his life. Because these letters show how the friendship
persisted, they may more suitably be given here than in their
strict chronology.

In explanation of their actual incidence it should be stated
that during 1869 and 1870 Kate became a well-known lecturer
on literary and imaginative themes and a copious writer for
various periodicals. In June 1871 she came to London, just
missing the Trollopes, who sailed for Australia at the end of
May.

Anthony clearly knew (and so early as in April 1870) that
she was coming, for he wrote the following letter to her in
response to an inquiry as to her prospects as a lecturer in
England:—

The Athenæum.
April 15 1870.

DEAR KATE,

I am not a grumbler, and you are very—impertinent.
All the same I am delighted to think that you should have
made $8000—and I congratulate you with all my heart. I
am sure of this; that in whatever way you earn money, it
will be both honest and honourable; that the money will
represent hard work, mental culture and much thought;
and that as you have never been depressed by poverty, so
will you never be puffed up by your wealth.

You write as though I should find fault with your lecturing. I am not in the least disposed to do so. I think writing

nicer for either man or woman;—but that perhaps comes
from the fact that I am better paid for writing than for
lecturing. I like your account of yourself—with your handsome dress, looking as well as you can, and doing your work
colloquially. I have no doubt you look very well. You
could do that when you were not handsomely dressed;—
and I should like to hear you lecture amazingly. Only I
should want to go home to supper with you afterwards and
be allowed to express my opinion freely. But in truth I
am not patient under lectures, and much prefer lecturing
myself—as I dare say you do also.

As for your lecturing here, I do not doubt you would
have very large audiences;—but they do not pay well.
£10 a lecture is about the mark if you can fill a large room
—600 or 700—for our rooms are not so large as yours—and
our lectures are chiefly given to audiences who do not pay
for tickets, but pay by the year. So that the managing
committees cannot afford to pay much. I had a word to
say the other day about fiction, and I lectured in four places,
receiving £15 in two and £10 in two. All of which information may, I hope, be useful to you soon, as I should so greatly
delight in having you here.

I don't in the least understand why you fly out against
me as to matrimony—or as to what I have said on that
subject in regard to you. I have said, and I say again, that
I wish you would marry. But I have never advised you to
marry a man for whom you did not care. You tell me I
don't know you. I think I do—as to character and mind.
As to the details of your life, of course I do not.

You may at this moment be violently in love with some
impossible hero, and I know nothing about it. What I have
meant to say in the way of counsel is this: that you should
not so bind yourself to an idea of personal independence as
to allow that feeling to operate in your mind against the
idea of marriage. I think that it does so, and has done so:
—not that I have any notion of any individual sent about
his business on those grounds, but that I think such to be
the tendency of your mind. As I think that at any rate in

middle life, married people have a better time than old bachelors and spinsters, I do not like that tendency in you. Now I think that is all very straightforward and decorous, and I don't know why I am to be flown at.

I have given up, or rather am now just giving up, my magazine, and therefore have no longer any power in that line. But in truth I myself hate Fechter as an actor, and I think the people here are sick of him. To me he was never a pleasant actor.[1]

I would tell you all about the magazine but that I am at the end of my letter. Our chief news is that early next year we go out to Australia to see a son of ours who is settled there. I hope to induce my wife to return via San Francisco.

Kate Field remained in England, with occasional journeys on the Continent, until 1873. She renewed her acquaintance with George Eliot; met for the first time Reade,[2] Wilkie Collins and other men of letters; lectured, journalised and followed untiringly the social-intellectual round. She came to England again in May 1874 for a few months; again in 1877; again and for a longer visit during 1878 and 1879.

During her later sojourns in London she saw the Trollopes frequently, and there would have been little need for correspondence, save of the frenzied brevity suitable to the arrangement of meetings or of "seeings off." Nevertheless fragmentary letters passed between them, which show that the old friendly sparring between pugnacious plain-sense and advanced idealism continued to the end.

He was always ready to make fun of her feminism. In July 1873 he sent her a little note: "Two of the wildest of your countrymen—Joachim Miller and Mark Twain—dine with me at my club next week. Pity you have not established the rights of your sex, or you could come and meet them and be as jolly

---

[1] Kate had conceived a great admiration for Charles Albert Fechter's rendering of Hamlet, and wrote criticism of his art and a biographical sketch. She had, it appears, suggested the publication of some essay on the subject in *St. Paul's*.

[2] One result of this acquaintance was her appearance in the title rôle of Peg Woffington in New York late in 1874. She was not a successful actress.

as men!" And four years later, they are still debating the propriety of female-lecturers, Kate having declared her faith in an article, and bravely enough, sent it to Trollope for his confounding.

39 Montagu Square.
8 *Feb.* 1877.

MY DEAR KATE,

I read your paper at once, and ought to have sent it back sooner. Had I been able to speak nicely of it you may be sure I should have done so.

It is gay and lively and in that way pleasant;—but it slaughters giants that have no existence. Who is the man of the world who exclaimed that "a lecturing woman is a disgrace to her sex"? It is like the good little books which say that Tom told a lie and broke his leg, whereas Dick spoke the truth and was at once made a lord. There is no evidence of the facts but the statement of the writer.

All your points can be argued pro and con as to women lecturing;—but you do not, I think, catch the objections which are made;—that oratory is connected deeply with forensic, parliamentary, and pulpit pursuits for which women are unfitted because they are wanted elsewhere;— because in such pursuits a man is taken from his home and because she is wanted at home. I am not arguing the question now. But I do not think you have hit the real objection.

Your fun is, I think, better than your facts;—but they are so mixed together that one cannot separate them. That Aspasia taught Socrates, I doubt much. That Cornelia whipped the Gracchi, I suppose to be true;—but not that she taught them eloquence.

But all this is trifling. The question is whether an Editor would publish your paper. I think *not* as it stands now. Were I an Editor, the first 8 pages would deter me. The remainder, though it is not argumentation, is good fun. I should begin less brusquely. Then if you like it I will ask Bentley if it would suit him.

This letter is the final surviving document of what is—even in its incomplete form—the most revealing record we possess of Trollope's emotional self.   Only his fondness for the American girl seems to have released the tenderness and humour which were normally imprisoned behind the bars of his self-conscious gruffness.   It is not the least of Kate Field's claims to a surviving reputation that by her personality she threw down the barrier of shyness which walled in a very upright but a very human man, and set free—for a brief while at any rate—his natural masculinity.

X

"ST. PAUL'S" WAS NOT A SUCCESS. The magazine itself lasted from October 1867 into the middle 'seventies; but Trollope resigned his editorial office in the summer of 1870, realising that he had not the particular sense of popular requirements necessary to make his paper such as its publisher would wish. "I was too anxious to be good" he says "and did not enough think of what might be lucrative."

He was disappointed that his strenuous attempt to be simultaneously literary and popular had not won greater favour; but it must be confessed that, although he worked far harder at his task than many a more successful editor, he did not produce a magazine of great distinction. Apart from his own contributions, the only items likely to survive are several poems by Austin Dobson, who was in effect "discovered" by Trollope as a poet and greatly helped.

The first Dobson poem ever published ("Une Marquise") appeared in *St. Paul's Magazine* for March 1868, and it was followed by many others. Letters have survived written by Trollope to Dobson which show real enthusiasm for the poet's work and editorial supervision of the most conscientious kind. Poem after poem Trollope examines line by line—praising, suggesting alterations, and incidentally expressing his idea of the true verse-requirements of his paper. "I think it is indispensable that poetry for a magazine should be so clearly intelligible that ill-constructed, uneducated but perhaps intelligent minds can understand it" (March 7 1868). "Such a poem as your *Pyramus and Thisbe* should be as clear as running water. No one should pause a moment to look for interpretation. If it is not fit to be read aloud so as to catch the intellects of not very intellectual people, it does not answer its proposed object" (November 8 1869).[1] "I lunched yesterday with my

[1] This particular letter is printed in *The Drama of the Doctor's Window*, a pamphlet privately issued by Austin Dobson in 1872.

dear friends George Eliot and G. H. Lewes. They were very loud in their praise of your *Autumn Idyll*, and George Eliot asked me to tell the author what she thought of it" (Dec. 8 1869). "I will use both your poems—on the condition that you will ease a prejudice on my part by expunging the joke about Gibbon's 'Decline and Fall'" (April 18 1869).

In May 1870, when on the point of relinquishing his editorship, Trollope writes: "In my endeavour to establish *Saint Paul's* on what I considered to be a good literary footing, I insisted on myself naming the remuneration to be paid. It has not been very great, but it has been fairly good. The object now is to make the magazine *pay*. What may be the result of that resolve to contributors in the way of remuneration will never be known to me after June.[1] I fear it may not be altogether satisfactory." A little later in the same letter he laments the indifference of the magazine public to work of literary promise: "I must own to a vexation of spirit when I have found that literary work which I have *known* to be good has not made that mark which it has deserved. As to your own poems I have heard great praise from some few whose praise is really worth having; I have myself felt that they would grace our literature hereafter; but I have been disappointed at finding—as regards yourself and others—that good work has not been more widely recognised."

These letters throw light on the reason for Trollope's retirement from *St. Paul's*, and on the real cause of his failure. He tried—as in Dobson's case—to adjust by verbal alteration work written from pure literary impulse to his own artificial conception of the capacities of a magazine public; conversely, he tried to improve magazine-writing proper into at least an imitation of literature. Inevitably he forfeited two potential popularities and achieved mediocrity. In other words, as editor of *St. Paul's* he fell between two stools; and that he did so was in some sort symbolical of the course his literary life was now to take.

Although at the time this was not evident, the year 1869 was

---

[1] In actual fact the last number to appear under his editorship was that for July 1870.

K*

in fact the "peak" year of Trollope's reputation. He crossed
the watershed of his fortune some time between 1868 and
1870.

Since 1860 he had been climbing steadily upward and to ever
loftier heights of success and popularity. *The Last Chronicle
of Barset* had had an enormous circulation; for *Phineas Finn*
and for *He Knew He Was Right*—the contracts for which were
made in January and December 1867 respectively—he had been
paid the highest prices that he had ever yet been offered. He
had become the unchallenged leader of contemporary novelists,
the despot of the lending-libraries, and the acknowledged interpreter of the mentality and sentiment of the England of the
day. Remarkable evidence of the extent to which his novels
and characters were at one time household words is provided
by Thomas Seccombe, who recorded a memory which must
have dated from about 1870 "of an intellectual clown at
Hengler's making a sort of rigmarole of patter out of the titles
of Trollope's books, and the product being received by salvos
of cheers." [1] Not many novelists have attained to such an
extreme of popularity.

But a change was coming. For a little while—between the
last upward slope and the first gentle stages of the downward
grade—his path ran level on the heights. For a little while he
appeared as easily supreme as ever. Nevertheless there was
a different feeling in the air. The social atmosphere was
changing. The 'seventies were already restless with the
menace of a new and different epoch.

Portents of change, then, were implicit in the curious
sequence of inefficacies (they were something less tangible
than failures) which occurred between the autumn of 1868
and the spring of 1870. As matters turned out, the prices
paid for *Phineas Finn* and for *He Knew He Was Right* were
the highest he was destined to receive. Further, the peak
had not only been reached, it had been overreached. Neither
Phineas nor its successor sold well enough to bring back
their cost.

The fact had more than a technical publishing significance.

[1] *The Bookman*, June 1915.

For the first time Trollope had *obviously* been paid beyond his value—"obviously" because the doings of a best-seller are never very secret, and the book trade and the craft of authorship had then, as now, a strange intuitive sense of the reality or otherwise of current values. The knowledge percolated through publishers' offices and from desk to editorial desk that the two latest Trollope novels had not earned their keep. Automatically, and in response to this disquieting rumour, his estimated value as a book or serial proposition suffered a check. There was no catastrophic fall; but the rise had stopped. For a while the actual reduction in payments was slight. His contracts show that for the six years from 1870 to 1876 his prices were, though with some difficulty, stabilised at a point well below the rate paid by George Smith or by Virtue, but not so very far below that paid by Chapman & Hall in 1861 for *Orley Farm* and in 1864 for *Can You Forgive Her?* He was in the first stage of a decline. The second stage began in 1876, after which date the market sagged dangerously. From then to the end of his life there was rapid decadence.

Trollope's fortunes as an author earning a livelihood are a compendium of the possibilities and dangers open to all professional fiction writers. His successes were partly due to good fortune, mainly to good sense and to industry; his failures to a blend of bad luck and of mistaken judgment.

The circumstances in which he crossed the summit of success merit examination.

When he accepted the offer of an editorship and of bill-top publicity from such a man as Virtue, he took a greater risk with his future reputation than he realised. It would have been better for him to continue one of a galaxy of stars with Smith, Elder, with Chapman & Hall or with Longmans—even though in actual cash he might have been less highly paid—than to become the only planet in a less traditional firmament. For Virtue—though in himself an admirable man, with all the honesty and sweetness proper to his name—was in a publishing sense a parvenu. He had hardly been a book-publisher at all before he started *St. Paul's*. He did not know how difficult

was the business into which he blithely ventured. In consequence he spent more money than he need have done to gain
insufficient results; also, by leaving complete control of his
magazine to the literary man whom he had chosen as editor,
he took in effect as partner—and as a partner financially irresponsible—a person as inexperienced as himself. Trollope
later came to realise his own unfitness as a man of letters to
perform what is really a business duty. He declares in the
Autobiography:—

> Publishers themselves have been the best editors of
> magazines when they have been able to give time and
> intelligence to the work. The proprietor knows what he
> wants and what he can afford and is not tempted to fall into
> that worst of literary quicksands, the publishing of matter
> not for the sake of the readers but for the sake of the writer.

That Virtue had misjudged his values became general knowledge with all the travelling speed of evil news. Rightly—
though pathetically, for he was a good man and deserved
success—he paid the penalty of his optimism. Realising that
his publishing ambitions were costing him too dearly to be
longer endured, he sold his general business and his magazine
to Strahan and, cutting his losses, retired to the old safety of
his printing and engraving.

But he was not the only one to pay. Though his mistakes
of inexperience had indeed damaged his own new and costly
property beyond repair, they also damaged Trollope's reputation in the general world of publishers.

When Virtue liquidated his responsibilities, Trollope found
himself involved (through sale of copyrights) with Strahan,
with Strahan's connections, Daldy, Isbister and, later, with
Isbister. Implication with these firms was bad for his repute.
Their imprints lowered his status, and the results of this loss
of status were soon manifest. He could not regain his old
place in the esteem of such a man as Smith; as a serious novelist
he was slightly blown upon. Wherefore he became primarily
a writer of novels for serial, of novels whose subsequent book
issue was less important than their magazine appearances.

And this, in an author of Trollope's capacity and achievement, is a sure mark of decadence.[1]

The numerous stories published during the last period of his life carry many and varied imprints—Hurst and Blackett, Sampson Low, Macmillan, Tinsley, Strahan, Isbister, Chatto & Windus. Few of these represent direct contracts between author and publisher. They resulted from the sub-sale to a book-publisher, by a magazine proprietor who had bought the copyright, of book-rights in a story purchased primarily for serialisation. With one or two exceptions, only those novels of the late period which bear the imprint of Chapman & Hall or of Blackwood are genuine novel-ventures by a book-publisher. In such cases the contracts were made directly with Trollope and reflected the publisher's belief that the novel *as a book* was worth the purchase.

Trollope's experience, therefore, affords good evidence, alike of the harm which may be caused to an author by a period of over-payment, and of the importance to his continuing reputation of the imprint on his books.

In the first regard—inflation brings its retribution to literature as to other things. No market will for long tolerate an inflated price, and literature is, in its economic aspect, as much a commodity for market as anything else.

In the second—the trademark on a book (the publisher's imprint is and should be regarded as a trademark) comes to represent a guarantee of quality as surely as does the name of any good manufacturer of any article which depends on quality for its acceptance.

Trollope's misfortunes at this time were not confined to

---

[1] Charles Reade had this same experience and at about the same time. After the outcry against his *Terrible Temptation* (published in book form in 1871), for which he could only secure from Chapman & Hall a price much lower than that previously paid, Reade noted bitterly in his private diary : " This is a pitiable decline. The serial in its first form will soon be the only considerable market open to me."

Charles Lever also met a similar fate. His last three or four novels were bought for serial, and so perfunctorily published in book form when serial was over, that they are nowadays more rarely seen than any of his earlier work.

his literary economics. In the autumn of 1868 he fought an unsuccessful election at Beverley. His quaint declaration in the *Autobiography* that "I have always thought that to sit in the British Parliament should be the highest object of ambition to every educated Englishman" cannot wholly account for the ill-judged rashness of this venture. But it helps to explain why, when he had been defrauded of the offer of a safe Essex seat which had been promised him, his obstinacy should have overcome his practical good sense and have driven him into a hopeless fight far away from his own countryside, rather than admit that the chicanery of a political caucus could cheat an Anthony Trollope of his ambition.

This election—a task both uncongenial and unsuited to his talents—cost him nearly £2,000 and several months of valuable time. More seriously, and in the most public manner possible, it advertised him as having failed of an enterprise.

One item, however, stands on the credit side of Beverley. Just as, from the unprofitable experiment of *St. Paul's*, came his series of *Editor's Tales* (which James Payn rightly describes as providing "as convincing a proof of the genius of the author as anything he ever wrote" [1]), so from the election fiasco resulted the novel *Ralph the Heir*. This book contains election episodes unsurpassed in English fiction and, because it is a record of personal experience, a vivid and humorous interpretation of Trollope's own sufferings as a carpet-bagger.

---

[1] *Some Literary Recollections*, by James Payn. London, 1884. The paragraph reads :—

> I could tell stories without end of my editorial experience, some humorous, some pathetic ; but the impersonality of the mysterious " We " ought, I feel, to be respected. If the reader wishes for more revelations of this description, I refer him to the *Editor's Tales* of Anthony Trollope, which are not only very charming in themselves, but unconsciously betray the kindness of heart of the writer, and the tender conscientiousness with which he discharged his trust. I may add, considering the slenderness of his material, and the strong impression that each narrative produces on the mind, that the volume is as convincing a proof of the genius of the author as anything he ever wrote. I once expressed this opinion to Trollope, who assented to my view of the matter, but added, with a grim smile, that he doubted whether anybody had ever read the book except myself, by which, of course, he meant to imply that it had had a very small circulation as compared with that of his novels.

Wherever he appears as victim of political wire-pullers, as rebel against their lack of scruple, as waverer from their parroted idealisms, Sir Thomas Underwood is Trollope himself. Sir Thomas receives the invitation to stand for Percycross as Trollope himself received the invitation to stand for Beverley. "I daresay I'm a fool for my pains. It will cost me some money that I oughtn't to spend. If I get in, I don't know that I can do any good or that it can do me any good." Sir Thomas being introduced by an agent he detests to influential supporters whom he does not trust is Trollope, growling uneasily under the tutelage of his own "Mr. Trigger" and trying to think of tactful things to say to the mustard-maker, the paper-maker and the two manufacturers of boots. Sir Thomas among the denominations is Trollope, acting perforce the Wesleyan to Mr. Pabsby, the Anglican to the Vicar of the parish. Sir Thomas declares himself for purity of election and finds his agent turns the subject hastily. Sir Thomas, with a timid weariness, goes canvassing from door to door, hating himself for an impertinent intruder and, by this very self-consciousness, suggesting to the persons visited that he is indeed intruding. Sir Thomas has little pleasure from his victory and infinite distress from the protracted squalor of the petition-inquiry which ultimately unseats him. In every one of these predicaments—with such slight alterations in detail as novelists (ostrich-like) are apt to introduce into fiction which is really fact—Sir Thomas Underwood is Anthony Trollope aspiring foolishly to a seat in Parliament.[1]

To a generation lacking the awe of Parliament and of members of Parliament which was so distinctive a feature of mid-Victorian mentality, it seems strange that Trollope should have stood for Beverley at all. But it is stranger still to realise the queer frivolity with which he wore his solemn Liberal aspirations. He went hunting in the middle of the short campaign, cancelling speeches and conferences rather than miss a likely meet. Also, after the defeat, after the petition had unseated his opponents and Beverley had been dis-

[1] Trollope's testimony at the Beverley Election Trial is given on p. 210 of the Minutes of the Trial, ordered to be printed in 1869 by the House of Commons.

franchised, he tackled the sequel to *Phineas Finn* in a jaunty spirit of defiance, as with a snap of the fingers at the fate that made him chronicler of Parliament and not a part of it. Of *Phineas Redux* he says: "As I was debarred from expressing my opinions in the House of Commons, I took this method of declaring myself." And certainly there is a sting about the second tale of Phineas in so far as it describes the world of politics which is not present in its predecessor.[1] The book was Trollope's revenge for Beverley, a challenging counterpart to the humorous self-abasement of *Ralph the Heir*.

St. Paul's Magazine; an unlucky change of publishers; a lost election—these three misfortunes befell Trollope in 1868 and 1869. In each of them, as has been said, he tumbled between two stools. As editor he was at once too literary and too commonplace; as author he was highly paid but by second-rank publishers; at Beverley he was at once too docile a candidate and too scrupulous a citizen. But two further frustrations were to come. In 1869 recurred the misadventure of *The Vicar of Bullhampton*, in which Trollope came to grief between a disingenuous publisher and a revolution in popular habits of reading. In 1870 appeared his brave edition of *The Commentaries of Cæsar*, by which he earned the scorn of scholarship and little uninstructed praise to balance it. *The Vicar of Bullhampton* was commissioned in February 1868 by E. S. Dallas, editor of *Once a Week* and a friend of Trollope's at the Garrick Club. Bradbury and Evans, the proprietors of the paper, purchased the copyright and stipulated that the book be of the same length as *The Claverings*. "Mind!" wrote Dallas. "I expect a stunner." The novel was finished by November 1st and due to begin publication in May 1869.

Then wrath began. Early in 1869 the editor found that it would suit his paper better to defer the serial issue of *The Vicar of Bullhampton* until later in the year. To this proposal Trollope objected. He was not unjustified in so doing; he had bound himself not to allow another work of his to run serially side

---

[1] Cf. particularly the description of the Tankerville election and Phineas' fight for "purity."

by side with *The Vicar* during the first six months of its career, and a sudden delay on the part of *Once a Week* would dislocate his careful plans. However, after a brief correspondence and because Dallas seemed rather injured than repentant, Trollope grew weary of his own annoyance and consented to postponement. *The Vicar* was scheduled to begin publication in the first week of July.

But worse was yet to come. On March 22 1869 the author received the following letter from the editor:—

MY DEAR TROLLOPE,

We are in great perplexity about your novel, and I write to ask you if you will agree to a proposal which will relieve us from this serious difficulty.

Messrs. Bradbury, Evans & Co. bought Victor Hugo's new story in November last on the faith of a promise from the French publisher that it would be issued in January. It has been delayed, however, from week to week through the incessant corrections of the author, so that it cannot be published in Paris before the first week in April, and we cannot begin to publish the translation in *Once a Week* before then. The result of this is that, supposing we begin to publish Victor Hugo in the first week in April and begin to publish your novel in the first week of July, you and he will be running on side by side in *Once a Week* for three or four months. Now this is death to us. *Once a Week* consists of 24 pages, of which 2 are devoted to advertisements and 2 to illustrations. Four from twenty-four leaves twenty. An instalment of your novel added to an instalment of Victor Hugo will take up 15 or 16 pages, leaving us from 4 to 5 pages for Table Talk, padding and correspondence which we proposed to begin when we begin V. Hugo. It is impossible to carry on in this fashion without increasing the size of *Once a Week*, which is impossible without serious loss to us.

Under these circumstances we make the following proposition to you and beg that you will give it your favourable consideration. Bradbury & Evans propose to publish *The*

Vicar of Bullhampton in the *Gentleman's Magazine*, beginning the publication of it on the 1st of May and running it on to the period at which it would have come to an end in *Once a Week*. If you will consent to this arrangement you will get us out of a very great difficulty. Do, like a good fellow, say that you agree. The *Gentleman's Magazine* is raised in character—is extremely well done—and will do you no discredit.

I fear this letter will not find you at home, and the publishers hope that you will permit them to announce the proposed arrangement in the forthcoming (April) number of the *Gentleman's Magazine* with which they go to press on Wednesday. If you could let me know your decision by letter or by telegraph on Wednesday morning, you would do me and the publishers a great favour. I hope it will be "yes." I am sorry to trouble you—but you will see the difficulty.

Yours always truly,

E. S. DALLAS.

This time Trollope was really angry. Not only was the *Gentleman's Magazine* a very inferior paper with a lower class of reader and a poor general reputation; not only was Hugo a Frenchman, whose later work was in Trollope's opinion bad and his interposition to the disadvantage of an Englishman in an English magazine intolerable, but the incident of itself offended—and deeply—the injured novelist's stern sense of a business engagement. He had always kept literal faith alike with publishers and editors; generally they had repaid the courtesy. But here was ill-treatment which he could not tolerate. That a fellow-clubman should thus behave to him (and on Garrick notepaper) aggravated an already grave offence.

And there is reason to think that behind this pugnacious resentment lay a second outraged principle. At this juncture Bradbury and Evans were out to dazzle the literary market. They had begun offering big money to this author or that—not because they thought the goods purchased worth the price, but in order to disturb existing author-publisher relations and from the fracas to have pickings of their own.

Such troubling of the literary waters by deliberate plunging is a trick not unknown to publishers, and has often the sequel that the author, once secured, is asked to consent to some unexpected adjustment of the contract. This had happened to Trollope, who was therefore doubly angry. Not only had he been manœuvred into the position of taking money for a story which, he now began to suspect, had always been intended for a second-rate magazine; he had also been made the victim of a proceeding economically subversive. He felt personally insulted and rejected the *Gentleman's Magazine* with indignation.

The anger was righteous; and the affray was not of his own seeking; yet it was he who suffered. The publishers solved the problem by issuing *The Vicar of Bullhampton* in monthly numbers, to which independent publication the author could not possibly object. But the day of monthly numbers was over. With the rise of the shilling magazine, serial novels had replaced part-issue in the favour of the fiction-reading public. *The Vicar*, presented in an unpopular form, fell flat. No doubt Bradbury & Evans lost money, as they deserved to do; but with equal certainty Trollope lost reputation and a section of his public, both of which penalties were wholly unmerited.

The story of *The Commentaries of Cæsar* is, in contrast to its predecessor, free from anger or doubtful dealing. Indeed it shows Trollope at his most hard-working and at his most generous, making a new friend and strengthening the affection of an old one. Yet though the generosity was deeply appreciated, and though the friendships—old and new—persisted till his death, Trollope had more disappointment from his labour than pleasure, less of satisfaction than wounded pride.

Blackwoods were launching a popular series of "Ancient Classics for English Readers" under the editorship of the Rev. W. Lucas Collins, rector of Lowick in Northamptonshire. Trollope accepted the task of condensing into one little English reader the ten books of Cæsar's Commentaries. For three months he toiled at his task: "I do not know that for a short period I ever worked harder" he says; and one can believe how laborious must have been an undertaking so completely different from his normal occupations. Brief extracts from the correspondence relating to the book tell the story of its composition.

(*To John Blackwood*)

Office of St. Paul's.
March 10 1870.

Since I got home from my lecturing expedition I've been at work on the *Cæsar* and find it very hard work. However, I have done the first and longest of the two commentaries. Before I attack the other I should like to know what you and Mr. Collins think of the one I have done. I do not like myself sending a half-completed work; but the job is so very stiff a one and so much subsidiary reading is necessary that I would spare myself six weeks' labour on the second commentary if, as may be probable, you or Mr. Collins do not like what I have done. If you approve, I will go to work again with a will.

The next letter, sent from Waltham on March 29, expresses pleasure that Blackwood "is satisfied with my little endeavour." The writer accepts a number of hints for the improvement of his book, but protests that he cannot put in battle descriptions, as these would make the work too long. He says:—

You can hardly guess how great was the necessity for condensation. I was bound to give some analysis of the seven books and was driven to measure myself by lines at last to get the thing into the pages I had allowed.

There is next a letter to the editor of the series, who was to become one of Trollope's most intimate friends.

(*To W. Lucas Collins*)

Waltham Cross.
April 7 1870.

I am very glad you like the *Cæsar*.

As to the phrases which strike you as too colloquial—
"thick as blackberries," etc.—you will, I do not doubt,
understand the spirit in which they are used. The intention is to create that feeling of lightness which is produced
by the handling of serious matters with light words, and
which is almost needed in such a work. I would not admit
slang, but such phrases as may be held to be admissible in
ordinary easy conversation do not seem to me to be objectionable. "As fast as he could lay leg to ground" seems a
fair colloquial translation for "quam magnis itineribus."
But let the phrases go if they displease you. . . .

I do not know Lewin's books. My books have been:
Long's *Cæsar*, Merivale's *Roman Empire*, Napoleon and
Plutarch. The less one allows oneself to be tempted into
would-be learned disquisitions the better, I think, in such a
work.

On April 16 he wrote to John Blackwood:—

It has been a tough bit of work, but I have enjoyed it
amazingly. It has been a change to the spinning of novels
and has enabled me to surround myself with books and
almost to think myself a scholar.

Then, on May 7, came the crowning gesture. Trollope, the
most professional and most businesslike of authors, made of
the copyright of this toilsome little book a birthday present
to his publisher:

I send down the whole work corrected [he wrote from
the Athenæum on May 7], having, as I think, complied
with every suggestion made by you or Collins. It is a dear
little book to me and there is one other thing to be said
about the little dear. I think the first of June is your birth-

day. At any rate we'll make it so for this year and you will accept *Cæsar* for a little present.

Blackwood was deeply touched,—and rightly, for Trollope had shown a generosity rare in the annals of authorship.

On June 1st 1870 *Cæsar* was published. It must have proved a valuable property to John Blackwood, for as a school reader it enjoyed—and has since continued to enjoy—a considerable sale. But its unlucky writer was to have (as he admits) "very little gratification from the work." The public who buy school readers rarely give that audible thanksgiving so grateful to an author's ears. One buyer indeed, so far from feeling gratitude, made hostile notes upon his copy of the book, remarking, "How unjust is the Gnat Trollop (*sic*) to the Lion Cæsar!" Apart from Lucas Collins' friendship and Blackwood's gratitude, Trollope received nothing for his months of strenuous work save casual sneers or silent indifference. He was deeply wounded. The Press was carelessly superior. An aged pundit, to whom a copy had been sent, returned laconic thanks for "your comic *Cæsar*." "I do not suppose," says Trollope, "that he intended to run a dagger into me." And then, with a typical understanding of the intolerance of vested intellectual interests, he adds: "There was probably a feeling in his mind that a man who has spent his life in writing English novels could not be fit to write about Cæsar. It was as when an amateur gets a picture hung on the walls of the Academy. What business had I there?"

Perhaps Trollope had the last word.

XI

ON MAY 24 1871 Trollope and his wife sailed from Liverpool to visit their farmer son in Australia. Trollope's children were now grown men, earning their own livelihood; Waltham Cross had been finally abandoned; *St. Paul's* was in other hands. For eighteen months he meant to move about the world with no responsibilities save the personal comfort of his wife and of himself; then he would return home—but to a different way of living, almost to a different England.

Trollope had reached a moment in his life as significant as that day in 1859 when he first undertook to write the opening serial for the *Cornhill*. Then he passed from the bright morning of his aspirations into the blazing noonday of success; now the long shadows were preparing to fall, and through the level gold of afternoon he was content to travel into a silver dusk.

To many prolific and once-popular authors old age—or what in the calendar of their lives does duty for old age—has brought a quadruple misery of loneliness, ill-health, poverty and a vanished reputation. From most of this misery Trollope was mercifully excused. He did not live so long that friends and family had gone before and left him solitary. Physically he remained hale until the very end; his body and his mind grew weary (few men have made such harsh demands upon them), but both were undiseased. His livelihood would have been amply secured by prudent investment and economy, even if the falling off in earning power had been more catastrophic than it was. Only in reputation came a noticeable loss and that, when life is drawing to a close, is of the four sufferings the most easily endured.

The series of misjudgments which, between 1867 and 1870, had blunted the edge of his attack on publishers and editors, dulled also—and in consequence—his attraction for contemporary intellectuals. There is no sarcasm at the expense of the cognoscenti in the suggestion that their interest in Trollope's work relaxed simultaneously with that of persons trained to judge him as a speculation. In the case of such an author as Trollope—a novelist writing for the public and one proud to please the normal taste of educated readers—the value set upon his work by editors and publishers has a critical as well as a material significance. The intelligentsia, whether they wish it or no, are inevitably influenced in their judgments of contemporary work by the fluctuations of a literary market. Some are themselves editors, others are friends of editors, all hear their publishers talk. A moment comes when they find that eager competition for the work of some living and eminent author has given place to a kind of standardised respect. Forthwith they lose interest. The man's writing has, apparently, reached its greatest limit of development, is now "placed," will offer no further surprise nor opportunity of discovery.

This was precisely Trollope's fate from 1870 onwards. When he ceased to be the *gros lot* in the lottery of publishing, he ceased also to be an exciting theme for literary gossip. Once a "dish of the day" and, as such, an object of greedy curiosity, he had become a printed item on the menu of contemporary letters. Henceforward he was taken for granted, and the reputation-makers of Belgravia and Hampstead passed to other and more adventurous personalities. In time this acceptance became neglect, neglect indifference, and indifference—though only gradually and not openly until after he was dead—contempt.

In this evolution of his fame there was nothing to cause Trollope personal surprise and little to cause him pain. He had never been very sensitive to the disapproval of the intellectuals, preferring to pay his court to the great public and by them to be cherished or rejected.

But when this great public, who had for so long and with such ardour cherished him, showed signs of weariness, then indeed came melancholy. The desertion was gradual and never, during Trollope's lifetime, complete; but he was sensitive to every sign of it. The early 'seventies brought him one popularity—that of *The Eustace Diamonds*—as great as any he had previously enjoyed; but he was too shrewd a judge of public feeling to be misled by a single triumph or to mistake a continuing (and largely automatic) library-success for a genuine renewal of reputation.

He realised that he was regarded as *démodé*; that he had become a survival from the 'sixties, too obviously a star-novelist of an earlier epoch for the impatient liking of a rising generation. A little angrily he turned his immense dexterity to the fashioning of further novels—some in the new manner of psychological analysis, others to the new design of ruthless realism. They were very good novels—better than most of those they challenged; but they did not impress the revolutionaries so much as they displeased his former adherents. Many of the old faithful lovers of Barchester could not stomach the Trevelyans, the Cousin Henrys, the Melmottes and the Scarboroughs, whom they found too intricate, too sordid, and too brutal for their liking. So once again he fell between two stools. The failure of *The Prime Minister* (published in 1876) shook him badly. One critic declared that the author had out-written his time and should for the future keep silence. The cruel words struck home; Trollope could not understand why *The Prime Minister* of all books should have provoked them.

2

On the verge of starting for Australia he is in great spirits. For all his regret at leaving Waltham Cross, he feels light-hearted and at peace with the world. But although on holiday, work is still his gospel and for work he has provided. He himself on journey and his second "printed" personality (which while he is away will stay at home and appear on further title-pages) can both be busy. Scribbling blocks are in his cabin trunk. He has contracted for a book about his journey and a series of travel letters to the *Daily Telegraph*. To satisfy the second self, three finished novels are left behind to wait their turn in the thronged calendar of his publishing future.

The Eustace Diamonds is with the editor of the *Fortnightly*; *Phineas Redux* and *An Eye for an Eye* are with his elder son Henry, at this time reader for the firm of Chapman & Hall. Then, at the last minute, a three weeks' delay in sailing irks him by its enforced idleness. He writes to Alfred Austin:—

Athenæum.
May 5 1871.

Very many thanks for your introduction and kind farewell letter. Alas for us, the wretched ambition which wrecked the "Queen of the Thames" on its homeward journey has caused our vessel to be postponed eighteen days, and we do not sail until the 24th—which is an incredible nuisance to us, busy as we homeless wanderers are. We are in all the misery of living about among friends and pot-houses, going through that very worst phase of life, which consists in a continuous and ever-failing attempt to be jolly with nothing to do. I cannot believe the Old Testament, because labour is spoken of as the *evil* consequence of the Fall of Man. My only doubt as to finding a heaven for myself at last arises from the fear that the disembodied and beatified spirits will not want novels.

In due course he really sails. A desk is set up in the cabin. He starts writing as they leave Liverpool; the day before the boat reaches Melbourne are set down the final words of *Lady Anna*. For fourteen months he travels ceaselessly about Australasia, writing his newspaper articles, collecting information for his book, absorbing such local Australian colour as will be used later in *Harry Heathcote of Gangoil* and in *John Caldigate*. Returning home via America he calls on Brigham Young, who has never heard of him, will not believe that he writes stories and insists that he is a miner. He lands in England in December 1872 carrying the immense manuscript of his book *Australia and New Zealand*, weather-beaten, blusterous but indomitable, while a tolerant but rather breathless wife trails behind him and asks a little anxiously about the luggage.

But at home is no peace. During his absence Charles Reade had blandly stolen the plot of *Ralph the Heir* and made a play of it. The piece—entitled *Shilly Shally*—had been produced at the Gaiety Theatre on April 1 1872, and considerably failed. The *Morning Advertiser* charged it with indecency. Here were all the materials for a first-class explosion. Trollope and Reade, old Garrick friends but both men of violent temper, plunged into a quarrel of the most comic intensity. Trollope was furious that his story had been stolen; Reade explained that he had intended half the profits for his unconscious collaborator. There were no profits. Trollope demanded how a man so aggressive as Reade over the rights of authors could even have imagined this shameless robbery; Reade, who was getting angry, said that he was sorry if his action had been over-hasty but—— Trollope roared him down. Reade, he declared, was guilty not only of theft and hypocrisy, but also of so altering another author's tale as to render it obscene. At this Reade flew into a rage and began laying about him on all sides. He sued the *Morning Advertiser* for slander; he stamped about London calling Trollope a literary knobstick and a publishers' rat. In the street the two men crossed the road rather than meet face to face; in the club they glared at each other in speechless fury. It is even said that they would play whist at the same table, communicating with each other through third parties.

Unbelievable though it may seem, this preposterous quarrel continued until 1876. By then it had become so ludicrous that both disputants must soon have forgotten it in laughter, had not two unlucky coincidences stoked the furnaces of wrath. Early in 1876 John Blackwood, writing to Reade about *A Woman Hater*, in which novel he had suggested some most unwelcome alterations, rashly referred to Trollope as more reasonable in his reception of a publisher's criticism. This, of course, set Reade off again, and for a short time the anger blazed more furiously than ever. By a second piece of bad fortune, it was during this Indian summer of their indignation that Trollope wrote his *Autobiography*, and there set down what has seemed to some a rancorous version of the dispute.

It must be borne in mind that the *Autobiography* dates from
1876, and not from the end of Trollope's life. The rancour
did not last. The quarrel was made up in 1877 and Trollope
forgot that his friend had ever been an enemy. Unfortunately he also forgot to re-read the manuscript of his
Autobiography, and so allowed to remain for the misunderstanding of posterity a sentence he would have been the first
to disavow.

3

At 39 Montagu Square Trollope spent eight happy and productive years. Every summer he travelled on the Continent;
during the winters of 1873, 1874 and 1875 he hunted from London
and with undiminished zeal. For eight months in 1875 he was
for a second time in Australia, for the greater part of 1877 he was
on journey to and about South Africa, in 1878 he went to Iceland.
At home and on tour novels and tales were written and in due
course published, friends were entertained, visits were enjoyed.

His life in London settled to a busy regularity. His orphan
niece, Florence Bland, who had come to live at Waltham Cross
in 1863 as quite a little girl, was very much the daughter of
the house at Montagu Square, and acted also as a faithful and
essential secretary. She helped to arrange the now numerous
books in their new home, ticketing each one with a shelf-letter
and its number on that shelf, fixing the little blue-paper book-
plate of her uncle's crest. Still more important was her secretarial work. Trollope began to suffer at intervals from writer's
cramp, and Florence Bland would sit and write to his dictation.
Of the later novels several were largely written by her hand.[1]
During dictation she might not speak a single word, offer a
single suggestion. One day he tore up a whole chapter and
threw it into the waste-paper basket, because she ventured on an
emendation. On such outbreaks family jokes were gaily built.
Florence Bland would be asked at breakfast if Trollope ever
took a stick to her; she would smile, and he would laugh aloud

---

[1] *Cousin Henry; Kept in the Dark; Dr. Wortle's School; An Old Man's Love;
The Fixed Period; Marion Fay; Mr. Scarborough's Family. The Life of Cicero*
was written entirely by Rose Trollope's hand.

and bang the table and, with his black eyes bright behind his spectacles, declare that some such punishment was sadly overdue.

At Montagu Square, as at Waltham Cross, Trollope was early at his desk. Most of the day's writing was over by eleven o'clock. Then he would ride out or drive or attend to such committee work as might arise from the numerous undertakings in which he was interested. Whist at the Garrick was a daily ceremony between tea and dinner. At night he dined abroad or entertained his many friends at home.

Mrs. Oliphant's letters give glimpses of him at this period. "The Lord Mayor's dinner was amusing. Matthew Arnold, Anthony Trollope, Tom Hughes and Charles Reade and myself were the sole representatives of literature. But oh, how fine they were!" (July 1874). "The systematic way in which Mr. Trollope grinds out his work is very funny. It must have answered, for he seems extremely comfortable; keeps a homely brougham, rides in the Park, etc." (May 1876).

Other folk knew him for an unfailing ally in distress. One friend, ailing and thrown upon the doubtful cookery of London lodgings, was visited regularly by Trollope on his way to the club, who would bring each day a pheasant, some fruit or other delicacies for a tarnished appetite. An old Irishman, fallen on evil days, was rescued from a slum and kept in decent comfort till he died, and for no other reason than that Trollope loved the Irish and had known this man slightly in his Mallow days.

A few letters on very miscellaneous themes will illustrate his unfailing cheerfulness, his readiness to help; his humorous modesty, his amused observation of the world and its ways, and—by implication if by no other means—his own philosophy of life.

To a lady who deplored the misalliance of the heroine of *Lady Anna* he wrote:—

> 39 *Montagu Square*.
> 21 *June* 1873.

Of course the girl has to marry the tailor! It is very dreadful, but there was no other way. The story was originated in my mind by an idea I had as to the doubt which would (or might) exist in a girl's mind as to whether she ought to be true to her troth, or true to her lineage, when, from early circumstances, the one had been given in a manner detrimental to the other. And I determined that in such a case she ought to be true all through. To make the discrepancy as great as possible, I made the girl an Earl's daughter, and the betrothed a tailor. All the horrors had to be invented to bring about a condition in which an Earl's daughter could become engaged to a tailor without glaring fault on her side.

Another lady—a novelist—asked his advice as to terms of publication offered to her by Chapman & Hall, and not to her mind sufficiently favourable. His reply is interesting. It gives data of publishing costs and conditions at the time, and it suggests also that part of his own success as a writer was due to a real understanding of the publisher's problem. This understanding saved him from the unpractical expectations of amateur vanity and spared him the disillusion which follows exaggerated hopes.

> 39 *Montagu Square.*
> 25 *March* 1876.

I think you must be wrong in your ideas about your novel. You would wish to limit Chapman to 600 copies. That means (after free copies) a sale of 550. He now gets 15/- each for three-vol. novels. The total realised would be £412 : 10:—. The expense of a three-vol. novel (including paper, printing and advertisements) with some few extra publishing expenses is about £200. This does not leave him enough to pay you a fitting price, let alone his own profit. If you only sell 600 copies, I do not think he could give you above £150, which is a very small sum. I shall be most glad to act for you if I can, and would think nothing a trouble; but before doing so I should have to see you. Could you come up here some morning and breakfast at 11.30, or later in the day if it suited you better, as I feel it would?

In a letter about Arabella Trefoil—heroine in fact, if not in

conventional parlance, of *The American Senator*—he shows how
shrewd and clearly cut was his conception of her character.
This certainty of delineation is very characteristic of him. To
the meticulous care with which he thought all round his
personages is principally due the smooth reality of all his
novels, and such a note as that which follows gives a glimpse
of the structural accuracy which lay below the apparently
effortless serenity of his characterisation.

> 39 *Montagu Square.*
> 17 *Feb.* 1877.

Your little note of commendation was just a Valentine,
but very pleasant. I have been, and still am, very much
afraid of Arabella Trefoil. The critics have to come, and
they will tell me that she is unwomanly, unnatural, turgid,—
the creation of a morbid imagination, striving after effect
by laboured abominations. But I swear I have known the
woman—not one special woman, not one Mary Jones or Sarah
Smith—but all the traits, all the cleverness, all the patience,
all the courage, all the self-abnegation—and all the failure.

Will such a one as Arabella Trefoil be damned? If so,
why? Think of her virtues; how she works; how true she
is to her vocation; how little there is of self-indulgence
or of idleness. I think that she will go to a kind of third-
class heaven in which she will always be getting third-class
husbands.

There have been preserved quite a series of letters written
home by Trollope during his trip to South Africa in 1877.
Some of these have a gay intimacy that is very charming;
others bear witness to his relentless industry.

> (*To Henry M. Trollope*)

> S.S. "*Caldera*" (on the way to South
> Africa) *July* 2.

I don't like anyone on board, but I hate two persons.
There is an old man who plays the flute all the afternoon and

evening. I think he and I will have to fight. And there
is a beastly impudent young man with a voice like a cracked
horn who will talk to me. He is almost unsnubbable, but
I think I will silence him, at least as far as conversation with
me goes. . . .

I fancy from what I hear and the little I see that I shall
find the Cape a most uninteresting place. The people who
are going there on board this ship are just the people who
would go to an uninteresting colony.

On landing in Cape Town he wrote to Blackwood announcing the completion on the voyage out of *John Caldigate* and
confirming his worst anticipations of the place that he had
reached.

Cape Town.   21 *July.*

As I have yet only been on shore twelve hours, I am not
prepared to give a full and comprehensive description of
the country; but it seems to be a poor, niggery, yellow-
faced half-bred sort of place, with an ugly Dutch flavour
about it.

The letters to Henry Trollope take up the tale again:—

Cape Town.   23 *July.*

Cape Town is very poor as a town—much inferior either
to Melbourne or Sydney.

Cape Town.   *August* 3.

I have begun my new book (on South Africa) and written
a chapter and a half. But at starting it is very hard to know
what to write about. If it were possible, such a book
should be written all at once, just when the journeyings
and inspections are done.

Port Elizabeth.
August 9.

I am getting on with my work, but have not come to the
heavy bone-breaking part of it yet. I own I look forward
with dread to some of the journeys I shall have to make
on postcars. 500 miles at a stretch with 4, 5 or 6 hours

allowed at night, according to the fancies of the black drivers. However, others have got through and I suppose I shall. I am working hard at my book and the letters, doing a bit piecemeal here and there as I get on. It is the best way with such a work, but it is troublesome and requires continual thought.

King Williamstown. Aug. 22.

This morning about 20 Kaffir chiefs were brought in to town to talk to me. They came with an interpreter, who explained the conversation backwards and forwards. Only one chief talked, and he declared that everything was as bad as it could be; that the Kaffirs were horribly ill-treated by the English; that they were made to wear breeches instead of paint, which was very cruel, and that upon the whole the English had done a great deal more harm than good. He was a dirty, half-drunken savage who wore a sixpenny watch key by way of an earring in one ear. He ended by begging tobacco and "God's blessing" me for giving him 2/6d. The other 19 stood by silent and went away when he went.

Pietermaritzburg. Sept. 3.

Here I am at the extreme of my journey as far as distance is concerned. . . . I think I shall bring my book nearly finished with me. I am writing very hard, tasking myself to write 1300 words a day—which as I am travelling all the time is hard enough.

Potchefstroom,
Transvaal. Oct. 7.

I do so long to get home! South Africa is so dirty. But I shall I hope do so before the first week in January. Not all the books in Christendom shall make me later than that.

Kimberley. Oct. 8.

Buy for me so that I may have it on my arrival C.O. list of 1877. I also want the blue book about the Transvaal, I think No. C 1748, published early in 1877, before the

L

annexation.   I have the continuation treating of the annexation. . . .

Heat here: 96 shade, 160 sun; supposed heat in infernal
regions: 94 shade (if any), 156 full brimstone.

Mossel Bay.   Oct. 9.

I am at this moment in an awful scramble, going off in
twenty minutes on an expedition with a man I never saw till
an hour and a half ago, in quest of grand scenery.   The
grandest scenery in the world to me would be Montagu
Square.

I expect to be back in Cape Town in about ten days and
to leave that place for England about the 17th of December,
which should land me at Plymouth on the 8th January, and
bring me to London on the 9th.

Griqualand.   Oct. 15.

I will not describe to you this most detestable place
because I must write about it and you must read what I write.
I have been handling diamonds till I am sick of them.   But
the great hole out of which they come is certainly the most
marvellous place I have ever seen.

We have had such adventures with our cart and horses,
but sold them yesterday by auction for £100.   All that,
however, will also be in the book.   But I shall not put in the
book that I had to get the governor to send the inspector of
police to the auctioneer before I could get my money!

Bloemfontein.   Oct. 24.

Since this morning I have seen the president of the
Orange Free State.   He seems to be a good sort of old
gentleman, very quiet, with a good sort of old wife, very
quiet too.   Everything here is very quiet. . . .

Trollope reached home again in January 1878.   He brought
back the manuscript of his two-volume book about South
Africa, which was published during March.   There is a legend
that he brought back also news of a novel of South African life
then being slowly written by a young woman named Olive

Schreiner. But it is only a legend and, on the authority of one familiar with Olive Schreiner's early life, must be declared apocryphal. When five years later (early in 1883) Chapman & Hall published *The Story of an African Farm* by "Ralph Iron," they acted on no word of Trollope's, but were persuaded by the critical enthusiasm of George Meredith.

Nevertheless, though Trollope must be denied any share in the establishment of Olive Schreiner's fame, he rendered good service to South Africa, which service has been acknowledged by Sarah Gertrude Millin—the second outstanding figure in the dynasty of South African woman-writers. Trollope's book on South Africa was, when it appeared, the least successful of his travel-books. Froude (not disinclined to regard South Africa as a special province of his own since he had toured it officially a year or two before) spoke sneeringly of "the buzzings of an intellectual blue bottle." Yet, nearly fifty years after it was published, Trollope's *South Africa* came into a reputation. The very first words of Mrs. Millin's book *The South Africans* [1] are these:—

> When Anthony Trollope came to South Africa in the year 1877, he went through it—its provinces and its problems—with his characteristic swift and imperturbable thoroughness. He dined with governors, slept in Boer farmhouses, inspected mission-schools, chatted with Kaffirs, with Hottentots, with poor whites, with Dutchmen, with Englishmen. He bought a cart and a team of horses, and travelled across land as yet untracked by railways. He entered a Transvaal recently annexed by Sir Theophilus Shepstone, his eight Civil servants and twenty-five policemen. He chronicled, as he went on his way, a new revolt by Kreli and his Galekas. He realised the importance of the diamond-fields, but barely foresaw the consequences of the gold-fields. He stood, that is, at the very point in history where the old Africa ended and the new Africa began. He looked at what was shown him and listened to what was told him and said: "I shall write my book and not yours."

[1] London, 1926.

He built up, as day by day he discharged on paper his clear and detailed impressions, as sane and wise a book on South Africa as has ever been written, a book which, despite some mistakes, has still, for our own times, its meaning.

Here is a tribute of the kind Trollope would have liked the best. Mrs. Millin gives credit where credit should be given— to his perception, to his judgment of men and policies, to his good sense. It is fair to say that she has avowed his genius also. It is no small thing for a man, after a six months' tour of many thousand miles in a strange country, so to gauge that country's character and problems that his judgment can be re-quoted half a century later as still essentially correct.

4

A decision—made about this time—finally to give up hunting was the first sign that Trollope felt the burden of his age. Though he was not long past sixty, his life had been unusually laborious, and the short sight which had always handicapped him in the field could no longer be counterbalanced by muscular energy.

Alas, alas [he wrote to Blackwood in March 1878] my hunting is over. I have given away my breeches, boots and horses. The abnegations forced upon us by age should be accepted gracefully. I have not therefore waited to drain the cup to the last drop.

There is wistfulness also in this later note, condoling with John Blackwood over his son's accident:—

October 11 1878.

I am very sorry to hear about William B. I suppose it will not much interfere with his hunting, as you say the fracture is not bad. To a hunting man a broken leg out of the season is nothing. Many a man would think it simply a beneficent arrangement of Providence so to break all his limbs about the middle of April as to have them again fit for the saddle on the first of November.

But although hunting had to be abandoned, Trollope was still more than equal to work, to social duties and to holidays. Of his trip to Iceland in the yacht "Mastiff" he made an article for the *Fortnightly* [1] and also left a genial record in the book *How the "Mastiffs" went to Iceland*, which was printed privately by John Burns of Castle Wemyss (afterward Lord Inverclyde), the yacht's owner and the organiser of the voyage. Among the persons to whom copies were presented was Miss Thora Pjetursson, daughter of the Bishop of Iceland, whom Trollope describes in his book as "the heroine of Reykjavik." This young woman, delighted with her appearance in the chronicle, wrote to one of the ladies of the party:—

Reykjavik.
29 March 1879.

Mr. Burns sent me the book entitled *How the "Mastiffs" went to Iceland.* I very much enjoy reading it, and to look at the pictures, which I think are very good. I think I know every one, so like they are. I like to read books of travels, especially about Iceland. I think Mr. Trollope writes very well about the country, and everything he mentions in his book.

If Mr. Trollope comes once more to Iceland, I will tell him that I feel so much flattery, in his book—about me— that I scarcely know myself when I read it. I will tell him when I come some day to Scotland, I hope then to meet him and then I will put him in my book of travels. No! I will write a special book about him, and then I hope he will not feel him lesser flattered than I do, when I read his book. I am afraid if he saw this letter, he would not speak so high of my English as he does in his book; I am sorry that I cannot write better English, than I do, but I am too lazy to study it thoroughly, as I ought to do.

To which Trollope, through the same lady, replied:—

April 10 1879.

I am very much obliged to you for sending me Thora's letter,—the divine Thora. I now return it. You ought to

---

[1] *Fortnightly Review*, August 1878. The article was also issued as a pamphlet.

send it to Wilson—Whether it would be a comfort who could say, because she makes no mention of him! Do you remember when she gave Wilson the bit of grass to eat?

Tell Thora that I shall look forward anxiously to her book of travels in which she is to mention me.

In August he was in Switzerland and wrote to George Eliot:—

Felsinegg.
August 13 1878.

DEAR FRIEND,

Your kindest letter has at length found me here.

After seeing you last, there came to me an invitation to join a party in a trip to Iceland, and to Iceland I went. How I fared in Iceland and was driven to talk Latin to my guide —in which accomplishment I was barely his inferior,— you may see in the *Fortnightly*.

Here we are on the top of a mountain, where I write for four hours a day, walk for four hours, eat for two, and sleep out the balance satisfactorily. I am beginning to think that the more a man can sleep the better for him. I can take a nap of nine hours each night without moving in these latitudes.

But as the months passed the weariness of age increased.

When I am written to [he wrote in January 1879] I answer like a man at an interval of a week or so. But in truth I am growing so old that, though I still do my daily work, I am forced to put off the lighter tasks from day to day. I do not feel like that in the cheery morning; but when I have been cudgelling my over-wrought brain for some three or four hours in quest of words, than I fade down and begin to think it will be nice to go to the club and have tea and play whist.

In 1880 it was decided to leave London and, for the relief of the asthma which was seriously troubling him, to settle at South Harting, near Petersfield. Visits to London were occasionally made, Trollope staying at Garland's Hotel in Suffolk Street, calling on his publishers, attending his meetings. But he spent most of his time in the country, watching the seasons with a quiet detachment, oddly aloof from the world in which once he loved to jostle and gesticulate. The letters to Henry Trollope have now a new quality of melancholy patience:—

> *39 Montagu Square.*
> *June* 27 1880.

In one week more we start from town. . . . It makes me melancholy;—though I believe I shall be happier there than I am here. I hate the dinner parties and all going out.

> *Harting.*
> 21 *December* 1880.

I miss you most painfully. But I had expected that. I only hope that you may come back with the summer. This is the longest day of winter and I shall begin now to look to the lengthening days. Ah, me! How I used to look for the shortening days when I was hunting, and had the first of November as a golden day before me for which my soul could long. I have now to look for the time when the green things in the garden may begin to show themselves. But the expectation of green things in another garden prevents me from being sad.

I finished on Thursday the novel I was writing, and on Friday I began another. Nothing really frightens me but the idea of enforced idleness. As long as I can write books, even though they be not published, I think that I can be happy.

> *Jan.* 24 1881.

Mamma and I have just settled that you are a pig. You promised to get cards and got none. Here we are snowed up in a most exigent manner. I went to-day up to the top of the White Hill, but to get there was a wonderful undertaking. To get down was worse. There were 3 or 4 feet of snow and a white mist blinding everything. When will it go away? We have had a week and not a grain has moved as yet: It is very melancholy.

To Alfred Austin he writes more cheerfully:—

Yes, we have changed our mode of life altogether. We have got a little cottage here, just big enough (or nearly so) to hold my books, with five acres and a cow and a dog and a cock and a hen. I have got seventeen years' lease, and therefore I hope to lay my bones here. Nevertheless I am as busy as would be one thirty years younger, in cutting out dead boughs, and putting up a paling here and a little gate there. We go to church and mean to be very good, and have maids to wait on us. The reason for all this I will explain when I see you, although, as far as I see at present, there is no good reason other than that we were tired of London.

In July comes a flash of the old pugnacity. The editor of the *Graphic* had imprudently complained of the serial possibilities of *Marion Fay*. Many difficulties had been raised as to American and Australian publication, to convenient division of the chapters, to adjustment of contract dates and periodical commitments. Memories of Dallas and of the now distant quarrel over *The Vicar of Bullhampton* warmed the old novelist's indignation.

My dear Sir [he wrote on July 13 1881] it is quite out of the question. Your letter would appear to me to be most unreasonable. You and Mr. Heaton must misunderstand each other.

I say in one of my letters to him, in which he had written about the American reprint: "I must beg it to be understood that the book will be published here in May 1882 whether completed in America or not."

You have had the book for months on your hands and have printed nearly all. The book is a regular 3 volume novel, *exactly* of the same length as my other 3 vol. novels. You have the advantage of the greater length than you expected. You have had more than a year to find out how to work it. It seems to me that you ask me to rectify your mistake by asking me to abandon my own interests.

You complain of the chapters. They are nearly all of the same length. No writer ever made work come easier to the editor of a periodical than I do.

With the dawning of 1882 the languor of fatigue becomes a definite admission of ill-health. From Cheshire, for example, in November 1881 he writes to his son:—

I am down here at Davenports, for a few days. Eating and drinking;—all eating and drinking! But as I dislike eating and drinking more than is usual, the time runs heavy.

But, alas, it has come to this—that all times run more or less heavy with me, unless when I am asleep.

Soon afterwards a London doctor diagnosed angina pectoris; a second doctor disagreed. Trollope writes to his son from Harting:—

What Dr. Murrell says is mainly true; but then what Dr. Cross said about me was also mainly true. I do not believe that I have any symptoms of angina pectoris, but I have got to be old, and nearly worn out by the disease of age.

They bade him go slowly, take life easily. His obedience was very intermittent. Old habits of impetuosity could not be cured in a few days by doctor's orders. Nevertheless with the spring came a renewal of strength and an inopportune excuse to make use of it.

The dreadful news of the Phœnix Park Murders on May 6 spurred the old man to an enterprise really beyond his strength. He had known Ireland well during her tragic 'forties; trouble had come upon her once again, and he must be there to see it and to help. Against the advice and wishes of his friends he obstinately journeyed across the St. George's Channel. When he returned he was much stronger and more cheerful. His asthma was relieved, and he made genial mock of those who would have kept him inactive. He began to write a novel— *The Landleaguers*—which should in some sort be a companion

L*

picture to *Castle Richmond*. Full of the interest of his task, he
spent the early months of summer happily at Harting, with
friends about him and the flowery garden and easy scented
walks along the hills to southward.

But in July *The Landleaguers* grew troublesome. The book
was not running easily. Trollope worried to find it limping
on its way, when usually his stories moved so lissomely. He
declared that another visit to Ireland must be made, in order
that new information and fuller details might be gathered for
the invigoration of his tale. Again his family protested; again
he was obstinate.

But from this second journey, taken in August heat, he
returned weary and dispirited. His wife, conscious of isolation
in the country and wishful to be within easy reach of doctors,
persuaded him to go to London for the winter. They left
Harting in late September and settled into rooms at Garland's
Hotel. . . .

THE FINAL SCENE

ON THE EVENING of November 3 1882 Sir John Tilley, his daughter, and Anthony Trollope his brother-in-law, were dining quietly in London. The old novelist was in exaggerated spirits. Indeed he was somewhat over-excited, for during the afternoon he had come to altercation with the leader of a German band which had played disturbingly under his window at Garland's Hotel. But in the gaiety of intimate talk his too-emphatic laughter passed unnoticed.

After dinner the little party settled in the drawing-room to read aloud from Anstey's *Vice Versa*. This story had just been published, and was the craze of every London gathering at which books were a theme of conversation.

The reading aloud progressed. Every now and again great gusts of laughter caught both listeners and reader, so that the tale was broken off and the room grew clamorous with shouted merriment.

But in the very midst of one such joyful interruption came realisation of a sudden silence. The loudest laugh of all had failed to sound. Trollope had had a stroke, and lay there speechless, propped crookedly against his easy-chair.

They moved him to a house in Welbeck Street. He rallied; sank again. For nearly five weeks he lingered on, hardly speaking, only intermittently aware of those about his bed. On the evening of December 6 1882 he died.

Thus, laughing, he passed out of a world of laughter; thus from the land of men and women whom he had so shrewdly understood, so tenderly described, he crossed over to that further shore, whence (in his own words) he stretches out his hand, bidding farewell.

HE WAS AT ONCE formidable and pathetic. Like a great dog he had strength and could use it; but beneath the strength was tenderness and in the bright eyes a something of appeal.

By superficial acquaintance the stranger did not often penetrate beyond the roughness of the outer man. Hence the Trollope of casual tradition—the "noisy bow-wow" Trollope, the Trollope of whose "dissatisfied rumblings" Browning used to speak.

"Tall, bearded, growling and spectacled, he was a tough customer for any stripling. I had cut myself shaving and he took care to tell me so at the outset." Such was Walter Sichel's first impression [1]; while Escott's story of an encounter in a train gives another vivid surface-picture.[2] It was during the 'seventies, and into a compartment of a night express at Euston already occupied by the young journalist, climbed a bulky figure in an enormous ulster. The two had previously met, and Trollope, acknowledging the young man's salutation, talked gustily for half an hour. Then, taking a large fur cap from his portmanteau and pulling it over his head, he said abruptly: "Do you ever sleep in the train? I always do." After snoring loudly in his corner for two hours, he woke as though by arrangement, got out his travelling lamp, his writing tablet and his pencil. Once more he spoke: "Do you ever write in the train? I always do." And he did, until his journey's end, saying no other word beyond a gruff farewell.

But all who experienced his asperity affirmed that no cruelty went with it. He might be brusque, but he was never venomous. Consequently the only people angered by his manner were unreasonable persons or themselves guilty of some meanness which he was castigating.

---

[1] *The Sands of Time*, by Walter Sichel. London, 1925.
[2] Told in his book on Trollope.

So much for casual acquaintances. His more intimate friends, who knew that with the gruffness would alternate boisterous gaiety, loved him the better for his contrasts. In cheerful company he was always noisy and vociferous; at times he was addicted to a mild horseplay. He was a great— almost a ruthless—talker, with a loud voice and many opinions. One personal memory tells of a dinner at the Friths, and of Trollope capturing the whole conversation and by sheer lung-power holding it a prisoner. The children at a house where he would often dine can still recall hanging over the banisters as the guests came to the big drawing-room and seeing Trollope —all rosy cheeks and bushy whiskers—pause for a moment at a mirror by the door, ruffle his hair and plunge into the room with a huge roar of greeting. The Committee table at the Garrick was, when Trollope sat there, the most resounding table in the coffee-room. At dinner with the Blackwoods he would make loud jest of the fierce loyalty and conservatism of "Maga." "Now, Blackwood, what possible effect would the Queen's death have on *you*? You know perfectly well that you would eat just as good a breakfast the next morning!" "Confess, Blackwood, that you think about Dizzy exactly as I do. You'd be delighted to hear he had been caught shop-lifting." On the links (John Blackwood's beautiful home Strathtyrum was near St. Andrews) he was as much buffoon as golfer. When he missed a shot he would pretend to faint, falling so heavily upon the sandy ground that the very earth shook.

Abroad he was the same naïve but emphatic creature as at home. He loved the jostle, the comic discomforts, the brusque encounters of journeys about the world, enjoying his own strength, relishing his own absurdity, stubborn in his assertion of the minor decencies of travel. His records of globe-trotting are full of personal misadventure. In British Guiana he tries in vain to escape behind his bedroom door from the persistent civilities of the black chambermaid, who must curtsey to him even when he is in his nightshirt. The voyage to Iceland is memorable for the siege of the deck cabin, during which someone emptied a pail of water on his head. Australia and

South Africa each provide experience, embarrassing but pleasurably ludicrous. Small calamities continually form the theme of his short stories. The mustard-plaster incident of *Thompson Hall* and the adventure of *The Man Who Kept his Money in a Box* did not actually (as did several others of their kind) befall Trollope himself; but he heard tell of them and relished their implications of dilemma.

As a travelling Englishman he would stand no nonsense. Once on the Alps he and his elder brother Tom returned from wayside *déjeuner* to find two Frenchmen seated in their places in the diligence. Expostulation had no effect. "Stand below, Anthony" cried Tom "and I will hand them down!" Whereupon he climbed the diligence, lifted the Frenchmen in his arms and dropped them over the edge to Anthony, who set them side by side upon the ground.

Toward freshness or presumption he was unmerciful. The young man with the cracked voice on board the liner to South Africa was, one may be sure, not unsnubbable for long. There was a lady once who ventured an impertinence. Sitting next Trollope at dinner she noticed that he partook largely of every dish offered to him. "You seem to have a very good appetite, Mr. Trollope" she observed. "None at all, madam" he replied "but, thank God, I am very greedy."

Another story is of his treatment of a consequential parvenu. A bumptious little man, very fine in his red coat, mounted on several hundred guineas' worth of horseflesh and wearing a peaked cap, forced his conversation on Trollope at a covertside. One remark struck the novelist as too ill-bred to be endured. "Get away!" he cried. "You monkey in top boots!"

That anecdote became part of the traditions of the hunt and has in consequence survived. But Trollope himself preferred its quaint companion-incident, which he put verbatim into a novel, so much did he enjoy his own discomfiture.

Kate Masters, though fifteen and quite up to that age in intelligence and impudence, was small and looked almost a child. "That's a nice pony of yours, my dear," said Lord

Rufford. Kate, who didn't quite like being called "my dear," said that it was a very good pony.

"Suppose we change," said his lordship. "Could you ride my horse?"

"He's very big," said Kate.

"You'd look like a tomtit on a haystack," said his lordship.

"If you got on my pony," said Kate, "you'd look like a haystack on a tomtit."

It was felt that Kate Masters had had the best of that encounter.[1]

2

In personal appearance Trollope was fresh-coloured, upright and sturdy. Although not quite six feet in height, his broad shoulders, fine head and vigorous power of gesture gave an impression of size beyond his actual inches. Everyone who met him remarked on the extraordinary brilliance of his black eyes, which, behind the strong lenses of his spectacles, shone (as one memorist records) "with a certain genial fury of inspection." There was little enough that those piercing eyes overlooked. On entering a roomful of people or on taking his seat at table, he would throw one quick, searching glance over the company and then sit awhile, his eyes downcast to carpet or to tablecloth. He was arranging his first impressions. Later and at leisure he would amplify with further observation his memory of such personal traits or mannerisms as had caught his attention.

His voice was bass and resonant. Lady Ritchie in her journal for 1865 speaks of his "deep, cheerful, lispy voice." His laugh was, at its healthiest, a bellow.

For so large a man he was easy of movement and could sit a horse, if not with elegance, at least with monumental certainty. He was a strong walker, a good eater, a connoisseur of wine and an insatiable disputant. In everything he did, in his every taste and talent, he was full-blooded and thorough, having the health and strength sufficient for his moderate but manifold enjoyments. Extreme short sight was, indeed, his only dis-

[1] *The American Senator.* Vol. I, p. 116.

ability. This, in the hunting field, was a continual source of mishap. "I am too blind" he says in the *Autobiography* "to see hounds turning. . . . My eyes are so constituted that I can never see the nature of a fence. I either follow someone or ride at it with the full conviction that I may be going into a horse-pond or a gravel pit. I have plunged into both one and the other." Now and again his spectacles would fall off. Then he would sit his horse and roar for help, not daring to dismount or move an inch lest they be trampled to pieces.

In *Can You Forgive Her?* he satirises himself as hunting man in the person of Mr. Pollock "the heavy-weight sporting literary gentleman."

"By George, there's Pollock!" said Maxwell. "I'll bet half a crown that he's come down from London this morning, that he was up all last night, and that he tells us so three times before the hounds go out of the paddock."

Shortly afterward:—

"Well, Pollock, when did you come?" said Maxwell.
"By George," said the literary gentleman. "Just down from London by the 8.30 from Euston Square, and got over here from Winslow in a trap with two fellows I never saw in my life before. We came tandem in a fly, and did the nineteen miles in an hour."
"Come, Athenian, draw it mild" said Maxwell.
"We did, indeed. I wonder whether they'll pay me their share of the fly. I had to leave Onslow Crescent at a quarter before eight, and I did three hours' work before I started."
"Then you did it by candlelight" said Grindley.
"Of course I did; and why shouldn't I? Do you suppose no one can work by candlelight except a lawyer?"

Off they go, and in the forefront of the hunt is Burgo Fitzgerald.

But almost neck to neck with Burgo was Pollock. Pollock had but two horses to his stud and was never known to give much money for them:—and he weighed without his boots,

fifteen stone! No one ever knew how Pollock did it;—
more especially as all the world declared that he was as
ignorant of hunting as any tailor. He could ride, or when
he couldn't ride he could tumble,—men said of him,—and
he would ride as long as the beast under him could go. But
few knew the sad misfortunes which poor Pollock sometimes encountered;—the muddy ditches in which he was
left; the despair with which he would stand by his unfortunate horse when the poor brute could no longer move
across some deep-ploughed field; the miles that he would
walk at night beside a tired animal, as he made his way
slowly back to Roebury.

In his study at Montagu Square he kept a dozen pairs of
spectacles upon the mantelpiece. A caller, ushered in upon
him, would see a heavy figure rise from the desk, hurry to the
fireplace and there fumble feverishly among the littered
spectacles for the pair best able to reveal the visitor's identity.

3

But the fierceness, the jollity, and the large healthy vigour
of his flesh and blood were not all of Trollope. Beneath them
lurked an under-self, a timid, melancholy wraith of past unhappiness, of whose existence only the very intimate or the
very perceptive were aware. Fortunately one of the latter has
borne testimony. Julian Hawthorne, son of Nathaniel, met
Trollope for the first time in 1879. His description of the
incident and his reading of the novelist's character are so
detailed and so wise that in them the old man almost lives
again.

> During the winter of 1879, when I was in London, it
> was my fortune to attend a social meeting of literary men at
> the rooms of a certain eminent publisher. The rooms were
> full of tobacco-smoke and talk, amid which were discern-
> ible, on all sides, the figures and faces of men more or less
> renowned in the world of books.
> Most noticeable among these personages was a broad-

shouldered, sturdy man, of middle height, with a ruddy countenance, and snow-white tempestuous beard and hair. He wore large, gold-rimmed spectacles, but his eyes were black and brilliant. He seemed to be in a state of some excitement; he spoke volubly and almost boisterously, and his voice was full-toned and powerful, though pleasant to the ear. He turned himself, as he spoke, with a burly brisk-ness, from one side to another, addressing himself first to this auditor and then to that, his words bursting forth from beneath his white moustache with such an impetus of hearty breath that it seemed as if all opposing arguments must be blown away. Meanwhile he flourished in the air an ebony walking-stick, with much vigor of gesticulation, and narrowly missing, as it appeared, the pates of his listeners. He was clad in evening dress, though the rest of the com-pany was, for the most part, in mufti; and he was an exceedingly fine-looking old gentleman.

At the first glance, you would have taken him to be some civilized and modernized Squire Western, nourished with beef and ale, and roughly hewn out of the most robust and least refined variety of human clay. Looking at him more narrowly, however, you would have reconsidered this judg-ment. Though his general contour and aspect were massive and sturdy, the lines of his features were delicately cut; his complexion was remarkably pure and fine, and his face was susceptible of very subtle and sensitive changes of expres-sion. Here was a man of abundant physical strength and vigor, no doubt, but carrying within him a nature more than commonly alert and impressible. His organization, though thoroughly healthy, was both complex and high-wrought; his character was simple and straightforward to a fault, but he was abnormally conscientious, and keenly alive to others' opinion concerning him. It might be thought that he was overburdened with self-esteem, and unduly opinionated; but, in fact, he was but over-anxious to secure the goodwill and agreement of all with whom he came in contact. There was some peculiarity in him—some element or bias in his composition that made him different from other men; but, on the other hand, there was an ardent solicitude to annul or reconcile this difference, and to prove himself to be, in fact, of absolutely the same cut and quality as all the rest of the world. Hence when he was in a demonstrative, expository or argumentative mood, he could not sit quiet in the face of a divergence between himself and his associates; he was incorrigibly strenuous to obliterate or harmonise the irreconcilable points between him and others; and since these points remained irreconcilable, he remained in a constant state of storm and stress on the subject.

It was impossible to help liking such a man at first sight; and I believe that no man in London society was more generally liked than Anthony Trollope. There was something pathetic in his attitude as above indicated; and a fresh and boyish quality always invested him. His artlessness was boyish, and so were his acuteness and his transparent but somewhat belated good-sense. He was one of those rare persons who not only have no reserves, but who can afford to dispense with them. After he had shown you all he had in him, you would have seen nothing that was not gentlemanly, honest and clean. He was a quick-tempered man, and the ardour and hurry of his temperament made him seem more so than he really was; but he was never more angry than he was forgiving and generous. He was hurt by little things, and little things pleased him; he was suspicious and perverse, but in a manner that rather endeared him to you than otherwise. Altogether, to a casual acquaintance, who knew nothing of his personal history, he was something of a paradox—an entertaining contradiction.[1]

When he wrote this, Hawthorne wrote something more than a skilful reminiscence; he diagnosed (and with rare subtlety considering the slightness of their acquaintance) the cardinal element in Trollope's character—its intriguing, wistful, lovable duality. Never in one man was there a greater contrast between the manner and the spirit; between the outward assurance and the inward uncertainty; between the

---

[1] *Confessions and Criticisms*, by Julian Hawthorne. Boston, 1887.

seeming asperity and the actual tender-heartedness; between the rough insensibility of gesture and the delicate transparency of mind. This fundamental conflict between the inner and outer man symbolises his whole life story. Within the vehement shell which the world knew as Trollope the successful novelist, cowered a secret Trollope—diffident, defenceless and forlorn. Behind the prosperous years at Waltham and in London lay—shadowy but unforgotten—a tormented childhood.

The circumstances of his upbringing explain of themselves why his later self-assertiveness, so far from seeming arrogant, struck the sensitive American as obscurely depreciatory. They must inevitably have produced an eagerness to justify himself, to prove his oneness with his kind. He never outgrew the nervousness which had made a torture of his schooldays— the terrified conviction that he was not like the other boys, that he was odd or dowdy, in some way liable to the contempt or the cold-shouldering of those more securely placed, more certain of their right to live. By courage and perseverance, indeed, he won success, and with the consciousness of that success armed himself against his shyness. But although he could pretend to ease of manner and, pretending, could deceive the world, he did not deceive himself. Despite the many warm affections of his later years and despite all that he won of dignity and influence, always deep down in the secret chamber of his being lingered self-consciousness and dread of loneliness and a tremulous conviction of his own inferiority.

He fought against these spectres of despondency, and part at least of his habitual jollity was due to a determination to control tremors which he held to be unmanly. But at intervals— and often when jogging homeward alone from the hunting-field—melancholy would steal over him. "It is, I suppose, some weakness of temperament that makes me, without intelligible cause, such a pessimist at heart" he once confessed to Millais. The cause lay, not in the temperament, but in the circumstances which had formed it. A child's agonised knowledge of inferiority had become a man's infirmity.

To this unhappy obsession must directly be attributed several further characteristics of his maturity. He was always quick to take offence, sometimes where no offence was meant. Impulsive in everything, he would magnify a disagreement into a hatred, a slight discourtesy into a deliberate insult. But the reaction to forgiveness—often to the point beyond forgiveness where blame is gladly shouldered by the very one who blamed —came as quickly as the original irritation. Trollope was incapable of bearing malice or of cherishing a grudge, which fact was well known to most of those with whom he came in conflict. In consequence, the wrath provoked in others by his own rapid tempers was also apt to go as rapidly as it had come, leaving no trace.

And to a suppressed expectation of persecution may also be attributed his ready pugnacity toward superiors and equals. Passages in the *Autobiography* dwelling on the duties and qualities of good breeding have been used by unfriendly critics to support a charge of snobbery. No accusation could be wider of the mark. It is only necessary to read his novels to realise that to him men and women are (or should be) men and women all the time, whatever their circumstances or social standing. He never judges a man by his position, his riches or his successfulness, but by the use he makes of them. To him a good man is one who lives up to or rises above his opportunities, a bad man one who abuses them or betrays the code of honour and kindliness which is the heritage of every living being.

With such a philosophy it was obviously necessary for opportunities to be classified and code defined. That is why so many of his books lay stress on the family influences and surroundings of the chief characters, why so many actions are judged by their achieving, or failing to achieve, a definite standard of gentility. Those who by upbringing and tradition are of the world of "gentlemen" sin more venally in that their every falling-off is sin against the light; those who adopt the code of gentlemen by their instinctive honourableness and not by mere inheritance win more thoroughly to grace, because their victory is of their own contriving.

Express this in terms of current social acquaintanceship, and it accounts for Trollope's upstanding aggressiveness toward the strong, and its natural converse—his sympathy and tolerance for the weak. The affection felt for him by country folk, by servants and by all who, whether from age or status, were in a position inferior to his own, is evidence of his accessibility and his unaffected kindliness. To Rowland Hill he was a torment and insubordinate; to the Glasgow postmen he was a god. To the intellectual conceit of cultured Anglo-Florentines or of Morleyite Radicals his pawky mediocrity was—as he meant that it should be—intolerable. But persons in distress, or young people who came to him for help or for advice, found him untiring in assistance, shrewd and fertile in suggestion.

> I wish [says Walter Herries Pollock in a memorial essay on Trollope] that I could give anything like an idea of the hold which he all unconsciously acquired on the affections of all who were fortunate enough to be thrown in his way. To younger men his ways and manner had a special charm that, without for a moment losing dignity, put them on an equality with himself. He happened to be older and therefore more experienced than they were—I do not think it ever occurred to him that he was more clever or more gifted —and whatever help might come to them from his greater experience was at their service as between comrade and comrade.[1]

And if in daily life he was less friendly to the prosperous than responsive to the claims of sorrow or perplexity, as a chronicler of the world about him he was readier to defend the erring than to applaud the virtuous.

Ethel Colburn Mayne once wisely wrote [2]:—

> Trollope achieved his immortality by his perception of the value—the artistic value—of humanity's incompetence.

---

[1] This admirable article—perhaps the best of the memorial tributes written after Trollope's death—was published in *Harper's Monthly Magazine* for May 1883.

[2] Reviewing " The Obstinate Lady," by W. E. Norris, in the *Daily News* on May 10 1919.

All his humour and his sympathy went out to this and made an undercurrent running through the endless pasture of his work, which keeps that and his memory green. This sense of our helplessness and puzzlement and his inexhaustible compassion for it, makes what he tells us so convincing that we can accept his optimism at the end.

One may go further, and to "incompetence" add "wrong-doing." There is hardly a sinner in his books who is not in some way also a claimant on our sympathy. A review of *Orley Farm* published in the *Cornhill* speaks of Lady Mason and her crime of forgery. "It is the sinner we pity, not the sin we absolve. We estimate the nature of her act; we estimate her temptation; we estimate her character; and the sum total of our judgment is that she sinned where a woman of stronger character would have resisted temptation, but nevertheless apart from this she is pitiable, lovable. We do not murmur at her punishment; but we feel with her, feel for her." This is true, not only of Lady Mason, but of other wrong-doers in Trollope's novels. Is not Lady Ongar pitiable? And Lady Laura Kennedy? Is there not an appeal even in such a rascal as George Vavasor?

This understanding of human helplessness and frailty was only possible to one conscious of his own infirmities. Trollope was sympathetic to incompetence, because he held himself fated to be incompetent. But because he was now captain of his soul, he could hold out to others caught in the tangle of their own mismanagement the prospect of release.

This great personal achievement gave him a forcefulness which impressed others with a complete confidence alike in his advice and in his judgment. Everybody trusted him. The influence which he exercised was based on trust—trust in his wisdom, his sense of justice, his honesty and his tolerance.

He was tolerant partly from experience but mainly because he had that understanding of human foibles which is neither intellect nor intelligence, but a sort of super-sense of the power of temptation and the means to overcome it. He always liked to think the best of everybody, and in his books he is at pains to bring out the good points even of persons in the main contemptible.[1]

In the advice which he so gladly gave and in the consolation which was never asked in vain, he blended commonsense with an instinctive reading of the heart. Also, his stern philosophy of individual effort kept him—and quite consistently—from that censoriousness which is really moral tyranny. His personal code of morality was a strict one, but he never sought to impose it upon other people. Partly because he wished to allow to others the liberty of private action, he claimed for himself, partly because the prying insolence of gossip and of Watch Committees offended his sense of charity towards one's neighbour—he was, to a degree unusual in his period, broad-minded and free from prejudice.

Two interesting letters illustrate, the one his opposition to conventional disapproval, the other his refusal to betray the privacy of a dead friend.

(*To Rhoda Broughton*)

Washington. 28 *June* 1868.

DEAR MADAM,

I have just read your novel *Not Wisely but too Well* and wish to tell you how much it has pleased me. I should not write you on such a matter if I were not also a novelist and one much interested in the general virtues and vices, shortcomings and excellences of my brethren. Some months since I was told by a friend,—a lady whom I know to be a good critic,—that *Cometh Up as a Flower* was a book that I ought to read; that your later published novel was also very clever, though not equal to the one which was earlier given to the public. This lady, who is an intimate friend of mine, told me either that she knew you or that some mutual friend created an interest on her behalf in

---

[1] One example may suffice—that of Sowerby in *Framley Parsonage*. Trollope's plea for a charitable judgment on Sowerby occupies pp. 141-142 of the second volume.

your writings. I do not often read novels, but I did the
other day, here in America, purchase, and have since read,
the one I have named. I must tell you also that I have
heard that your stories were written in a strain not becoming
a woman young as you are—not indeed becoming any
woman. I tell you this without reserve, as doubtless the
same report must have reached your ears.

In the story which I have read there is not a word that
I would not have had written by my sister, or my daughter
—if I had one. I do not understand the critics who, when
there is so much that is foul abroad, can settle down with
claws and beaks on a tale which teaches a wholesome lesson
without an impure picture or a faulty expression. I will
not say that your story is perfect. Having been probably
ten times as many years at the work as you have, I think,
were I with you, I could point out faults here and there
against nature. You fall into the common faults of the
young, making that which is prosaic in life too prosaic, and
that which is poetic, too poetic. The fault here is of exaggeration. But I read your tale with intense interest. I
wept over it, and formed my wishes on it, and came to the
conclusion that there had come up another sister among us,
of whose name we should be proud.

Yours with much admiration.

It is difficult nowadays to realise the tempest of shocked
indignation that raged about Rhoda Broughton's early novels
and in particular *Not Wisely*. She was attacked for immorality, for tarnishing the fair name of womanhood, for leading
the young and innocent astray. A little scared, she was in
danger of retreating into sullen defiance, when at the critical
moment came this letter from the famous Trollope.

One cannot doubt that the letter gave her poise and confidence, but it is sad to have to record that she soon forgot whatever gratitude she may have felt. An essay about Rhoda
Broughton printed in another book of mine[1] quotes exten-
sively from her letters to her publisher, in the course of one

[1] *Things Past*, p. 90.

of which she makes a peevish reference to Trollope as a man who is never known to praise any of his fellow-writers.

The second letter is a reply to an inquiry from Kate Field for certain details of George Eliot's private life. Kate was writing a memoir of the woman-novelist, who had died on December 22 1880.

> Harting,
> Petersfield.
> Jan. 17 1881.

DEAR KATE,

I hardly know how to answer your letter because, though I was very intimate with George Eliot, she never spoke to me of her life before I knew her, nor, as far as I am aware, did she to her other friends. Nor did he. He was a friendly affectionate man,—but very reticent, especially as to the matters which concerned her.

I do not know where G. E. and Lewes became acquainted. I think it was in the pages of *Blackwood's*, if the word can be applied to a magazine. I think I may say that the two were acquainted some time before *Adam Bede* came out. I knew them, being together, shortly after the publication of *Adam Bede*. But my impression, though I feel sure of it for my own purposes, cannot be taken as a positive assertion. You may say that she had lived down evil tongues before Lewes's death. She was asked to dine with Queen Victoria's daughter (Crown Princess of Prussia), when the Princess was in England. I mention this because the English Royal family are awfully particular as to whom they see and do not see. That at any rate is true, because I was there.

But in truth she was one whose private life should be left in privacy.

Affectionately yours.

With Trollope's tolerance went wisdom. He was wise because he knew the world; and, unlike many who boast that knowledge, knew men and women even better than their institutions. His sense of justice was notorious. Certain aspects of it have been revealed in letters earlier quoted; others are shown—and repeatedly—in his novels. Every meanness or betrayal which in the books is punished with righteous violence is a meanness personally hated by Trollope, and (almost without exception) one with which the law cannot deal. It is as though he promised himself that, if in life a certain type of scoundrel can go scatheless, he should not miss his due of chastisement in the imaginary world of Trollope fiction.

There remains his honesty, his disinterested zeal for genuine work and for that work's reward. Once again his own record is his best testimonial. The *Autobiography* contains a trenchant statement of the critic's duty to the author, but also one no less trenchant of the author's proper demeanour toward the critic:—

> I made up my mind that I would have no dealings with any critic on my own behalf. I would neither ask for nor deplore criticism, nor would I ever thank a critic for praise or quarrel with him for censure. To this rule I have adhered.

And in another place:—

> A critic showed me the manuscript of a book recently published—the work of a popular author. It was handsomely bound and was a valuable and desirable possession. It had just been given to him by the author as an acknowledgment for a laudatory review. I said I thought the token should neither have been given nor have been taken. I was told that I was straitlaced, visionary and unpractical.

Such preaching was but the culmination of years of practice. A young friend once went to him and said: "A book of yours has been sent to me for review. I don't think I ought to review it, but I have come to ask you." "No, my boy" Trollope replied. "I don't think you ought to review a book of mine any more than I ought to review one of yours."

Another incident is recorded by Alfred Austin, who was present when Trollope read a highly eulogistic article on his books from the pen of a partial writer. Though sensitive to praise and at times pathetically eager for it, Trollope could not tolerate any eulogy based on personal friendship rather than an admiration for his work. With the look and manner that Wilkie Collins once described as "an incarnated gale of wind," he threw the magazine across the room; then wrote to the well-meaning eulogist a most discouraging letter:—

> I don't like such notices. I would much rather be left to the mercies of the real critics. Sydney Smith used to say it was impossible to say how much melted butter a gentleman would bear to have poured into his dresscoat pocket; I dislike it almost as much when it is poured down my back.[1]

Because it was known that he maintained an extreme of independence; because, whatever help he might give to others, he never swerved from the determination himself neither to accept nor to solicit a literary favour—the effect of his stern idealism on his reputation was final and complete. It set a pinnacle of incorruptibility upon the temple of his sturdy commonsense, which towered—serene, solid and trustworthy —above the crowded buildings of the mid-Victorian literary scene.

4

"I do not think it ever occurred to him that he was more clever or more gifted than they," says Walter Herries Pollock in the article above quoted. The critic is speaking of Trollope's bearing toward his juniors, but the words apply equally to his bearing throughout life and toward all and sundry. He was the most modest of men, and wholly without jealousy.

Modesty is one of the dominant flavours of the *Autobiography*. It is continually noticeable, and yet blends so naturally with the general narrative that its genuineness is never once in doubt. False humility provokes embarrassment; the downright modesty of Trollope puts one at ease.

It is unnecessary to quote from the *Autobiography* the phrases and passages of self-depreciation so plentifully sprinkled through its pages. They are well known, having been more

[1] " Last Reminiscences of Anthony Trollope," *Temple Bar*, January 1884.

frequently quoted than almost any other section of the book. To them, however, may be added one or two stories less generally familiar, which illustrate the unassuming candour of his self-valuation, and his readiness, even in this matter of modesty, to make fun of himself.

Dining with the Leweses he was discussing modes of writing with his hostess. George Eliot quivered with all the sensibility of genius to hear of the scheduled hours of productivity from half-past five (even in winter-time) until the breakfast gong. "There are days together," she groaned, "when I cannot write a line." "Oh, well," replied Trollope, "with imaginative work like yours that is quite natural; but with my mechanical stuff it's a sheer matter of industry."

Toward Carlyle's inability to write without absolute silence he was less charitable. But then he did not like Carlyle, either as an author or a man.

A young relative sent him word of someone who had praised *Barchester Towers*, making particular reference to a certain passage which, he surmised, Trollope had long since forgotten. The old man replied:—

> *Harting.*
> *Dec.* 5 1881.

> *Barchester Towers* was written before you were born. Of course I forget every word of it! But I don't. There is not a passage in it I do not remember. I always have to pretend to forget when people talk to me about my own old books. It looks modest. But the writer never forgets. And when after 30 years he is told by some one that he has been pathetic, or witty, or even funny, he always feels like lending a five-pound note to that fellow.

Trollope's recorded judgment of his own work was, of course, absurdly—even mischievously—harsh. During his lifetime he seldom talked to others of his books, and the low value which after his death the *Autobiography* set upon them was taken disastrously on trust by the generation who succeeded him. Nor did he court posterity's disfavour only by critical depreciation of his books. By stressing his personal qualities of materialism and automatic precision he put words into the very mouths of his detractors.

Whence it came ironically to pass that at the hands of his literary successors he suffered more for his virtues than for his failings. The *Autobiography*, in its extreme of shy defiance, distorted the perspective even of its author's finest qualities. He was, for example, a worker of the most dogged and scrupulous kind. Yet, by his manner of describing this admirable industry he harmed his reputation more seriously than if, in self-revelation, he had shown himself disgruntled, quarrelsome or mean. His contented modesty, his lack of jealousy, his generous candour, were all overshadowed in the estimation of the critics who came after him by his avowed habit of writing to time, by his contemptuous denial of the need for literary inspiration.

That he should thus have written his own sentence to oblivion is comprehensible to those who understand his character. In his heart he was at once vain and a little ashamed of his quantity and methodicality of output—vain, in that by sheer labour he had trained invention to perpetual wakefulness and his pen to write at any moment and at a uniform rate of speed;—ashamed, because even during his lifetime his colleagues laughed at him. To subdue the vanity, he mocked himself more loudly than his critics mocked; to stifle shame, he over-emphasised the very tendency which embarrassed him. In consequence, the *Autobiography* offers in its descriptions of his working method a blend of self-detraction and of defiant jauntiness which arms his enemies against him but disarms his friends:—

When I have commenced a new book, I have always prepared a diary, divided into weeks. . . . In this I have entered day by day the number of pages that I have written, so that if at any time I have slipped into idleness for a day or two, the record of that idleness has been there, staring me in the face and demanding of me increased labour. . . . According to circumstances, I have allotted myself so many pages a week . . . and as a page is an ambiguous term my page has been made to contain 250 words. . . . I have

Harry Clavering—35 a week for 22 weeks—770 pages.   Pages at 260.

1864 Aug.		5	}	23	.....
24	No. 1. 1–5	6	} Paris with Harry.	24	No. 13. 1–3
25	6–15	7	}	25	4–16
26	16–20	8	}	26	17–21
27	.....	9	}	27	22–33
28	21–30	10	} Isle of Wight with	28	34–37
29	31–40	11	} Rose.	29	38–48
30	41–48				
		12	}	30	}
		13	}	Dec. 1	}
		14	33–36	2	} Alas !
31	No. 2. 1–10	15	37–48. No. 8. 1–3	3	}
Sept. 1	11–20	16	4–16	4	}
2	21–30	17	17–28	5	}
3	.....	18	29–38	6	}
4	31–38	19	39–45	7	}
5	39–48	20	46–48	8	} Ramsgate.
6	.....	21	.....	9	}
		22	No. 9. 1–16	10	}
7	} Writing *Malachi's*	23	17–22	11	} Alas !
8	} Cove.	24	23–30	12	}
9	}	25	31–37	13	}
10	No. 3. 1–12	26	.....		
11	13–24	27	.....	14	No. 14. 1–4
12	25–36	28	.....	15	5–16
13	37–48	29	.....	16	17–28
		30	38–48. No. 10. 1–4	17	29–32
14	.....	31	5–19	18	33–44
15	.....	Nov. 1	20–31	19	45–48. No. 15. 1–2
16	No. 4. 1–10	2	32–43	20	3–6
17	11–20	3	44–48. No. 11. 1–7		
18	21–30	4	8–19	21	7–18
19	31–40	5	20–29	22	19–28
20	41–48	6	30–37	23	29–38
		7	.....	24	39–42
21	No. 5. 1–12	8	.....	25	43–48
22	13–24	9	38–48	26	No. 16. 1–10
23	25–36	10	}	27	11–22
24	37–48	11	}		
25	No. 6 1–12	12	} Trollopes to stay.	28	23–34
26	13–24	13	}	29	.....
27	25–32	14	}	30	35–43
		15	}	31	44–48
28	33–42	16	No. 12. 1–12		
29	43–48	17	13–24		768
30	No. 7. 1–8	18	.....		
Oct. 1	9–20	19	.....		Finis.
2	21–32	20	25–36		
3	.....	21	37–48		
4	.....	22	.....		

WORKING TABLE FOR *THE CLAVERINGS*
(Originally entitled *Harry Clavering*)

₊ An examination of the Calendar of Events in Trollope's life (see below, Appendix II (*a*), pp. 406–413) will show from another aspect the dogged sequence of his work.   Hardly any interval was permitted between the conclusion of one book and the beginning of the next.

prided myself on completing my work exactly within the proposed dimensions.

So much in way of over-detailed candour. Immediately the expected criticism is forestalled:—

> I have been told that such appliances are beneath the notice of a man of genius. I have never fancied myself to be a man of genius.

Elsewhere in the *Autobiography* he states that daily at Waltham Cross he was at his desk by half-past five in the morning; that sometimes he would time his writing by the clock. His slighting words to George Eliot describing his own work as "mechanical stuff," and the letter (already recorded) claiming that no man ever made easier the life of a periodical editor, were expressions of the same rueful self-derision. Nor was this mood assumed for the challenging of outside opinion. Even in a private note to his son, who is endeavouring to write a book, he says:—

> I do not suppose your words are really shorter than mine, but that you have not as yet quite got into the way of writing for lengths. One cannot do all these mechanical tricks at once.

It is easy to understand that a later generation—and particularly one so conscious of its own inspiration as the generation of the æsthetic 'eighties—would shudder (as George Eliot shuddered) at this denial of all grace and mystery of authorship. If, however, the matter be viewed dispassionately, if Trollope's own aggressiveness and the unjust contempt of his opponents are both discounted, the details of his working-method become impressive if a little comic. It must not be forgotten that this method was originally forced on him by circumstances. When he began to write, he had only odd times at his disposal. Because every half-hour was precious a certain system was inevitable. First, then, he had recourse to early rising to give himself the extra hours that were so badly needed; next, he evolved his "diary" or "working-table." The first such working-table ever used was drawn up in 1856 for *Barchester*

Towers. From that date to the time of the unfinished *Landleaguers* no single novel but had its ruled and dated calendar.
For interest's sake one of these "working tables" (see page
351) has been transcribed. It will be seen that incidental
journeys and visitors are recorded, that lamentations mark
two wasted weeks.

But even an aid to industry so systematic as a "diary" could
not of itself cause chapters of fiction to flow smoothly and at
will from an unready pen. Behind the physical training lay a
mental training, thorough and in its results miraculous.

> Three hours a day [he says] will produce as much as a
> man ought to write. But he should so have trained himself
> that he shall be able to work continuously during those
> three hours—so have tutored his mind that it shall not be
> necessary for him to sit nibbling his pen and gazing at the
> wall before him, till he shall have found the words with
> which he wants to express his ideas.

How was the mind of Trollope tutored, so that it could produce, steadily and without waste of time, the long, unbroken,
satisfying series of his novels? By one means only—that of
continual concentration at all times and seasons on the themes
and persons of his imaginary world. The secret of Trollope's
writing mastery lay in a perpetual preparatory shaping of his
stories and his characters. Of this he was well aware:—

> The novelist desires to make his readers so intimately
> acquainted with his characters that the creatures of his
> brain should be to them speaking, moving, living human
> creatures. This he can never do unless he knows his
> fictitious personages himself, and he can never know them
> unless he can live with them. They must be with him as he
> lies down to sleep and as he wakes from his dreams. He
> must learn to hate them and to love them. The depth and
> the breadth, and the narrowness and the shallowness of
> each should be clear to him. It is so that I have lived with
> my characters and thence has come whatever success I have
> obtained.

M

Does not this fact of Trollope's unceasing exploration of the moods and possibilities of his characters explain the practicability of his writing method and dispose of a great part of the uncharitable comment passed upon it? When Whistler was asked: "Is the labour of two days, then, that for which you ask two hundred pounds?" he replied: "No. I ask them for the knowledge of a lifetime." Similarly, when Trollope settled to his three hours of early morning writing, he wrote indeed for three times sixty minutes, but what he wrote was the result of days, weeks, months and years of searching thought. Sometimes he made an advance-schedule of the characters as they were forming in his mind; [1] sometimes he carried all the *dramatis personæ* in his head, until each one was so complete that he or she could step ready-made from the busy, crowded brain on to the white paper.

There is a letter to Blackwood about *John Caldigate*. The publisher had suggested changes in the plot. Trollope replied:—

Sept. 12 1878.

I am bound to say that I have never found myself able to effect changes in the plot of a story. Small as the links are, one little thing hinges on another to such an extent that any change sets the whole narrative wrong. There are so many infinitesimal allusions to what is past that the whole should be re-written or it will be faulty.

It was no ordinary mind which could conceive in full and interacting detail a complex tale (not only *John Caldigate* but most of the novels are structurally elaborate), set it convincingly on paper and, at a stipulated rate of words per day, complete three volumes-worth of manuscript for a publisher, punctually and without one important inconsistency or contradiction.

5

The portrait is nearly complete. Trollope emerges from the shadows of the past a sturdy, manly, unaffected figure, a man

[1] Two such schedules are transcribed in Appendix IV (*a*) and (*b*).

high-minded and high-principled, a tireless worker, a brave fighter, a faithful friend, a generous judge. Only the spiritual element remains in need of definition. What were the inner convictions of his staunch, honourable soul? What were his beliefs? By what code of ethics did he administer his life?

To some extent Trollope deliberately veiled his spiritual self, and it is not the business of posterity to draw that veil aside. But it is permissible to ask what, broadly, were his spiritual preoccupations, seeing that many critics of his work have been influenced by its materialism to set him, for lack of wedding garment, in a lower room.

He was a Christian and (though without great conviction) a conforming member of the Anglican Church. But, as one who knew him well observes, "he was something of a *frondeur* in these matters." His dislike of caste-supremacy, his instinctive reaction against an imposed code, whether of belief or morals or social deportment, disposed him to be exceptionally critical of Church dogma and of Church discipline.

Once in a letter to a young friend, he declared that taking Orders was crippling to a man's mentality. The novels are full of the sense of contrast between the practice and profession of those clergymen and ministers who think more of their Order than of their faith.

But when he encountered (or set out to create) a person whose actual character was Christian, his appreciation was respectful and wholehearted, and the more respectful if the man happened to be in Holy Orders. The Reverend Frank Fenwick, Vicar of Bullhampton, may be taken as Trollope's ideal of what a parson should be, and with that ideal the world will sympathise.

Conversely, he was convinced that unhappiness must inevitably come from unbelief. By "unbelief" he meant denial of God, and not at all refusal to subscribe to any one religious creed. Sir Thomas Underwood, the forlorn central figure of *Ralph the Heir*, is described as an "unbeliever," and Trollope implies that much of his isolation and gloom is due to the absence of spiritual conviction, to want of faith in a watchful and affectionate Deity.

Of such an ultimate faith Trollope himself was firmly possessed. Behind his religious indocility was staunch belief, alike in the existence of a beneficent Almighty and in the authority and supremacy of Christian ethics.

Castle Richmond contains a solemn declaration of his belief in God, his conception of the workings of the Supreme Intelligence. He has explained that the Irish peasantry attributed the failure of the potato crop to divine anger, and continues:—

> For myself, I do not believe in such exhibitions of God's anger. When wars come, and pestilence, and famine; when the people of a land are worse than decimated, and the living hardly able to bury the dead, I cannot coincide with those who would deprecate God's wrath by prayers. I do not believe that our God stalks darkly along the clouds, laying thousands low with the arrows of death, and those thousands the most ignorant, because men who are not ignorant have displeased Him. Nor, if in His wisdom He did do so, can I think that men's prayers would hinder that which His wisdom had seen to be good and right.
>
> But though I do not believe in exhibitions of God's anger, I do believe in exhibitions of His mercy. When men by their folly and by the shortness of their vision have brought upon themselves penalties which seem to be overwhelming, to which no end can be seen, which would be overwhelming were no aid coming to us but our own, then God raises His hand, not in anger, but in mercy, and by His wisdom does for us that for which our own wisdom has been insufficient.

His faith embraced not only God, but the Son of God also. When the *Fortnightly* was founded, he made the stipulation that nothing should be said to challenge the divinity of Christ. At Harting he would go riding with a nephew of whom he was very fond, and talk widely and thoughtfully of religion and of metaphysics, showing that he had pondered (and in the light of Christian revelation) many matters which have no place in his books; showing further that the actions of his daily life were regulated according to a coherent and a considered philosophy.

Put shortly, that philosophy was one of honest common-sense, tempered with generosity and deriving sanction from the achievement of a definite standard of personal behaviour. There are wisdoms and there are follies; but there is something higher than either prudence or recklessness—the duty a man owes to his own sense of what is right. Cruelty and meanness are the ultimate sins; misfortune is more likely to be unmerited than success.

There has been preserved Trollope's own copy of Bacon's *Essays*, which he read from cover to cover, recording his impressions at the end of each essay. These notes are of great evidential value to an understanding of his personal philosophy. He is in the main hostile to Bacon, as a writer who envelops platitudes in pretentious folds of language, whose counsel is more crafty than courageous, who is selfish even in well-doing. Throughout the annotations Trollope expresses his hatred of high-falutin, of humbug, and of that ingenuity which is really slyness. Such hatreds were among the directing principles of his life; and it is only necessary to imagine a being who governs himself in accordance with them, to imagine Trollope and to realise what manner of man he was.

Here is a selection from the marginalia to Bacon. On the essay "Of Truth" he says:—

Bacon begins by accusing those who differ from him of being false in their search after truth. It is as though he should declare that a man who did not believe revealed religion were a liar.

Concerning the essay "Of Death," he says:—

"Oh death, where is thy victory?" contains all and more than all that is here.

Concerning "Of Simulation and Dissimulation," he says:—

There is nothing here to solve the acknowledged difficulty in Ethics as to the right a man has to hold back that which is his own, and the duty incumbent upon him not to lie. Bacon studies that which is politic rather than that which is proper, when he recommends "a Power to faigne if there be no Remedy."

Writing "Of Love" Bacon remarks: "You may observe that amongst all great and worthy persons, there is not one that hath been transported to the mad degree of love."

> What of Cæsar and Cleopatra? [writes Trollope in the margin]. What of Achilles and Briseis? What of Wolsey and the brown girl?

At the end he writes:—

> Lust is ever bad and love ever good. That, I take to be the truth as arranged by God.

Concerning "Of Atheisme" Trollope significantly says:—

> He fails to be clear because he has in his mind that Atheism and Religion are the two opposites. Conviction of the existence and of the goodness of God is compatible with the absence of all Religion so-called.

When Bacon writes "Of Cunning" Trollope accuses him of showing "a great love for the cunning which he condemns"; and the essayist's blame of selfishness in the next essay, "Of Wisdome for a Man's Selfe," is declared to be "on selfish principles, because he never uses the idea of doing good to others because of those others."

"Of Friendship" moves the commentator to indignation.

> With Bacon friendship is all policy. Is there a word of the delight of serving your friend? Selfishness is the source and the object of all Bacon's teaching.

He is satirical over the essay "Of Expence."

> Do not spend but seem to spend! Who but Bacon would have dismissed a good servant from caution? The habit of parsimony is no doubt the making of wealth—and the mother of misers!

After "Of Followers and Frendes" he writes: "The meanness of it all!" After "Of Negociating": "All these counsels

are counsels to the crafty—how they may best take advantage
of the passions, weaknesses, follies and inferior cunning of
others."

In the Golden Treasury edition of Bacon's *Essays* the Fragment of 1597 entitled: "Of the Coulers of Good and Evil"
is printed at the end of the volume. Trollope's note on the
work is a kind of summary of his general attitude, not only to
Bacon's philosophy, but to all instructional punditry:—

> As to these colours of good and evil, the philosophy
> seems to lie in the crabbed language. The axioms are
> truthlike and have been accepted commonly when put
> forward in ordinary language; but they are here produced
> in stiff Latin riddles, in which the meaning is intentionally
> hidden by the uncouthness of the phraseology.
>
> All this is child's play in reasoning, but by the crabbed-
> ness of Bacon's Latin is made to stand for deep learning.
>
> *The depths of philosophy often owe their marvels to the conceits
> of philosophers.*

To the ideal of honourable self-forgetfulness, to the doctrine
of moderation and willing service from which he declares
Bacon recusant, Trollope himself rigorously conformed.
Loyalty in friendship, self-control and the doing with all one's
might of the work that lay to hand became to him duties so
obvious that it never occurred to him to neglect them. They
were the truisms of behaviour, and he brushed aside as meddle-
some pomposity organisations and philosophies which sought
to propagate what were merely platitudes. No doubt he was
over-impatient, for exhortations and professed moralities can
be of real help to persons less self-reliant, less sturdily opinionated. Also, by bluntly insisting that man must govern himself
and along lines instinctively familiar to any decent being, he
lost in subtlety what he gained in ease of mind. But he would
have declared that other folk's morals were not his to improve,
and that a man's first duty is to make himself a good man and
a good citizen. According to his lights he performed that
duty.

Some comment has already been passed on the emotional

side of his nature. His fondness for poetry was very great, though he spoke of it reluctantly and with the shyness of his characteristic humility. He was strongly susceptible to pathos —in life, in fiction and on the stage. His collection of the old dramatists was a large one, and at the end of many of the volumes are notes, which show him keenly aware of false emotionalism, readily responsive to passages of genuine feeling.

Near the end of the *Autobiography* is a paragraph in which the warmer delights of manhood are touched on with a rare dignity, almost with nobility. There were, to his mind, betrayals even of self which may not be committed, indulgences that honest men may practise, but only to the strict limits of their spiritual caste. In this paragraph is contained the essence of Trollope's personal morality. Without doubting or hesitation he honoured it.

6

The heroine of that remarkable novel *The Rector's Daughter*,[1] is tormented by doubts and made miserable by a love-episode gone awry. She has no one to whom to turn for counsel; her father, remote with age and scholarship, has neither inclination nor capacity for sympathy. In loneliness and bewilderment she turns to Trollope's novels for distraction and for comfort. She has found comfort in them before, but her present grief has so sharpened her appreciation of Trollope that she now feels the man himself behind the books.

> She did not exactly wish it had been possible to exchange her father for Trollope, but she felt if he had been more like him, he might have had more mercy, more understanding.

There could be no truer estimate of the personality of Anthony Trollope than that of this forlorn and solitary woman. The qualities which would have made him the ideal helper and comforter in her distress are the qualities which carried him through his untiring life of hard work and hard play. His mercy and his genius for understanding brought him

[1] By F. M. Mayor. London, 1923.

during his lifetime a crowded happiness, a livelihood and the love of a million readers; they should now secure to him the affectionate admiration of posterity. Staunch beyond the ordinary run of men, he could endure. He could take blows and, if they were deserved, take them in silence; but an unjust blow he as doughtily returned, having in himself too much of the common clay of obstinate humanity to suffer fools gladly or to submit to bullying. Of fame he took little thought; toward social prejudice he had no softness. In early youth he felt himself an individuality, solitary in a world of strangers, conscious of unattraction and of the shyness born of gaucherie. But where a weaker or a vainer man might have tried to cloak his self-distrust with nonchalance, Trollope turned to solid work as a road—slow perhaps but certain—to control of self and, after self, of fate.

He was not a brilliant man nor a handsome one; he achieved no sensational fame, centred no dramatic happening. Yet in retrospect we admire and love him, and in perplexity the thought of him brings comfort. He was honest, strong and tender-hearted; also he loved his kind. He alone of the great fiction-writers of the past truly appreciated the power in human life of mutual tolerance and of mutual affection, because these were qualities which he himself abundantly possessed. "Trollope" wrote Sir Walter Raleigh "starts off with ordinary people and makes an epic of them, because he understands affection." [1] That is truly said, and not of the novels only but of the man also.

His friend the Reverend W. Lucas Collins once remarked to him: "Trollope, you are too good for this world," and said a wise thing foolishly. Trollope was upright and sturdy beyond the run of human men. But his courage depended on his war against himself, and his nobility upon the failings of his fellows. Therefore, save in terms of this world, he is hardly definable at all, and if he be denied this world, he is excluded from the only sphere in which he could have thriven or even have survived.

[1] *The Letters of Sir Walter Raleigh.* London, 1926.

M*

THE HISTORY, from his death to the present day, of Anthony Trollope's writing reputation is among the most sensational of its kind. It is also to an unusual degree illustrative of his quality as a writer. His novels are so intimately interwoven with the social life of their period, are so much more obviously remarkable for their expression of period-psychology than for their literary texture, that their effect on posterity seems—and very curiously—to have varied according to the social rather than the literary preoccupations of those who read them.

Already when he died in the winter of 1882, the dispraises of a new and rebellious generation were mingling with the respectful compliments due to a vanished eminence. The obituary notices, in so far as they were written by men who had known and loved him, were sympathetic, sorrowful and moving; but those briefer ones that recorded the death of a novelist and not of a man, were at best tolerant, at worst contemptuous.

The Times was typical. A leading article was published on the very day following his death in which, after an agreeable reference to his personality, his work was relegated—firmly, contemptuously and (as matters have turned out) mistakenly—to a respectable oblivion.

Loud and emphatic in speech, peremptory in argument, bluff in manner, thoroughly good-natured and kind-hearted, trustworthy in great matters and small, his own pen never drew a finer picture than he presented of the hearty, frank, English gentleman, well-cultivated, but somewhat ostentatiously contemptuous of the petty refinements of the modern drawing-room. A thorough man of business and man of the world, an ardent sportsman, especially in riding after hounds, familiar with every aspect of home life, a visitor to every continent, Mr. Trollope combined the qualities of the

English official, the English country gentleman, the traveller and the man of letters. . . .

He could not manage very deep passion and had the sense rarely to attempt it. He could still less manage intellectual difficulties and had the sense still more rarely to attempt them. . . . No deep riddles, no unconquerable troubles diversified Mr. Trollope's stories. . . . It would be rash to prophesy that his work will long be read; most of it lacks some of the qualifications which that stern official who draws up the passports for the Land of Matters Unforgot insists upon.[1]

These sentences were prophetic of what was yet to come. Because they were written within a few hours of the passing of a brave lovable personality, they are affectionate even in condescension. But their verdict on Trollope's literary work is the verdict of an age of intellectual snobbery and economic restlessness, of an age which found beauty in abnormality, which despised contentment and quiet friendliness, which—because subversiveness was due to be the *chic*—throve on disgruntlement and judged complacency the deadliest sin.

This revolt from the long domination of mid-Victorian philosophy would of itself have driven Trollope to a temporary oblivion. He himself made matters worse by taking a posthumous hand in his own discomfiture. A few months after his death his *Autobiography* appeared, and from beyond the grave he flung in the face of fashionable criticism the aggressive horse-sense of his views on life and book-making. Then it was that affectionate depreciation became malevolent hostility; then did the tempest of reaction against his work and against all the principles and opinions it represented break angrily and overwhelm him.

Rarely can the convictions and assumptions of a vanished age have made so untimely and so uncompromising an appearance as did those of mid-Victorianism, when Trollope's

---

[1] *The Times*, December 7 1882. Reference may also be made to an article in the *Spectator*, December 9 1882, and to a waspish essay by Edmund Yates published in the *World* at about the same date. Only the *Saturday Review* gave the dead man true and generous credit for his qualities.

Autobiography fell with a splash into the elegant waters of æstheticism. The book is a compendium of all that was most offensive to the new modishness. It is the self-portrait of a man who went out of his way to deny his literary caste; of a man physically exuberant and morally unadventurous; of a man (and this perhaps was worst of all) who was blatantly English. And not content with being personally distasteful to the generation of his supplanters, Trollope by his expressed views on authorship flouted their every artistic prejudice. He put the writing of books on a level with the practice of any other trade; he glorified industry and perseverance; he spoke a little sceptically of genius; he reckoned the rewards of literature in pounds sterling and the calendar of its creation in hours by the clock. It would have been difficult to challenge more directly the studied attitudes and the proclaimed indifference to the rewards of literature so characteristic of the æsthetic 'eighties.

And Trollope was guilty of yet a third offence. To an uncongenial personality and to unpalatable teaching he added self-depreciation. His aggressive modesty was in actual fact sincere and genuine; but to the offended 'eighties it appeared merely an aggravation of insult. Not only was this dowdy, *démodé* scribbler disloyal to the conventions of his craft; he also disarmed criticism by, as it were, disclaiming the right to be regarded as a worthy antagonist at all.

Debarred from obvious personal retort by their enemy's blunt insistence on his own mediocrity, the new generation were driven to vilification of his works. This they undertook most zestfully. Trollope's novels were dubbed "superficial and trivial"; "monotonous"; "commonplace"; "vulgar"; "low"; "without charm or imagination." [1] And the source of such opinions was not always negligible. Critics both learned and discriminating were so far affected by the prevail-

---

[1] A. Edward Newton, one of the American enthusiasts who had much influence in re-establishing the novelist's reputation, quotes several of the foolish and insolent things said of Trollope's work by criticasters in an essay " A Great Victorian " published in the *Amenities of Book Collecting* (New York and London, 1920). This essay is a rewritten version of a booklet entitled *Trollopeana* privately printed by Mr. Newton in 1911.

THE REVIVAL

ing opinion of the day as to penalise Trollope for the short-comings of his period and to echo Richard Garnett's disparagement of "the chronicler of small beer." But some at least of these have since made their courageous recantation. Re-reading Trollope in the atmosphere of an age more critical of Baudelaire and Beardsley even than of Tennyson and, perhaps, unconsciously mellowed in their views by the passage of time, they are now conscious of his qualities where once they recognised only his limitations.[1] Further, we are now sufficiently removed from Trollope's period to be able to give it credit for its good qualities, and to admire his novels for their perfect expression of these qualities, if for no other reason.

Time, therefore, and the evolution of opinion which it brings, have given to Trollopians a second chance. May it be taken soberly and without exaggeration. Though period prejudice destroyed him, the prejudice of another period must not be allowed to overstress his resurrection. It is true that his flavour is as agreeable to contemporary mentality as it was repellent to the eighteen-eighties; that his candour and his lack of affectation are grateful to an epoch which inevitably is an epoch of reaction from elaborate trifling. It is true that the last thirty years of declared and undeclared war have given a sudden lustre to such normal peaceful things as form the theme of his many novels. But Trollope deserves graver consideration than as a mere escapist author, and at the same time a judgment more stringent than would be passed by a new-found enthusiasm for his Victorianism. The duty of our time is not to deify or to pet him (no processes could be more distasteful to his spirit or unsuitable to his aggressive bulk), but to appraise him fairly and dispassionately; to take account,

[1] Contrast particularly George Saintsbury's essay on Trollope in *Corrected Impressions* (London, 1895) with that entitled "Trollope Revisited," and contributed by him to Volume VI of *Essays and Studies by Members of the English Association* (Oxford, 1920). Seldom can the influence of the actual age of a critic on his opinions have been shown more clearly. The effect of personal maturity on critical judgment and the manner in which the instinctive subversiveness of youth gives place to the more tolerant understanding of middle age are brilliantly set forth in Havelock Ellis' preface to the new edition (1926) of his book *The New Spirit*, first published in 1890.

neither of period-whim nor of his own expressed ideals, but only of his right to hold a place in the imperishable pageant of the English novel.

2

The initial obstacle to a sober-minded definition of Trollope's novels is that they provide a sensual rather than an intellectual experience. A smell, a pain or a sound is not more difficult to describe than the effect—at once soothing and exciting—produced on the reader's mind by the leisurely, nonchalant commentaries on English social life which carry his name on their title-pages.

The phenomenon is partly explicable by the fact that a Trollope novel is of the very essence of fiction. At its best it represents a distillation of that element in story-telling on which all other elements depend, without which no blend—however skilful—of fact, incident, idea and description can be recognised for fiction at all—the element of characterisation.

There are novels more spiritual than his, more heroic and more beautiful; but there are none more faultless in this most delicate of all novel-writing problems. "Trollope" one critic has declared "is more than the painter or the sculptor of his people; he is the biographer of them all." That is high praise, but it is praise deserved.

Power of characterisation, then, is the superlative quality of Trollope as a novelist. And as revealed by him, it is not a power of observation nor of imagination; not a power of knowledge nor of intuition; but a compound of all four, with a something added of the author's personality, giving to the whole a peculiar but elusive flavour.

For even granted characterisation, Trollope's quality remains intangible, baffles resolution. In theme familiar, in treatment undistinguished, his work is nevertheless potent in appeal, unrivalled in its power to hold the attention of readers of any kind and of any generation. And its elusiveness is the more extreme for being unexpected. It seems hardly fitting that a being, who in himself was so definite and so solid, who —like a solitary tower upon a hill—was visible for miles around in the wide landscape of Victorian England, should as a literary phenomenon be so difficult to seize and to describe; it is almost irritating that books in themselves so lustily prosaic should be so hard of definition.

There are, of course, certain qualities that Trollope as a novelist emphatically does not possess. He is no great philanthropist like Dickens; he has not Thackeray's pointed brilliance nor George Eliot's grave enthusiasm; he does not, like Meredith, paint a familiar scene in colours so vivid as to be of themselves a challenge; he has not the passionate sense of Nature's oneness with humanity that lights the sunset over Egdon Heath. Even in comparison with Jane Austen—the writer nearest to him as a novelist of manners—his curiosity seems suave rather than searching, his observation to have more of scope than of discrimination.

But not by elimination only can the quality of Trollope be appraised. He may be neither teacher nor word-painter, neither pantheist nor social reformer, but he is definitely something. What is he? Wherein lies that strange potency, which renders work so featureless, so sober and so undemonstrative an entertainment than which few are more enthralling?

It lies surely in his acceptance and his profound understanding of ordinary daily life. In the tale of English literature he is—to put the matter in a phrase—the supreme novelist of acquiescence.

> I know there are artists [says a modern writer] whose work bears witness to a complete acquiescence in the world and in life as it is. But in the most clumsy and bungled work (if it has been born of the desire for beauty) we should doubtless find, could we but pierce through the dead husk of it to the hidden conception, that divine homesickness, that longing for an Eden from which each one of us is exiled.[1]

Trollope is the great exception that proves the rule herein laid down. He seeks for no doorway of escape. He is content with life, engrossed in it, never weary of its kaleidoscope of

---

[1] *Apostate*, by Forrest Reid. London, 1926.

good and evil, of tears and laughter. Not only does he agree to the terms proposed by life, but he glories in them. And yet his work is born of a desire for beauty. He finds all of romance and courage and achievement within the unpretentious limits of the social existence of his day. He believes in individual capacity for perfection, but in terms of things as they are; his ideal of beauty and of proportion, whether in character or in happening, lies in the suave adjustment of personality to circumstance.

Trollope, then, is never a writer of revolt. But so complete is his acquiescence that he is not even a critical despot over the society of his imagination. Like a man in a crowded street who views his fellow-men, he is at once genially disposed but fundamentally detached. Also, to the point inevitable in detachment, he is cynical. He is without superiority; without presumption of omniscience. He has his own idea of what is right; but if the crowd of passers-by have a different idea and act accordingly, their ultimate salvation is no concern of his.

It is this almost pugnacious acceptance of reality that distinguishes him from all other novelists of standing. It lies at the root of his difference from Jane Austen, from Sir Walter Scott, from Dickens, from Thackeray and from George Eliot. It explains why his social pictures differ in basic impulse from theirs. And they do differ, even from such as belong in theme and treatment to an identical school of novels of manners. *Middlemarch*, for example—which is the most Trollopian of all George Eliot's novels [1]—is never wholly free of the intellectual superiority of its author towards the non-intellectual middle class. As Oliver Elton wisely says: "George Eliot is apt to be hard on the upper bourgeois, and Trollope's light, unassuming way is really sounder than hers." [2] As for Thackeray and Jane Austen, behind the whimsical elegance of the former, behind the latter's shy sense of the absurdity of other people,

---

[1] George Eliot herself told Mrs. Lynn Linton that, but for Trollope, she could hardly have persevered with the extensive, patient study necessary to the completion of *Middlemarch*.

[2] *Op. cit.*

lies a conviction—unexpressed but unmistakable—that the satirist at least knows what is what. Thackeray when he tears at snobbery, Jane Austen when she laughingly lays bare the follies of the female heart, are passing judgment, basing a criticism on a code of manners of which they, at least, claim to possess the secret.

But Trollope arrogates to himself no general right of judgment, no knowledge of the true paths of virtue or of social decency more profound than that possessed by any of his characters. Punishment for wrong-doing he frequently inflicts; but it is punishment by one citizen of a fellow-citizen who has transgressed the civic code. For he himself, as has been said, is one of the throng of his imaginary persons. With the amusement of a casual acquaintance he can observe their little ambitions, disappointments, self-delusions. But if they are free to live their lives, so is he also. He will fall in love with his heroines as readily as he will take a hand in the discomfiture of villainy. Snobbery, infidelity, dishonesty are as displeasing to him in his fictional as in his real life; but in the former, no less than in the latter, he is pugnacious rather than censorious, touched in his sense of citizenship rather than in his moral consciousness. "Such things are," he seems to say; adding, more tritely still, "It takes all sorts to make a world." But at certain crises he is roused. "This sort of thing won't do," he declares. "We must put a stop to it." With the result that Crosbie gets a thrashing at Paddington; that Lord Brotherton is knocked into the fireplace of his hotel sitting-room by an angry Dean; that Mountjoy Scarborough lies senseless on the flagstones by the Junior United Service Club.

A curious, though not perhaps unnatural, result of Trollope's extreme acquiescence has been to set his work athwart the pattern of modern literary criticism. The long series of his books—so drab yet so mysteriously alive, so obvious yet so impossible of imitation—evade every criterion of what has become an academic judgment. They will stand no school-tests save those of the school of real life. They cannot but violate the modish canons of good fiction, as continually and as shamelessly as does life itself. Like life, they are diffuse, often tedious, seldom arrestingly unusual. Their monotony is the monotony of ordinary existence, which, although while actually passing it provides one small sensation after another, emerges in retrospect as a dull sequence of familiar things.

For in this queer sense of the absorbing interest of normal occupations lies the true realism of Trollope. He can reproduce the fascination of the successive happenings of the daily round, in the absence of which the human spirit would perish or go mad. Existence is made up of an infinite number of tiny fragments of excitement, interest and provocation, which carry men on from day to day, ever expectant, ever occupied. It is the second part of Trollope's claim to be a novelist that, by building up from just such multifarious trivialities the big absorptions which are his books, he gives the illusion that is of all illusions the most difficult to create—the illusion of ordinary life.

3

The art of Trollope, therefore, has two predominant qualities: power of characterisation and power of dramatisation of the undramatic. Within the limits of these rare capacities he designed and peopled a second England, virtually a replica of the London and counties of his day. But although in his imaginary England life seems (as indeed it is) utterly, almost exasperatingly, a series of unsensational sensations, a slow progression of meals and small ambitions, of love-making and disappointments, of sport and business, it would be an error to regard the Trollopian world as—other than superficially—without violent happenings. Accompanying a rather offensive "Spy" cartoon of Trollope published in *Vanity Fair* in April 1873 was a still more offensive paragraph of critical text. "Mr. Trollope has had by far the greatest success in writing books with the ordinary young lady always in mind—books sufficiently faithful to the external aspects of English life to interest those who see nothing but its external aspects, sufficiently removed from all the depths of humanity to conciliate all respected parents." The implication of these words—that Trollope for profit's sake was a writer of goody-goody un-

reality—is grotesque.   Julian Hawthorne in the article already
quoted was much nearer the mark when he wrote:—

> There may be, perhaps, as many murders, forgeries,
> foundlings, abductions, and missing wills, in Trollope's
> novels as in any others; but they are not told about in a
> manner to alarm us; we accept them philosophically; there
> are paragraphs in our morning paper that excite us more.
> And yet they are narrated with art, and with dramatic
> effect.   They are interesting, but not uncourteously—not
> exasperatingly—so; and the strangest part of it is that the
> introduction and intermediate passages are no less interest-
> ing, under Trollope's treatment, than are the murders and
> forgeries.

And to murders and forgeries may be added—if one is agog
for crime—adulteries and bigamies.   It is one aspect of his
amazing truth to life that he could contrive at the same time to
be a novelist for the *jeune fille* and a most knowledgeable realist.
For his books are lifelike in this also—that though compounded both of innocent and guilty, the guilt (as in life) is
shrouded from the innocent, so that only such as know the
signs of it may realise its presence or its nature.

This fact indicates those two of his personal qualities which
most influence his handling of an imaginary social scene—his
worldly proficiency and his good manners.   There is nothing
that he does not know; there is very little that, in his quiet
skilful diction, he is not prepared to say.   Socially speaking he
is the wisest of English novelists; but because a large part of
social wisdom is restraint, alike of gesture and of word, his
books are restrained—not in incident or necessarily in emotion
—but in expression.   He writes adult books for adult people.
But because he writes in terms of polite society, because he is
in the truest sense a "man of the world," he is too civilised
and too experienced to forget the social decencies for the sake
of the social sins.

And not only had he a well-bred man's distaste for ugly
realism; he was himself more interested in the deceptive calm
of society's surface than in details of the hidden whirlpools

beneath. The incident of Madame Max Goessler and the old
Duke of Omnium in *Phineas Finn* provides a case in point.
The inclination of the great nobleman to make the pretty widow
his mistress is treated adequately but briefly; all of the author's
skill in dramatic dialogue goes to the fashioning of the subsequent scene between Madame Goessler and Lady Glencora
Palliser, in which the latter (representing the *convenances*)
appeals to the former (as likely to represent irregularity) to
forgo a personal triumph for the sake of social decency.
Always, as here, the clash between conventional poise and
secret catastrophe, the delicate adjustment of repute and disrepute which kept the life of upper-class England outwardly
serene for all its inward hazard, appealed to Trollope's
sophisticated and rather cynical mind.

For in all things he was sophisticated and in social things
more than a little cynical. Carlyle compared his work to alum,
and the fancy is a shrewd one. Contrast his books with those
of the sensation-writers of his day or with those of novelists
from a later generation who have been praised for their
courageous realism. Trollope in geniality, in satire or in
bitterness is calm; but to the others, in one way or another,
existence is perpetually and disproportionately exciting. Wilkie
Collins and Miss Braddon; Zola, Hardy and George Moore—
all of these have beside Trollope a certain callowness. One or
two of them may excel him in other, perhaps higher qualities;
but none can rival his controlled indifference in the face of life.
The sensationalists are thrilled by their own catalogues of
crime; the reforming realist shudders to read his own ex-
posures of cruelty and bestiality; the child of nature makes
discoveries as to the shifts and sorrows of humanity that have
been made in every generation for centuries; the amorist
regards his love successes as of a piquancy unrivalled. But
Trollope is beyond such elementary stimulus. To him everything is material for observation, nothing for declamation or
for vanity. He approves virtue and deprecates vice, but he
refuses to become excited either over ugliness or beauty. Like
a connoisseur of wine he sips at this vintage and at that, selects
to his taste and lays a cellar down. We, who inherit it, have

but to drink at will, and in the novels that he left behind to savour the essence of life as once it was, as it still is, as in all likelihood it will remain.

4

Indeed, general observations apart, a reading of Trollope is worth a volume of critical analysis. But there is interest in a consideration of the evolution of his talent and of his changing tendencies as fiction-writer, while to a wholesale recommendation of the novels should be added some degree of special definition.

A schedule of the various categories into which the stories fall is given below.[1] Some such classification is necessary in an age of scanty leisure and with work of such intimidating bulk. But toward actual comment on each single novel no attempt can be made. Such book-by-book examination would result only in repetitions, and it has seemed more practical to call attention mainly to the less familiar tales, and to those more famous ones which have a direct bearing on their author's literary development.

Trollope's work is of unusually constant quality, and at frequent intervals during his writing life he would revert to earlier loves and to earlier models. Nevertheless, during his long and crowded career of authorship, not only did he come to gradual technical mastery, but also his work underwent a definite transformation in kind. There came a moment at which—perhaps in unconscious obedience to the new tendency in fiction—he sought to abandon pure narrative, to leave behind the type of novel in which many characterisations are blended to produce a complex but evolving tale, and to experiment in psychological analysis of one character reacting to a single set of circumstances. There came another moment when, stirred to indignant protest by what he deemed the vulgar degeneration of his beloved England, he wrote one of the most savage satires in social fiction and became, instead of an amused and tolerant observer, an envenomed castigator of the age.

[1] See Appendix II (c).

That the early Irish novels and the historical romance *La Vendée* were the unskilful fumblings of a writer who had not found himself, has already been shown; and in a survey of his work those books can be ignored. The Trollope of posterity appeared in 1855, when *The Warden* first gave sign of a new and individual talent. One may salute *The Warden* and respect it for the sake of the admirable books it heralded; but one may not deny that this inaugural fiction, with its exaggerated sentiment and its clumsy caricature, is very elementary Trollope. The two years that followed its completion were years of vital education—how vital the author's next novel was to prove. *Barchester Towers* shows a wonderful advance, alike in literary technique and in forcible use of selected material *solely in the interests of the novel's plot*. There is virtually no beating of the propagandist air in *Barchester Towers*; hardly an incident or a character but goes to strengthen the book's legitimate fictional aim—the portrayal of society in a southern cathedral city.[1] "*Barchester Towers,*" says Oliver Elton "is crowded and rich and harsh." [2] The epithets are happy, and may be applied not only to this book, but to most of Trollope's successful work. He was a generous writer. He loved to populate his novels thickly, and felt the more at home the more his characters jostled one another in his mind. Also, beneath the suavity, was always harshness—not the harshness of cruelty, but the asperity of a man who was impatient of false sentiment, on the rock of whose aggressive commonsense the waves of flummery beat in vain.

But in the excellence of *Barchester Towers* was an element of fluke. That Trollope himself was not aware of the book's real quality was shown by its immediate successor. *The Three Clerks*, whatever its value as a document in autobiography, is a bad novel. Beside *Barchester Towers* it is shrill and facetious;

[1] The only strident lapse from this laudable detachment is the rather foolish reference to a descendant of the " Sidonia " who shines flamboyantly in Disraeli's *Coningsby*. Trollope, in his rôle of anti-humbug, detested Disraelian fiction for rococo unreality. His Sidonia—" a dirty little old man, who positively refused to leave his villa till he had got a bill on Doctor Stanhope's London bankers " —is proof that he had not yet shuffled off the chains of topical prejudice.
[2] *Op. cit.*

its background is a mere "painting in" and not a fertile soil from which spring character and happening. Indeed it is a novel born some fifteen years too late, and was, no doubt, written with a mistaken idea of emulating the picaresque novel of incident which bloomed and faded in the 'forties. Formless and flaccid for all its sprightliness, *The Three Clerks* is not redeemed even by the character of Undy Scott, who introduces what was to become a Trollopian speciality—the gentleman who is also a cad. Perhaps the book's female characters betray most completely its essential feebleness. The young women are pretty dolls in simpering bourgeois homes, or lovely daughters of the people, exposed to sordid sights and much temptation but with a virtue repellently impregnable. The freshness and frankness that distinguish the true Trollope girl are lacking even from Katie Woodward, for whom (and perhaps this is the reason of her unreality) Trollope himself cherished a romantic memory.

Undoubtedly *The Three Clerks* was derivative—in ultimate resort from Dickens, nearer at hand from such a Dickens imitator as Frank Smedley; and to the fact of its derivativeness may be attributed its popularity among contemporary intellectuals. Neither Thackeray nor the Brownings could have felt for such genuine Trollopianism as (for example) *The Belton Estate* the enthusiasm they had for a book written to a more familiar recipe. Thackeray was himself a novelist of the 'forties, and knew where he was in a novel written to the specification of his own period; the Brownings, out of touch with changing England and perforce judging their own country by its appearances in such fiction as came their way, accepted *The Three Clerks* for a continuing reality, whereas in fact it was a picture—and an inexpert picture—of a vanished age.

Trollope himself, although he clung—and for very obvious reasons—to his affection for this book of reminiscence, must during 1857 have had a vision of his real writer's destiny. How otherwise may be explained the sensational perfection of *Doctor Thorne*, one of the five (in a technical sense) faultless books he was to write? In nearly every novel—even in novels so outstanding as *The Small House at Allington*, *The Last Chronicle of Barset*, the two chronicles of Phineas Finn, *He Knew He Was Right*, *The Eustace Diamonds*, *The Vicar of Bullhampton*, *The Way We Live Now* and *Mr. Scarborough's Family*—it is impossible not to deplore a sub-plot or an exaggeration, a long-windedness or a more than normally aggressive repetition. But in five books—*Doctor Thorne*, *The Belton Estate*, *The Claverings*, *Sir Harry Hotspur of Humblethwaite* and *Dr. Wortle's School*—though there may be an extreme of tranquillity there is not a loose end, not a patch of drowsiness, not a moment of false proportion.

And *Doctor Thorne* has this distinction also—that it contains the loveliest of all his lovely heroines. Mary Thorne must take precedence even of Lily Dale. She is Trollope's most complete creation of the normal English girl as she was then, as (despite her detractors from Mrs. Lynn Linton to the latest angriest sociologist) she has ever since remained.

5

The importance of this tale of *Doctor Thorne* to an appreciation of the good qualities of Trollope as a novelist is so great, and its plot, bias and handling are so typical of his genius, that an examination in some detail of its construction and texture may profitably (and with ultimate economy of words) interrupt a survey of the author's general development.

Doctor Thorne is a sensitive, humorous, and even passionate delineation of an elderly doctor of noble character; of a fine young man; of a crowd of arrogant stupidities; of a downright heiress; of some fortune-hunters; and, above all, of a most entrancing girl.

The village of Greshamsbury in East Barsetshire owns as squire John Newbold Gresham, who, though impoverished, still lives majestically and is regarded as the first commoner of the county. His wife is sister of the Earl de Courcy, a magnate in the western (Whig) division of the county and the father of many unprofitable children. Through Lady Arabella Gresham, de Courcy influence and de Courcy views pervade the

Hall at Greshamsbury more than the squire could wish and much more than his son Frank Gresham means to tolerate. In particular it is an article of the de Courcy creed that Frank must marry money and restore the Gresham fortunes. Unless he does this the Greshamsbury relatives by marriage will disgrace their noble connections at Courcy Castle, which will never do, seeing that the de Courcys are of the great upon earth.

Unluckily Frank's love fancy has already strayed. Already he has slipped through childhood friendship into tenderness for a girl who lives with an old uncle in the village near the squire's gates, a girl without a penny, and a girl whose very origins are obscure.

Old Doctor Thorne was settled in Greshamsbury before the action of the novel starts. He has for long been intimate with the squire, doctored his children, advised him about money matters, and had free entrance all and every day to the Gresham household. When his niece Mary came to live with him, she naturally romped with Frank Gresham and his sisters and shared their lessons and their playrooms, and became as one of them.

The mystery of Mary's birth is only a mystery to the numerous characters in the tale. It is one of Trollope's most insistent principles to take the reader into full confidence, and *Doctor Thorne* is a good example of his method.[1] He explains in the first few chapters just who Mary is, and tells of the seduction by the doctor's elder brother of the sister of a stonemason in Barchester. He tells how the stonemason—Roger Scatcherd —avenged the girl's disgrace and, striking harder than he

---

[1] He had already made a solemn declaration of this principle in *Barchester Towers* :—

  Here, perhaps [he says, in the chapter entitled "The Widow's Suitors"] it may be allowed to the novelist to explain his views on a very important point in the art of telling tales. He ventures to reprobate that system which goes so far to violate all proper confidence between the author and his readers, by maintaining nearly to the end of the third volume a mystery as to the fate of their favourite personage. . . . Our doctrine is, that the author and the reader should move along together in full confidence with each other. Let the personages of the drama undergo ever so complete a comedy of errors among themselves, but let the spectator never mistake the Syracusan for the Ephesian ; otherwise he is one of the dupes, and the part of a dupe is never dignified.

meant, killed Henry Thorne outright. He tells how the dead man's brother saved the stonemason from the worst consequences of crime, visited him in prison, tended the wretched girl whose bastard was now quick within her. At last the child was born, and a faithful former lover of poor Mary Scatcherd forgave her tragedy and married her and took her to America. But the two sailed without the child, whom the good Doctor Thorne took and put to school, and in her thirteenth year fetched home to Greshamsbury. Now all of this was long ago, so that when Trollope's story proper is begun Mary is twenty years of age and Frank—the squire's son—turned twenty-one.

The doctor's secret was not known even to Roger Scatcherd. It was believed—by those few who cared to remember the sorry tale of the stonemason's sister—that the babe had died. Nevertheless there is a mystery about Mary; and when Lady Arabella wakes with a shock to the unpleasant fact that Frank —her only son, and heir to all the Gresham poverty and pride —is playing the lovesick over this girl, she finds in Mary's unexplained parentage a likely weapon against the, to her unthinkable, alliance.

There remains one further major character—or rather nucleus of character and incident—which, with the Gresham household and its haughty Courcy hinterland and with the quiet home of Doctor Thorne himself, supports the structure of the novel's plot. When Roger Scatcherd had served his period of prison, he disappeared to seek his fortune. He found it, becoming in due course a railway contractor of enormous wealth and purchaser of a baronetcy. Unluckily sobriety has not come with fortune, and Scatcherd is slowly drinking his way to death. Ever since the tragedy of twenty years before, the contractor has put all his trust—mental and physical—in Doctor Thorne. He now reappears in Barsetshire and, as Sir Roger Scatcherd, puts himself under the doctor's care. To ease the stringent poverty of Greshamsbury, the doctor has persuaded one friend, Squire Gresham, to sell to another friend, Sir Roger Scatcherd, a portion of the Greshamsbury land; in return Sir Roger has promised to advance money to the squire on terms more generous and against security less formidable than would elsewhere be possible.

Thus the stage is set. Between the weak, impoverished Gresham, with his domineering wife and arrogant "in-laws" at Courcy Castle, and the rough-diamond, brandy-soaking millionaire Sir Roger Scatcherd in his grand new mansion-house on Boxall Hill, stands Doctor Thorne, intimate with both, loving and loved by both, but powerless either to strengthen Gresham against Lady Arabella's social scheming or to restrain the new-made baronet from the indulgence which must ultimately kill him. And behind Doctor Thorne is Mary, timid and unassuming, a thing of gentle charm rather than of beauty, happy in the knowledge of her uncle's love, incurious as to the story of her birth, contented with her simple lot.

Because the tale of *Doctor Thorne* is a tale of successive dilemmas, all of which centre in a marriage that would conventionally be termed a misalliance, it is in theme, as well as in treatment and choice of characters, very typically Trollopian. The problem of misalliance tempted the novelist in Trollope time and time again; dilemma—social or ethical—remained throughout his active writing life his favourite among all the phases of the mind. Consequently in such a novel as *Doctor Thorne*—a novel compounded of perplexities and hinged on misalliance—he is at his best, because most thoroughly himself.

Of the dilemmas the first to emerge is that of Lady Arabella. She loves devotedly her only son; that part of her at least is genuine humanity. But having been brought up within the narrow boundaries of de Courcy social pride, she cannot escape the conviction that love alone does not make marriage suitable. Further she has a husband, and the squire is frankly difficult. He glides unhappily through life, pondering his stringencies. He knows that he himself inherited an unembarrassed property; that his extravagance (or rather that which, in his early married life, was forced upon him by the determined splendour of his wife's relations) has loaded mortgage upon mortgage, has indeed all but sold the title-deeds of land which has been the Gresham pride for generations. His crowning misery is that his only son, Frank, will not inherit wealth enough for his position, and *must marry money*. Nevertheless he will not join his wife in schemes to bring about that golden matrimony. He sees what must be, but tarries, making no virtue of necessity, but merely an excuse for dawdling melancholy.

Poor Lady Arabella—for with all her selfishness and all her cruelty to Mary Thorne and all her foolish pride, one pities her, so deft is Trollope's evocation of a soul three-quarters snob, one quarter mother-love—poor Lady Arabella has perplexities enough. And as the tale proceeds they multiply. Her husband becomes ever more elusive; he will not tell her how near or how far away is bankruptcy; he will not take advice from Courcy Castle; persistently he sees and talks with Thorne, until the good doctor—for all that long ago he saved the lives of three of her young children—becomes to Lady Arabella a menace and almost an object of hatred. Further, her daughter Beatrice, always a special friend of Mary Thorne, is loyal to a brother's steadfast passion rather than to maternal strategy, and visits Mary with such regularity that at last the exasperated mother forbids all intercourse. Then Beatrice sulks resignedly, and her father gives sympathetic looks, and Lady Arabella comes near to distraction.

The squire's quandary needs no labouring. Throughout the book he is torn between love and admiration for his son and contempt for himself. It is *his* fault that Frank must marry thousands rather than maiden sweetness; it is *his* mismanagement which stands between an only son and happiness. He cannot encourage the boy in a love meaning family disaster; he is too devoted a father (and incidentally too fond of Mary Thorne herself) to exercise authority and try to force on Frank a marriage of convenience.

Perhaps instinctively he knows the last course to be in any case impossible. Certainly the father is weak just where the son is strong. Frank's faithfulness to Mary never wavers. No strain can break him down. If Trollope was not always happy in his creation of young men, with Frank Gresham at least he makes no mistakes. Alone among the characters in *Doctor Thorne*, Frank sees his goal and, clear-eyed, holds upon his way. His mother's entreaties, his father's mournful prophecies of poverty and disaster, only strengthen his determination to win Mary and to keep her. His real obstacle is the person from whom opposition might least be expected—Mary herself.

But before Mary, with her courage, dignity and tenderness comes to take the place of honour which in any analysis of her story is her due, the influence of Sir Roger Scatcherd on the tale, and the cruel dilemma into which that influence thrusts Doctor Thorne, must briefly be revealed.

Sir Roger Scatcherd is Trollope's sole full-length portrait of a self-made man. The financial adventurer he was, in later novels, to describe more than once; there is Lopez in *The Prime Minister*, there is Melmotte in *The Way We Live Now*. Of money magnates, also, he made good use; but they, like Sir Thomas Tringle in *Ayala's Angel*, were successful business men, or, like Martha Dunstable and Moffat in this very novel *Doctor Thorne*, inheritors of fortunes made by trading parents.

It may at first thought seem strange that the effectiveness of Scatcherd did not encourage Trollope to use such men more frequently. Not only might their dramatic possibilities have been expected to appeal to him, but also his sensitiveness to social change must have impressed upon him their increasing frequency. Yet the uniqueness of this character is explicable. Scatcherd—for all the power of his presentment—is not wholly Trollope. He was an invention of the inventor of the novel's plot, who was not Anthony at all but his brother Tom. So in one sense at least Scatcherd is extraneous to the Trollopian conception of *Doctor Thorne*. One savours an outside influence in the very style of portraiture, in the queer colloquies of brandy-rotted parvenu and gin-sipping, submissive clerk, in the strong shading of the death-bed scene.

But the millionaire is extraneous only in one sense. His share in Mary's destiny is of the very essence of the tale, and that share begins when, under incessant drinking, the man's rugged physique at last gives way. Half-paralysed, but still the headstrong violent man he ever was, Scatcherd summons the doctor to his bedside and tells the details of his will. Of these the most important is that Boxall Hill and quite £200,000 are left in trust to Sir Roger's only son, left in the absolute control of Doctor Thorne, and not to be surrendered until young Louis Scatcherd reaches the age of twenty-five. Should Louis, by any hazard, die before reaching that delayed majority, the money is to go to the eldest child of Roger Scatcherd's sister, that very Mary Scatcherd who years before had fallen victim to the doctor's brother and then had married and migrated to America.

Now Louis Scatcherd is a dissolute inebriate, feeble and just turned twenty-one. The doctor knows that, left alone, he will surely kill himself with alcohol before the four years are run between now and the fulfilment of Sir Roger's will. Suppose he does? The money goes to Mary Scatcherd's eldest child, and only the doctor knows that this child is his own niece, his almost daughter, Mary Thorne.

For fully two-thirds of the novel's length poor Doctor Thorne labours beneath a cruel burden of uncertainty. At first he tries to make the dying Sir Roger name the residuary legatee; then in desperation tells who Mary is. But the baronet only laughs, and curses Thorne for keeping him ignorant of his niece's whereabouts, and laughs again, and coarsely hints that Mary and the wretched weakling Louis make a match of it. Joking, he dies. The next day, swathed in furs, degenerate and resentful, Sir Louis comes. Then life for Doctor Thorne becomes hell indeed.

Three separate intricacies confront him. He knows that Frank Gresham loves his Mary, but that Mary, for Frank's own sake, will not hear him; he knows that Greshamsbury is as good as sold to the Scatcherds; that, if the new owner of Boxall Hill insists, the very title-deeds may have to be surrendered; he knows that Lady Arabella is persecuting Mary in order to save her son from his own infatuation; he knows that, if Louis Scatcherd dies, Mary becomes an heiress and in effect owner of Greshamsbury. Shall he tell anyone of Mary's actual position, or shall he keep his counsel? Shall he encourage Frank and help him win the girl he wants, or give the victory to Lady Arabella by leaving Greshamsbury and taking Mary with him? Shall he use his authority and skill to save the useless selfish life of Louis Scatcherd, or shall he let him die?

In all his suffering the doctor has the warm comfort of his niece's love and loyalty. Beautiful, with steadily increasing beauty, is Trollope's tale of the relationship between Mary and her uncle. The old man, torn by uncertainty, watches the girl's heart turn towards Frank and lose itself in him, sees the girl's courage as she denies her love and sends the lover constantly away. Knowing that these two would give to one another a lifetime of happiness, he must yet keep silent as to the fortune which might so well be Mary's and would so smoothly conquer Greshamsbury debts. His duty to the dead Sir Roger is, if it be achievable by human skill, to keep dying Sir Louis among living men. His every inclination and desire is to let Louis die, to pile those golden sovereigns into Mary's lap, to watch the cruel Lady Arabella turn from frowns to smiles, to see the cloud of worry lift from Squire Gresham's brow. Shall it be duty or desire? Which shall he choose?

As matters turn out the choice is made for him—partly by circumstance, mainly by Mary herself. Obscure and unassuming, she is yet the despot of the novel's kingdom. In her the light and beauty of the whole book are centred; from her they radiate over the fields and parklands of East Barsetshire.

"I know one thing" says Beatrice Gresham to her sister after the Thorne ship has at last come home; "Mary will be as mild and as meek as a little dove. If she and the doctor had lost every shilling in the world, she would have been as proud as an eagle."

And that indeed is Mary Thorne. Her story takes 200,000 words to tell; but, when it ends, one lays the book aside, happy to think of Mary and her uncle happy, but wishing all the same fulfilment had not come so soon.

In the realm of fictional womanhood Mary and her less happy sister Lily Dale divide the loyalty of Trollopians. The latter was, by inference, the novelist's own ideal, and many readers worship in his company. Certainly Lily is perfect—whether, as at first, she is blithely mischievous; whether, as when doubts of Crosbie begin to gather, she is reserved and watchful; whether, as when betrayal is complete, she walks with head bravely high, but with a broken heart; whether, as on her welcome reappearance in *The Last Chronicle of Barset*, she keeps at arm's length, gently and tenderly, but always without flinching, the faithful love of Johnny Eames. But without treachery to the Pearl of Allington, it may be claimed that in Mary Thorne is embodied the true essence of the Trollope heroine. This heroine in her purest form is no tremendous beauty, certainly no minx. She is of small stature and of retiring mode; her woman's strength and her woman's tenderness come forth to meet the crises of her life, but for the rest she lives obscure and quietly dutiful. She typifies the "little brown girls" whom Trollope loved (the phrase is his, and he employs it more than once), and of her kind are his most delicate delineations of maids in love. In Mary's train come Lucy Robarts, Clara Amedroz, Ayala Dormer, Rachel Ray; others—essentially of the same gentle-forceful breed, though in their trappings more the aristocrat—are Violet Effingham (afterwards Lady Chiltern), Emily Hotspur, and Lady Mary Palliser, daughter of the Duke of Omnium.

All of these—so mild and yet so strong—reflect their creator's idea of the essential domination of womanhood over the contacts and crises of society, and of the proper means to its attainment. Modest of mien, low-voiced, by modern standards strangely feminine, each of these young women yet proves herself the ultimate despot of her social world. Claiming nothing of equality she achieves supremacy, and Trollope —English as he is—loves to be ruled by her but loves as much to criticise her faults.

"Women have no political honesty" he declares in *Framley Parsonage*. "A woman will turn" he wrote in one of the last letters of his life "so will a worm or a fox or a politician— often with no honest ground for turning. The truth is a woman delights to have the opportunity of turning so that she may make herself out to be injured." But he would not have her otherwise. His letters to Kate Field and such a character as the Baroness Banmann in *Is he Popenjoy?* express his scorn for feminist theory and ambition. Violet Effingham in *Phineas Finn* (who first declares "I do not think I shall marry Oswald.

I shall knock under to Mr. Mill and go in for woman's rights,"
and then, having nevertheless married her Chiltern, achieves
the fullest, happiest and most influential life to which, in
Trollope's view, a woman can aspire) may stand for his conception of the triumphant feminine.   Such conception is, of
course, a masculine one.   But Trollope was unashamedly
masculine, and lived in an age when traces of masculine
civilisation still remained.

Further, being not only a man but also a man of the world,
he had the attitude toward young girls natural to the experienced male.   Simpering sweetness made a first and last appearance in his work with Katie Woodward; but the minx—all
shrill impertinence and callow vanity—is more than once
daubed with a touch of angry satire.

"Unmarried girls are a mistake," wrote Sir William Hardman in 1863. "Set them down to sober conversation with
men of the world and they are little better than idiots.   The
humanising influences of matrimony are required to fit a
woman for the society of men." [1]

Similar, though perhaps less bluntly conceived, was Trollope's view of the virgin in society.   That is why he urged
matrimony even on Kate Field; that is why his stories of
young women are all love stories, his young wives faultlessly
perceived, and his maiden portraiture the more vivid the
nearer that its models are to a surrender of their maidenhood.

6

With *Doctor Thorne* Trollope had definitely found himself;
two books later he was to find his public also.   Between *Doctor
Thorne* and *Framley Parsonage* intervened two novels which,
although they did little to advance his fame, were influential by
their very faults and helped in the perfecting of his education.

The Bertrams is a considerable literary failure.   It is lop-
sided, cumbrous in humour and informative in landscape-
background.   But it lies in the direct line of Trollopian
evolution; it attempts situations and characters of a kind

[1] *The Letters and Memoirs of Sir William Hardman.*   London, 1925.

N

which later he was to make essentially his own. It was published at an important moment in his career, and foreshadows —clumsily enough—much of his subsequent development.

Caroline Waddington rejects George Bertram for reasons of income and prospects, marrying instead his prosperous lawyer friend. She finds that she has sold herself to a greedy tyrant, and the three volumes of the novel tell the story of her repentance and of her tragic liberation. Perhaps *The Bertrams* may claim to be a "try-out" for *The Claverings*; Julia Brabazon becomes Lady Ongar much as Miss Waddington becomes Lady Harcourt, living to rue her own ambition even more bitterly. Further, *The Bertrams* has to its credit several advance indications of a Trollope more controlled and more mature. The close-fisted old man, the disposal of whose money provides the *motif* of much of the incident, points the way to other enigmatic and tyrannical fortune-holders; there are touches in the description of Society at Littlebath—with Miss Todd [1] and her friends, with Colonel Sir Lionel Bertram, padded, corseted, sixty but sprightly—which prepare the reader for *Miss Mackenzie*; the final union of George and Caroline, though brought about by a suicide as timely as most fictional suicides, is admitted with a rather bleak contempt, characteristic at once of Trollope's tenderness toward lending-library prejudice and of his rough dislike of pretty-pretty and of wedding-bells. But when so much has been said in favour of *The Bertrams*, the rest is fault-finding. From the flat opening scenes of undergraduate life (Trollope avoided Oxford and Cambridge as staging for his later novels, and may be applauded for his prudence) [2] to the unTrollopian "Methinks" which begins the final chapter, the book is laboured and insufficiently compact. The central idea is too slight for its framework; subsidiary plots and rather heavy knockabout (the comic elements in *The Bertrams* are a mistaken tribute, partly to Dickens, mainly to Thackeray) cluster about the central theme and

[1] Miss Todd is said to have been modelled on Frances Power Cobbe, a fat jolly lady who was prominent as a humanitarian and an anti-vivisectionist.

[2] Much of the action of *John Caldigate* takes place in or near Cambridge, but the city appears in the capacity of county town and hardly as the seat of a great university.

overshadow it. The novel is unmistakably a Trollope novel and proved, maybe, part parent of several handsome children; but it is technically a bad book and (this is a rare fault in Trollope's fiction) not always easy to read.

If *The Bertrams* is Trollope of poor quality, *Castle Richmond* is not in the classic sense Trollope at all. It has earlier been stated (and why) that it was a reversion to the early didactic Irish novels. But it is difficult even to detect in its pages promise of work yet to come or qualities noticeably characteristic of its author. Perhaps the Countess of Desmond is the first of the tragic, passionate ladies whose sad procession winds through important later stories. Perhaps the plot, in so far as it turns on the doubtful death of Lady Fitzgerald's first disreputable husband, may be considered a foretaste of the plot of *Dr. Wortle's School*; maybe the style has here and there the biblical lilt to which the mature Trollope (a little unexpectedly) showed himself frequently inclined; [1] certainly one already mentioned characteristic of his method—a refusal to keep the reader in suspense, as though he scorned to save himself work of characterisation by erecting between himself and the public a screen of mystery—is strongly and disastrously evident, for the secret power exercised by the unsavoury Molletts over Sir Thomas Fitzgerald, just because it early ceases to be secret, proves a foundation too weak to carry the story's bulk. But, these details apart, *Castle Richmond* must claim the attention of readers of Trollope for its "Irishism" and not for its fictional significance.[2] It is a document, not a work of art; its appeal is to nationalist enthusiasm, not to the literary appreciation that knows no nationality.

The writing of *Castle Richmond* was interrupted in favour of *Framley Parsonage*, which, although in itself a minor link in the chain of Barset chronicles, won for Trollope the big public that

[1] *e.g.* "The battle had gone altogether against him, and now there was nothing left for him but to turn his face to the wall and die. Absolute ruin through his fault had come upon him and all that belonged to him. In that the glory was gone from the house of his son, and of his son's mother, the glory was gone from his own house." (*Castle Richmond*, chapter xxix.)

[2] An interesting survey of Trollope's novels, which pays particular attention to his exceptional understanding of Irish folk and Irish problems, was published in the *Dublin Review* for October 1872.

never wholly forsook him. The book is pleasant, at places highly amusing, and of great evidential value as to political views, sense of property and social manners prevalent at the time. But it is a little artificial in impulse and betrays signs of the great haste with which it was composed.

Orley Farm, the book which followed on the delayed completion of *Castle Richmond*, is much more significant of Trollope's growing mastery of his craft and of the qualities which, for good or ill, were permanently his. The tale was published in monthly numbers, and this method of issue set its mark upon the construction of the work. In fact *Orley Farm* is the first of the too numerous Trollope novels which suited themselves, though at the expense of conciseness and arrangement, to the exigencies of publishing. Again and again was the call for three-volumes worth of fiction to stretch a delicate and charming story to a dangerous tenuity; sometimes the proportions of a tale were damaged by the addition of sub-plot after sub-plot, so determined was the author to do his duty by the publisher, to give full measure for his money. The effect of publishing conditions on *Orley Farm* was of the kind peculiar to part-issue. The tale is episodic; it switches abruptly from grave to gay, from one set of characters to another, as do the successful novels of other authors who published in monthly or in weekly numbers. The periodical public required variety and sectional incident; *Orley Farm* (and its later counterpart *Can You Forgive Her?*) gave to the public what it wanted and suffered in the giving. Yet not irrevocably. The novel contains a wealth of characterisation and much agreeable humour of a "period" kind. The long-drawn tragedy of Lady Mason, the noble dignity of Sir Peregrine Orme, Madeline Staveley the heroine, and the grotesqueries on virtues of many of the minor characters have the vital reality that lingers in the mind. And there remains to *Orley Farm* a further, if ironic, distinction. It contains an ambitious trial scene—serving as climax to the whole crowded tale—at which appears the lawyer Chaffanbrass, who made his bow in *The Three Clerks* and was to make a sensational reappearance in *Phineas Redux*. But this trial, according to expert opinion, is a tissue of impossibilities and technical mistakes. Seldom, it seems, has a novelist trifled more recklessly with truth. And the sinner is Trollope—the faultless observer, the unrivalled realist! One cannot help feeling that the author of *Orley Farm*, could he read the savage attack on his legal accuracy made by an eminent barrister of our own day,[1] would rather chuckle than growl. Having lost no opportunity of scarifying lawyers, he would attribute some part at least of the professional hostility provoked by *Orley Farm* to the sting of his deliberate sarcasm. And yet, as to the charge of inaccuracy, he might well cry guilty. It is probable that he did not for long remain in ignorance of the faults of procedure in the trial of Lady Mason. *Phineas Finn* contains a lament over the difficulty to novelists of legal technicalities, and declares outright that the mumbo-jumbo is deliberate;[2] and when, in *The Eustace Diamonds*, he tackled a further problem involving such technicalities, he went to the trouble of getting written expert opinion on the point at issue. It may be hazarded that the precaution served its purpose; the law in *The Eustace Diamonds* (and for that matter in *Phineas Redux* also) has remained unchallenged.

With the writing of *Orley Farm* Trollope may claim to have mastered once and for all the technique of his craft. The days of tilting at windmills of contemporary abuse or misery, of airing personal distaste for other folks' opinions, were over. He had become a fictionist pure and simple; and one so skilful that, whether he varied theme and *mise-en-scène* or served up a familiar mixture in slightly different guise, he could produce without fail a story fresh and convincing and (to use his own word) "readable." The novels of the first years at Waltham are of a uniformly high standard. From the fine achievement of *The Small House at Allington*—with Lily Dale running a close second to Mary Thorne; with the subtle self-portraiture of

---

[1] "Anthony Trollope and the Law," by Sir Francis Newbolt, K.C. (*Law Journal*, Feb. 10 1923.)

[2] "And then those terrible meshes of the Law ! How is a fictionist in these excited days to create the needed biting interest without legal difficulties ; and how again is he to steer his little bark clear of so many rocks—when the rocks and shoals have been purposely arranged to make the taking of a pilot on board a necessity ? " (*Phineas Finn*, Vol. 1, chapter xxix.)

Johnny Eames; with the masterly entanglement of Crosbie
in the repellent scheming of the ladies of Courcy Castle—he
passed to the delicate brevity of *Rachel Ray*. It has been
suggested that the short story *The Courtship of Susan Bell*[1] was
a sketch for Rachel Ray, and so—in so far as Mrs. Ray and her
two daughters are concerned—it may have been; but the novel
has qualities peculiar to itself, particularly a ferocious caricature
of an evangelical minister, a pleasantly natural hero, and some
excellent studies of small-town snobbery. The Rev. Mr. Prong,
who marries Rachel's sister, out-Vicars the Vicar of Wrexhill
in his dour hypocrisy. He is the first and angriest of several
such pastiches, others being the Rev. Mr. Gibson in *He Knew
He Was Right* and Mrs. Bolton, mother of the heroine of
John Caldigate.

Can You Forgive Her? was a return to episodic bulk, to
comic relief, and to a crowded, motley cast of characters. As
is known, the book was a transformation into novel-form and
into modern dress of the author's rejected drama *The Noble
Jilt*; it offers also a foretaste of one of the strongest elements in
Phineas Finn. Alice Vavasor, heroine of *Can You Forgive Her?*,
jilts John Grey because he is too virtuous, and prefers the risk
of unhappiness and poverty with her rascally but engaging
cousin George; Laura Standish in *Phineas Finn*, shirking
poverty and fearing her own emotion, marries the blameless
but oppressive Kennedy to escape a handsome lover. A
weakness of *Can You Forgive Her?* is that Alice, after her period
of revolt, bows to propriety, marries her paragon and lives
happily. But Lady Laura Kennedy, having made her choice,
must abide by it; and strangely, tragically she does so. It is
possible that Trollope regretted the return of his earlier heroine
to her too admirable Grey and sought, in *Phineas Finn* and its
successor *Phineas Redux*, ruthlessly to gauge the price a girl
will sometimes pay for making a marriage of convenience.

In this respect *Can You Forgive Her?* is ancestral to the
Phineas books. So also is another, finer tale, *The Claverings*.
The powerful Phineas-Laura element in *Phineas Finn* and in
Phineas Redux (for the physical collapse and spiritual agony of

[1] *Tales of All Countries* (1st series).

Laura Kennedy are very powerfully portrayed) is anticipated—though differently and less grimly—by the tale of Julia Ongar and Harry Clavering. To the writing of *The Claverings*, after the shabby gentilities of the amusing but faintly sordid *Miss Mackenzie*, Trollope devoted six months of 1864. Though without the cumulative power of *The Last Chronicle of Barset*, *The Claverings* is the best wrought of the novels designed for the *Cornhill*, and as surely conceived as any book he ever wrote. Into the characterisation of young Harry Clavering are deftly woven a dozen social and spiritual dilemmas, from the tremendous hesitation between a first love and a second, to the trivial disconcertment of a young man who invites an elder to a club he has just proudly joined, only to find that the guest knows more of the club and of its members than he does himself. It is typical of Trollope, with his keen understanding of the torture-power to men of tiny social misadventure, that he should by such means swell Harry Clavering's mounting embarrassment. As for Julia Ongar—the super-jilt, the once ambitious now repentant, lonely, tragic woman—she is the perfect example of the novelist's skill in rousing pity even for a deserved misfortune. It is true that she sold herself; it is true that (as Trollope continually, effectively repeats) "she had the price in her hand"; but though she sinned for self-advantage, though all her misery was due to her own money-greed and love of luxury, she remains pitiful and the heart bleeds for her.

The qualities of sure-footed subtlety which distinguish *The Claverings* are equally present in *The Belton Estate*. But because this story is quieter and less obviously dramatic, its distinction is—or was until lately—apt to be overlooked. *The Belton Estate* has to a greater degree than any other of Trollope's books that art of concealing art which delights one type of mind, but by another is misapprehended or ignored. Henry James reviewed *The Belton Estate* when he was a young man of twenty-one and—partly because he was but twenty-one, partly because he was Henry James—his judgment of its qualities was unfavourable.

Our great objection to *The Belton Estate* is that we seem

to be reading a work written for children, a work prepared for minds unable to think, a work below the apprehension of the average man or woman. *The Belton Estate* is a *stupid* book . . . essentially, organically stupid. It is without a single idea. It is utterly incompetent to the primary function of a book of whatever nature—namely, to suggest thought.[1]

These words have a significance beyond that of mere excoriation of the particular novel they concern. Henry James was to become one of the typical minds of the æsthetic period. His own complex fiction of intricate impulse and of the half-expressed desires of remote and superior people was to come into fashion as the Trollopian novel faded to oblivion. Already, therefore, in 1866, in the scornful dislike of an impatient youth for the calm proficiency of an older man, may be remarked the beginning of the struggle which was to end with the defeat of mid-Victorianism and the triumph of the 'eighties. In this review of *The Belton Estate* are expressed the desire for technical perfection, the contempt for ordinary people, the love of elaboration, the disdain of simplicity, which were to become the religion, not only of the mature Henry James, but also of the whole æsthetic period. And it is suitable enough that *The Belton Estate* of all books should have provoked this early outburst of the anti-Trollope spirit. In no other novel is the essence of Trollope so concentrated. Using a cast of four principal and as few subsidiary characters, he fills three volumes with the matrimonial dilemma of Clara Amedroz, who has to choose between the uncouth farmer Will Belton— to whom has passed her thriftless father's estate—and the polished, self-seeking Captain Aylmer, who offers her marriage because at the death-bed of his rich aunt, and as part condition of becoming her heir, he swore to do so. The theme is commonplace; the incidents unsensational; the treatment unassuming and serene. Perhaps to those who demand of fiction what Trollope does not pretend to give, it may be an

[1] *The Nation* (U.S.A.), January 4 1866. Reprinted in *Notes and Reviews*, by Henry James. (Cambridge, Mass., 1921.)

aimless irritation—undistinguished, a waste of time and labour, incompetent (in the Jamesian sense) to suggest a single thought. But to a reader in sympathy with the Trollopian method and mentality the book is a delight, for its smoothness, its subtlety and its faultless adjustment of character and circumstance.

7

It was almost exactly three years after the completion of *The Belton Estate* (during the interval he had written *The Last Chronicle of Barset*, *Phineas Finn* and three short romantic tales of foreign life) that Trollope began *He Knew He Was Right* and for the first time based a novel on careful psychological analysis rather than on a study of social manners.

He Knew He Was Right (originally entitled "Mr. Trevelyan") is a long and detailed study of the gradual falling into madness of a suspicious husband. From obstinate egoism to proud and dangerous reserve, from reserve to desolate monomania, Trevelyan travels with tragic certainty. The final stages of his mental and moral dilapidation have a wild affliction unusual in the controlled world of Trollope characters. Certainly the novel has also its more familiar elements—there is an excellent sub-plot centring round the Cathedral Close of Exeter, with rich "Aunt Stanbury" to uphold the honourable tradition of caustic elderly spinsters [1]—but the pathological study of Trevelyan is at once the book's main theme and its importance in the chronology of Trollope's work. It is significant to read in the *Autobiography* the author's lament over his failure to create sympathy for Trevelyan. A modern reader must inevitably find the unhappy, haunted creature rather pathetic than repellent; but to contemporary criticism he was a monster. This was not the only occasion upon which Trollope showed himself in advance of the taste of his time.

From *He Knew He Was Right* descended quite a family of "novels of the mind" which tended to become shorter and

---

[1] The Exeter scenes, and to some extent also "Aunt Stanbury" herself, were memories of visits paid to Miss Fanny Bent, an old friend of Frances Trollope and of her sons, who lived near the Close.

simpler in plot, as their author realised the impossibility of blending successfully the old manner of episodic realism with the new concentration on psychological analysis. These novels, and in the order of their composition, are *An Eye for an Eye* (written in 1870, although not published until 1879); *Cousin Henry* (1878); *Dr. Wortle's School* (written in 1879, published in 1881); *Kept in the Dark* (1882) and *An Old Man's Love* (written in 1882, posthumously published in 1884). *An Eye for an Eye* describes the struggle in the mind of a young Englishman of family between the claims of tradition and of personal comfort and those of moral obligation toward the Irish girl who has become his mistress. *Cousin Henry* tells of the finding of a hidden will between the pages of a book by the very man to whom its discovery would mean the loss of an inheritance. The hesitations and agony of Henry Jones in his dilemma between self-interest and honesty are the theme of the story, which paints a shrewd portrait of a mean but pathetic man, not strong enough either for villainy or generosity, tortured in mind, suspected and insulted by his neighbours, but clinging with the obstinate tenacity of weakness to his unhappy secret.

The most memorable of this series of brief novels is *Dr. Wortle's School*, a book no reader of Trollope should neglect. Of the stories of its class it most successfully combines the psychologist with the student of manners. Further, being in effect a study of social prejudice, it gives scope to the author's great knowledge and understanding of the simultaneous cruelties and justifications of convention, and at the same time offers opportunity for delicate delineation of motive and dilemma. Finally, in the personality of Doctor Wortle, the reader has an admirable portrait of Trollope himself. The book was written at Lowick Rectory, which Trollope had been lent for the summer of 1879 by the Rev. W. Lucas Collins. He had written amusingly in acceptance of the invitation to occupy his friend's parsonage:—

That I, who have belittled so many clergymen, should ever come to live in a parsonage! There will be a heaping of hot coals! You may be sure that I will endeavour to behave myself accordingly, so that no scandal shall fall upon the parish. If the bishop should come that way, I will treat him as well as e'er a parson in the diocese. Shall I be required to preach, as belonging to the Rectory? I shall be quite disposed to give every one my blessing. . . . Ought I to affect dark garments? Say the word, and I will supply myself with a high waistcoat. Will it be right to be quite genial with the curate, or ought I to patronise a little? If there be dissenters, shall I frown on them, or smile blandly? If a tithe pig be brought, shall I eat him? If they take to address me as "The Rural Anthony," will it be all right?

Dr. Wortle's School is an interesting product of a sojourn undertaken in so gay a spirit. With the scene before his eyes, living in the midst of the landscape and society that was to compose his novel, Trollope plots the theme. Lowick becomes "Bowick"; the parsonage becomes a fashionable private school conducted by the Rev. Jeffrey Wortle, who combines rectorship with pedagogy. To the staff of the school is added a Mr. Peacocke, whose efficiency and charm are exceptional, but over whose marriage hangs a cloud of mystery. It comes to be whispered that Mrs. Peacocke is not, in fact, Mrs. Peacocke at all; the whisper swells to muttering; the county grow uneasy at the thought of their sons thus tutored by depravity. Finally Dr. Wortle is faced with a dreadful choice. He must dismiss his dear friend and his most treasured helper, or see his school shrink and wither away, as one by one children of wealthy respectability are withdrawn and sent elsewhere. In his dilemma the doctor acts precisely as Trollope himself would have acted. Perhaps the novelist was at pains to imagine himself the rector-pedagogue, entangled with the problems of his private school, coming to loggerheads with his bishop, torn between personal loyalty to a friend and prudent care for the livelihood of his wife and child. But whether he did so or no, whether the self-portraiture were conscious or fortuitous, there are sentences describing the pugnacious but warm-hearted doctor, there are words put into his mouth in self-justification, in bewilderment and in vehement argument, which might have been written of Trollope or spoken by him. The book therefore may claim the dual significance of fictional power and self-revelation. On the one hand, the story is a good one and well told; on the other, in his generous tolerance of Peacocke's "sin," in his stubborn determination not to be bullied by gossiping women and a nervously conventional prelate, and in his keen appreciation of the practical element in a man's duty to himself and family, Jeffrey Wortle is Anthony Trollope.

Inevitably, as a successor to *Dr. Wortle's School*, *Kept in the Dark* seems something of an anti-climax. It is a study of a morbid obsession—*He Knew He Was Right* in tabloid form—with a very "modern" cynical beginning but subsequent periods of perfunctory efficiency which hint at author's weariness. Nevertheless it reads agreeably, and ranks among the brief studies in individual psychology as *Ayala's Angel* ranks among the more usual full-length stories of the later period—that is to say, as a book which must be read to be realised, and which, when read, will be found to offer genuine, if conventional, Trollope to such as seek him.

8

If it be said that of the rest of Trollope's work one novel only (*The Way We Live Now*) is of supreme importance to an understanding of his evolution, no disrespect is meant to the numerous good qualities of a dozen others. There are indeed two among them that, because they are too long drawn out and in their inspiration mechanical, belong definitely to the second class. These are *Lady Anna* and *Marion Fay*. But of the rest, one can claim technical perfection; several within their familiar limits are a delight to read; and there is not one without some quality or other which entitles it to survival.

Of the outstanding merits of *Sir Harry Hotspur of Humblethwaite* and of *Mr. Scarborough's Family* something has already been said. The former is a study of female constancy of a poignancy to which Trollope rarely aspires and still more rarely attains. The latter—cynical and, for its period, daring —shows his power of sustained and dexterous raillery.

The Prime Minister and *The Duke's Children* carry further the adventures of characters already familiar, and for that reason, if for no other, will not be forgotten.[1] *The American Senator* will be read for the sake of its opening chapters, which set before the reader in a few pages the whole geographical and social pattern of an English county; for the sake of its hunting episodes, which are among the best not only in Trollope,[2] but in the whole of English fiction; and for the sake of Arabella Trefoil, a masterly study of a girl without a heart, who may be compared with Molière's Célimène and even with Beatrix in *Esmond*.

Is He Popenjoy? will survive for the Dean of Brotherton— a Trollope dignitary of the first water; for his gay, loving, whimsical daughter; for her husband Lord George Germain, with his excessive sense of duty and inadequate sense of humour; for her aristocratic sisters-in-law, shrouding in ill-nature and good works the emptiness of their lives and purses; for the feminist lecturer Baroness Banmann; for a society siren and society match-maker; and for the ill-tempered, dissolute marquess, on the legitimacy of whose son turns the whole mechanism of the story.

Maybe *Ralph the Heir*, apart from its personal memories of election-time and the pathetic determination of Neefit the tailor to buy a bankrupt young squire as husband for his daughter, is rather flaccid stuff. But *The Vicar of Bullhampton* has a sure title to enduring reputation. Ostensibly a novel written in defence of the "fallen woman," it has a quaintly solemn preface in which the author apologises to his public for venturing on ground so indelicate. But the book itself fails admirably to fulfil its proclaimed intentions. It is as

[1] See Appendix II (*c*).
[2] Lord Willoughby de Broke included two chapters from *The American Senator* in his hunting anthology *The Sport of Our Ancestors* (London, 1921). In his introductory note he says : " These chapters are chosen because they set forth in a few touches, but with unerring precision, almost every point of view from which fox-hunting can be regarded. . . . The book should be read by all those who wish to study the influences that are at work upon 'The Sport of our Ancestors.'"

characteristically Trollopian in plot and staging as the preface
in its self-conscious propagandism is uncharacteristic. A
vigorous story of village life, *The Vicar of Bullhampton* presents
a delightful parson, several charming ladies, a gruff miller, a
pompous marquess and some aggressive nonconformity.
Mary Lowther, its heroine, was condemned at the time of her
appearance for fickleness and lightness in her loves; [1] to-day
she seems sensible enough and, as a young woman, wholly
natural. The story, like all Trollope's really good work,
impresses the reader forcibly with its Englishry. It has the
quiet humour, the shy sympathy masquerading as indifference,
the delicate sense of kindliness, the occasional heaviness and
the occasional irritability which mark a book no less clearly
than a man, as shamelessly and irrevocably English. In
consequence, if Trollope is to come back to the affection of
his countrymen, *The Vicar of Bullhampton* must come with him,
for author and book have identical faults and qualities, and
both and all are English.

But more important than any of the novels thus summarily
appraised is the long and trenchant satire on the ways of the
changing world to which was given the ironic, angry title of
The Way We Live Now. In later years Trollope expressed
regret for this novel, declaring it to be ill-natured and over-
satirical. But one cannot wish it other than it is. The author's
impulse to its composition was twofold. In the first place,
the England of 1873 was to Trollope, no less than to Henry
Adams, an England in the grip of evil and transforming
powers. The international financial adventurer had settled on
London in his swarms; embarrassed country gentlemen,
touched with the fever of speculation, were selling their names
to shady directorates; the wrong Jews came ever more blandly
to the right houses; success was wealth and wealth was God.
To such as Trollope, this alien tarnishing of the bright shield
of English manners, this betrayal of a self-contained suavity in
the interests of a hustled luxury, were bitter indeed. He would
discuss the sinister tendencies of the time with his friend John
Delane. At this very moment Delane had written and pub-

[1] Cf. *Blackwood's Magazine*, May 1870.

lished in *The Times* a signed denunciation of a swindling
Californian Colonel, who had ruined a prominent English
nobleman by trailing the nets of rotten speculation before feet
that wandered on the path of bankruptcy. Doubtless the fears
and thunders of Delane made Trollope the more fearful for his
England, the more indignant with her enemies. But he had
also, and simultaneously, a personal spur to fictional energy.
The critics were beginning to contrast his leisured comedies of
county-manners with the glorious actuality of business and
efficiency. His clerics and his country gentlemen, his political
aristocrats, his dutiful daughters and despotic wealthy aunts,
were shrugged aside as out of date. He was declared to represent a moribund and frumpish England, an England which had
already abdicated in favour of popular sport and advertising
and the glories of cosmopolitan modernity. Trollope was not
the man to remain meekly inactive under such treatment. He
bestirred himself to beat the grumblers at their own game.
With a gesture half impatient, half appealing, he sent out into
the world the searing, crowded realism of *The Way We Live
Now*. He would prove that the old hand could still out-
modernise the youngsters, and at the same time expose the
new magnificence for the hollow bombast that it was.

Into his commentary on "things as they ought not to be"
he crowds the various dishonesties which most offend his taste.[1]
The first chapter of the novel is a caustic exposure of literary
log-rolling in the person of Lady Carbury, novelist and
intriguer, who plays her charms on editors and publishers,
securing contracts on account of favours yet to come. That
she schemes rather for her children's sake than for her own and
is in consequence more to be pitied than reviled, is but another
expression of her creator's belief that a good motive is present
in most human error. Very soon Melmotte—alien, million-
aire, company-promoter and swindler—makes his appearance.
Trollope was later accused of having copied Melmotte from
Merdle in *Little Dorrit*, but he asserted that he first read
that novel in 1878, and the similarity—at best a doubtful one

---

[1] See Appendix IV (*b*) for Trollope's preliminary lay-out of *The Way We
Live Now*.

—was therefore pure coincidence. Mrs. Hurtle, Paul Montague's "secret woman," is by her nationality a bitter insinuation that even in wild oats an American brand had become the mode. Gilded youth (or rather pseudo-gilded youth, for almost every character in *The Way We Live Now* is in one way or another a sham), its dissipations and its squalid knock-about are satirised in the group of young bloods at the "Bear-garden" —a club "lately opened with the express view of combining profligacy with parsimony" and one where "everything was provided by a purveyor, so that the club should be cheated only by one man." Of the members of the Bear-garden the most important to the story are Sir Felix Carbury, the ne'er-do-weel son of the log-rolling novelist, and Dolly, heir to Adolphus Longestaffe of Caversham in Suffolk and of Pickering Park in Sussex. The family of Longestaffe are Trollope's most merciless comment on the degeneration of the squirearchy. Ambitious and scheming, they are also meanly inefficient. They put an honoured name in pawn to city charlatans; on borrowed cash they lord it arrogantly over the local countryside. At home they snarl and scrape and plot for pin-money and husbands; abroad they haughtily maintain at least the attitudes of a betrayed nobility.

To every feature of the changed and changing face of England, Trollope applies his pitiless, resentful scrutiny.

What are we coming to [asks Roger Carbury (the honest John Bull of the novel, the old-style Englishman who lives unhappily amid the new promiscuities)] when such as Melmotte is an honoured guest at our tables? You can keep your house from him and so can I mine. But we set no example to the nation at large. They who do set the example go to his feasts, and of course he is seen at theirs in return. And yet these leaders of fashion know—or at any rate they believe—that he is what he is because he has been a swindler greater than other swindlers. Men reconcile themselves to swindling. Though they themselves mean to be honest, dishonesty is of itself no longer odious to them. . . . Of course he's a failure—a miserable imposition, a hollow vulgar fraud from beginning to end. But his position is a sign of the degeneracy of the age.

In Melmotte's train, with Lady Pomona Longestaffe and the smart rowdies of the Bear-garden, came others—shady, common or contemptible. Squercum the lawyer, "who, though an attorney, would hardly have been taken for a gentleman,—a sign in his way that the old things are being changed"; Breghert the Jew; Sir Damask Monogram, who, because he "shot pigeons at Hurlingham, drove four-in-hand in the park, had a box at every racecourse and was the most good-natured fellow known, had really got over the difficulty of being the grandson of a butcher and was now as good as though the Monograms had gone to the crusades"; Lord Alfred Grendall, brother of a duke, professional whist player, waster and sponge, who becomes tame aristocrat to every money-rigger of the Melmotte consortium—these there are, and half a dozen more, all striving to be what they can never be, pretending to a dignity they have not, living by sham, or bluff, or on the largesse of the rich parvenus to whom they cringe.

Such, in brief, is *The Way We Live Now*, a sour and pitiless picture of a sordid scene. Trollope was angry when he wrote it; and the anger burns through its four hundred thousand words, until one fancies that the whole jerry-built society of scheming women, money-grubbing aristocrats and blatant millionaires must needs go up in the fierce flame of the old novelist's disgusted rage. At times one wonders whether this fierce tremendous book is not the greatest novel Trollope ever wrote. But when the thought of Mary Thorne returns, and because beauty is more permanent than anger and sweetness more abiding than even righteous cruelty, the satire falls into the second place, leaving perpetually enthroned at the proud apex of the pyramid of Trollope fiction the tale of Doctor Thorne.

APPENDICES

I

(a) CALENDAR OF EVENTS IN THE LIFE OF FRANCES TROLLOPE

1780.		Birth of Frances Milton, second daughter of the Rev. William Milton of Heckfield, Hampshire.
1809.	May 23.	Marriage of Frances Milton and Thomas Anthony Trollope.
1810.		Birth of T. Adolphus Trollope. [Died 1893.]
1811.		Birth of Henry Trollope. [Died 1834.]
1812.		Birth of Arthur William Trollope. [Died 1824.]
1813.		Birth of Emily Trollope. [Died at birth.]
1815.	Apl. 24.	Birth of ANTHONY TROLLOPE at 6 Keppel Street, Bloomsbury.
1816.		Birth of Cecilia Trollope at Harrow; afterwards Mrs. John Tilley. [Died 1849.]
1816.		Thomas and Frances Trollope move from London to Julians, near Harrow.
1818.		Birth of Emily Trollope (the second). [Died 1836.]
1827.		Thomas Trollope moves from Julians to Julians Hill. ("Orley Farm.")
	Nov. 4.	Frances Trollope sails to America.
1828.		The Trollope Bazaar ("Trollope's Folly") starts building in Cincinnati.
1828–9.		*Domestic Manners of the Americans* begun.
1830.		Thomas Trollope moves from Julians Hill to Harrow Weald.
1831.	Aug. 5.	Frances Trollope returns to England from America.
1832.	Mar. 19.	Frances Trollope publishes her first book, *Domestic Manners of the Americans*. The Trollopes return to Julians Hill.
1834.	Apl. 18.	The bailiffs occupy Julians Hill. The Trollopes leave England and settle at Bruges.
	Dec. 23.	Death of Henry Trollope at Bruges.

1835. Oct. Death of Thomas Anthony Trollope at Bruges. Frances Trollope returns to England and settles at Hadley.

1846. After ten years spent in various houses in England and in foreign travel, Frances Trollope and her eldest son settle in Florence.

1863. Oct. 6. Death of Frances Trollope in Florence.

(b) BIBLIOGRAPHY OF FRANCES TROLLOPE

Domestic Manners of the Americans. With illustrations by A. Hervieu. 2 vols. London. Whittaker, Treacher. 1832.

The Refugee in America: A Novel. 3 vols. London. Whittaker, Treacher. 1832.

The Mother's Manual: or Illustrations of Matrimonial Economy. An Essay in Verse. With illustrations by A. Hervieu. 1 vol. London. Treuttel and Würtz and Richter. 1833.

The Abbess: A Romance. 3 vols. London. Whittaker, Treacher. 1833.

Belgium and Western Germany in 1833. 2 vols. London. John Murray. 1834.

Tremordyn Cliff. 3 vols. London. Bentley. 1835.

Paris and the Parisians in 1835. With illustrations by A. Hervieu. 2 vols. London. Bentley. 1836.

The Life and Adventures of Jonathan Jefferson Whitlaw: or Scenes on the Mississippi. With illustrations by A. Hervieu. 3 vols. London. Bentley. 1836.
[Re-issued in 1857 under the title: *Lynch Law.*]

The Vicar of Wrexhill. With illustrations by A. Hervieu. 3 vols. London. Bentley. 1837.

Vienna and the Austrians. With illustrations by A. Hervieu. 2 vols. London. Bentley. 1838.

A Romance of Vienna. 3 vols. London. Bentley. 1838.

The Widow Barnaby. 3 vols. London. Bentley. 1839.

The Widow Married: a Sequel to The Widow Barnaby. With illustrations by R. W. Buss. 3 vols. London. Colburn. 1840.

The Life and Adventures of Michael Armstrong, the Factory Boy. With illustrations by A. Hervieu, R. W. Buss and T. Onwhyn. 3 vols. and 1 vol. (8vo.) London. Colburn. 1840.

One Fault: A Novel. 3 vols. London. Bentley. 1840.

Charles Chesterfield: or the Adventures of a Youth of Genius. With illustrations by "Phiz." 3 vols. London. Colburn. 1841.

The Ward of Thorpe Combe. 3 vols. London. Bentley. 1841.
  [Re-issued in Ward, Lock's Parlour Library, and later as a
    Routledge Railway Novel under the title: *The Ward.*]
The Blue Belles of England. 3 vols. London. Saunders and Otley.
  1842.
A Visit to Italy. 2 vols. London. Bentley. 1842.
The Barnabys in America: or Adventures of the Widow Wedded. With
  illustrations by John Leech. 3 vols. London. Colburn.
  1843.
Hargrave: or the Adventures of a Man of Fashion. 3 vols. London.
  Colburn. 1843.
Jessie Phillips: A Tale of the Present Day. With illustrations by John
  Leech. 3 vols. London. Colburn. 1843. 1 vol. (8vo.)
  1844.
The Laurringtons: or Superior People. 3 vols. Longman, Brown,
  Green and Longmans. 1844.
Young Love: A Novel. 3 vols. Colburn. 1844.
The Attractive Man. 3 vols. London. Colburn. 1846.
The Robertses on their Travels. 3 vols. London. Colburn. 1846.
Travels and Travellers: A Series of Sketches. 2 vols. London. Col-
  burn. 1846.
Father Eustace: A Tale of the Jesuits. 3 vols. London. Colburn.
  1847.
The Three Cousins. 3 vols. London. Colburn. 1847.
Town and Country: A Novel. 3 vols. London. Colburn. 1848.
  [Re-issued in 1857 under the title: *Days of the Regency.*]
The Young Countess: or Love and Jealousy. 3 vols. London. Col-
  burn. 1848.
  [Re-issued under the title: *Love and Jealousy* in Ward, Lock's
    Railway Library, and later by C. H. Clark.]
The Lottery of Marriage: A Novel. 3 vols. London. Colburn.
  1849.
The Old World and the New: A Novel. 3 vols. London. Colburn.
  1849.
Petticoat Government: A Novel. 3 vols. London. Colburn. 1850.
Mrs. Mathews, or Family Mysteries. 3 vols. London. Colburn.
  1851.
Second Love, or Beauty and Intellect: A Novel. 3 vols. London.
  Colburn. 1851.
Uncle Walter: A Novel. 3 vols. London. Colburn. 1852.
The Young Heiress: A Novel. 3 vols. London. Hurst and Blackett.
  1853.

The Life and Adventures of a Clever Woman. Illustrated with Occasional Extracts from her Diary. 3 vols. London. Hurst and Blackett. 1854.

Gertrude: or Family Pride. 3 vols. London. Hurst and Blackett. 1855.

Fashionable Life: or Paris and London. 3 vols. London. Hurst and Blackett. 1856.

II

(a) CALENDAR OF EVENTS IN THE LIFE OF ANTHONY TROLLOPE

1815.	Apl. 24.	Birth at 6 Keppel Street, Bloomsbury.
1822.		Sent as day-boy to Harrow.
1825.		Sent to Arthur Drury's private school at Sunbury.
1827.		Sent to Winchester.
1830.	Spring.	Removed from Winchester; sent again to Harrow.
1834.	Apl.	Leaves Harrow in consequence of the family's migration to Bruges.
	Summer.	Becomes for six weeks a classical usher in a Brussels school.
	Autumn.	Accepts a junior clerkship in the General Post Office. Settles in London.
1840.	Spring.	Has serious illness.
1841.	Aug.	Becomes Deputy Postal Surveyor at Banagher in Ireland.
1843.	Autumn.	*The Macdermots of Ballycloran* begun.
1844.	June 11.	Marries Rose Heseltine. Is transferred to Clonmel.
1845.		Promoted Surveyor and stationed at Mallow. *The Macdermots of Ballycloran* finished. [Published 1847.]
1847		Writes *The Kellys and the O'Kellys*. [Published July 1848.]
1849.		Writes *La Vendée*. [Published June 1850.]
1850.		Writes *The Noble Jilt*. [Published July 1923.]
1851.	Spring.	Transferred to western England on special postal mission.
1852.	July 29.	*The Warden* begun.
1853.	Autumn.	Returns to Ireland. *The Warden* finished in Belfast. [Published January 1855.]
1854.	Autumn.	Leaves Belfast and settles at Donnybrook near Dublin.

1855.	Feb.	Writes *The New Zealander*. [Never published.]
	Apl.	*Barchester Towers* begun.
1856.	Nov.	*Barchester Towers* finished. [Published May 1857.]
1857.	Spring.	*The Three Clerks* begun.
	July.	*The Struggles of Brown, Jones and Robinson* begun.
	Aug. 18.	*The Three Clerks* finished. [Published Nov. 30 1857.]
	Sept.	Visits Frances Trollope in Florence.
	Oct. 20.	*Doctor Thorne* begun.
1858.	Feb. 11.	Leaves London on an official postal mission to Egypt.
	Mar. 11.	Leaves Alexandria for Palestine.
	Apl. 1.	*Doctor Thorne* finished. [Published June 1858.]
		The Bertrams begun.
	Apl. 22 to May 10.	Travels home via Malta, Gibraltar and Spain.
1858.	May to July.	Occupied with a series of official visits to towns in Scotland and the north of England.
	Aug. to Oct.	At home in Ireland.
	Nov. 16.	Leaves London on official postal mission to the West Indies.
	Dec. 20.	*The Bertrams* finished. [Published March 1859.]
1859.	Feb.	*The West Indies and the Spanish Main* begun.
	Summer.	Returns to London with complete MS. of *The West Indies and the Spanish Main*. [Published Oct. 1859.]
	Aug. 4.	*Castle Richmond* begun.
	Sept.	On holiday in Pyrenees.
	Oct.	Commissioned to write *Framley Parsonage* for the *Cornhill*.
	Nov. 4.	*Framley Parsonage* begun.
	Dec.	Leaves Ireland finally and settles at Waltham Cross.
1860.	Jan. 1.	*Castle Richmond* resumed.
		Framley Parsonage begins serialisation in *Cornhill*.
	Mar. 31.	*Castle Richmond* finished. [Published May 1860.]
	Apl. 1.	*Framley Parsonage* resumed.
	June 30.	*Framley Parsonage* finished. [Published May 1861 after completion of serial.]
	July 4.	*Orley Farm* begun.
	Oct.	Visits Frances and T. Adolphus Trollope in Florence. First meeting with Kate Field.

1861. Aug. to   Writing short stories. [*Tales of All Countries.*
        Apl.   Published 1861 and 1863.]

        Mar.   *Orley Farm* begins publication in monthly numbers.

        June 15.   *Orley Farm* finished. [Published 1861/2, after completion of part issue.]

        Spring.   Elected member of the Garrick Club.

        June 23.   *The Struggles of Brown, Jones and Robinson* resumed.

        Aug. 1.   *Brown, Jones and Robinson* begins serialisation in *Cornhill*.

        Aug. 3.   *Brown, Jones and Robinson* finished. [Published Nov. 1870, eight and a half years after completion of serial.]

        Aug. 24.   Leaves London on official postal mission to the United States.

        Sept. 16. *North America* begun.

1862. Apl.   *North America* finished. [Published May 1862.] Returns home from New York.

        May 20.   *The Small House at Allington* begun.

        Sept.   *The Small House at Allington* begins serialisation in *Cornhill*.

1863. Feb. 11. *The Small House at Allington* finished. [Published March 1864, just prior to completion of serial issue.]

        Mar. 3.   *Rachel Ray* begun.

        June 29.   *Rachel Ray* finished. [Published October 1863.]

        Aug. 16.   *Can You Forgive Her?* begun.

        Oct. 6.   Death of Frances Trollope.

        Dec.   Death of Thackeray.

1864. Jan.   *Can You Forgive Her?* begins publication in monthly numbers.

        Apl. 28.   *Can You Forgive Her?* finished. [Published 1864/5 after the completion of the part issue.]

        May 22.   *Miss Mackenzie* begun.

        Summer.   Elected member of the Athenæum Club.

        Aug. 18.   *Miss Mackenzie* finished. [Published March 1865.]

        Aug. 24.   *The Claverings* begun.

        Dec. 31.   *The Claverings* finished. [Serialised in the *Cornhill* from Feb. 1866 to May 1867. Published Apl. 1867.]

1865. Jan. 30. *The Belton Estate* begun.

1865.	Feb.	The *Pall Mall Gazette* starts publication.
	Feb. 9.	First Hunting Sketch published in *Pall Mall*.
	Mar. 20.	Last Hunting Sketch published in *Pall Mall*. [Collected and issued in book form May 1865.]
	May 15.	First number of *Fortnightly Review* published, containing first serial instalment of *The Belton Estate*.
	Aug. 3.	First Travelling Sketch published in *Pall Mall*.
	Sept. 4.	*The Belton Estate* finished. [Published Dec. 1865, shortly before conclusion of serialisation.]
	Sept. 6.	Last Travelling Sketch published in *Pall Mall*. [Collected and issued in book form Feb. 1866.]
	Sept. 11.	*Nina Balatka* begun.
	Nov. 20.	First Clerical Sketch published in *Pall Mall*.
	Dec. 31.	*Nina Balatka* finished. [Serialised in *Blackwood's Magazine* from July 1866 to Jan. 1867. Published Feb. 1867.]
1866.	Jan. 20.	*Last Chronicle of Barset* begun. [Issued in weekly numbers from Dec. 1. Published in 1867 after completion of part issue.]
	Jan. 25.	Last Clerical Sketch published in *Pall Mall*. [Collected and issued in book form under the title *Clergymen of the Church of England*, March 30 1866.]
	Sept. 15.	*The Last Chronicle of Barset* finished.
	Nov. 17.	*Phineas Finn* begun.
1867.	Jan.	Writes *Palmerston*. [Published 1882.]
	May 15.	*Phineas Finn* finished. [Serialised in *St. Paul's Magazine* from Oct. 1867 to May 1869. Published March 1869.]
	June 2.	*Linda Tressel* begun.
	July 16.	*Linda Tressel* finished. [Serialised in *Blackwood's Magazine* from Oct. 1867 to May 1868. Published May 1868.]
	Aug.	*Lotta Schmidt* published. [Collection of stories written during the preceding four years.]
	Sept. 1.	*The Golden Lion of Granpère* begun. Resigns from the Post Office and leaves the Civil Service.
	Oct. 1.	*St. Paul's Magazine* starts publication.

1867. Oct. 22.   *Golden Lion* finished. [Serialised in *Good Words* from Jan. 1872 to Aug. 1872. Published May 1872.]

       Nov. 13.   *He Knew He Was Right* begun.

1868. Mar.   Leaves London for the United States on official postal and copyright missions.

       June 12.   *He Knew He Was Right* finished. [Issued in weekly numbers from Oct. 17 1868 to May 22 1869. Published May 1869.]

       June 15.   *The Vicar of Bullhampton* begun.

       July (end).   Returns home from United States.

       Nov.   Stands unsuccessfully as Liberal candidate for Beverley in the General Election. *The Vicar of Bullhampton* finished. [Issued in monthly numbers from July 1869 to May 1870. Published Apl. 1870.]

       Dec.   *Sir Harry Hotspur of Humblethwaite* begun.

1869. Jan. 30.   *Sir Harry Hotspur of Humblethwaite* finished. [Serialised in *Macmillan's Magazine* from May to Dec. 1870. Published Nov. 1870.]

       ? Feb.   Dramatises *The Last Chronicle of Barset* under the
       or Mar.   title *Did He Steal It?* [Never performed. Text of play privately printed.]

       Apl. 4.   *Ralph the Heir* begun.

       Aug. 7.   *Ralph the Heir* finished. [Issued in monthly numbers and simultaneously as Supplement to *St. Paul's Magazine* from January 1870 to July 1871. Published April 1871.]

       Dec. 4.   *The Eustace Diamonds* begun.

1870. Jan. 29.   *The Commentaries of Cæsar* begun.

       Mar.   Resigns editorship of *St. Paul's*.

       Apl. 25.   *The Commentaries of Cæsar* finished. [Published June 1870.]

       May.   *An Editor's Tales* published. [A collection of stories written during the preceding two years and published in *St. Paul's Magazine*.]

       Aug. 25   *The Eustace Diamonds* finished. [Serialised in the *Fortnightly Review* from July 1 1871 to Feb. 1 1873. Published December 1872.]

1870. Sept. 13.   *An Eye for An Eye* begun.

       Oct. 10.   *An Eye for An Eye* finished. [Serialised in the

1870.   *Whitehall Review* from Aug. 24 1878 to Feb. 1 1879. Published Jan. 1879.]

     Oct. 23.   *Phineas Redux* begun.

1871.   Apl. 1.   *Phineas Redux* finished.

     Apl.   Gives up Waltham House.

     May 24.   Sails from Liverpool for Australia to visit his farmer son.

     May 25.   *Lady Anna* begun at sea.

     July 19.   *Lady Anna* finished at sea. [Serialised in the *Fortnightly Review* from Apl. 1873 to Apl. 1874. Published May 1874.]

     July 20.   Lands in Melbourne.

     Oct. 23.   *Australia and New Zealand* begun.

1872.   Jan to

     Oct.   Travelling Australia and New Zealand.

     Apl.   *Shilly Shally*, by Charles Reade, produced at the Gaiety Theatre. [This play was a pirated dramatic version of *Ralph the Heir*.]

     Dec. 15.   *Australia and New Zealand* finished. [Published Feb. or Mar. 1873.]

     Dec. 20.   Arrives home via the United States from Australia and settles at 39 Montagu Square.

1873.   May 1.   *The Way We Live Now* begun.

     June 1.   *Harry Heathcote of Gangoil* begun.

     June 28.   *Harry Heathcote of Gangoil* finished. [Issued as the Christmas number of the *Graphic* on Dec. 25 1873. Published Oct. 1874.]

     July 3.   *The Way We Live Now* resumed.

     Dec. 2.   *The Way We Live Now* finished. [Issued in monthly numbers from Feb. 1874 to Sept. 1875. Published July 1875.]

1874.   Apl. 2.   *The Prime Minister* begun.

     Sept. 15.   *The Prime Minister* finished. [Issued in monthly numbers from Nov. 1875 to June 1876. Published May 1876.]

     Oct. 12.   *Is He Popenjoy?* begun.

1875.   Feb. 28.   Leaves London via Brindisi for Ceylon.

     Mar. 27 to

     Apl. 14.   In Ceylon.

     May 3.   *Is He Popenjoy?* finished at sea between Ceylon and Australia. [Serialised in *All the Year*

1875.   *Round* from Oct. 13 1877 to July 13 1878.
                               Published Apl. 1878.]

        June 4.   Arrives in Australia. *The American Senator*
                   begun.

        Aug. 28.   Sails for England from Sydney.

        Sept. 24. *The American Senator* finished at sea. [Serialised
                   in *Temple Bar* from May 1876 to July 1877.
                   Published July 1877.]

        Oct.   Arrives home from Australia. The *Autobio-*
                   graphy begun.

1876.   Apl. 30.   The *Autobiography* (save for a few notes added
                   later) finished. [Published posthumously
                   Oct. 1883.]

        May 2.   *The Duke's Children* begun.

        Oct. 29.   *The Duke's Children* finished. [Serialised in *All*
                   the Year Round from Oct. 4 1879 to July 24
                   1880. Published June or July 1880.]

1877.   Feb. 3.   *John Caldigate* begun.

        Feb. 22   First part of *The Life of Cicero* written. [Date of
        to Mar. 12. its completion not recorded. Published
                   autumn 1880.]

        June 29.   Leaves London for South Africa.

        July 22.   *John Caldigate* finished at sea. [Serialised in
                   Blackwood's Magazine from April 1878 to
                   June 1879. Published June 1879.]

        July 23.   *South Africa* begun.

        Dec. 12.   Leaves South Africa for home.

1878.   Jan. 2.   *South Africa* finished at sea. [Published Mar.
                   1878.] Arrives home from South Africa.

        Apl. 25.   *Ayala's Angel* begun.

        June 21 to
        July 24.   Travels to Iceland in the yacht "Mastiff."

        Aug.   *How the "Mastiffs" went to Iceland* written. [Pub-
                   lished (?) Oct. 1878.]

        Sept. 24. *Ayala's Angel* finished. [Published June 1881.]

        Oct. 26.   *Cousin Henry* begun.

        Dec. 8.   *Cousin Henry* finished. [Serialised simultaneouely
                   in the *Manchester Weekly Times* and the *North*
                   British Weekly Mail from Mar. 8 to May 24
                   1879. Published Nov. 1879.]

        Dec. 23.   *Marion Fay* begun.

1879.   Feb. 1.   *Thackeray* begun.

1879. Mar. 25. *Thackeray* finished. [Published early summer 1879.]

    Apl. 8. *Dr. Wortle's School* begun.

    Apl. 29. *Dr. Wortle's School* finished. [Serialised in *Blackwood's Magazine* from May to Dec. 1880. Published Jan. 1881.

    Aug. 6. *Marion Fay* resumed.

    Nov. 21. *Marion Fay* finished. [Serialised in the *Graphic* from Dec. 3 1881 to June 3 1882. Published May 1882.]

1880. July 4. Gives up 39 Montagu Square and settles at Harting Grange, near Petersfield.

    Aug. 18. *Kept in the Dark* begun.

    Dec. 15. *Kept in the Dark* finished. [Serialised in *Good Words* from May to Dec. 1882. Published Aug. or Sept. 1882.]

    Dec. 17. *The Fixed Period* begun.

1881. Feb. 28. *The Fixed Period* finished. [Serialised in *Blackwood's Magazine* from Oct. 1881 to Mar. 1882. Published Mar. or Apl. 1882.]

    Mar. 14. *Mr. Scarborough's Family* begun.

    Oct. 31. *Mr. Scarborough's Family* finished. [Serialised in *All the Year Round* from May 27 1882 to June 16 1883. Published May 1883.]

1882. Jan. or *Why Frau Frohmann Raised her Prices* published.
    Feb. [A collection of stories written between 1876 and 1878.]

    Feb. 20. *An Old Man's Love* begun.

    May 6. Phœnix Park murders in Dublin.

    May 9. *An Old Man's Love* finished. [Published posthumously Nov. or Dec. 1883.]

    May Travels to Ireland to collect data for an Irish
    (middle). novel.

    June. *The Landleaguers* begun.

    August. Visits Ireland a second time to get fresh material.

    Sept. 2. *The Landleaguers* resumed. [The story was never finished and was published in an incomplete form in October 1883.]

    Sept.
    (late). Leaves Harting to spend winter in London.

    Dec. 6. Dies in London.

(b) BIBLIOGRAPHY OF ANTHONY TROLLOPE

[*In the original edition of this book indications were given of those novels of Trollope's which had been more or less recently reprinted and were therefore obtainable. Such information cannot be given at the present moment (summer 1944) because the paper shortage has driven virtually every Trollope text off the market, and his books can only be purchased by chance and secondhand. When times become normal again, would-be readers should consult the list of the "World's Classics" published by the Oxford University Press. The service done by this series to Trollope's memory cannot be too warmly acknowledged.*]

The Macdermots of Ballycloran. 3 vols   London. Newby. 1847.

The Kellys and the O'Kellys: or Landlords and Tenants. 3 vols. London. Colburn. 1848.

La Vendée: An Historical Romance. 3 vols. London. Colburn. 1850.

The Warden. 1 vol. London. Longman. 1855.

Barchester Towers. 3 vols. London. Longman. 1857.

The Three Clerks: A Novel. 3 vols. London. Bentley. 1858.

Doctor Thorne: A Novel. 3 vols. London. Chapman & Hall. 1858.

The Bertrams: A Novel. 3 vols. London. Chapman & Hall. 1859.

The West Indies and the Spanish Main. 1 vol. London. Chapman & Hall. 1859.

Castle Richmond: A Novel. 3 vols. London. Chapman & Hall. 1860.

Framley Parsonage. With illustrations by J. E. Millais. 3 vols. London. Smith, Elder. 1861.

Tales of All Countries. 1 vol. London. Chapman & Hall. 1861.

Orley Farm. With illustrations by J. E. Millais. 2 vols. London. Chapman & Hall. 1862.

North America. 2 vols. London. Chapman & Hall. 1862.

Tales of All Countries: Second Series. 1 vol. London. Chapman & Hall. 1863.

Rachel Ray: A Novel. 2 vols. London. Chapman & Hall. 1863.

The Small House at Allington. With illustrations by J. E. Millais. 2 vols. London. Smith, Elder. 1864.

Can You Forgive Her? With illustrations by "Phiz" and E. Taylor. 2 vols. London. Chapman & Hall. 1864.

Miss Mackenzie. 2 vols. London. Chapman & Hall. 1865.

Hunting Sketches. 1 vol. London. Chapman & Hall. 1865.

The Belton Estate. 3 vols. London. Chapman & Hall. 1866.

Travelling Sketches. 1 vol. London. Chapman & Hall. 1866.

Clergymen of the Church of England. 1 vol. Chapman & Hall. 1866.
Nina Balatka. 2 vols. Edinburgh & London. Blackwood. 1867.
The Last Chronicle of Barset. With illustrations by George H.
    Thomas. 2 vols. London. Smith, Elder. 1867.
The Claverings. With illustrations by M. Ellen Edwards. 2 vols.
    London. Smith, Elder. 1867.
Lotta Schmidt: and Other Stories. 1 vol. London. Strahan. 1867.
Linda Tressel. 2 vols. Edinburgh & London. Blackwood. 1868.
Phineas Finn: The Irish Member. With illustrations by J. E. Millais.
    2 vols. London. Virtue. 1869.
He Knew He Was Right. With illustrations by Marcus Stone. 2 vols.
    London. Strahan. 1869.
The Vicar of Bullhampton. With illustrations by H. Woods. 1 vol.
    London. Bradbury, Evans. 1870.
An Editor's Tales. 1 vol. London. Strahan. 1870.
The Struggles of Brown, Jones and Robinson: by one of the Firm. With
    illustrations. 1 vol. London. Smith, Elder. 1870.
The Commentaries of Cæsar. 1 vol. Edinburgh & London. Black-
    wood. 1870.
Sir Harry Hotspur of Humblethwaite. 1 vol. London. Hurst &
    Blackett. 1871.
Ralph the Heir. 3 vols. London. Hurst & Blackett. 1871. Also
    1 vol. (8vo.) With illustrations by F. A. Fraser. London.
    Strahan. 1871.
The Golden Lion of Granpère. 1 vol. London. Tinsley. 1872.
The Eustace Diamonds. 3 vols. London. Chapman & Hall. 1873.
Australia and New Zealand. 2 vols. London. Chapman & Hall. 1873.
Phineas Redux. With illustrations by Frank Holl. 2 vols. London.
    Chapman & Hall. 1874.
Lady Anna. 2 vols. London. Chapman & Hall. 1874.
Harry Heathcote of Gangoil: A Tale of Australian Bush Life. 1 vol.
    London. Sampson, Low. 1874.
The Way We Live Now. With illustrations by Luke Fildes. 2 vols.
    London. Chapman & Hall. 1875.
The Prime Minister. 4 vols. London. Chapman & Hall. 1876.
The American Senator. 3 vols. London. Chapman & Hall. 1877.
South Africa. 2 vols. London. Chapman & Hall. 1878.
Is He Popenjoy?: A Novel. 3 vols. London. Chapman & Hall. 1878.
How the "Mastiffs" went to Iceland. With illustrations by Mrs. Hugh
    Blackburn. 1 vol. London. Virtue. 1878.
An Eye for an Eye. 2 vols. London. Chapman & Hall. 1879.
Thackeray. 1 vol. London. Macmillan. 1879.

John Caldigate. 3 vols. London. Chapman & Hall. 1879.

Cousin Henry: A Novel. 2 vols. London. Chapman & Hall. 1879.

The Duke's Children: A Novel. 3 vols. London. Chapman & Hall. 1880.

The Life of Cicero. 2 vols. London. Chapman & Hall. 1880.

Dr. Wortle's School: A Novel. 2 vols. London. Chapman & Hall. 1881.

Ayala's Angel. 3 vols. London. Chapman & Hall. 1881.

Why Frau Frohmann Raised her Prices: And Other Stories. 1 vol. London. Isbister. 1882.

Lord Palmerston ("English Political Leaders"). 1 vol. London. Isbister. 1882.

Kept in the Dark: A Novel. With a frontispiece by J. E. Millais. 2 vols. London. Chatto & Windus. 1882.

Marion Fay: A Novel. 3 vols. London. Chapman & Hall. 1882.

The Fixed Period. 2 vols. Edinburgh & London. Blackwood. 1882.

Mr. Scarborough's Family. 3 vols. London. Chatto & Windus. 1883.

The Landleaguers. 3 vols. London. Chatto & Windus. 1883.

An Autobiography. 2 vols. Edinburgh & London. Blackwood. 1883.

An Old Man's Love. 2 vols. Edinburgh & London. Blackwood. 1884.

The Noble Jilt. 1 vol. London. Constable. 1923.

London Tradesmen. 1 vol. London. Mathews & Marrot. 1927.

(c) CLASSIFICATION OF TROLLOPE'S FICTION [1]

[*Books recommended are marked with an asterisk—several Baedeker fashion, with a double asterisk, a very few (in restrained imitation of the A.A.) with a triple asterisk.*]

I. THE CHRONICLES OF BARSETSHIRE.

> *The Warden* (1855).
> *Barchester Towers (1857).
> ***Doctor Thorne (1858).
> *Framley Parsonage (1861).
> *The Small House at Allington (1864).
> **The Last Chronicle of Barset (1867).

---

[1] In this classification of Trollope's fiction use has been made of the grouping carried out by Mr. Spencer van Bokkelen Nichols in his valuable monograph *The Significance of Anthony Trollope* (New York, 1925). From some of Mr. Nichols' allocations I differ, but the assistance afforded by his work is gratefully acknowledged.

These stories are not direct sequels one to another (save that in the author's original intention *Barchester Towers* was something of a continuation of *The Warden*),[1] but all concern the society of the imaginary county of Barset in south-western England and of its capital—the cathedral city of Barchester.

Certain persons reappear from novel to novel, and in the manner of their reappearance show Trollope's skill in so drawing his characters as to depict them gradually growing older or altered in nature by altered circumstance.

Barsetshire serves as background to one or two other novels—notably to *The Claverings*, in which reference is actually made to "Bishop Proudie"—but to include such extra novels among *The Chronicles of Barsetshire* would tend to confuse unfamiliar readers and go beyond Trollope's own intention. He regarded Barsetshire as "a little bit of England which I have myself created," and for a novel to rank as a "chronicle" of this area, it must deal rather with local affairs than with problems common to humanity, must be written in terms of the county rather than in terms of England as a whole.[2]

II. THE POLITICAL NOVELS.

> *Can You Forgive Her?* (1864).
> ***Phineas Finn: The Irish Member* (1869).
> ***The Eustace Diamonds* (1873).
> **Phineas Redux (1876).
> **The Prime Minister* (1876).
> **The Duke's Children* (1880).

These novels are linked together by continuing character-study and, more loosely, by their frequent reference to parliamentary life; they share no common background or locality. Certain of the personages introduced into *The Chronicles of Barsetshire* reappear—for example, the old Duke of Omnium (from *Doctor Thorne*), and Griselda Grantley, daughter of Archdeacon Grantley, who becomes first Lady Dumbello and then Marchioness of Hartletop.

Can You Forgive Her?, although its main emphasis lies on the

---

[1] Cf. Trollope's preface to the collected issue of *The Chronicles of Barsetshire*. (8 vols. London. Chapman & Hall. 1879.)

[2] Trollope set so strict an interpretation upon the phrase "Chronicles of Barsetshire" that he was unwilling to reckon even *The Small House at Allington* among their number. When at last he yielded to pressure from friends and publishers, it was against his better judgment.

jilting of John Grey by Alice Vavasor, is chiefly interesting to the reader as introducing for the first time Lady Glencora, wife of the Plantagenet Palliser, who becomes Duke of Omnium. The love-impulse of Lady Glencora toward the handsome ne'er-do-well, Burgo Fitzgerald, and the stirrings of desire felt by Plantagenet Palliser for the empty loveliness of Lady Dumbello form the ironic overture to a married life which dominates five succeeding novels and shows no second sign of even conceivable collapse.

Phineas Finn and its direct sequel, *Phineas Redux*, are definitely novels of political life. Just as Trollope was interested in the social prestige of the clergy and not in their professed religion, so he concentrates in these and other political novels on the social background of Parliament and on the great influence of women over place and ambition, content merely to indicate the policies and measures of the various cabinets which come and go. It results from this preoccupation with political society and this indifference to political theory that the two chronicles of Phineas (and *The Prime Minister* also) can only with difficulty be treated as *romans-à-clé*. Suggestions have been made toward identification of the principal characters, but only two of these did Trollope himself endorse. He admitted that the Tory leader Daubeny was Disraeli (then in opposition to Gladstone) and that Turnbull was John Bright; but would not agree that in "Lord Chiltern" he was drawing Lord Hartington (afterward the eighth Duke of Devonshire) or that Gresham was a blend of the character of Peel with the position of Gladstone. Monk and Plantagenet Palliser were certainly imaginary. Phineas Finn himself had a dual inspiration. Physically he was Joe Parkinson, an English journalist who married a million-aire's daughter and became a wealthy director of companies; intellectually and politically he was John Pope Hennessy, a young Irish politician of brilliant parts who was a protégé of Disraeli and married the daughter of Sir Hugh Low.[1]

The Prime Minister draws the portrait of Plantagenet Palliser, now Duke of Omnium and first minister of the Crown. Trollope put much loving care into this delineation of "a perfect gentleman" and of his so feminine wife. "If" he says "Plantagenet Palliser be not a gentleman, then am I unable to describe one. The Duchess (Lady Glencora) is by no means a perfect lady; but if she be not all over a woman, then am I not able to describe a woman."

---

[1] This fact was recorded by T. P. O'Connor in *T.P.'s and Cassell's Weekly*, June 5 1926.

Between *The Prime Minister* and *The Duke's Children* Glencora, Duchess of Omnium, dies. The latter novel is the story of the unhappy widower, struggling alone with the problem of his two sons and of his daughter, for the solution of which the woman's wit of the dead Duchess is so sorely needed. For the Duke everything goes awry. His daughter gives her love to an unknown and penniless commoner; the younger son, after ragging through his University career, takes disastrously to cards and racing; finally the heir—Lord Silverbridge—stands for Parliament in the interest contrary to that of his father and, turning from the girl the Duke has chosen as his bride, throws his title and prospects at the feet of the lovely daughter of an American *savant*.

The Eustace Diamonds belongs to the political series only by virtue of the part played in it by Lady Glencora, by Lord Fawn, by the fashionable Jewish preacher Emilius and by one or two other characters who appeared in *Phineas Finn*. It is one of the best constructed of all Trollope's novels and the character of Lady Eustace —untruthful, insincere, but always seductive and appealing; pretending to the loss of her own superb diamond necklace in order to frustrate the jealous claims of her dead husband's family—is a masterpiece of subtlety. There is some excellent hunting in *The Eustace Diamonds*. The episode of Nappie's Grey Horse in the second volume was one actually witnessed by Trollope. One curious incidental feature of the book is that Trollope sends a group of his characters to the Haymarket Theatre to see performed his own, long pigeon-holed play *The Noble Jilt*.

III. NOVELS OF MANNERS, CONVENTION AND SOCIAL DILEMMA.

> *The Three Clerks* (1858).
> *Orley Farm* (1862).
> ***The Belton Estate* (1866).
> ***The Claverings* (1867).
> **The Vicar of Bullhampton* (1870).
> *Ralph the Heir* (1871).
> **Sir Harry Hotspur of Humblethwaite* (1871).
> Lady Anna* (1874).
> *The American Senator* (1877).
> **Is He Popenjoy?* (1878).
> *Ayala's Angel* (1881).
> Marion Fay* (1882).

IV. SOCIAL SATIRES.

> The Bertrams (1859).
> *Rachel Ray (1863).
> Miss Mackenzie (1865).
> The Struggles of Brown, Jones and Robinson (1870).
> ***The Way We Live Now (1875).
> **Mr. Scarborough's Family (1883).

V. IRISH NOVELS.

> *The Macdermots of Ballycloran (1847).
> The Kellys and the O'Kellys (1848).
> Castle Richmond (1860).
> The Landleaguers (1883).

VI. AUSTRALIAN NOVELS.

> Harry Heathcote of Gangoil (1874).
> *John Caldigate (1879).

These two novels were, of course, the outcome of the author's visit to his son in Australia. The earlier shorter tale is a mere ranch episode—dramatic, vividly told and with good local colour, but frankly the "Christmas Number" story that it set out to be. John Caldigate is more important. It is the only one of Trollope's books in which for the purpose of his plot he uses his knowledge and experience of the Post Office (the salvation of Caldigate from his enemies is achieved by an ingenuity not unworthy of the modern detective story), and the comments on the Civil Service contrast interestingly with those implicit in The Three Clerks, written twenty years earlier.

VII. HISTORICAL AND ROMANTIC NOVELS.

> La Vendée (1850).
> *Nina Balatka (1867).
> *Linda Tressel (1868).
> The Golden Lion of Granpère (1872).

VIII. PSYCHOLOGICAL ANALYSES AND STORIES OF SINGLE INCIDENT.

>   **He Knew He Was Right* (1869).
>   An Eye for an Eye* (1879).[1]
>   *Cousin Henry* (1879).
>   ***Dr. Wortle's School* (1881).
>   Kept in the Dark* (1882).
>   An Old Man's Love* (1884).

IX. FANTASIA.

The Fixed Period (1882).

This is the story of an imaginary country in the year 1980. The Wellsian romance of the future was as unsuited to Trollope's genius as any fictional genre could possibly be. His prophecies of the growth of invention and scientific ingenuity are not inspired. A steam tricycle which travels twenty-five miles per hour, a cricket-match with sixteen players a side and a steam-bowler, and an apparatus for the mechanical reporting of speeches are among the more daring flights of fancy. The main theme of the story depends on the voluntary suicide of all persons over sixty, which system of willing self-sacrifice quickly and thoroughly breaks down.

X. SHORT STORIES.

>   *Tales of All Countries.* First and Second Series (1861, 1863).
>   *Lotta Schmidt: and Other Stories* (1867).
>   **An Editor's Tales* (1870).
>   **Why Frau Frohmann Raised her Prices: and Other Stories* (1882).

---

[1] Mr. Nichols classifies this story as of the Irish series. But although the action takes place mainly in Ireland, the drama is one of human dilemma, and its protagonists could as well have played their parts in any other land.

III

THE INTRODUCTORY PAGES OF TROLLOPE'S PROJECTED
"HISTORY OF FICTION" TRANSCRIBED FROM THE MSS.

"I write this book to vindicate, not only or chiefly my own profession as a novelist, but also and more specially that public taste in literature which has created and nourished the profession which I follow. And I am led to do this by a conviction that there still exists among us Englishmen a prejudice in respect to novels, which may perhaps be lessened by the work which I here propose to myself. This prejudice is not against the reading of novels, as is proved by their general acceptance among us. But it exists strongly in reference to the appreciation in which they are professed to be held, and robs them of much (of) that high character which they may claim to have earned by their grace, their honesty, and good teaching.

No man can work long at any trade without being brought to consider much whether that which he is doing daily tends to evil or to good. I have written many novels and have known many writers of novels, and I can assert that such thoughts have been strong with them and with myself; but in acknowledging that these writers have received from the public a full measure of credit for such genius, ingenuity, or perseverance as each may have displayed, I feel that there is still wanting to them a just appreciation of the excellence of their calling and a general knowledge of the high nature of the work which they perform.

By the common consent of all mankind who have read, poetry takes the highest place in literature. That nobility of expression and all but divine grace of words which she is bound to attain before she can make her footing good, is not compatible with prose. Indeed, it is that which turns prose into poetry. When that has been in truth achieved, the reader knows that the writer has soared above the earth, and can teach his lessons somewhat as a God might teach. He who sits down to write his tale in prose makes no such attempts, nor does he dream that the poet's power is within his reach; but his teaching is of the same nature, and his lessons all tend to the same end. By either means false sentiment may be fostered, false notions of humanity may be engendered, false honours, false love, false worship may be created;—by either vice instead of virtue may be taught;—but by each equally may true honour, true love, true worship and true humanity be taught;—and that will be the greatest teacher which may spread such truth the widest. But at present, much as novels are sought and read, there still exists an idea that novels, even at their best, are negligible. Young women, and old men too, read more of them than they read of poetry, because such reading is easier than the reading of poetry; but they read them,—as men eat pastry after dinner,—not without some inward conviction that their taste is vain if not vicious. I take upon myself to say that it is neither vicious nor vain.

But all writers of fiction who have desired to be able to think well of their work will have had doubts in their minds before they have arrived at this conclusion. Thinking much of my own dark labour and of its nature I felt myself at first to be much afflicted; and then to be deeply aggrieved by the opinion expressed by wise and think-ing men as to the work done by narrators of novels in prose. As I write this, there is still living among us one whom I have ever revered as a thinker, and valued as an author, and whom I much esteem as a man,—one from whom, perhaps, I have myself learned more than from any other English writer; and I was astounded when I first came across the following words from him. It is thus that Mr. Carlyle has written of the novel-writers of his day:—

"How knowest thou," the distressed novel-wright exclaimed: "that I, here where I sit, am the foolishest of existing mortals; that this my long ear of fictitious biography shall not find one and the other into whose still longer ears it may be the means under Providence of instilling somewhat?" We answer: "None knows; none can certainly know. Therefore write on, worthy brother, even as thou canst, even as it is given thee."

I was at first astounded and as it were convicted of being a wind-bag. I and my friends—those whom I so greatly loved and esteemed—whose works to me were the objects of such close criticism and scrutiny—were all windbags. But when by degrees I dared to examine and sift this saying of Carlyle's I found it to be silly and arrogant. Our dear old English Homer—Homer in prose —nods sometimes, and had nodded then. But words such as those from such a man do not pass by one like the wind.

I then began to enquire what had been the nature of English novels since they first became common in our own language, and to be desirous of ascertaining whether they had done harm or good.

I could myself well remember that in my own young days they had not taken that undisputed possession of ladies' drawing-rooms which they now hold. Forty-five years ago when George the Fourth was King, they were not treated as Lydia had been forced to treat them in the preceding reign. When mamas came their way, *Peregrine Pickle* was not hidden under the bolster, or *Lord Ainsworth* put under the sofa. But the families in which an unrestricted permission was given for the reading of such books were very few; and from many they were altogether banished. The high poetic genius and correct morality of Walter Scott had not altogether succeeded in making men or women understand that lessons which were good in poetry could not be bad in prose. I remembered that an embargo lay upon novel-reading as a pursuit, very much heavier in its nature than that want of a full appreciation of which I now complain. . . ."

IV

ADVANCE LAY-OUTS FOR TWO OF TROLLOPE'S NOVELS TRANSCRIBED FROM HIS MSS. NOTES

(a) "SIR HARRY HOTSPUR OF HUMBLETHWAITE."

[*Originally entitled*: "*The House of Humblethwaite.*" *In the story as published* "*Brandon*" *becomes* "*Hotspur*" *and* "*Harry Brandon*" *becomes* "*George Hotspur.*"]

Characters:

GIRL: Tall. Thin; light-haired. Blue-eyed. Rather quiet. Had been sickly; now well. Very fond of her father, who is worshipped also by the mother. Very much in love with cousin.—EMILY BRANDON.

FATHER: Rich—£20,000 a year. Brandon Park. House in London. Very handsome. Passionate and self-willed. Devoted to his daughter. Fond of hunting and racing—but the soul of honour. Preux chevalier. Very fine fellow.—SIR HARRY BRANDON.

MOTHER: LADY BRANDON. Augusta. Devoted to her husband. Very good. Rather given to be ill. Somewhat weak in character.. Under her daughter's control.

LORD ALFRED GRESLEY: Member of Parliament. Second son of Marquis of Milnthorpe—Suitor favoured by Sir Harry. Good, honest, true, a gentleman. 12 years older than Emily. Rather stupid—is rejected—behaves well.

THE COUSIN: HARRY BRANDON—a thorough blackguard—handsome—clever—quite unprincipled. Is known to Lord Alfred.

THE COUSIN'S FRIEND: CAPTAIN STUBBER. Has some conscience. Tells the truth to Sir Harry at last—and has a quarrel with the cousin.

ABRAHAM HART: The Jew lawyer who has Harry Brandon in hand.

MRS. LAMLEY: Lucy—the woman with whom Harry Brandon is entangled—ill-used—true to him.

Time: Eight months

(*b*) "THE WAY WE LIVE NOW"

[*Novel in 20 parts.   32 pages.   520 words=5 volumes.   Presumed period 1873.*]

LADY CARBURY. Widow of late General Sir Michael Carbury, Bart.
(died in India)—left with £1000 a year—had left her husband,
but not in adultery (from his hard temper and her impetuosity)
—had gone back and been forgiven—but the evil report
remained. Living in Welbeck Street with son and daughter.
Spoiling the son and helping to pay his debts—clever and
impetuous. Thoroughly unprincipled from want of knowledge of honesty—an authoress, very handsome, 43—trying
all schemes with editors etc. to get puffed. Infinitely energetic
—bad to her daughter from want of sympathy. Flirts as a
matter of taste, but never goes wrong. Capable of great
sacrifice for her son. *The chief character.*

SIR FELIX CARBURY, BART. 25. Been in the Guards. Sold out
(enquire about this). Magnificently beautiful, dark with perfect features, brown eyes. Utterly selfish, reckless from
thoughtlessness, debts paid by mother, by sister's lover, by
the lady who loves him—but all is hopeless. His father left
him £1000 a year. He and his sister to divide the mother's
thousand at her death.

(Lady Carbury had run away. Felix a coward.)

HENRIETTA CARBURY. Hetty by some. Harry by her brother.
Almost as handsome as her brother, but thoroughly strong and
good—antagonistic to her mother's dodges. Courted by her
cousin Roger Carbury, the head of the family, a man of wealth
and position considerably older than herself. She 21. But in
love with Paul Montagu. She almost yields when she is made
to believe that Paul is bad, but never quite does so. Entitled
to £6000 on her marriage with the consent of either her mother
or her cousin, who is executor under her father's will. Loves
her brother.

ROGER CARBURY of Carbury Hall in Norfolk. 38. Straightforward.
About £2000 a year—ready money. Very good. Horribly in
love with his cousin. Hero of the book. Property will go to
the other Carburys. Takes Paul Montagu by the hand and
sacrifices himself at last.

Life at Carbury Hall with neighbours—the Bishop—R.C. Priest—
big squire in next parish who has large income and is in debt.

Doubts about his religion—finds it easier to love his neighbour than his God. Staunch old Tory.

PAUL MONTAGU (*sic*). Hetty's lover. Gets into some scrapes which must be devised. Marries at last under the auspices of Roger. A scapegrace. Has glimmerings of Radical policy for the good of the people and disgusts Roger Carbury. Lives at last at Carbury Hall and marries Hetty.

BISHOP OF ELMHAM—old Longley.

FATHER JOHN BARHAM. Pervert. Waltham priest. Very poor.

HEPWORTHS OF EARDLEY with £7000. Primeros. Spaniards by descent.

ADOLPHUS LONGESTAFFE ESQUIRE. Squire of Caversham, Norfolk (*sic*), and neighbour of Roger Carbury.

LADY POMONA LONGESTAFFE and YOUNG DOLLY the heir. Large property much involved. Hot-tempered and cross-grained. Country going to the dogs. All of them spending too much money. Sophia (Mrs. George Whitstable)—Georgiana—Squercum, lawyer.

MR. NICHOLAS BROUNE (Morrish), editor of the "Morning Breakfast Table." (Pall Mall office in Trafalgar Square.) Fond of ladies.

MR. BOOKER editor of "The Literary Chronicle," a supposed writer of criticism, very poor. (Alfred Shand.)

MR. FERDINAND ALF. Editor of "The Evening Pulpit." Great swell.

LEADHAM & LOITER. Publishers.

MARIE MELMOTTE. The heiress. Daughter of Augustus Melmotte, great French swindler.

MADAME MELMOTTE. Fat Jewess.

HERR VOSSNER. Purveyor to the Bear Garden.

DUCHESS OF STEVENAGE. Castle Abbey. Grendalls. Lord Alfred. Miles Grendall, second son.

RUBY RUGGLES. 23.

DANIEL RUGGLES OF SHEEPSACRE.

JOHN CRUMB.

MRS. HURTLE.   (? Caradoc, ? Carson.)—Winifred—Lives with
MRS. PIPKIN—five children—a widow.

SOUTH CENTRAL PACIFIC AND MEXICAN RAILWAY.

Roger's married sister in California, had befriended Montagu.

*** Two features of this lay-out merit notice. In the first place, it is clear that
Melmotte was not in the author's intention so important an element
in the book as in performance he turned out to be. In the second
place, a few of the minor characters (to judge from the names that here
and there follow the designations) were portraits of real people.

INDEX

Oxford Paperbacks

Oxford Paperbacks

PRINTED IN GREAT BRITAIN
AT THE UNIVERSITY PRESS, OXFORD
BY VIVIAN RIDLER
PRINTER TO THE UNIVERSITY